# REFUGEE CRISIS IN INTERNATIONAL POLICY
## VOLUME II
## REFUGEE POLICIES OF THE EU AND EUROPEAN COUNTRIES

# REFUGEE CRISIS IN INTERNATIONAL POLICY

## VOLUME II

### REFUGEE POLICIES OF THE EU AND EUROPEAN COUNTRIES

Edited by

Hasret Çomak, Burak Şakir Şeker, Mehlika Özlem Ultan, Yaprak Civelek, Çağla Arslan Bozkuş

TRANSNATIONAL PRESS LONDON

2021

MIGRATION SERIES: 29

REFUGEE CRISIS IN INTERNATIONAL POLICY

VOLUME II - REFUGEE POLICIES OF THE EU AND EUROPEAN
COUNTRIES

Edited by Hasret Çomak, Burak Şakir Şeker, Mehlika Özlem Ultan,

Yaprak Civelek, Çağla Arslan Bozkuş

Copyright © 2021 Transnational Press London

First Published in 2021 by TRANSNATIONAL PRESS LONDON in the United Kingdom, 13 Stamford Place, Sale, M33 3BT, UK.
www.tplondon.com

Transnational Press London® and the logo and its affiliated brands are registered trademarks.

Requests for permission to reproduce material from this work should be sent to: sales@tplondon.com

Paperback
ISBN: 978-1-80135-012-9
Digital
ISBN: 978-1-80135-013-6

Cover Design: Nihal Yazgan
Cover Photo by Julie Ricard on Unsplash.com

Transnational Press London Ltd. is a company registered in England and Wales No. 8771684

# CONTENTS

# PREFACE

Every day, in many parts of the world people are giving the hardest decisions of their lives. With these decisions, they have to leave their homes behind for a better and safer life. Many people in the world, by giving the decision to leave where they grew up, move to a close settlement. Some have to leave their country for a short period of time or for a lifetime.

In many parts of the world, there are many reasons why people try to re-establish their lives in other countries. Some leave their home country to find a job or for education. Others are forced to escape from human rights violations such as inhuman treatment and torture. Millions run away from armed conflicts or violence. These people who do not feel safe; might be targeted due to their characteristics that establish their identity or faith such as their ethnic origin, religious beliefs, gender, and political thoughts.

These journeys that have begun in pursuit of a better future, might be full of danger and fear; some might fall into the trap of human traffickers or other forms of exploitation. Also, some are taken into custody by authorities as soon as they arrive in a country. Many, who settle in a country and start a new life face racism, xenophobia, and discrimination almost every day. They may feel lonely and isolated.

There are many reasons which make it difficult and dangerous for people to stay in their country of origin. Violence, war, hunger, and poverty are the most important ones. Sexual preferences and sexual identity also take an important place. People may also have to leave their home country because of climate change and natural disasters. Mostly, it is possible to encounter many of these difficult conditions all at once.

Fleeing danger is not the only reason people leave their country. Some think of becoming a part of a qualified workforce or gain capital in another country. Moreover, they suppose there is a higher possibility of finding a job in a foreign country. Others seek to live with their relatives and friends currently living abroad. Also, there might be those who aim to begin and continue their education in another country. Therefore, there are many reasons why people might start out to establish a new life in another country.

It is noteworthy to mention the words "refugee", "asylum seeker" and "migrant" in terms of International Law.

The refugee is the person who leaves his home country due to the threat of being subjected to grave human rights violations and persecution. These people have to leave their home country and seek asylum in another country due to security threats and threats against their lives. As they have no other choice and they feel their governments cannot or will not protect them

1

against these threats, they are forced to take this decision.

According to the provisions of the "United Nations Convention Relating to the Status of Refugees", adopted on 28 July 1951 by the United Nations Conference of Plenipotentiaries on the Status of Refugees and Stateless Persons convened under General Assembly resolution 429 (V) of 14 December 1950 and entered into force on 22 April 1954, refugees have "the right for international protection".

An asylum seeker is a person who has left his home country to seek asylum in another country to be protected from persecution and grave human rights violations. However, in this case, one only has the status of asylum applicants and legally has not yet been accepted as a refugee. Seeking an asylum application is a human right. This means everyone should be given permission to enter a country to seek asylum.

Migrants, on the other hand, are those who live outside their home country thus who are not asylum seekers or refugees. Migrants in general, leave their home countries to work, to have an education, or to live with their family members in another country. Some feel the need to leave their home country for the reasons of poverty, political turmoil, natural disasters, or other difficult conditions.

The issue that should be emphasized here is the situation that many people who do not fit into the "refugee" definition might get be in danger once they are returned to their home country. Even if they may not be escaping from persecution, no matter what their legal status is in the country they established themselves, migrants' human rights must be protected, and these rights must be respected.

States must protect all migrants against violence based on racism and xenophobia, exploitation, and forced labor. Migrants should not be detained without legitimate reasons or forcefully send back to their home country.

Human rights have become both a subject and a legitimate instrument of international politics. Therefore, the human rights of refugees, asylum seekers and migrants must always be protected at the international level. States must fulfill their joint responsibility to protect the rights of refugees, asylum seekers and migrants.

People are not the source of the problem. The main problem is the reasons that force families and individuals to cross borders. Those who cause these reasons have responsibilities. The attitude of authorities who are trying far-sighted and unrealistic approaches matters in the creation of this problem.

States must ensure that refugees, asylum seekers and immigrants are safe, not subject to torture, discrimination and living in poverty.

2

States should assess the applications of asylum seekers according to international rules except for those who:

- has committed a crime against peace, a war crime, or a crime against humanity, as defined in the international instruments drawn up to make provision in respect of such crimes;
- has committed a serious non-political crime outside the country of refuge prior to his admission to that country as a refugee;
- has been guilty or suspicious of acts contrary to the purposes and principles of the United Nations.

The situation of asylum seekers should not be left in a state of uncertainty for years. Unlawful detention practices should not be carried out and the necessary diligence should be taken in this regard. Also, international regulations must be made in order to protect migrants against the exploitation of employers or human traffickers and abuse.

States must take responsibility for and fulfill these responsibilities meticulously for refugees, asylum seekers and immigrants to be able to rebuild their lives safely against serious dangers. Sharing responsibility for global problems is fair in the 21st century.

Welcoming people from other countries might empower host communities by making them more diverse and more flexible in a rapidly changing world. Some of the successful, impactful, and productive people in the field of arts, politics, and technology can be refugees, asylum seekers, or migrants. There are very successful people in the international community who have been given the opportunity to start a new life in another country and become a member of a new community.

In the 21st century, leaders, by showing sufficient political will, should produce and develop new projects to relocate people fleeing conflict and persecution in their countries.

Furthermore, the practice of other safe approaches should be implemented to enable refugees to start a new life. Providing the necessary financial support for refugee families to come to the country and granting them a study or work visa might be considered as an appropriate method for them to establish a new life.

States should not force anybody to return to a country where they might be subjected to human rights violations. Instead, states should ensure a safe place for refugees and asylum seekers, and migrants to live, a job, access to education, and health services.

Refugees, asylum seekers, and immigrants should be treated with dignity without being deprived of their freedom as stated in the United Nations

Universal Declaration of Human Rights. Under all the circumstances which require detention and retention, refugees, asylum seekers, and immigrants should be informed about their current rights as well as their fundamental rights. Their detention conditions should comply with international standards in terms of rights and freedoms.

Comprehensive programs should be prepared with the United Nations Member States and the United Nations High Commissioner for Refugees on the provision of social and legal assistance to refugees, asylum seekers and migrants. For this purpose, a valid and secure "country of origin information system" should be established. This system should be targeted to be structured as an "international joint system".

All these developments have revealed the necessity of preparing a multidimensional, original, up-to-date, original and rich content about refugees, asylum seekers and immigrants in the international community and presenting it to science.

This six volume book series is titled "Refugee Crisis in International Politics" are prepared with the aim of clarifying the above-mentioned issues and enriching the content, context, and depth to the field of science.

The second volume presents comparative and detailed analyses on the refugee policies of not only the European Union but also the European countries. Contributions in this volume are as follows: Neriman Hocaoğlu Bahadır "The Refugee Policy of the EU and the Status of the Refugees"; Sertif Demir "The European Union Migration Policy: Evolution Through Refuge Crisis"; Mesut Şöhret "Historical Development of the Refugee Crisis in the European Union"; Ayşegül Gökalp Kutlu "Gender, Migration and Security: The EU's Responses to the Refugee Crisis"; N. Aslı Şirin and Ebru Dalgakıran "Re-Bordering Europe?: Refugees and 'Temporary' Internal Border Controls"; Mesut Şöhret "Securitization of Refugee Problem Within European Union"; Sinem Bal "Normative Elusiveness of Europe in Terms of Refugee Crisis"; Burulkan Abdibaitova Pala "Refugee Policies of the Baltic Countries"; Serkan Baykuşoğlu "A Historical and Contemporary Analysis of the British Immigration Policies and their Implications for Settlement and Integration: The Case of Turkish Immigrants in the United Kingdom"; Ferda Özer "Migration Policy of Spain"; Sinem Eray "Populism and Refugee Policies of Austria"; Ebru Dalğakıran "Belgium's Immigration Asylum Policies in Times of Crisis"; N. Aslı Şirin "Hungary's Asylum Policy before and after the Refugee Movement in 2015"; and Ayşegül Bostan "The Asylum Policy of Republic of Serbia: The Case of the Humanitarian Route".

We would like to thank all the contributing and researching colleagues who supported us with their research and findings.

4

We would like to express our gratitude to Prof. Dr. İbrahim Sirkeci who made the publication of "Refugee Crisis in International Politics" possible.

Special thanks should be given to the staff of Transnational Press London (TPLondon) for their valuable guidance and technical support on this process, for preparing our books for publication, and for designing the covers.

We sincerely hope that the work will be useful and useful to the world of science.

Hasret Çomak, Burak Şakir Şeker, Mehlika Özlem Ultan, Yaprak Civelek, Çağla Arslan Bozkuş

ISTANBUL, MARCH / 2021

# CHAPTER 1

# THE EU REFUGEE POLICIES AND THE STATUS OF REFUGEES

Neriman Hocaoğlu Bahadır[1]

## Introduction

The European Union (EU) is a sui generis organization. Its establishment can be traced back to the European Coal and Steel Community. It has many characteristics which make it different than many other international organisations. European integration started in a specific area but day by day, it was deepened and widened. Cooperation spread to many different areas, such as agriculture, trade, economy, environment, education, culture and many more. It started with six member states and today it has 27.[2]

The EU can be seen as a success story that started after the World War II, especially in terms of peace and welfare. This attracts many people who are looking for better social, political and economic conditions. It is accessible for many people living geographically nearby. For this reason, the EU attracts people who have a reason to move. These reasons may be war, sometimes poverty and sometimes better education. The Migration/Refugee Crisis in 2015 is a good example of the flow of thousands of people in search of a safe and economically better place to live. However, long before this crisis, the EU had started developing its refugee policy, as migration to Europe started long before 2015. Christof Van Mol and Helga de Valk note the historical migration flows in three periods: the period between the 1950s and 1974, the second one between 1974 and the end of the 1980s and the last one from the 1990s to 2012.[3] This is quite a general classification of the history of migration to Europe, but it is important to show that there has always been a movement to the EU.

This chapter aims to draw the general framework of the refugee policy of the EU to provide a clear understanding of this policy area which consists of many official documents and a complex structure. First, this chapter focuses

---

[1] Asst.Prof. Dr., Kırklareli University, Faculty of Economics and Administrative Sciences, International Relations Department.
[2] The UK left the EU on 31 January 2020, concluding a long withdrawal process initiated by the 2016 Brexit referendum.
[3] Christof Van Mol, Helga de Valk, "Migration and Immigrants in Europe: A Historical and Demographic Perspective", Integration Processes and Policies in Europe Contexts, Levels and Actors, Blanca Garces-Mascarenas, Rinus Penninx (Ed.), Springer Open, 2016, pp. 32-37.

on the policy itself and what it is understood from it. Here, the general concepts of this policy area are also stated. Then, the historical development of this policy area is given to present a holistic approach. After the historical developments, this chapter clarifies the status of the refugees.

### What is the refugee policy of the EU?

The EU consists of 27 member states that act together in some policy areas. Even though it is not a fully integrated organization it has some common points, and some decisions are made at the union level and for that reason the member states have to be in harmony with the EU acquis communautaire. The acquis of the EU consists of *"common rights and obligations that are binding on all EU countries."*[4] Within EU law, there are treaties, regulations, directives, decisions, recommendations and opinions. Some of these are binding and some of them are not.[5] For that reason, member states are free to make their own decisions and this makes the related policy a bit complex.

Here, some concepts should be noted to understand the refugee policy of the EU. Some of these concepts include: legal migration, illegal migration, irregular migration, migrant, asylum seeker, refugee, external border control, Schengen and internal borders.

The concept of legal migration can be defined as migration for which the law defines who can enter and have residence in a country. In terms of the EU's legal migration measures, there are various categories, such as: highly qualified workers, students and researchers, family members of the people who have a right to live in the EU, and long-term residents.[6] So, the migration of these groups are enacted within EU law, and their rights are regulated within the law.

Illegal migration is also another concept, but is contested. The EU has used this concept for some time but now prefers to use irregular migration *"as most irregular migrants are not criminals".*[7] This concept is defined as the *"movement of persons to a new place of residence or transit that takes place outside the regulatory norms of the sending, transit and receiving countries."*[8] These concepts are

---

[4] Eur-lex, Glossary of Summaries: acquis, Retrieved from: https://eur-lex.europa.eu/summary/glossary/acquis.html

[5] Europa, Regulations, Directives and other acts, https://europa.eu/european-union/law/legal-acts_en (Access 20.11.2020).

[6] European Commission, Migration and Home Affairs, Legal Migration and Integration, https://ec.europa.eu/home-affairs/what-we-do/policies/legal-migration_en (Access 21.11.2020).

[7] European Commission, Migration and Home Affairs, Irregular Migration, https://ec.europa.eu/home-affairs/what-we-do/networks/european_migration_network/glossary_search/irregular-migration_en (Access 22.11.2020).

[8] ibid.

about the act and it should also be evaluated in terms of subject of the act. Migrant or irregular migrant, asylum seeker and refugee are the other concepts to be defined.

The United Nations International Organization for Migration (UN IOM)[9] defines migrant as an umbrella term and as "a person who moves away from his or her place of usual residence whether within a country or across an international border, temporarily or permanently and for variety of reasons."[10] This is a broad concept and for that reason, it is used more than the other concepts and is sometimes even misused. Migrants also include irregular migrants who are defined in two contexts by the European Commission's Directorate-General for Migration and Home Affairs. The first is the global context in which an irregular migrant is defined as "a person who, owing to irregular entry, breach of a condition of entry, or the expiry of their legal basis for entering and residing, lacks legal status in a transit or host country".[11] The second context is the EU context, which is the primary context in terms of this chapter. The EU defines an irregular migrant as "a third-country national present on the territory of Schengen State who does not fulfil, or no longer fulfils, the conditions of entry as set out in the Regulation (EU) 2016/399 (Schengen Borders Code) or other conditions for entry, stay or residence in that EU Member State".[12] Here, it is explained and defined quite clearly that a person may not have legal right to enter, or after entrance may no longer have right to reside within, the Schengen Area.

Another term quite related with the refugee policy is asylum seeker. According to IOM, asylum seeker is defined, in short, as "*an individual who is seeking international protection*" and, in detail, as "*someone whose claim has not yet been finally decided on by the country in which he or she has submitted it*".[13] Here, it is clear that this concept is related to a person who seeks international protection and applies for such protection from a country in which he/she wants to stay. IOM notes that this person may be recognized as a refugee at the end if his/her application is evaluated positively.[14] The UN High Commissioner for Refugees (UNHCR) also defines asylum seeker as "*someone whose request for sanctuary has yet to be processed*".[15] The EU has a Common European Asylum

---

[9] IOM was incorporated into the UN system in 2016. In this research, it is mentioned as IOM for consistency.

[10] IOM, Key Migration Terms, Migrant, https://www.iom.int/key-migration-terms#Migrant (Access 22.11.2020).

[11] European Commission, Migration and Home Affairs, Legal Migration and Integration, https://ec.europa.eu/home-affairs/what-we-do/networks/european_migration_network/glossary_search/irregular-migrant_en (Access 22.11.2020).

[12] Ibid.

[13] IOM, Key Migration Terms, Asylum Seeker, https://www.iom.int/key-migration-terms#Asylum-Seeker (Access 23.11.2020).

[14] ibid.

[15] UNHCR, Asylum-seekers, https://www.unhcr.org/tr/en/asylum-seekers (Access 23.11.2020).

System (CEAS) which accepts asylum as a fundamental right and notes that *"asylum is granted to people fleeing persecution or serious harm in their country and therefore in need of international protection"*.[16] CEAS is mentioned in the following part as it is important for the EU because of its special borderless structure.

Another concept related to asylum seeker is refugee. As stated above, after the evaluation of the asylum application, the asylum seeker may be given refugee status. So, who is a refugee? The generally accepted definition is in the 1951 Convention Relating to the Status of Refugees. IOM, referring to the Conventions, notes that *"a person who, owing to a well-founded fear of persecution for reasons of race, religion, nationality, membership of a particular social group or political opinion, is outside the country of his nationality and is unable or, owing to such fear, is unwilling to avail himself of the protection of that country; or who, not having a nationality and being outside the country of his former habitual residence as a result of such events, is unable or, owing to such fear, is unwilling to return to it."*[17] This can be seen as the first definition and it is the mostly cited one. However, it is also criticized for being *"a very cautious attempt to find balance between the needs of refugees and the burden of protection for the contracting parties"* rather than consisting of *"desirable or best practices in granting protection to refugees"*.[18] There are other definitions but this one gives the general framework and what should be understood from the concept. The EU also uses nearly the same definition, but it prefers to use the terms "third-country national" and "stateless person"[19] in defining refugees, and references are given to the Convention and the 1967 New York Protocol in official documents of the EU. Among these three concepts, it should be noted that asylum seeking is the previous step before getting refugee status, but it should not be understood as an automatic process. It is not; asylum seeking process may not result in recognition of refugee status. Constant and Zimmermann define the process clearly by stating that *"Asylees usually arrive in the new country as displaced people or illegal immigrants and immediately seek asylum ... If their application is approved by the government of the host country, asylum seekers take the status of refugees."*.[20] So, these concepts are closely related, and it is a step-by-step process, and all steps should be well-defined, fulfilled and clear in order to reach an outcome.

Lastly, the focus is on external border controls and Schengen and internal

---

[16] European Commission, Migration and Home Affairs, Common European Asylum System, https://ec.europa.eu/home-affairs/what-we-do/policies/asylum_en (Access 23.11.2020).
[17] IOM, Key Migration Terms, Refugee, https://www.iom.int/key-migration-terms#Refugee-mandate (Access 23.11.2020).
[18] Kay Hailbronner, Detention of Asylum Seekers, **European Journal of Migration & Law**, Vol.9, No.2, p. 162, https://doi.org/10.1163/138836407X190415 (Access 25.11.2020).
[19] Eurostat, Glossary, Refugee, https://ec.europa.eu/eurostat/statistics-explained/index.php/Glossary: Refugee (Access 23.11.2020).
[20] Amelie F. Constant and Klaus F. Zimmermann, "Towards a New European Refugee Policy that Works", **CESifo DICE Report**, Vol.14, No:4, 2016, p. 3, https://www.econstor.eu/bitstream/10419/173104/1/PC-08-2017.pdf (Access 24.11.2020).

borders. These two concepts specify the borders within which the concepts are defined. The first one is related to the external borders of the EU and the second related to its internal borders. The external borders of the EU are the borders of its member states at the outer circle of its territory. They include land, air and sea borders.[21] The EU as a dynamic union took some preventive measures to protect its borders and secure itself after the migration crisis it experienced in 2014-15. Some of these measures include the establishment of European Border and Coast Guard Agency, the formation of Schengen Information System, cooperation with third countries, systemic checks, entry-exit system, a new online European travel information and authorisation system (ETIAS) and more interoperable databases.[22] Most of these measures have been developed or initiated after 2015 and some of them will be fully functional in the following years. Schengen and internal borders should also be explained generally. Even though the EU is a union which provided free movement within its borders for its citizens and for the third country nationals who have a Schengen visa, which gives the right to move within Schengen Area, some crises have caused a reintroduction of internal borders in the EU. At the beginning, free movement was provided for working population but after 1985 some changes occurred and some of the members signed Schengen Agreement (1985) and the Convention Implementing the Schengen Agreement (1990) and in 1995 the Schengen area became operational, starting as an intergovernmental initiative.[23] It includes most of the EU members and some non-EU members. In the last decade, internal border controls have been reintroduced twice related to the crises by several member states. The first one was related to the migration crisis and the second one came with the coronavirus pandemic. These crises caused the Schengen Area to be questioned because of the border controls. However, as Marketa Votoupalova discusses, reintroducing internal borders cannot be evaluated *"as a violation of Schengen"* because member states reintroduce these border controls within the rights stated in the acquis and she claims that the danger related to Schengen area is *"insufficient external border controls"*.[24] Here, it should be noted that both internal borders and external borders are important in terms of movements and regular/irregular migration.

Here, the concepts mostly referred to are explained so as to aid understanding of the EU's refugee policy and the status of the refugees. The

---

[21] European Council, Strengthening the EU's external borders, https://www.consilium.europa.eu/en/policies/strengthening-external-borders/# (Access 24.11.2020).

[22] ibid.

[23] European Commission, Migration and Home Affairs, Schengen Area, https://ec.europa.eu/home-affairs/what-we-do/policies/borders-and-visas/schengen_en (Access 23.11.2020).

[24] Marketa Votoupalova, "The wrong critiques: why internal border Controls don't mean the end of Schengen", **New Perspectives: Interdisciplinary Journal of Central & East European Politics &International Relations**, Vol.27, No.1, 2019, p.73.

aim of giving a conceptual framework of this policy area is that refugee policy cannot be thought separately from the asylum policy, visa policy or migration policy. They all form the general policy area and are integrated. It can be easily noticed in the next section that the developments related to this policy mostly refer to developments in the field of asylum and migration. Accordingly, it is important to evaluate this policy area in a broad scope.

## The historical development of the EU's refugee policy

In this chapter, legal documents, programmes and regulations are analysed in order to offer the framework of the EU's refugee policy. However, before stating the important developments within this policy area, it may be appropriate to start with the EU's confession: "The current system no longer works. And for the past five years, the EU has not been able to fix it."[25] This can be seen as an outcome of the recent migration flows and the unwillingness of some member states to cooperate in coping with the crisis together.

The EU refugee policy does not date back to the beginning of the union. The refugee related developments can be traced back to the 1980s when Schengen related issues began to be discussed. Before the implementation of Schengen Agreements there was an important development within this policy area. The issue of migration and asylum were included in the Maastricht Treaty under Title VI, which was about cooperation in the fields of justice and home affairs. Here, the refugee policy of the EU started to be shaped and was related with free movement, common interests and areas of cooperation of the member states in order to achieve the objectives of the EU. It was also noted that the issues would be addressed in relation to the Human Rights and Fundamental Freedoms Convention and the Geneva Convention. In the first three paragraphs of the Article K.1 asylum policy and persons' crossing the external borders and immigration policy were stated as matters of common interest. Immigration policy was mentioned in terms of entry, movement and residence of third country nationals and unauthorized immigration on the territory of the member states.[26] According to Scholten and Penninx, with the Maastricht Treaty "*a broader framework for intergovernmental cooperation in the field of asylum and migration under the so-called Third Pillar 'non-binding' cooperation*" was established.[27] So, the policy area became

---

[25] European Commission, A fresh start on migration: Building confidence and striking a new balance between responsibility and solidarity, Press Release, 2020,
https://ec.europa.eu/commission/presscorner
/detail/en/IP_20_1706?fbclid=IwAR1fPOogwXUzByDJbEZKVgkdKwX2kH8Lo4LyIet4cZnCG8Wo
qVd8RBoPiI (Access: 24.11.2020).
[26] European Commission, Treaty on European Union, pp.131-132, https://europa.eu/european-union/sites/europaeu/files/docs/body/treaty_on_european_union_en.pdf (Access: 24.11.2020).
[27] Peter Scholten and Rinus Penninx, "The Multilevel Governance of Migration and Integration",

part of the EU treaties even though it started with non-binding intergovernmental cooperation. This was an important step in the development of this policy area.

The Dublin Convention also has a crucial place in refugee policy of the EU. It was signed in 1990 but took seven years to come into force. This Convention regulates the responsibilities of the States in examining applications for asylum. It has 22 articles and gives concepts in the first article and then states which member state would be responsible for examining the asylum application and how the process would proceed.[28] Besides noting the general framework for applications, examinations and procedures, it also aims to prevent multiple applications as the Article 3 states "application shall be examined by a single Member State".[29] Even though the Dublin Convention is one of the first steps in the development of this policy, it has been criticized many times from different aspects. According to Hurwitz, *"the criteria for determining responsibility are too formal"*, there is an *"imbalance of the burden of 'outer' EU States such as Germany, Austria, Spain, Italy and Greece"* and there is not *"genuine co-operation between national administrations who refuse to accept responsibility on the basis of indicative evidence"*.[30] Niemann and Zaun also note that *"Dublin system -according to which border countries are responsible for any asylum-seeker entering the Schengen area through territory- broke down completely"*.[31] They add that some governments preferred to suspend the Dublin Regulation for Syrians in 2015.[32] So, it can be said that there are problems in applying this system, especially in the migration crisis as there was flow of people which could not be controlled. The most important reason for this break down is that the system was overloaded more than the border states could deal with.

The next step in the development of the EU's refugee policy was the Treaty of Amsterdam. In the first part of this Treaty, under the Substantive Amendments, migration was mentioned in an article. In this article, external borders, asylum and immigration were evaluated in terms of free movements of persons.[33] The other mentions related to migration are Article 73i and

---

**Integration Processes and Policies in Europe Contexts, Levels and Actors**, Blanca Garces-Mascarenas, Rinus Penninx (Ed.), Springer Open, 2016, p.95.
[28] Eur-lex, Convention determining the State responsible for examining applications for asylum lodged in one of the Member States of the European Communities, Official Journal of the European Communities, C254/1, https://eur-lex.europa.eu/legal-content/EN/TXT/PDF/?uri=CELEX:41997A0819(01)&from=EN (Access: 24.11.2020).
[29] ibid., p.3.
[30] Agnes Hurwitz, "The 1990 Dublin Convention: A Comprehensive Assessment", **International Journal of Refugee Law**, Vol.11, No.4, 1999, p.676, doi:10.1093/ijrl/11.4.646 (Access: 24.11.2020).
[31] Arne Niemann and Natascha Zaun, EU Refugee Policies and Politics in Times of Crisis: Theoretical and Empirical Perspectives, **JCMS**, Vol.56, No.1, 2018, p.4, DOI: 10.1111/jcms.12650 (Access: 24.11.2020).
[32] ibid.
[33] European Commission, Treaty of Amsterdam, p. 8, https://europa.eu/european-union/sites/europaeu/files/docs/body/treaty_of_amsterdam_en.pdf (Access: 25.11.2020).

Article 73k under the title of Visas, Asylum, Immigration and other Policies Related to Free Movements of Persons. Article 73i was related to the establishment of an area of freedom, security and justice and some measures were stated such as measures related to *"asylum, immigration and safeguarding the rights of nationals of third countries"*.[34] Here, there is a reference to Article 73k which is also closely related with the measures on asylum, refugees, immigration policy and nationals of third countries.[35] The Amsterdam Treaty is evaluated as a fundamental change because the abovementioned migration related issues were transferred from the third pillar to the first pillar of the Union which means the transfer from an intergovernmental framework to a supranational framework.[36] This is a kind of transfer of authority and it means that the Community may have more authority in an area where nation states had full control.

Another development in this policy area was the Tampere European Council 1999. In this meeting, a Common EU Asylum and Migration Policy was put forth for the first time. Under this policy area, there were some elements, such as: partnerships with countries of origin, a CEAS, fair treatment for third country nationals and management of migration flows. These all are critical to forming a common migration policy and under each of these headings, the Council stated its suggestions, calls and instructions.[37] As Halleskov notes, *"a hope for more communitarian and inclusive Community approach"* was reinforced with the Tampere European Council.[38] This can be evaluated as an initial step for a common policy in terms of migration and the future steps were noted in the Tampere European Council. However, it is important to see whether or not it turned out be a comprehensive policy area.

After the Tampere European Council, Dublin Regulation II was adopted in 2003.[39] This Regulation established the rules and mechanisms to determine which member state is responsible for examining the asylum applications.[40] The question of which member state is generally answered as the member state *"where the asylum seeker first entered the EU"*.[41] Here, it is important to note that Dublin system supposes that member states have common standards

---

[34] ibid., p. 28.
[35] ibid., pp.29-30.
[36] Kay Hailbronner, "European Immigration and Asylum Law Under the Amsterdam Treaty", **Common Market Law Review**, Vol.35, No.5, 1998, p.1047, https://kluwerlawonline.com/ journalarticle/Common+Market+Law+Review/35.5/188634 (Access: 25.11.2020).
[37] European Parliament, Tampere European Council 15 and 16 October 1999 Presidency Conclusions, https://www.europarl.europa.eu/summits/tam_en.htm (Access: 25.11.2020).
[38] Louise Halleskov, "The Long-Term Residents Directive: A Fulfilment of the Tampere Objective of Near-Equality?" **European Journal of Migration**, Vol. 7, No.2, 2005, p.181, doi:10.1163/1571816054762205 (Access: 25.11.2020).
[39] This is the formal/binding version of the Dublin Convention adopted in 1990.
[40] UNHCR, The Dublin Regulation, https://www.unhcr.org/4a9d13d59.pdf (Access: 25.11.2020).
[41] ibid.

related to asylum, even though it is not the case.[42] This causes differences in evaluation of the application and desire of the asylum seekers to apply from one country rather than the other country.

The Hague Programme is also an important step in developing a common refugee policy as ten priorities were stated in this Programme. Common migration policy was one of these priorities and there were refugee related issues such as internal borders, external borders, visa, asylum, and integration, as well. With this Programme, once again common rules and criteria related to migration issues were stated by noting the negative outcomes of having different policies because of the Schengen area which provides free movement.[43] The third Programme after Tampere and Hague (2004 - 2009) was the Stockholm Programme (2010-2014). It was also a five-year programme which included guidelines for common policies and measures in the migration field.[44] Brown, who evaluates the Stockholm Programme in terms of freedom, security and justice, states that *"'Stockholm solution' simply papers over pre-existing cracks, leaving the EU with a continued credibility gap in this important and developing area of co-operation"*.[45] This means that these programmes are far from presenting the needs of the EU. They simply offer cooperation, but the member states have different policies and priorities and some of them are not facing the threat as others. Therefore, they do not have any intention to cooperate.

The Lisbon Treaty, as the last treaty, has importance in this process to show the final position reached within the founding treaties. However, it should not be forgotten that there have been some other developments after the treaty, as well. The policies on border checks, asylum and immigration were noted under Chapter 2 in articles 62, 63, 63a and 63b in the Lisbon Treaty. Border checks and visa related issues were addressed in Article 62. Common asylum policy, subsidiary protection and temporary protection related regulations and measures were stated in Article 63. Immigration policy related issues were given in Article 63a and lastly in Article 63b drew attention to solidarity and fair sharing of responsibility in implementation of these policies. In these articles, common policies were aimed and measures to be taken were noted one by one in terms of each policy area, which include: common visa policy, common asylum policy and common immigration

---

[42] ibid.

[43] European Commission, The Hague Programme ten priorities for the next five years, 2005, https://ec.europa.eu/commission/presscorner/detail/en/MEMO_05_153 (Access: 25.11.2020).

[44] European Commission, Migration and Home Affairs, Stockholm Programme, https://ec.europa.eu/home-affairs/what-we-do/networks/european_migration_network/glossary_search/stockholm-programme_en (Access: 25.11.2020).

[45] Dan Brown, The Stockholm solution? Papering over the cracks within the area of freedom, security and justice, **European Security**, Vo.20, No.4, 2011, p.481, DOI: 10.1080/09662839.2011.617369 (Access: 25.11.2020).

policy.[46] Here, the emphasis on solidarity is important as there were some problems in terms of solidarity during the migration/refugee crisis in 2015. As noted above, some of the member states refuse to share the responsibilities imposed by the EU. Another important point was that immigration policy was 'normalized' by "introducing qualified majority voting in this domain and strengthening the role of the European Parliament and the European Court of Justice".[47] So, these developments are crucial steps in terms of developing the refugee policy.

The Dublin Regulation[48] was amended in 2013 according to the needs of the moment. As Brekke and Brochmann note, the Dublin Regulations have two challenges. One of them is "the principle of 'first country of arrival' lays a disproportional burden on the countries on Europe's southern border" and the second one is "differences in reception conditions, processing ability, and access to social rights prompt regime competition."[49] These are the problems most discussed in terms of the Dublin Regulations, and it caused differences in processing. In September 2020, the Commission President Ursula von der Leyn announced that the Dublin Regulation would be abolished and replaced with a new European migration governance system.[50]

Lastly, the Charter of Fundamental Rights of the European Union is a crucial document that has two articles related to refugee policy. One of them is Article 18, which covers the right to asylum, and the other one is the Article 19, which is about the protection in the event of removal, expulsion or extradition and prohibits collective expulsions.[51] These two articles regulate the rights and protect a person from sending him/her to a state where his/her life will be at risk.

In what fallows, the development of refugee policy is given with the treaties, programmes and regulations. However, all of them are not mentioned in detail so as to prevent extending the context. One of these developments is CEAS. As Cecilia Malmström has noted, it had been aimed at since 1999.[52] There are some directives and regulations which sustain the

---

[46] Eur-lex, Treaty of Lisbon Amending the Treaty on European Union and the Treaty Establishing the European Community, (2007/C 306/01), https://eur-lex.europa.eu/eli/treaty/lis/sign 617369 (Access: 27.11.2020).

[47] Scholten and Penninx, op.cit, p.95.

[48] This is actually called Dublin Regulation III. Dublin Regulation II is dated 2003. The Dublin Convention of 1990 is known as Dublin I.

[49] Jan – Paul Brekke, Grete Brochmann, "Stuck in Transit: Secondary Migration of Asylum Seekers in Europe, National Differences, and the Dublin Regulation", **Journal of Refugee Studies**, Vol.28, No.2, 2014, p.148.

[50] France24, "Dublin rule for asylum seekers to be replaced, EU's von der Leyn says", 16.09.2020, https://www.france24.com/en/20200916-dublin-rule-for-asylum-seekers-to-be-replaced-eu-s-von-der-leyen-says (Access 28.11.2020).

[51] Eur-lex, Charter of Fundamental Rights of the European Union 2012/C 326/02, https://eur-lex.europa.eu/legal-content/HR/TXT/?uri=celex:12012P/TXT (Access 28.11.2020).

[52] European Commission, A Common European Asylum System, Luxembourg, Publication Office of

implementation of this system. Those directives are asylum procedures directives consisting of two directives and regulating all process of claiming asylum; receptions conditions directives also include two directives which are about the access conditions of the asylum seekers; qualification directives are about the standards for granting international protection; Dublin regulations; and Eurodac Regulations which are about taking and processing the fingerprints of asylum seekers to use in the asylum seeking process.[53] With this system and all the directives and regulations which sustain the functionality and which is for asylum seekers, it is aimed to continue the process and reach an outcome, which is actually the refugee status. This System is realized to prevent applying for asylum in more than one country to collaborate on having a common, effective and well-functioning system.

A recent development came in September 2020 with proposal of the Commission for a new Pact on Migration and Asylum which covers improved, faster and effective procedures, responsibility and solidarity, a predictable and reliable migration management system, cooperation with non-EU countries and a comprehensive approach.[54] This Pact includes previously proposed but not concluded reforms and negotiations (2016-2018) and it will also include a series of initiatives such as an Action Plan on Integration and Inclusion, a Strategy on the Future of Schengen, another Strategy on Voluntary Returns and Reintegration, an Operational Strategy on Returns, an EU Action Plan against Migrant Smuggling and a Skills and Talent Package.[55] Here, it should be noted that the Commission released an Action Plan on Integration and Inclusion 2021-2027 on 24 November 2020.[56] The Commission has also announced a package of 9 instruments. Some of them have legislative features while some are recommendations and a guidance within the new Pact on Migration and Asylum.[57] This Pact is quite comprehensive and aims a common, fast, effective, well-functioning policy that will fulfil the needs of the EU. It is constructed with the consistent attitude of the EU, its experiences and needs.

To sum up, it should be noted that the EU's refugee policy related to asylum and migration has been developed day by day with treaties, programmes, directives, regulations and actions. It began with the Dublin

---

the European Union, 2014, https://ec.europa.eu/home-affairs/sites/homeaffairs/files/e-library/docs/ceas-fact-sheets/ceas_factsheet_en.pdf (Access 28.11.2020).

[53] ibid.

[54] European Commission, A fresh start on migration: Building confidence and striking a new balance between responsibility and solidarity, op.cit.

[55] European Commission, New Pact on Migration and Asylum: Questions and Answers, https://ec.europa.eu/commission/presscorner/detail/en/qanda_20_1707 (Access 28.11.2020).

[56] European Commission, Action Plan on Integration and Inclusion 2021-2027, 2020, https://ec.europa.eu/homeaffairs/sites/homeaffairs/files/pdf/action_plan_on_integration_and_inclusion_2021-2027.pdf (Access 28.11.2020).

[57] European Commission, New Pact on Migration and Asylum: Questions and Answers, ibid.

Convention. Then it became part of the treaties but over time due to crises a need for a better functioning and more effective system emerged. Even though it is difficult to act quickly in a union of 27 member states, recent developments show that policy is developing in accordance with needs.

### The status of refugees

The previous section stated the general developments related to the EU's refugee policy step by step. The Geneva Convention is the basis of this policy and the developments related to migration, and especially asylum, forms an important part of the refugee policy. Since the early 1990s, the EU has done much in terms of developing a common policy. Recent developments are also crucial to be able to reach a common point among the member states. However, it should not be forgotten that having instruments and legal basis does not always mean good implementation of these rules and proper use of instruments. In this section, the focus is on the EU's refugee status and statistics.

As stated earlier, there have been different migration flows to the EU. The last migration flow due to the war in Syria caused a migration/refugee crisis in the EU. The member states that constitute the external border of the EU had problems in dealing with the flow of people, asylum seekers and their applications for refugee status. This can be understood better with numbers. For example, first time asylum applicants to the EU were 184,270 in 2010 and it became 1,216,660 in 2015 before dropping to 612,685 in 2019.[58] These numbers show how tragic the situation was in 2015. Even though the EU had some rules, a system, standards and other instruments to deal with these applications, it is exceedingly difficult to cope with. In order to deal with the flow of people in 2015, the EU prepared a reallocation plan. Niemann and Zaun evaluate this plan as a temporary measure and note that "it fails to establish a longer-term sustainable alternative to Dublin."[59] However, as mentioned above, the Commission President's statement related to the Dublin Regulation is important. As seen in this statement, the Dublin Regulation is not enough for such crises and it does not fulfil the needs of the EU.

Refugee numbers are also important to see how the process is conducted. Here, the statistics related to recognition of refugees should be considered. According to EU sources, in 2019 only 38% of the decisions were positive. All of these positive decisions were not related to granting refugees status. The people who were granted refugee status were 109,000, the people granted

---

[58] Eurostat, Asylum Statistics, https://ec.europa.eu/eurostat/statistics-explained/index.php/Asylum_statistics (Access 28.11.2020).
[59] Niemann, Zaun, op.cit, p.7.

subsidiary protection status were 52,000 and 45,000 people received humanitarian status.[60] However, there were some other decisions made after an appeal, for that reason the numbers increased in 2019. For example, it became 142,000 for refugees, 82,000 for subsidiary protection status and 73,000 for humanitarian status. The last number, which gives another crucial piece of information, is the pending applications, which was 929,000 in 2019.[61] Hence, it can be said that the EU is not granting the refugee status easily since more than half of the positive decisions with the cases following an appeal are subsidiary protection status and humanitarian status. It should also be remembered that just 38% of the applications are positive which includes refugee status, subsidiary protection status and humanitarian status in 2019. These are total numbers for the EU and situation and numbers change according to the member states. As can be noticed here, according to the decisions of the applicants, different statuses are granted to the applicants. The one which is the subject of this chapter is refugee status but there are also statuses like subsidiary protection status, humanitarian status and temporary protection status.[62] Here it should be noted that "while both refugee and subsidiary protection status are defined by EU law, humanitarian status is granted on the basis of national legislation."[63]

The statistics of 2018 is parallel with the statistics of 2019. According to 2018 statistics, 333,400 asylum seekers were granted protection status in the EU 28, but it was nearly 40% less than the previous year, which was 533,000 in 2017. Granting protection status differs according to member states and in 2018 Germany granted 139,600 (more than 40% of all positive decisions) protection status, Italy 47,900 and France 41,400.[64] Here, the protection status types were not clarified. It cannot be known how much of these protection statuses granted as a refugee status. So, it is difficult to evaluate the situation in the EU with these statistics. But in general, according to 2019 statistics, 38% of positive decisions shows that the EU is unwilling to grant protection status and nearly half of positive decisions were refugee status. Rather than granting refugee status, the EU prefers to grant other types of protection status.

Another point which should be mentioned is that "each EU-State develops its own rules and interpretation, resulting in discrepancies and gaps

---

[60] European Commission, Statistics on Migration to Europe, https://ec.europa.eu/info/strategy/priorities-2019-2024/promoting-our-european-way-life/statistics-migration-europe_en (Access 28.11. 2020).
[61] ibid.
[62] European Commission, Glossary: Asylum Decision, https://ec.europa.eu/eurostat/statistics-explained/index.php/Glossary:Asylum_decision (Access 28.11.2020).
[63] Eurostat, Asylum Decisions in the EU, Newsrelease, 25 April 2019, https://ec.europa.eu/eurostat/documents/2995521/9747530/3-25042019-BP-EN.pdf/22635b8a-4b9c-4ba9-a5c8-934ca02de496 (Access 28.11.2020).
[64] ibid.

among countries"[65] and the EU tries to prevent it by proposing systems and pacts as mentioned in the previous section. Developing its own rules causes different processing and decisions. For example, average processing time for Germany was 219 days for the period of 1 January – 30 June 2016 while it was 75 days for Poland and 293 days for Sweden.[66] The EU is trying to make these numbers closer to prevent gaps among the member states. Having a common policy, standards and rules is crucial for the EU to be fast, effective and well-functioning.

To sum up, it should be noted that many of the asylum seekers who applied for refugee status cannot gain this status. Only 38% were able to gain protection status in 2019. This rate does not represent refugee status as it consists of all other protection statuses. This means the rate of granting refugee status is less and the EU in general shows unwillingness in granting refugee status. But it can differ among the member states. Here, each member state of the EU is not evaluated as it is not within the scope of this chapter.

## Conclusions

The EU as a union has been dealing with migration/refugee related issues for a long time. Since the 1990s, İt has been developing a refugee policy to prevent different practices. However, as the European Commission notes "migration is a complex issue, with many facets that need to be weighted together".[67] Comprehensive refugee policy is important as is a nation state's ability to manage the process started by an asylum seeker. However, it is more important for the EU, as a union with many different member states and borderless concept. And this is the challenge for the EU: to deal with migration, asylum and refugee related issues in the most efficient way.

Well-functioning and cooperative system is a must in this policy area and the EU is trying to develop a system to fulfil the needs of the EU as a union. However, it is quite difficult to move as a union in such a policy area with 27 member states which have different conditions, interests and priorities. Even though there are inefficiency or insufficiencies within the refugee policy, the EU is consistent in developing its refugee policy by learning from its insufficiencies. It has improved in this policy area and continues to improve. There are developments which have been initiated even during the coronavirus pandemic while the EU and the whole world are combatting the virus.

---

[65] Constant and Zimmermann, op.cit., p.4.
[66] Aida Asylum Information Database, The length of asylum procedures in Europe, October 2016, https://www.ecre.org/wp-content/uploads/2016/10/AIDA-Brief-DurationProcedures.pdf
[67] European Commission, A fresh start on migration: Building confidence and striking a new balance between responsibility and solidarity, op.cit.

In a nutshell, this chapter presents a snapshot of the EU refugee policy. Following a conceptual framework defining the policy area, it focused on the historical developments related to migration, asylum and refugees to understand how this policy area has been improved, supported and developed with reference to the official initiatives and documents. Lastly, the refugee status and its reflection in statistics were presented. It should be noted that the act of moving and people's need for protection will not stop. Therefore, the EU should continue to improve its refugee policy and processes to be speedier, more efficient and fairer.

# CHAPTER 2

# THE EUROPEAN UNION MIGRATION POLICY: EVOLUTION THROUGH REFUGEE CRISIS

Sertif Demir[*]

## Introduction

The issue of Refugee has become a main challenging issue for European Union (EU) after Arab Spring occurred in 2011. Nevertheless, the subjects of refugee and asylum have well integrated in the EU policies, law and those topics are well implemented in decision and organizational structure of EU. The EU founding treaties and acquis communautaire[1] constitute of norms, principles, values which take human rights as essential one. As the issue of refugee and asylum are considered as part of human rights, EU has always attached hug importance to them.

While bearing this fact in the mind, the EU has faced a challenging refugee problem notably after 2014-2015s, because of Syrian crisis-led refugees who wanted to migrate Europe. As the refugee burden intensified in Europe, the EU has encountered many hardship. In order to cope with increased huge number of refugees, EU has taken new policies and decisions. Furthermore, the EU has also rearranged its refuge and asylum policies.

Considering all above, the aim of this paper to analyze the EU refugee policies and implementations. In order to make that analysis, the first the general refugee and asylum policy will be discussed, then paper will focus on refugee challenges its implication on the EU refugee policies. Finally, the evolution of EU refugee policies will be scrutinized. The paper will be over with general evaluation of topic.

## An overview of migration policies

As the globalization has spread and it started to reduce the barriers, migration from one sate to another state has also enlarged for the purpose of working, education, commercial, business etc. These are called voluntary migrations, result of enlarging economic activities and volume of such migration is ignorable and has not huge implication on the migrated countries. Bearing in the mind that America is land of migration, its economic

---

[*] Prof.Dr., sertifdemir@gmail.com
[1] It covers all the EU laws related to the functioning of union.

growth can also be attributed to those migrated people, among other reasons.

However, forced migration is the different type of migration which take place because of wars, conflicts natural and man-made disasters such as poverty, famine, droughts, and earthquakes. People are enforced to migrate due to unwanted conditions. Political violence, persecutions, civilian wars, degrading ecosystems are major root causes of such enforced migrations. People who migrated for such reason seek also for political asylum which can provide any migrator with more protective rights. According to statistical information, the number of the forced displaced people have enlarged year by year. Seeking protection or shield for themselves and their families can take place either crossing international borders or it can occur displacement at the same country. They are called internally displaces persons (IDPs). Migrated people seeking protection outside home country are called refugees and asylum seeker. The 1951 Geneva Convention on the protection of refugees defined that group as "individuals who have fled their country due to a "well-founded fear of being persecuted for reasons of race, religion, nationality, membership of a particular social group or political opinion" and crossed an international border to seek safety."[2] Bearing in the mind that, asylum is a fundamental right; granting it is an international obligation, per 1951 Geneva Convention on the protection of refugees.[3]

At the end of 2019, 79.5 million enforced people were in need of protection and assistance as a consequence of forced displacement.[4] It requires to provide huge humanitarian assistance to those migrations for hosting countries. According to international laws, hosted countries need to provide basic human requirements with refugees and IDPs. They need to meet their safety and protection, free access to shelter, food and health needs. Hosting countries also need to take measure against any criminal activities, violence, abuse and exploitation of refugees. For the long duration, refugees also require education support as needed.

Forced dislocation is no longer a momentary issue because in our globalized world the displacement of human being has become an ordinary problem. Displacement lasts 20 years on average for refugees and more than 10 years for 90% of IDPs.[5] Unfortunately, "Up to 85% of the enforced displaced are hosted by low- and middle-income countries."[6] Additionally, it definitely leads to internal political crisis in a hosted country because of accommodating unexpected amount of migrated people. Nevertheless, if

---

[2] EASO Asylum Report 2020.

[3] https://ec.europa.eu/home-affairs/what-we-do/policies/asylum_en (Accessed 07.10. 2020).

[4] https://ec.europa.eu/echo/what-we-do/humanitarian-aid/refugees-and-internally-displaced-persons_en (Accessed 07.10. 2020)

[5] Ibid.

[6] Ibid.

duration of forced people takes longer in hosted country, the political frustration will rise. So, the situation in 2015 in EU was the same as some EU countries close their borders to any migrated people.

**Figure 1.** 79.5 Million Forcibly Displaced Persons at the Worldwide at the End of 2019.

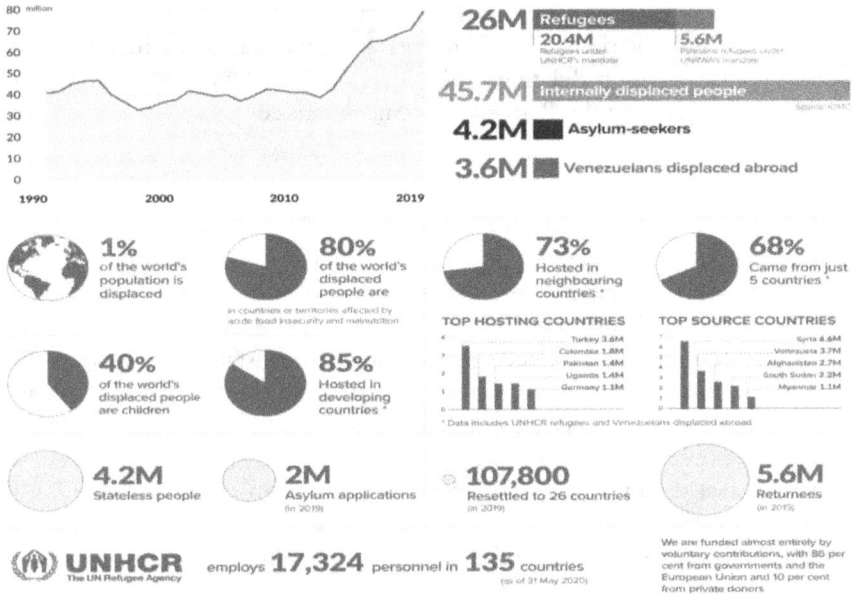

Source: UNHCR, https://www.unhcr.org/figures-at-a-glance.html

**Figure 2.** The Countries Hosting the Most Refugees

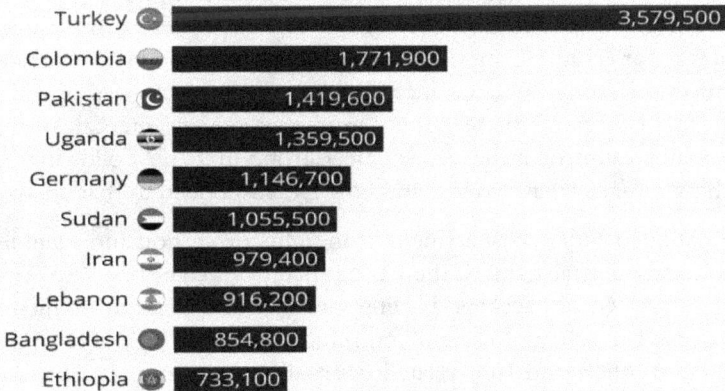

Excludes Palestine refugees under UNRWA's mandate.

Source: UNHCR and Statista

Regarding international law document that are approved by nations are as follows: The essential document for refugees are the 1951 Convention Relating to the Status of Refugees and 1967 Protocol Relating to the Status of Refugees. These documents outline the essential rights of refugees. Additionally, these documents are interrelated with the 1948 Universal Declaration of Human Rights and subsequent related documents as well as the four 1949 Geneva Conventions on international humanitarian law. On the other hand, the rights and obligations of stateless persons are included in the 1954 Convention Relating to the Status of Stateless Persons and in the 1961 Convention on the Reduction of Statelessness.[7]

## EU migration policies

Europe has a very different historical past. It has reached to its current development level after long periods of social, economic and political struggles and of religious and national originated conflicts. After the two world wars devastated the continent, powerful states of Europe understood to find solution how to live together without devastating each other. The economic integration based on common sharing and usage of valuable natural sources was seen a basic solution to overcome nationalistic purposes. This economic integration led to wider political integration based on functionalist theory. After long overhaul, it has been a venue of freedom, a venue of wealth, and a venue of social and political equities. The refugees view Europe where wealth and freedoms are guaranteed.

The issue of refugee has become very hot topic after 1990s. Because the end of Cold War led to political struggles in old Soviet Blocs countries and newly established countries. A wider reoccurrence of frozen conflicts after Cold War period led to rise war-originated refugees. Besides, globalization has also contributed to rise refugees across the world. The poor people living in Asia, Africa and Middle East countries wanted to come Europe through all illegal way for economic motives. On the other hand, political violence of Arab Uprising starting 2011 has increasingly contributed to rise of refugee problem for Europe. Notably, long-protracted Syrian internal war has become major cause of refugee to come Europe in 2015. Followings will explain how refugee crisis evolved and how EU responded to that crisis.

As mentioned earlier, pioneering human rights protection and a venue of the wealth and political stability, the EU has been viewed as first safe heaven by refugees and asylum seekers. Having said that, the EU and its member states also have a policy of asylum and refugee by being signature of 1951 Refugee Convention and later related international documents. Moreover,

---

[7] Expert Group on Refugee and Internally Displaced Persons Statistics — International Recommendations on Refugee Statistics Eurostat, March 2018, 19.

the EU composed of countries which have similar perspective on the protection rights and freedoms movement of refugees across Europe. Member countries share the same fundamental values to guarantee outlined necessary protection for refugees.[8]

Based on those facts and consideration, the EU Council takes the lead to establish an efficient and applicable migration policy.[9] Furthermore, the EU and its institutions have intensified their efforts to build a Common European Asylum System (CEAS).[10]

The most important document of the EU about refugee policy are the Common European Asylum System (CEAS) and A European Agenda on Migration. According to these documents the EU pledged to take immediate action to prevent further losses of life and to improve conditions for those seeking protection in Europe.[11]

As regards political development, the EU and the world have undergo deep and radical change. Populist rightest parties and radical right wings have gained huge popularity among voters because of prolonged global economic crisis of 2008-9, increasing unemployment, decreasing wages, xenophobia, etc. So, political climate are not so mild for the foreigners in the EU. The political conversion in Europe was the result of such political evolution. The current executive power is unprecedentedly against any kind immigration policy of the EU. The rise of autocratic leadership behavior in Hungary and Poland has created a new anti-refugee wave in Europe. The centralist parties in Europe have feared to openly support refugee policy in Europe because loss of voter's support in elections. Among that confusing situations, the refugee crisis have posed a threat to European Union integrity in 2015-2016.

Refugee were always an issue in the EU through years, however as explained above, Syrian crisis led to an unexpended rise in Syrian refugee in 2015 and 2016 in Europe. This was the huge influx of refugee that Europe experienced since World War II. In each of these two years more than 1.2 million asylum-seekers submitted their asylum claims in the EU as compared to 625,000 in 2014.[12] The EU was caught unprepared to such huge immigrant's influx although the EU was in a position to handle with refugees.

As for the emigration routes to Europe, there are three routes which

---

[8] https://ec.europa.eu/home-affairs/what-we-do/policies/asylum_en (Accessed 07.10. 2020).

[9] https://www.consilium.europa.eu/en/policies/migratory-pressures/ (Accessed 08.10. 2020).

[10] https://ec.europa.eu/home-affairs/what-we-do/policies/asylum_en (Accessed 07.10. 2020).

[11] A European Agenda on Migration, 2015 cited in Murat Necip Arman, "the Syrian Refugee Crisis and the European Union Conditionality", Doğu Anadolu Sosyal Bilimlerde Eğilimler Dergisi, Vol. 1, No. 2, 2017, pp. 10-20, p. 12-13

[12] Eurostat, 2017a; Eurostat, 2015, p. 4 cited in Arne Niemann · Natascha Zaun, "EU refugee Policies and Politics in times of Crisis: Theoretical and Empirical Per-spectives". *Journal of Common Market Studies*, Vol. 56. No. 1, 2018, pp. 3-22.

immigrants have mostly used. Those three routes have contained the Mediterranean Sea for transiting to Europe. First one is the Eastern Mediterranean route via crossing sea over Turkey. Most refugees used this direction to reach the EU land in 2015 and 16. The second most-applied route is the Western Mediterranean direction; immigrants from sub-Saharan and North Africa passes Morocco to reach Europe. The third used-route is the Central Mediterranean route easing the passage of migrants from sub-Saharan and North Africa through Libya to come Europe.[13] As understood from those explanations, the immigrants have tried to reach the costal line of Europe at very short routes. The Eastern Mediterranean route is the shortest one through which immigrants used to arrive to Aegean islands. On the other hand, land route over Bulgaria has not frequently used comparing to see routes. But it also remains a passage for refugees to exploit if other routes are blocked. Considering all those above, Turkey has seen focus point at the immigrants' journey to Europe. Therefore, the EU leadership has centralized its efforts on Turkey to find a logical solution in preventing the flow of immigrants to Europe.

Coming to member states' positions, the EU member states have generally presented a warm attitude towards the immigrants without any discriminations. However, as the burden and number of immigrant increased in 2015 and 16 some EU members such as Germany, Austria and Sweden closed their borders, hanging the Schengen system temporarily. This approach was overtly against the EU law which views freedom of movement, one of the key pillars of European integration[14] and an essential part of human right. On the other hand, Hungary reacted the EU policy of relocation of refugees across the EU territory.

After the human tragedy of immigrants in Mediterranean was seen on screen of TVs showing the deaths of innumerable refugees, and also their economic burden and political and social implications seemed unprecedentedly harmful, the leaders of the EU came a conclusion to find a solution to the refugee crisis. As mentioned, populist wave combined with media attention exacerbated the crisis and this had the potential to seriously damage the overall project of EU integration.[15] Fearing of the inflamed refugee crisis put pressure over the EU's integrity, and jeopardized the EU's future, the EU took the harsh measure in order to curb refugee flows. However, these measures were not on line with human basic rights and this put Europe in a position that disregards human rights whenever their national and/or EU interests are under threat. It was overtly not in line with the EU's

---

[13] https://www.consilium.europa.eu/en/policies/migratory-pressures/ (Accessed 08.10. 2020).
[14] Niemann and Zaun, op.cit., pp. 3-22.
[15] Ibid.

stance as it was seen as a promoter of human rights in the world.[16] Those action further exacerbated the reliability of the EU in protecting the people under persecution or under political, cultural and social pressure in their country.

## The Evolution of the EU Migration Policy through Refugee Crises

As mentioned above, the refugee crisis stressed the EU and its member states from various perspective. First, economically it was very huge burden for the EU to accommodate such huge member of immigrants. From domestically political perspective it had a potential risk to damage political establishment and social structure of member states. For example, there has been ongoing rise of populist parties and ultra-nationalism in the EU member states. Furthermore, new refugee means the less job opportunity for The EU citizen. In order to cope with the refugee crisis, the EU needed to consider those factors, otherwise it would face huge problem in internal politics. But, the EU must always rethink its pioneering role at the field of human rights. Therefore, the EU should provide a fair asylum procedures with anyone who seeks for safe shelter and who flees from "political terrorism and despotic prosecution", as expressed, "Humanism does not stop at national borders."[17]

Having assessed all the implication of the immigrant on the EU's political and economic integrity, the EU understood that a simple, fair, swift and acceptable plan was required to overcome emigrant crises in 2015. After long discussion, the EU came to conclusion to accept some measures to be implemented. Those measure played a critical role in decreasing the number of refuges coming to the EU. Based on those measures, migration to the EU have been reduced by more than 90%.

The first measure was to help the member countries who were under dire strait because of hosting refugees under threat of influx of refugees. In this perspective, Greece and Italy were the members encountering the highest numbers of refugees at its external borders. Therefore, the EU decided to employ the EU Agencies Frontex, the European Asylum Support Office (EASO), Europol, and Eurojust to provide operational support at the Mediterranean Sea.[18] This policy has largely reduced the passage of emigrants at Mediterranean but have not totally blocked. As expressed below, Turkey's collaborative efforts have played critical role at the reducing emigrants' transit to Europe.

The another policy of the EU was to relocate refugees from most

---

[16] Ibid., pp. 3-22.
[17] Thomas Straubhaar, Towards a European Refugee Policy, Intereconomics, 2015, 5, Leibniz Information Centre for Economics
[18] Niemann and Zaun, op.cit., pp. 3-22.

suffering countries to less suffering member states in order to fare share economic and political burden among the Union. Later, the EU initiated relocation and resettlement of refugees among the members in September 2015. The EU relocated 160,000 refugees from Italy, and Greece[19] to other member such as Hungary and Poland. Nonetheless, those relocation and resettlement policy created frictions among member states. Hungary aggressively reacted to this policy, but accepted to host a certain number of refugees.

Another measure was to make cooperation with refugee–related international organizations, refugee-originated countries and refugee-transit countries. Therefore, the EU focused on finding external solution to prevent the migration of refugees.[20] and international organizations. The EU aimed at containing the refugee at origin countries as IDPs or keep them at transit country or non-EU refugee-hosting countries. This policy had fruitful results as expressed below.

Firstly, the EU intensified its efforts to alleviate or remove the root causes of immigration in origin countries. In this perspectives, the EU has tried to improve the political economic and, social situation in origin countries, like Afghanistan and Iraq and other third world countries. Economic aid was considered as tool to ameliorate for economic improvement of citizen of origin countries. Fund for refugees was established to meet the cost of refugees. The member states were asked for to contribute such fund for collective effort. Additionally, political pressure was selected as instrument, in some case, to prevent political pressure and, persecution. Overall, "Carrot and stick" tactic have being implemented to contain refugees in their origin countries.

For the conflict-originated refugees, the EU has focused on ending the confliction or war among the warring parties. Thus, it aimed at removing or alleviating the conditions led to migration of people as IDPs or refugees. In this perspective, role of mediation and economic aid have been most relevant ones that the EU applied. However, the enforcing policies such as use of force threats or actually force through with UN Security Council resolutions and finally imposing sanctions to rulers of states causing instability are other policies that could be implemented.

As expressed that coordination and collaboration with international organizations such as United Nations High Commission for Refugees (UNHCR), Food and Agricultural Organization of UN (FAO), World Health Organization (WHO) are considered basic remedy for alleviating refugee burden. The European Council has executed such policies for the EU to

---

[19] Ibid.
[20] https://www.consilium.europa.eu/en/policies/migratory-pressures/ (Accessed 08.10. 2020).

organize a collective answer.

The other reactive policy has been to collaborative with the non-EU refugee hosting countries or transit countries. In this perspective, Turkey, Jordan and Lebanon are important countries which hosted most of Syrian refugees in their land. Among them, Turkey is the one of key country that the EU deadly required to collaborate. Because Turkey, as transit and hosting country of refugees, has had a critical role in preventing, reducing or diverting the immigrant strain over the EU. Based on those facts, the EU has had attached huge importance to Turkey in the refugee subjects as Syrian refugees put huge strain on the EU and member states in 2015 and 2016.

The EU-Turkey Statement of 18 March 2016 was the central policy of precluding migration from third countries to the EU. One of the solutions was to make an agreement with Turkey to keep Syrian refugees in Turkey while the EU would share the economic cost. The EU and Turkey agreed on a Joint Action Plan on 29 November 2015. In return for hosting Syrian refugees, the EU committed to re-energize Turkey's accession process by opening new negotiation chapters, accelerate the lifting of visa requirements for Turkish citizens by October 2016, and provide an initial three billion Euros to improve the situation of Syrians in Turkey.[21] An additional disbursement of 3 billion Euros was also planned, however, it has not realized yet. Although Turkey has not received promised funds all, the EU-Turkey Statement has achieved the substantial reduction of refugees entering Greece via Turkey for example refugees' number dropped by 98% between 2015 and 2016.[22] This is definitely not in line with the Turkey-EU statement of 2015 and 2016. Turkish President Erdogan several time criticized the EU for not fulfilling its promises.

The immigrant problem has demonstrated that the EU cannot resolve the refugee issue by just closing border and containing the immigrant at the third countries' land. The key to solving the refugee crisis lies in the countries of origin and in the hands of their political leaders.[23] In summary, the problem might disappear through the prevention of poverty, increasing wealth and affluent of poor people, fair sharing of national incomes, increasing political freedoms and promoting democracy, and finally clearing the cause of wars and conflicts inter-states or internal wars. If these can be achieved, the issue of immigrant would be vanished due course.

As Turkey is major partner in curbing the illegal immigration to Europe,

---

[21] Sertif Demir- Muzaffer Ercan YILMAZ, "An Analysis of the Impact of the Syrian Crisis on Turkey's Politic-Military, Social and Economic Security", Gaz' Akademik Bakış, Cilt 13 Sayı 26, Yaz 2020, pp. 1-19.

[22] Niemann and Zaun, op.cit., pp. 3-22.

[23] Straubhaar, op.cit., p. 5.

Turkey has sometimes used refugee policy as instrument of foreign policy. For example, Turkey opened its border and eased the border crossing for the refugees as the EU and the major powers of the EU did not voiced anything against Russian air attack on Turkish outposts in Idlib-Syria at the end February 2020. However, the widespread pandemic of Covid-19 has led to alleviate this problem.

### Conclusion

The EU has faced a challenging refugee problem notably after 2014-2015s, because of Syrian crisis-led refugees who wanted to migrate Europe. As the refugee burden intensified in Europe, the EU has encountered many hardship. In order to cope with increased huge number of refugees, EU has taken new policies and decisions. Furthermore, the EU has also rearranged its refuge and asylum policies. We should not forget the EU has been seen as safe shelter/heaven for the person under threat of persecution and political terrorism. On the other hand. The EU has also viewed as land of wealth and opportunities at the fields of politics, economics, social, and commercial. Therefore, people who undergone poverty, wars, civilian conflicts, and natural disasters want to migrate Europe for better future.

The EU faced very complex immigrant crisis in 2015 since the Second World War. So, the EU required a simple, fair, swift and acceptable plan to overcome emigrant crises in 2015. After long discussion period the EU came to conclusion to implement some measure and to change its refugee policy.

Assisting member countries which bear the most burden of refugees, creating fund for immigrant prevention, establishing border control system or strengthening those control systems, discriminative asylum policies for safe countries, relocation and resettlement policies of refugees in the EU lands to share burden of refugee and finally making cooperation with non-EU countries which hosting and transmitting refugees are some key refugee policies implemented by the EU. Those measure played a critical role in decreasing the number of refuges coming to the EU. In summary, through leadership of Germany, the EU has attained a successful result to cope with increasing number of emigrants.

# CHAPTER 3

# HISTORICAL DEVELOPMENT OF THE REFUGEE CRISIS IN THE EUROPEAN UNION

## Mesut Şöhret[*]

## Introduction

The new world order established after the end of the Cold War has fragmented the nature of the elements perceived as "threats" as in many other fields, and the issue of migration and refugees have started to be debated in the field of "high politics". At the same time, this period includes a process in which the association between international migration, threat and security becomes clear and migration has been politicized and securitized by its reflection on the policies implemented. Actually, when evaluated in general, it is seen that immigrants, who were regarded as necessary and efficient and encouraged by European states from after the Second World War until the 1974 Oil Crisis, and later on started to be regarded as undesirable people and even threats in Europe.

Especially it is seen that the issue of migration and refugees have been involved in a political construction process since the 1980s and has taken its place in social memory as a factor that threatens societies in political, cultural, political, economic and social terms. This evident change in the policies implemented against immigration and refugees, especially the perception of immigrant identity as criminal identity and its inclusion in the field of securitization within this framework has been supported by political discourses.

Immigrants, refugees and asylum seekers have been perceived as foreigners who have exploited the opportunities provided by the state, and this situation has caused them to be classified as 'others' within Europe. This evident change in the policies implemented against immigration and refugees, especially the perception of immigrant identity as criminal identity and its inclusion in the field of securitization within this framework has been supported by political discourses. In the meantime, this issue has become an issue that is constantly kept on the agenda by the right-wing parties in order to increase their voting potential. However, to be able to an issue to be perceived as a security problem by the society, discourses and actions must

* Assist. Prof. Dr. Gaziantep University, Faculty of Economics and Administrative Sciences, Global Politics and International Relations, sohretmesut@yahoo.com, ORCID No: 0000-0003-4052-9286

act on a common plane. At this point, the EU as a supranational structure made bilateral and multiple agreements with the countries from which they received immigration. This ensured that the securitization was accomplished by European societies thanks to the political tools and institutions that became active in time. For example, readmission agreements signed by the EU with many countries enabled the society to perceive migration as a security problem and laid the groundwork for the legitimacy of extraordinary methods that could be applied. Therefore, it is seen that a security-oriented perspective has been effective in the process of creating a common migration policy of the EU.

Securitization, which is an issue already shown as a threat, has granted absolute priority over the other issues. If this issue cannot be resolved, there is a perception that no other issue will matter. Thus, the relevant actors gain the legitimacy to solve this issue by using extraordinary means or by taking measures. In this regard, it is possible to say that the European Union, which was founded on certain humanistic values and principles, resorted to extraordinary measures, especially by making the migrant problem safe. One of the points that should be stated is that the migration that countries face within the scope of problems and threats is illegal and irregular migration rather than legal immigration.

This process brought along more restrictive and oppressive policies towards immigration issue. Although there has been progress towards developing a common migration policy within the EU with the signing of the Amsterdam Agreement in 1997, in the current situation it is not possible to talk about the existence of a common policy on immigration among member states as a whole. On the other hand, the problem of immigration is not only a problem that threatens EU countries, but also a very comprehensive discussion area that concerns both emigrant countries (sending immigrants), countries receiving immigration and transit countries.

**Migration issue and historical development in the European Union**

Migration is a phenomenon that has persisted for a variety of reasons and forms throughout the history of the world. This phenomenon has gained a global character in today's world, which is the product of a dynamic process and its impact has reached a potential that can be felt at every corner of the world.[1] In other words, globalization has brought about an increase in human movements and migration, and its effects are intensely felt on different cultures. People leave their own lives behind by various reasons and migrate

---

[1] Yaşar Aldırmaz, "Değerler Avrupası'ndan Duvarlar Avrupası'na Göç, Sığınmacılar ve Mülteci Krizi Çerçevesinde AB Hukuku ve Politikaları". **Kastamonu Üniversitesi İktisadi ve İdari Bilimler Fakültesi Dergisi**, Vol. 16, No. 2, 2017, p. 83, pp. 83-103.

for a new life; however, no country can isolate itself from the results of this process. Regardless of the nature of international migration, many states not only have been exposed to migration but have also globally felt the effects of this process almost in every aspect.[2]

Although international migration policies vary from country to country, the only constant is to ensure the continuity of the economic, social, political and cultural institutions of the nation-states. In this sense, nation-states are faced with international migration movements within the framework of a market relationship established in the context of supply-demand or repulsion-attraction factors. However, keeping immigrants under quantitative and qualitative control is at the center of migration policies as a precondition for nation-states to protect and reproduce themselves. Sometimes, when the interests of the country are in that direction, the arrival of immigrants is encouraged more, and sometimes, on the basis of the interests of the country, the arrival of immigrants is intensely prevented. Countries' migration histories are shaped by different immigration policy practices that occur within this framework and may change over time.[3]

Global migration, which is largely due to economic reasons, has been moving towards the economically developed regions of the world for about 200 years, and the migration policies of the receiving countries are shaped on the axis of economy and security. In this context, regular migration policies are developed to meet the need for cheap and qualified workforce, while many preventive measures are taken to prevent migrants with humanitarian reasons from being accepted as much as possible. The most important dynamics driving global migration movements in the 20th century are, on the one hand, deeply rooted in the poor regions of the world. The supply of migrants has been due to reasons such as poverty and unemployment. On the other hand, there has been demand for migrants for economic reasons to close the labor gap in the most developed regions with cheap labor. Therefore, in the face of this supply and demand, migration movements in the 20th century stemmed from Africa, South Asia, South America and Asia were directed to Europe and North America, the richest regions of the world.[4]

### Guest worker demand period: 1945 – 1973

In fact, the European continent was not a popular immigration

---

[2] Cansu Güleç, "Avrupa Birliğinin Göç Politikaları ve Türkiye'ye Yansımaları" **TESAM Akademi Dergisi**, Vol. 2 No. 2, 2015, p.82, pp. 81-100

[3] Doğuş Şimşek and Ahmet İçduygu, Uluslararası Göç, Politika ve Güvenlik, **Toplum ve Bilim Dergisi**, No. 140, 2017, p. 6, pp.6-10

[4] Hasan Canpolat and Hakkı Onur Arıner, **Küresel Göç ve Avrupa Birliği İle Türkiye'nin Göç Politikalarının Gelişimi**, ORSAM Rapor No. 123, Haziran 2012, p.9-10

destination until the Second World War. On the contrary, before this date, there was much immigration from Europe to the America. For example; it is thought that approximately 55-60 million Europeans immigrated to America from 1820 until World War II. After the war, the developments, especially the increase in the welfare of Europe and the conflicts that occurred in the regions around Europe, caused the phenomenon of immigration from Europe to migration to Europe.[5] This change brought along the diversity in the characteristics of migration. In this respect, immigration went through a period of ups and downs soon after World War II, especially due to economic developments. Many European countries, such as Austria, Belgium, Germany, Netherlands, France, Luxembourg, Sweden, Switzerland, which they opened their doors to many foreign "guest workers" during the economic growth period in the post-war period in Europe and in whichguest workers settled in time.

In this respect, migration policies in the EU since the Second World War can be examined in three stages as follows:

1. Inviting unskilled "guest workers" from the southern periphery countries to the industrialized countries in the north to be employed in the reconstruction works after the World War II.

2. The reunification of the immigrants who established their lives there with their families in the Europe

3. It was carried out by people who came for asylum in the West with the collapse of the communist regimes in the Eastern Bloc countries.[6]

Immigrants who came to Europe with the labor force agreements made with various countries especially between 1945 and 1970 have greatly supported the continent's re-development process after the war and thus Europe has gained economic momentum in a short time. However, the unification of immigrants with their families in the later times brought about the formation of ethnic communities in the countries of immigration. This has shown that immigrants are no longer guests.[7] Thus, they started to take steps to make guest workers stay there permanently, instead of letting them return to their countries of origin. As a matter of fact, over time, some of these workers acquired the citizenship of the countries they stayed and started

---

[5] Ufuk Alkan, "Avrupa'da Refah Devleti ve Göç İlişkisi: Refah Şovenizmi Örneği" **Ankara Üniversitesi SBF Dergisi**, Vol. 70 No. 3, 2015, p.756, pp.751-768.

[6] Channe Lindstrom, "European Union Policy on Asylum and Immigration. Addressing the Root Causes of Forced Migration; A Justice and Home Affairs Policy of Freedom, Security and Justice?" **Migration, Immigration and Social Policy**, Catherine Jones Finer (Ed.), MA, Oxford, Carlton Victoria, Blackwell Publishing, 2006, p.11-12, pp.9-47

[7] Jeroen Doomernik and Michael Jandl, **Modes of Migration Regulation and Control in Europe**, Amsterdam, Amsterdam University Press, 2008, p.19-20

to establish a permanent life in these countries. At this point, the rate of increase of foreign workers in Europe has increased significantly over time. Thus, while the ratio of foreign workers to the general population in the Western European region was 1.3% in 1950, this rate increased to 3.6% after 10 years. By 1990, this ratio increased to 10.3%.[8]

In fact, it can be said that there was a liberal and positive attitude towards migrants and guest workers in general throughout Europe until the 1973 Oil Crisis. Of course, although immigrants sometimes experienced problems with the societies in which they lived, there was not much of problem other than some individual incidents. However, when the oil embargo imposed by OPEC in 1973 started to cause a rapid increase in the unemployment rate in Europe as in the whole world, the positive attitude towards the immigrants suddenly started to reverse.Local people started to see migrants as responsible for losing their jobs and started to take an anti-immigration attitude.

### Control-oriented immigration policies: 1973-1990

The Oil Crisis that started in 1973 deeply affected the labor market in Western European countries. At this point, countries started to implement some policies such as ending immigration flux and applying quotas for immigrants, encouraging migrant workers to go to their own countries. However, although these policies caused a relative decrease in the number of migrant workers in Europe, it seems that to be that they did not give the desired result. Because the migrant workers did not lean towards returning because they did not want to stop benefiting from the social rights and services such as unemployment benefits, child benefits and health services in which they lived in Europe. Instead of returning to their home countries, they tried to bring their families they left in their home country with them legally or illegally. For instance, as of November 1973, the number of immigrants who were legally immigrated to Germany was 4 million, but in 1980 this number increased to 4.5 million.[9]

Anti-immigrant policies and restrictive measures across Europe have by-passed the way for arrivals in Europe through their legal routes. In the period between 1973 and 1980, the issue of immigration started to be criminalized by European governments in general, and it was seen as a problem that should be tackled within the security concepts of countries.[10] This period

---

[8] Paola Subacchi, "Temporary Immigration: A Viable Policy for Developed Countries", **International Economics Programme**, Chatham House Briefing Paper, 2005, p.2

[9] Ayhan Gençler, "Avrupa Birliği'nin Göç Politikası" **Sosyal Siyaset Konferansları Dergisi**, No. 49, 2005, p.175, pp.173-197.

[10] Rinus Penninx et. all, "**Migration and Integration In Europe: The State of Research**", Centre on Migration, Policy and Society, Oxford, Oxford University Press, 2008, p.4

refers to a period in which "tolerant" immigration policies in Europe changed towards "control-oriented" policies.[11] In other words, it refers to a period in which the issue of immigration in Europe began to be securitization. It is the period in which the emphasis is on the wow that immigration can cause serious problems that cannot be ignored. As temporary foreign worker admission programs and other programs regulating migration were reviewed, a controlled attitude towards migration began to be developed both nationally and internationally in order to prevent illegal migration flows.[12]

In this regard, it is possible to say that since the second half of the 1970s, European societies and governments have started to show a radical change in their view of immigrants. At this point, immigrants and asylum seekers are no longer people who require humanitarian aid and protection or serve an economic purpose such as worker migrants, but the above-mentioned "organizational" and "conceptual" scheme (trying to extract shares from the state's social services and / or endangering the social order) started to be seen as the label of these people.[13]

Since the mid-1980s, there has been a significant increase in the number of refugees and asylum seekers worldwide. Apart from economic, political and social reasons, these people are forced migrants fleeing from conflict and violence. During this period, serious migration waves started to be seen not only in Europe but also in other continents of the world. Western Europe started to become an important target country for immigrants fleeing from military conflicts, economic difficulties and political reasons in Western Europe?, Asia and Africa, especially the Balkans, especially due to its proximity and ease of transportation. Therefore, "the issue of asylum and immigration became one of the most important agenda items in Western European countries."[14]

## Supra-nationalization of immigration issue: 1990-2010

With the collapse of the communist regime in Eastern Europe and the Soviet Union, European countries faced an intense wave of immigration and asylum, and the perspective of the migration regime, which was previously expressed with the slogan 'Europe surrounded by castle walls', has now turned into a more conservative political atmosphere.[15] Undoubtedly, the biggest reason for this situation is the collapse of the regimes in the Soviet

---

[11] Jef Huysmans, "The European Union and the Securitization of Migration", **Journal of Common Market Studies**, Vol. 38, No 5, 2000, p.754, pp.751-777
[12] Stephen Castles and Mark J. Miller, **Göçler Çağı: Modern Dünyada Uluslararası Göç Hareketleri**, Çev. Bülent Uğur Bal and İbrahim Akbulut, İstanbul, İstanbul Bilgi Üniversitesi Yayınları, 2008, p.131
[13] Canpolat and Ariner, Ibid., p.12
[14] Castles and Miller, 2008, p.144
[15] Ahmet İçduygu, Türkiye-Avrupa Birliği İlişkileri Bağlamında Uluslararası Göç Tartışmaları, İstanbul, TÜSİAD Yayınları, 2006, p.41

Union and the Eastern Block, which caused a major paradigm shift in international relations. After this change, the irregular flow of immigrants from Central and Eastern European countries and from the Balkans to Western European countries suddenly caused the issue of immigration to turn from a national problem to an international problem for the European Union countries. In other words, this issue of migration has turned from a national dimension to a supranational problem and has become a priority problem for the European Union that needs to be solved.

Since the collapse of Soviet Union, migration and refugees have been constructed as a barrier that poses threats to the security, identity and wellbeing of European states and societies, and they have been the target of policies aimed at reducing the risks posed by it. While securitized discourses, politics and policy responses are often articulated at the national level, the European Union has been the locus of both discourses and practices securitizing migration in the European context.[16]

Until the 1990s, in addition to migrants mainly from Asia and Africa, after the collapse of the Eastern Bloc, immigrants from Central and Eastern European countries, who were described as "old enemy brothers", were also added to the immigration influx. After the planned and centralized economic model, the workforce in the former Eastern Bloc countries trying to adapt to the capitalist economic model turned seriously to the European Union countries in this period in order to reach a better living condition. After this influx from Eastern Bloc, the immigration has officially turned into Europe's internal and external problem.

Instead of going to countries such as Spain, Portugal, Greece, which had had low income at that time and had just joined the Union, it is seen that they preferred to go to countries such as Germany, France, the Netherlands, Belgium, England and Sweden which had developed economies. Immigrants think that they can provide them with better living conditions and they can have easier employment opportunities. However, the main problem at this point was that the union countries with these developed economies, which had started to adopt a negative attitude towards immigrants after the oil crisis, did not want the immigrants, but there were many Eastern Bloc countries that fell apart due to reasons such as geographical proximity and border controls were not good enough at that time. Immigrants and asylum-seekers entered the countries with developed economies, as was mentioned above, illegally and irregularly.

Thus, the phenomenon of immigration for Europe has become

---

[16] Lena Karamanidou, "The Securitisation of European Migration Policies: Perceptions of Threat and Management of Risk" **The Securitisation of Migration in the EU Debates Since 9/11**, Gabriella Lazaridis, Khursheed Wadia (Ed.), London, Palgrave Macmillan, 2015, p.37, pp.37-61

increasingly included in the security area; on the other hand, it has become difficult to control and more harmful for the union.[17] The data of the UN High Commissioner for Refugees confirm that there became a significant increase in asylum applications to European Union countries during this period (1989-1994).[18] Over four million asylum seekers came to Europe in the 1990s. Again, in the same period, it is estimated that 800.000 irregular migrants entered Europe annually.

Considering all this human mobility, the European Union, which thinks that it has enough reasons to create a common migration policy, has laid the first foundations for a common migration policy.[19] Especially, European countries, faced with immigration waves that were not their own preference, turned towards stricter policies towards immigration from the 1990s to the early 2000s. As of this period, ethnic diversity, which was formed due to migration, can be shown as the source of negative reactions against international migration and immigrants in the EU because many European Union countries seem very eager to see the increasing number of foreign immigrants as a potential security threat to their population. Another development that supports this de facto situation is that xenophobia, which emerged in the Western world after the September 11, 2001 attacks, started to be utilized increasingly by the governments of the European Union countries to produce anti-immigrant policies.

On the other hand, with the immigrants coming from the Balkans to the European Union countries during the dissolution process of Yugoslavia, this problem has gradually started to raise the issue of protecting the external problems of the Union. After the Schengen Agreement, which was signed in 1990 and entered into force after its ratification in 1995, not only caused the borders to become ambiguous within the European Union, but also revealed the necessity of the union to act jointly to ensure the security of external borders. After the Schengen Agreement, refugees who succeed in entering the borders of the European Union through legal or illegal means can find the opportunity to go to the target country s/he wants without encountering any problems. In this respect, the necessity of keeping refugees outside the borders of the EU, that is, strengthening the borders of the union has become clear.

With the signing of the Maastricht Treaty in 1992, the European Community, which was named "European Union", evolved from economic

---

[17] Hakan Samur, "Avrupa Birliğinde Göçe Yönelik Global Yaklaşım", **Uluslararası İnsan Bilimleri Dergisi**, Vol. 5, No. 2, 2008, p. 4, pp.1-16.

[18] İçduygu, Ibid., p.49

[19] Yusuf Furkan Şen and Gözde Özkorul, "Türkiye–Avrupa Birliği İlişkilerinde Yeni Bir Eşik: Sığınmacı Krizi Bağlamında Bir Değerlendirme", **Göç Araştırmaları Dergisi**, Vol. 2, No. 2, 2016, p.97, pp. 86-119.

integration to political integration. In the "Justice and Home Affairs" column of the EU, which is built on three pillars, the field of immigration and asylum has been an important policy title. With the Maastricht Treaty, nine policy areas are defined as "issues of common interest" regarding internal security:

✓ Asylum policy

✓ Inspections at external borders,

✓ Immigration policy for third country nationals,

✓ Drug trafficking

✓ Fraud

✓ Criminal and judicial cooperation,

✓ Customs cooperation,

✓ Police cooperation (particularly with regard to drug trafficking and other serious crimes) related)

✓ Common knowledge within the Union through the European Police Office (Europol) exchange system[20]

With the Maastricht Treaty the issue of immigration and asylum was addressed as a common issue for the first time. Following the determination of a common policy and area of interest regarding migration management with the Maastricht Treaty, the Amsterdam Treaty came into force in 1999. With the agreement, common approaches were adopted in the field of visa, residence and asylum, and efforts were made to harmonize asylum policies and practices in member countries.[21] In fact, with the Amsterdam Treaty, it is a noteworthy development that the Union has authority in important areas such as immigration, which the states have included in the national independence areas.[22]

The Amsterdam Treaty is the second turning point in the formulation of a common policy regarding migration and asylum policies within the framework of the EU structure. Within the framework of the agreement, an "area of freedom, security and justice" was created and the "justice and domestic affairs cooperation" column, which is one of the basic principles of the Maastricht Treaty, became operational. Free movement of persons and

---

[20] Julliet Lodge and Mustafa Bayburtlu, **Avrupa Birliği'nin Adalet ve İçişleri Alanındaki Müktesebatı ve Türkiye'nin Uyumu**, İstanbul, İktisadi Kalkınma Vakfı Yayınları, 2002, p.13
[21] Zerrin Savaşan, "AB'de Sığınma Hakkı: Ortak Sığınma Sistemi Oluşturma Amacı ve Devam Eden Kısıtlamalar", **İnsan Hakları Yıllığı**, No. 27, 2010, p.22-24, pp.13-34.
[22] Petra Bendel, "Everything Under Control? The European Union's Policies and Politics of Immigration" **The Europeanization of National Policies and Politics of Immigration**. Thomas Faist and Andreas Ette (Ed.) London, Palgrave MacMillan, 2007, p.33, pp.32-48

goods, controls at external borders, asylum, immigration and protection of the rights of non-member country citizens, judicial cooperation in civil matters have been transferred to the first column called "European Communities."[23]

Since 1999 establishing the "Common European Asylum System" (CEAS) initiatives have been taken on behalf of member states and attempts have been made to establish minimum standards to be complied with. In this context, it is aimed to increase the sense of responsibility and solidarity between EU countries with the relevant regulations of the refugees, as well as cooperation between the member states to harmonize EU member states with non-EU states. In this framework, the minimum standards expected to be implemented by the member states between 1999-2005, which is called the first stage of CEAS, have been determined. Negotiations on EU regulations, which are qualified as the second stage and will allow the further harmonization of the legal regulations of the member states regarding refugees, are still going on.[24]

The most important development regarding the common immigration policies developed after the Maastricht and Amsterdam Agreements is the Tampere (Finland) Summit held on 15-16 October 1999. It was emphasized that four areas are necessary for policies to be developed within the borders of the Union and with third countries. These areas include the development of cooperation with the countries of origin of immigrants and asylum seekers, the common asylum system, fair treatment of third-country citizens and the management of migration flows, including heavy sanctions for those engaged in illegal immigrant trafficking.[25] The main issues addressed at the Tampere Summit are listed below.

✓ Managing migration flows

✓ Developing a viable policy on visas and other illegal documents

✓ Establishing EU joint visa issuing offices within the framework of closer cooperation between third countries and EU consulates

✓ Serious sanctions against human trafficking in illegal immigration and criminals who abuse migrants economically,

✓ Union member states to work together with Europol to make more efforts to identify such criminal organizations and to

---

[23] Enver Bozkurt et all, **Avrupa Birliği Hukuku**, Ankara,Yetkin Yayınları, 2012, p.63
[24] Enes Bayraklı and Kazım Keskin, **Türkiye, Almanya ve AB Üçgeninde Mülteci Krizi**, SETA Yayınları, No. 143, 2015, p.11, pp.1-32
[25] Aslı Şirin Öner, "Göç Çalışmalarında Temel Kavramlar", **Küreselleşme Çağında Göç: Kavramlar, Tartışmalar**, Suna Gülfer Ihlamur Öner and N. Aslı Şirin Öner, (Ed.) İstanbul: İletişim Yayınları, 2016, p.556

capture these criminal networks

✓ Active control of the future borders of the Union[26]

✓ Voluntary return incentives as a result of cooperation with transit and source countries involved in this process and signing readmission agreements with these countries

In fact, with the Tampere Summit, it was not aimed to establish a new asylum system, but to create a common system by harmonizing existing policies and practices. One of the most important results of Tampere Summit is that the "external dimension" constitutes the cooperation within the scope of migration and asylum. In line with the idea of solving the problem from its main source, the partnership with the mentioned source and transit countries appeared as legal outputs in line with the supportive studies developed in the following period. It is the work of the High-Level Working Group (HLWG), to focus on the root causes of people's migration and to define and to implements action plans to protect refugees in their country of origin, and to design common readmission policies within a short period of time. These are the prominent developments compared to the studies conducted. Within the framework of these results, a program was created to achieve the targets agreed at the summit and this program was put into practice between 2000-2005.[27]

The Hague Summit was held in 2003 in line with the goals set out in the Tampere Summit. As a result of the summit, a plan that will continue until 2010 emerged. In this plan; studies on the following issues were envisaged.

✓ Strengthening the asylum systems of source and transit countries

✓ Developing cooperation with third countries

✓ Combating irregular immigration

✓ Development of resettlement programs

✓ Increasing efforts to ensure border security[28]

With these developments, an issue such as asylum and immigration that has progressed in the direction of human rights has ceased to be an issue considered within the scope of migration, and the issue of migration has now begun to be addressed on the axis of security in a way that supports the examples given before. This axis shift has been one of the most important

---

[26] Anneliese Baldaccini and Helen Toner, "From Amsterdam and Tampere to the Hague: An Overview of Five Years of EC Immigration and Asylum Law" **Whose Freedom, Security and Justice**. Anneliese Baldaccini, Elspeth Guild and Helen Toner (Ed.) Portland, Hart Publishing. 2007, p.3-4, pp.1-22.
[27] Fatma Elmas Yılmaz, **Avrupa Birliği Göç-Dış Politika İlişkisinde Paradigma Değişimi**, (UnpublishedPhD Dissertation), Ankara: Ankara Üniversitesi Sosyal Bilimler Enstitüsü, 2016, p.42
[28] Güleç, Ibid., p.86-87

factors affecting the asylum and immigration policies implemented in the current period.[29]

As a result of the Hague program covering the period between 2005 and 2010, guidelines were drawn up for the establishment of funds to regulate activities in the field of freedom, security and justice, the signing of readmission agreements, the preparation of EU joint resettlement programs, the establishment of a European migration network and in the return of unregistered migrants.[30] On the other hand, the "2008 European Union Asylum and Migration Pact", put forward during the Presidency of France, was formed around five principles:

1. The regulation of legal immigration as determined by each member country's own priorities, needs and acceptance capacities

2. Controlling illegal immigration by making sure that illegal migrants are returned to their country of origin or transit countries

3. Making border controls more effective

4. A single asylum procedure and a single status for refugees

5. Establishing inclusive partnerships to support interaction between countries of origin and transition and migration and development[31]

One of the most effective regulations in the structure of the European Union's immigration regulations has been the Lisbon Treaty, which came into force on 1 December 2009. The Lisbon Treaty touched upon an issue that had been omitted in previous agreements and determined the purpose of establishing a common migration policy. Within this context, the Lisbon Treaty is an agreement that changes the structure of the agreement establishing the European Community. It states that the Union should develop a common immigration policy in order to effectively manage migration flows, ensure the fair life of third-country citizens legally residing in member states, and legal protection in the member states of the Union at each stage. In addition, he stated that illegal immigration and human trafficking should be fought.[32] However, the Lisbon Treaty has made amendments in a way to strengthen outward-oriented actions, including the external dimension of migration action, and redesign the actors involved in

---

[29] Canpolat and Ariner, Ibid., p.16

[30] Nurcan Özgür and Yeşim Özer, **Türkiye'de Sığınma Sisteminin Avrupalılaştırılması**, İstanbul, Derin Yayınları, 2010, p.67

[31] Hasan Canpolat and Hakkı Onur Ariner, Ibid., p.13

[32] Sevinç Çetinkaya, AB Göç Politikalarının Güvenlikleştirme Ekseninde İncelenmesi, (UnpublishedPhD Dissertation), Bolu, Bolu Abant İzzet Baysal Üniversitesi Sosyal Bilimler Enstitüsü, p.74-75

this action. Innovations for the foreign policy of the Union, such as the implementation of the High Representative of the EU Foreign Relations and Security Policy, have outlined the institutional framework for a more effective cooperation to blend the relationship between immigration and foreign policy.[33]

The Stockholm Program, which was accepted at the Brussels summit in December 2009, was announced as the third five-year plan, which is the other phase of the area of freedom, security and justice. This program is a continuation of the Tampere and The Hague Summits and the aim Program were to guide the studies on migration in the 2010-2014 periods.[34] The Stockholm program aims at ensuring security by making legal arrangements for combating illegal immigration and cross-border crime, while facilitating concessions for legal entries into the territory of the Union. Within the Stockholm Program, the Council of the European Union focused on the risks and opportunities brought about by the increase in human mobility and opened the discussion of the idea that a well-managed migration would be beneficial for both emigration and immigration parties. At the summit, which examined the process for affirmation rather than 'securitization' policies against migration waves, it was stated that a worker deficit might occur in the future due to the demographic structure of the union and in this case, flexible migration policies would contribute to the economic development and performance of the Union. As stated in the meetings and summits held until this period, the Council at the Stockholm Summit called for a comprehensive and sustainable common immigration policy in line with the aim of managing migration flows, taking into account all these prospects for the future.[35]

### The Transformation of Europe into a Fortress after the Arab Spring: From 2010 to Present and Future

The second decade of the 21st century started with a process called the Arab Spring, which is considered to be one of the most important turning points in world political history. This period, which started in Tunisia in 2011 and resulted in the change of many authoritarian regimes in the Middle East and North Africa region, was not limited to its own geographical area, but also had different effects on many regions of the world. In other words, The Arab Spring revolutions have brought about major changes in the Arab world and its neighboring countries, the revolutions have generally been followed by years, perhaps even decades, of instability, resulting in deep and comprehensive changes. The changes taking place in the Arab world have

---

[33] Yılmaz, Ibid., p.48
[34] Uğur Özgöker and Ferhat G. Batı, "Avrupa Birliği Hukukunda Göç Sorunu Parametreleri. Ekonomi", **İstanbul Arel Üniversitesi Yönetim ve Sosyal Araştırmalar Dergisi**, Vol. 1, No. 2, 2016, pp.1-10.
[35] Çetinkaya, Ibid., p.75-76

significantly affected migration, asylum seekers, and people's movement, as well as the policies pursued by countries on migration-related issues.[36]

In this respect, undoubtedly, the region most affected by these population movements was the European continent. Because the destination countries that irregular migrants and refugees from the Middle East and North Africa desire to go to for a better life have generally been European Union countries. This situation has caused the problem to increase more in the European Union countries, which already have a big problem in the issue of refugees, and by ignoring the humanitarian dimension of the problem; mostly the member countries of the Union develop policies to protect the external borders of Europe. In other words, it is possible to say that the main phenomenon shaping the refugee policy of the EU, which was subjected to an intense influx of refugees and migrants after the 2010 Arab Spring, is trying to keep refugees away from the European border with security-based practices.

In fact, while the developments that started in the 1990s on the way to form a common migration policy within the EU to be experienced, a security-oriented approach was generally adopted in the context of the external dimension of migration. As a result of the conflicts and instabilities in various parts of the world as well as economic concerns, the EU has always been a target for irregular migrants.[37] The idea of "Fortress Europe"[38], in which the security of external borders was increased as a result of the increasing irregular migration movements towards the EU in the 2000s, gained weight in the eyes of many member states.

When revolts broke out at the end of 2010, the region was home to almost 8 million first-generation migrants; 62% of them were living in an EU member state, 27% in another Arab state (20% in the Gulf) and 11% in another part of the world. By world standards, most of these countries were above average senders of international migrants with first-generation emigrants representing between more than 2% of the total population in Syria and 12% in Lebanon, compared with a 3% world average. Libya, a major receiver of international migrants, was the only country with a small

---

[36] Mohammed Torki Bani Salameh, "Migration from the Arab Spring Countries to Europe: Causes and Consequences" Smart Technologies and Innovation for a Sustainable Future. Advances in Science, Technology & Innovation, Al-Masri A., Curran K. (Ed.) (IEREK Interdisciplinary Series for Sustainable Development). Springer, Cham. 2019, p. 1.

[37] Hanifi Sever and Muhammed Sever, "Avrupa Birliği ve Türkiye Ekseninde Yasadışı Göç ve İltica Paradoksu: Domino Etkisi Sonrası Yaşananlar", **Polis Bilimleri Dergisi**, Vol. 15, No. 2, 2013, p.89, pp.85-108

[38] Contrary to the official discourse of the EU, it is the concept used to define its boundaries on the basis of ethnic culture and express that it can be exclusionary rather than inclusive against different cultures.

percentage of emigration (1% of its population).[39]

Although the refugee influx seen at the end of 2010 was at a high rate for Europe, the rebellion movement that started against the Assad regime in Syria during this period triggered a very serious migration movement for the European Union countries after a short time. The search for asylum of millions of people who were displaced from their homes as a result of the turmoil that started in Syria in 2011 has led to the biggest refugee crisis after the Second World War. So much so that, according to UNHCR? Syrian crisis data, approximately 5,6 million people had to leave their country in Syria alone, and more than 6,6 million people were internally displaced.[40] With this situation, Syria has become the first among the countries that have been the source of migration, passing Afghanistan.

The immigration movement, which started with the conflicts in Syria, primarily affected neighboring countries. This resulted in migration movements. According to data from UNHCR Syria Crisis Intervention, the majority of Syrian refugees are in Turkey, Lebanon, Jordan and Iraq. With the Syrian crisis, there was a noticeable increase in the number of Syrians among these irregular migrants. Irregular immigration movements, which have increased as a result of mass influxes, have become one of the most important topics of the EU security agenda. In this context, many operations were initiated under the coordination of FRONTEX? in order to prevent irregular migrants from reaching the EU borders.[41] Despite all these efforts of the EU, according to the UNHCR 2015 Global Trends Report, more than 1 million people reached Europe in 2015, 50% of which were Syrians.[42]

In fact, it is possible to say that 10 years have passed since the beginning of the Syrian Crisis, but the EU has not been able to act in common at the point of solving the refugee crisis as a whole. So, Hungary, which was the focus of discussions during the summer of 2015, when the refugee crisis reached an acute level, claimed on 23 June 2015 that the number of refugees coming to the country had reached 60 thousand since the beginning of the year, and announced that it suspended the Dublin System as there had been no signs of solidarity for the solution of the problem within the EU. Faced with a controversial reaction from Brussels, Hungary had to announce its reversal the next day. Despite this, when the Hungarian Parliament decided to put barbed wire on the border with Serbia on July 7, 2015, there was no

---

[39] Philippe Fargues and Christine Fandrich, **Migration after the Arab Spring**, Migration Policy Center Research Report 09, 2012, p.6
[40] Syria Emergency (19 April 2018), https://www.unhcr.org/syria-emergency.html (Access 09.01.2021)
[41] Yusuf Furkan Şen and Gözde Özkorul, 2016, p.103-104
[42] UNCHR Global Trends Forced Displacement in 2015 Report, (2015), p.7
http://www.unhcr.org/statistics/unhcrstats/576408cd7/unhcr-global-trends-2015.html (Access 09.01. 2021)

negative reaction from Germany. With this decision, Hungary aimed at preventing refugees from coming through Greece from reaching the country by crossing Serbia.[43]

Despite all the obstacles and the barbed wire, the migration flow towards the European Union countries continued increasingly between 2015-2020. The relapse of different practices in the union regarding the Refugee Crisis has also led to the inability to develop a common policy for the solution of the ongoing crisis. Externalization of this crisis cannot be solved within the Union; in order to prevent the mobility of immigrants towards the EU is trying to resolve with the cooperation with Turkey. In addition to that, in 2015, the EU Commission made a decision to reduce the burden on Italy and Greece, which were at the forefront of the migration crisis, by relocating 160,000 asylum seekers through the mandatory quota system of the member states. Czech Republic, Hungary and Poland objected to this decision and refused to take asylum seekers. There upon, the EU Commission filed a lawsuit against the three countries in question in the European Court of Justice. Although the court finds the countries that do not want to accept the mandatory quota application unfair after 5 years, these countries still resist not applying the court decision.[44] The common European asylum policy proposed on the basis of basic EU values such as solidarity and fair sharing of responsibility among the Union countries has been met with serious objections, especially in the eyes of Eastern and Central European countries, both discursively and in action. Considering that the objections coincide with the narrow Member State interests and feed from the exclusion of "Fortress Europe" in some places, it is clear that the EU falls short of its vision of being a value-based community in the management of the refugee crisis.[45] Although the European Union tries to establish a common policy on refugees, immigration policies and how many refugees will be accepted come into consideration by sovereign of member states. For this reason, countries prefer to act by prioritizing their own interests.[46]

2015 was a difficult year for both Turkey and EU, because when terrorist activities spread beyond Syrian territory and illegal immigration and asylum requests exploded, both actors faced security impasse. During this period, 99 % of the illegal immigrants entered the EU from Italy and Greece reached to

---

[43] Bayraklı and Keskin, Ibid., p.16

[44] ECJ condemns refusal to take in refugees (03 April 2020), https://www.eurotopics.net/en/238291/ecj-condemns-refusal-to-take-in-refugees# (Access 09.01.2021)

[45] Beken Saatçioğlu, "AB'nin Mülteci Krizi: Normlar-Çıkarlar Dikotomisi Üzerinden AB'yi Yeniden Değerlendirmek", **Türkiye-AB İlişkilerinde Yeni Bir Konu: Mülteci Sorunu ve Türkiye-AB İşbirliği**, Yaprak Gülcan, Sedef Akgüngör ve Yeşim Kuştepeli (Ed.), İstanbul, İktisadi Kalkınma Vakfı Yayınları 2017, p.226

[46] Deniz Karakaş, "Mülteci Sorunu Çerçevesinde Avrupa Birliği–Türkiye İlişkileri", **Ormer Perspektif Serileri**, No 16, 2016, p.3

850,000 using the Eastern Mediterranean route.[47] In fact, 10,000 people a day have been found to make the entry into EU territory from Turkey.[48] EU realized it could not fight irregular and illegal immigration without Turkey and began refugees' dialogue process with Turkey rapidly.

The dialogues that started in October 2015 with many legal gaps and integration deficiencies turned into bargains within the framework of mutual national interests.[49] But efforts to intervene in the problem outside the borders of the EU have made it advantageous to Turkey in the first place. For this reason, Turkey had the opportunity to gain the visa liberalization. In addition, the agreement text to which financial support was added had actually been made win-win for the parties. By waiving interest for all EU readmission agreements to use the conditionality principle in the text of the agreement were signed on March 18, 2016 with Turkey. Thus, the process to be completed was brought forward 1.5 years and illegal entries to the Union were prevented to a great extent with the gradual returns that started on 20 March. The agreement provided the EU with the targeted benefit for.[50] But immediately after the agreement, the Union and Turkey began questioning the value of the asymmetric advantage. Because the purpose of the agreement from the beginning of the Union, was securitization and externalization with curbing illegal immigration from Turkey and it was to ensure that those arrested would have been sent back to Turkey.[51]

The Most Challenging point of the agreement was to declaration of Turkey as a safe third country. Because, according to the EU acquis, return and acceptance agreements can only be signed by providing the safe third country condition. According to international law, there should be no geographical restrictions in safe third countries.[52] However, the Union has ignored the condition here for its strategic interests. Response to ongoing violence in the country of origin, and the security conditions in Turkey, it is also appropriate to thematize of the rule of non-refoulement. It has found the area to support the decision taken by the Union. But Turkey was charged with many responsibilities and costs. Those illegal immigrants who were unable to return to the country of origin did not receive refugee status in

---

[47] Yusuf Adıgüzel, **Göç Sosyolojisi**, Ankara: Nobel Yayıncılık, 2019, p.130.

[48] Yonca Özer,"Mülteci Sorununun Türkiye-AB İlişkilerine Yansımaları", **Türkiye-AB İlişkilerinde Yeni Bir Konu: Mülteci Sorunu ve Türkiye-AB İşbirliği**, Yaprak Gülcan, Sedef Akgüngör and Yeşim Kuştepeli, (Ed.) İstanbul: İktisadi Kalkınma Vakfı Yayınları, 2017, p.45, pp. 37-69.

[49] Yeliz Yazan, Avrupa Birliği'nin Yasadışı Göç Politikası: Türkiye Örneği Çerçevesinde İnsan Hakları Sorunsalı, İstanbul: Milenyum Yayınları, 2016, p.183

[50] Özer, Ibid., p.46-47

[51] Canpolat and Ariner, Ibid., p.17

[52] Ahmet Ceran, "Türkiye-AB Mülteci Uzlaşısına İnsan Hakları Düzleminde Alternatif Bir Bakış: Türkiye 'Güvenli Ülke' Midir?", Türkiye-AB İlişkilerinde Yeni Bir Konu: Mülteci Sorunu ve Türkiye-AB İşbirliği, Yaprak Gülcan, Sedef Akgüngör and Yeşim Kuştepeli (Ed.), İstanbul: İktisadi Kalkınma Vakfı Yayınları 2017, p. 73

Turkey due to geographical constraints. They could not be deported in accordance with the principle of non-refoulement.[53] The EU tried to create a buffer zone by externalizing illegal immigration through safe third country and readmission agreements. Transit countries created disparity in the number of people being sent back to Turkey. It has also been turned into a win-lose deal and agreements not provided all the promised financial support to Turkey.[54] By the end of 2019 the number of illegal immigrants arrested in Turkey reached 454 000.[55] As a result of military casualties after airstrike of Esad regime in Idlib in February 27, 2020, Turkish President Recep Tayyip Erdogan announced that Turkey would no longer stop Syrian refugees from reaching Europe.[56] Thus, readmission treaty between the EU and Turkey was canceled. This situation led to a new twist to the EU-Turkey relations. In this case, once again the EU shown that Turkey was a vital partner to combat illegal immigration. However, as long as the European Union does not give up its Fortress Europe stance, it seems unlikely that it will be successful in the refugee crisis.[57]

## Conclusion

Integration policies in the European Continent are actually highly intertwined with migration policies, and the development of the EU can be read through the development of migration policies. From this point of view, the essence of the EU's immigration policies is based on bringing the immigrants whom they need to support the EU area on one hand while integrating them within itself. In this respect, the EU has paved the way for free movement by strengthening the integration within itself after the World War II. Here, the needs of European countries are at the forefront. On the other hand, it aimed at keeping irregular migration at the lowest level by developing practices that strengthen the protection of its external borders. While the integration dimension of immigration policies has created a free movement zone in the continent that has not been seen before in world history. On the other hand, external borders protection policies and integrated border management as unique examples have gradually

---

[53] Barış Özdal, "Uluslararası Göç ve Nüfus Hareketleri Bağlamında Türkiye", Bursa, Dora Yayınları, 2018, p. 301.

[54] Adıgüzel, Ibid.,p.141-142, p.188

[55] Murat Erdoğan, "Açık Kapı Politikasından Açık Sınır Politikasına Türkiye'deki Suriyeliler", March 9, 2020, https://www.uikpanorama.com/blog/2020/03/09/acik-kapi-politikasindan-acik-sinir-politikasina, (Access 09.01.2021)

[56] Turkey says will not stop refugees from reaching Europe after troops killed in Syria, February 28, 2020 https://www.france24.com/en/20200228-turkey-says-will-not-refugees-from-reaching-europe-after-troops-killed-in-syrian-air-strike (Access 09.01.2021)

[57] Merve Zorlu and Mustafa Yetim, "Yasa Dışı Göçle Mücadele Bağlamında Avrupa Birliği ve Türkiye Politikalarının Karşılaştırması", **Ortadoğu Etütleri**, Vol. 12, No. 2, 2020, p. 342, pp.325-348

transformed the EU into a European fortress.[58]

The 1973 Oil Crisis can be considered as a turning point in the emergence of the refugee problem across Europe. The unemployment problem that emerged after this crisis changed the perspective of refugees and caused them to be considered as harmful people who exploit the resources of the states. The second important turning point in the refugee problem in the European Union was the migration wave that emerged as a result of the collapse of the Soviet Union in 1989. Therefore, one of the most fundamental issues and problems faced by the European Union in the last 30 years is illegal and irregular immigration from outside the Union territory to Europe? Many political, social and sociological effects caused by immigration within legal boundaries or illegally are corresponded with concern within the Union and reflect negatively on the deepening process. Therefore, it has been compelled to create new policies regarding the control of migration.[59] Since the first half of the 1990s, the European Union has started to develop a holistic approach to migration. However, it was not possible for the member states to determine a common policy due to their different approaches to the refugee problem and the sovereign rights of this issue.

The attacks of September 11 caused states to increase their border security and to reconcile migration and security issues. In line with the legal regulations created in this conjuncture, illegal immigration has been defined and has become a controversially securitized area. National and international measures have been taken on illegal immigration, which is also associated with international crimes. The actors most affected by this illegal immigration problem were EU member states, because of their proximity to source countries and their attraction. Especially in times of crisis and war, countries consider migrants as a major threat to their national security. The bombs exploded in Madrid in 2004 and London in Europe in 2005. Fears about the association between migration and terrorism have further increased. When we consider the recent terrorist incidents in Europe, we can say that the vast majority of these acts have been carried out by foreign citizens. At this point, immigrants are seen as a major threat to national security. Therefore, Europeans do not want immigrant population within the EU borders. Especially immigrants who enter the country illegally are dangerous because they cannot be controlled. The EU has been making various regulations for years to protect and secure its borders. However, with the help of human smugglers, immigrants use many different routes to enter Europe. The national interests and security of each EU member state are of particular importance. Therefore, approaches and policies towards immigrants may differ among countries because when it comes to security, countries put all

---

[58] Canpolat and Arıner, Ibid., p.11
[59] Samur, Ibid., p. 1.

their interests aside and prefer to ensure their national security first.[60]

After the regime changes in the Middle East and North Africa after 2010, millions of irregular and illegal immigrants from these countries trying to reach Europe by sea and road caused a serious problem in the European Union. In this respect, the number of refugees increased after Syrian Civil War and millions of Syrian populations tried to reach Europe in a very short time. The migrant crisis that emerged as a result of the Syrian Civil War necessitated EU member states to act together. Because the unexpectedly prolonged Syrian Civil War produced results that these actors could not cope with national measures. Having difficulty in dealing with this situation, the EU tried to protect its own borders and tried to keep irregular immigration outside of its borders within the framework of Fortress Europe, but did not do much out of this.

From the beginning of the process, the EU has tried to protect the borders of with the externalization method that it has made an extension of securitization to combat illegal immigration. Increasing immigrant numbers brought about deepening of the segregation within the Union. When the European Union realized that they could not solve the problem with unilateral policies than they preferred to sign Readmission Treaty with Turkey to be able to close the most preferred route of refugees. The agreement, which caused many debates in legal and ethical areas, has became a way that only the EU benefited. The agreement for the deal the buffer zone created by the EU through Turkey has become questionable. Because the terms of the treaty remained in force as long as the treaty Turkey agrees. Turkey has fulfilled its responsibilities. In this way, the influx of irregular migrants a route to Europe via Turkey has decreased to the lowest level. On the other hand, EU countries did not comply with the terms of the treaty regarding the economic aid and Visa Liberalization that they had to make within the scope of the readmission agreement. Following the withdrawal of Turkey's Readmission Treaty, the number of irregular migrants arriving to the European Union has begun to increase again. Especially after the cancellation of the Readmission Treaty, the violence and abuse inflicted by the Greek military forces on the immigrants who collapsed on the Greek border have shattered the human conscience.

Recent developments show us that the European Union does not want to see any more immigrants or asylum seekers within its borders. For this reason, it follows a security-oriented policy by increasing security measures at the point of protecting both land and sea borders as much as possible. In this context, the Union wants to exclude irregular migrants and asylum seekers as

---

[60] Hilal Zorba, "AB'nin Göçmenlere Yönelik Politikalarını Etkileyen Faktörler" **Barış Araştırmaları ve Çatışma Çözümleri Dergisi**, Vol. 4, No. 1, 2016, p.12-13, pp.1-17

much as possible. Although this approach is considered as correct policy in terms of the Fortress Europe approach, but in practice immigrants find their way and reach Europe. In addition, this strategy does not seem to be sustainable in the medium and long term. By following such a policy, the European Union contradicts its own universal values and human rights principles.

For the European Union, perhaps solving the problem at its source may be considered as a wiser strategy in the long run. The irregular wave of refugees, mostly from countries with military, political and economic crises, could perhaps be prevented by helping to resolve ongoing crises in these countries. It should not be forgotten that many countries that irregular migrants come from are countries that were under the control of the European Union member states in the past and are now economically and politically dependent on these European countries. In this respect, the former colonies of the EU member states have the capacity to have an impact on the establishment and stability of these countries. Thus, people living in these countries may not be so keen to come to this undesirable continent.

# CHAPTER 4

# GENDER, MIGRATION, AND SECURITY: THE EU'S RESPONSE TO THE REFUGEE CRISIS

Ayşegül Gökalp Kutlu[*]

## Introduction

Gender equality is a fundamental value of the European Union (EU). The EU Member States pledged to prohibit discrimination based on sex or sexual orientation and ensure equality between women and men in all areas by accepting the Charter of Fundamental Rights of the European Union. In its Gender Equality Strategy 2020-2025, the European Commission declares that "the promotion of equality between women and men is a task for the Union, in all its activities, required by the Treaties"[1]. The EU also pledged to ensure a secure environment for everyone, no matter what their racial or ethnic origin, religion, belief, gender, age or, sexual orientation is[2].

The EU is not only committed to achieving gender equality, but it is also a global leader in the area: in terms of gender equality, 6 of the top 10 countries in the world are EU Member States[3]. Even though the EU has made significant progress in the field of gender equality in the last decades, the recent refugee crisis seems to be its litmus test. The question to be asked in this context is whether the EU can develop a response that recognizes the refugees' gendered vulnerabilities. This article aims to find out how gender mainstreaming, which the EU committed itself with the Amsterdam Treaty, is incorporated in the refugee and asylum policies.

But what is meant by the incorporation of gender mainstreaming into refugee and asylum policies? What does this article expect of the EU? International crises produce gendered vulnerabilities; men, women, and the LGBTI may experience migration differently. Gender is influential in

---

[*] Assistant Prof. Dr., Kocaeli University, Faculty of Economics and Administrative Sciences, International Relations Department
[1] European Commission, Communication from the Commission to the European Parliament, the Council, the European Economic and Social Committee and the Committee of the Regions, A Union of Equality: Gender Equality Strategy 2020-2025, 2020, https://eur-lex.europa.eu/legal-content/EN/TXT/HTML/?uri=CELEX:52020DC0152&from=EN (Access: 29.11.2020)
[2] European Commission, Communication from the Commission to the European Parliament, the European Council, the Council, the European Economic and Social Committee and the Committee of the Regions on the EU Security Union Strategy, 2020, https://ec.europa.eu/info/sites/info/files/communication-eu-security-union-strategy.pdf (Access: 29.11.2020)
[3] World Economic Forum, **Global Gender Gap Report 2020**, http://www3.weforum.org/docs/WEF_GGGR_2020.pdf (Access: 29.11.2020)

deciding to leave the home country, the experiences in the journey to safety, the asylum application process, evaluation of asylum applications, the experience of being resettled in a new country / or the experience of asylum rejection and being sent back to the home country. Women and girls may be victimized by human traffickers, young male refugees might be seen as potentially dangerous or as a threat to economic well-being, LGBTI may face additional discrimination in their asylum application because of their sexual orientation. Gender, when coupled with multiple other disadvantages such as race, age, religion, or economic status, will add to the existing vulnerabilities in the migration process. Even though the EU is aware of these vulnerabilities (see, for example, the 2013 EU Directive on Reception, the 1984 Resolution and 2016 Report of the European Parliament, the 2017 Staff Working Document of the Commission – all of which will be explained below), its increasingly securitized refugee policies result in the EU's disregard of these vulnerabilities. The EU is responding to the current refugee crisis by using various internal and external policy tools. Fortifying the 'Fortress Europe' automatically results in tougher refugee policies, and tougher refugee policies result in easily disregarded gendered vulnerabilities. While the EU is the champion of gender equality internally, gender sensitivity in its external policy is limited.

The article will start by analysing Europe's history of refugee "crises". The social construction of refugee flows as 'crises' makes it easier to impose a security perspective on migration. Later, the EU's formation of a common refugee policy and its development of internal and external response tools will be explained. The first two sections aim to show that Europe's history of refugee flows has been influential in adopting the securitization perspective. Lastly, a gender analysis of the EU's responses to the latest refugee crisis will be analysed by looking at the various documents and policy statements adopted by the EU institutions.

### Europe's history of refugee crises

Neither forced migration flows towards Europe, nor calling them as 'crises' is new. Indeed, scholars have utilized the term migration/refugee 'crisis' almost once in every decade following the First World War. It is possible to say that the first academic usage of the term 'crisis' referring to the huge flows of people fleeing into Europe is by Zolberg et. al. in their book titled "Escape from Violence: Conflict and the Refugee Crisis in the Developing World"[4]. While the authors claim that they aim to "foster a more critical and realistic understanding of the refugee phenomenon" by attempting to put forward a "comprehensive, theoretically grounded

---

[4] Aristide R. Zolberg, Astri Suhrke and Sergio Aguayo, **Escape from Violence: Conflict and the Refugee Crisis in the Developing World**, Oxford University Press, 1989.

explanation of refugee flows"[5], this outstanding work asserts that there have been three refugee situations to qualify as crises: The first crisis was during the post-World War I years. To cope with the refugee outflow from Russia after the Russian Revolution, the League of Nations appointed a 'High Commissioner on behalf of the League in connection with the problems of Russian Refugees in Europe'. Fridtjof Nansen (known for the infamous 'Nansen passports' for stateless refugees) was appointed as the High Commissioner. This office later assisted other refugees in Europe in the post-war setting and its workload increased vastly after the Great Depression and the following fascist takeovers in European countries. Italians, Portuguese, Spaniards were fleeing their countries, and later the Jewish exodus from Germany was added to this high flow. The League appointed a 'High Commissioner for Refugees coming out of Germany' for this special situation in 1933, which will evolve into the Intergovernmental Committee on Refugees in 1938. As the Second World War was taking its toll, the work of this office expanded to cover all European refugees.[6]

The second refugee 'crisis' in Europe was deeper than the first one. The number of the displaced people in Europe after the Second World War was around 30 million and, of these, 11 million people needed urgent assistance[7]. To these were added people fleeing the newly formed regimes in their countries; especially in Central and Eastern Europe. The International Refugee Agency was founded in 1946, and in 1949, the UN High Commissioner's Office for Refugees (UNCHR) was established to assist the displaced Europeans. In 1951, the Convention Relating to the Status of Refugees was adopted. The refugee crisis in the immediate post-Second World War Europe was mainly due to refugees of European origin, who were fleeing from communist regimes to Western European countries. These were mostly political refugees, and they were welcome for political reasons. Hence, the 1951 Convention covered only the then-known groups of refugees, who were "persons who had become refugees as a result of events occurring before 1st January 1951" (Article 1(A)(2)). The 1951 Convention originally contained temporal and geographical limitations, hence it grants refugee status to those people who became refugees as a result of events occurring *in* Europe and *before* 1st January 1951.

The 1956 Hungarian Refugee Crisis was a major post-War crisis, in which large numbers of Hungarians who protested the communist rule fled Austria and Yugoslavia after the severe crushing of the demonstrations by the Soviet Union. In less than a month, the number of people fleeing out of Hungary

---

[5] ibid., p.*v*
[6] ibid., pp.18-20
[7] ibid., pp. 21

reached 200.000.[8] The European states and the UNHCR acted unprecedently responsive. Even though there were uncertainties as to whether Hungarian refugees would technically fit into the definition of 'refugee' in the 1951 Convention (refugee status could only be granted to those who became refugees as a result of events occurring before 1st January 1951), the UNHCR came up with the incentive that they could be recognized 'prima facie'. Hence refugee status was accorded to the Hungarians arriving in Austria, and the individual determination for 'persecution' set out in the 1951 Convention was postponed to a later time. This will later turn into a practice that will help millions of other refugees in the upcoming crises.[9]

The third 'crisis' started in 1970s when asylum seekers all over the world saw Western Europe as a destination for protection.[10] Population movements from the developing world and post-colonies into Western Europe necessitated the expansion of the scope of the 1951 Convention. The geographical and time limitations of the Convention were removed in the 1967 Protocol, which was also changing the Europe-centred notion of who would be considered as a refugee. Meanwhile, labour migration to Western Europe started during the 1960s and 1970s. The importation of foreign labourers, either through former colonies or by bilateral agreements with third countries was beneficial for the European economies that needed the workforce. As the numbers of non-European workers started to increase, however, hostilities began to surface towards migrants, especially towards those who were at the lower strata of the society where the home population felt that their economic livelihood was imperilled. The period after the oil shocks of the 1970s corresponds to this new 'crisis' rhetoric. There was a decreasing need for labour and increasing discontent towards migrant workers. As a result, the recruitment of foreign labourers was halted. Voluntary return was encouraged, and many labour importing western European countries adopted restrictive definitions of citizenship in order to discourage potential newcomers. These policies did not produce the expected results, though. Despite the restrictive migration policies and worsening economic and social conditions in Western Europe, migration flows did not stop. Racial tensions in western Europe were rising by the mid-1980s since rising terrorist incidents and economic problems were being associated with unintegrated migrants. Hence, migration turned out to be a 'crisis'; immigration was criticized and politicized by politicians, decision-makers, scholars and commentators as destabilizing the social order.[11]

---

[8] https://www.unhcr.org/news/latest/2006/10/453c7adb2/fiftieth-anniversary-hungarian-uprising-refugee-crisis.html (Access: 20.11.2020)
[9] ibid.
[10] Zolberg et.al., op.cit., p.27
[11] see Klaus J. Bade, **Migration in European History**, Wiley-Blackwell, 2003.

The end of 1970s and the whole 1980s witnessed decreasing demand for labour in Western European countries, while numbers of asylum seekers both from Eastern Europe and the Third World were on the rise. As the demarcation line between 'the political refugee' and the 'economic migrant' was blurring, European states started to introduce more restrictive refugee resettlement programmes and deterring asylum systems. This was because of the declining number of European refugees and the increasing number of non-European migrants moving towards western markets for various reasons facilitated by globalization. As European countries were limiting opportunities for economic migration, economic migrants and political refugees from the Global South were forced into seeking asylum in Western countries.[12] Given the fact that the reasons for economic migration and political asylum seeking are very much intertwined in the Global South, the European countries started to perceive 'the economic migrant' and 'the refugee' as identical. The result is that 'the refugee' is increasingly perceived as the non-refugee, who is seen as an illegal immigrant looking for better economic opportunities in Europe. This is the period when "Cold War reasons for accepting refugees disappeared"[13].

Migrants and refugees coming from post-Soviet countries and refugees seeking asylum as a result of the ethnic persecution and wars in the post-Cold War Balkans started another round of 'crisis' rhetoric. The disintegration of Yugoslavia produced a sudden wave of mass displacement and migration. 2.3 million people fled their homes between 1989 and 1992 in what was called "Europe's worst since the 40's"[14] and 1,4 million Kosovo Albanians were later displaced because of the Kosovo War of 1998-1999[15].

Their experiences with migration flows have pushed the European states towards a process of developing a more comprehensive asylum and migration policy. The European integration was deepening; and the European Union was slowly developing a unified policy on migration, refugees and asylum. The Third Pillar on Justice and Home Affairs, the Schengen Agreements, and the Dublin Convention were the indicators of the formation of a restrictive migration policy and the construction of migration as a security problem. Meanwhile, increasing numbers of non-European refugees started meeting with the 'myth of difference'[16]:

---

[12] Emma Haddad, The Refugee in International Society: Between Sovereigns, Cambridge University Press, 2008, p.168

[13] Ibid, p.167

[14] https://www.nytimes.com/1992/07/24/world/yugoslav-refugee-crisis-europe-s-worst-since-40-s.html (Access: 22.11.2020)

[15] Organization for Security and Cooperation in Europe (OSCE), KOSOVO / KOSOVA As Seen, As Told: An analysis of the human rights findings of the OSCE Kosovo Verification Mission October 1998 to June 1999, 1999. p. 13

[16] B.S. Chimni "The Geopolitics of Refugee Studies: A View from the South", Journal of Refugee

"the nature and character of refugee flows in the Third World were represented as being radically different from refugee flows in Europe since the end of the First World War. Thereby, an image of a 'normal' refugee was constructed – white, male and anti-communist – which clashed sharply with individuals fleeing the Third World."

Towards the end of the 1990s; several scholars started pointing out the dangers of the 'crisis' discourse and showed how migration is 'securitized' by European countries. The first attempt to explain migration from a securitization perspective came from the Copenhagen School. In their book *Security: A Framework for Analysis,* Barry Buzan, Ole Weaver and Jaap de Wilde defined migration as one of the factors threatening the 'we identity'. For them, migration was securitized by the fears of "X people being overrun or diluted by influxes of Y people; the X community will not be what is used to be, because others will make up the population; X identity is being changed by a shift in the composition of the population".[17] The securitization perspective reveals that *securitizing actors* frequently utilize concepts such as 'influxes', 'being overrun', 'identity change' whilst referring to migration or refugees.

The 2000s witnessed a clear securitization of migration. After the 9/11 attacks in the United States and subsequent terrorist incidents in Europe, tolerance towards migrants/refugees (especially Muslims) reduced. In this context, it was easier for migration to be "presented as a danger to public order, cultural identity, domestic and labour market stability".[18] For Jef Huysmans, securitizing immigration and refugee flows produces and reproduces a political community of insecurity.[19] When migration is constructed as a security issue, the inclusion of immigrants, asylum seekers, and refugees in European societies becomes more difficult. Didier Bigo, while criticizing the Copenhagen School and their approach to securitization, claims that "[s]ecuritization of immigration is the result and not the cause of the development of technologies of control and surveillance."[20] In his perspective, one needs to look into the daily practices, routines and the workings of bureaucracy in order to understand securitization. The security professionals (all the members of "services such as customs, police, intelligence services, bankers engaged in risk assessment, and suppliers of

---

Studies 11, 4 (1998), 350–74, quoted in Haddad, op.cit., p.167-168.
[17] Barry Buzan, Ole Weaver, Jaap de Wilde, **Security: A New Framework for Analysis**, London:Lynne Rienner Publishers, 1998, p. 121
[18] Jef Huysmans, "The European Union and the Securitization of Migration", **Journal of Common Market Studies**, Vol. 38, No. 5, 2000, pp.751-777, p.752
[19] Jef Huysmans, The Politics of Insecurity: Fear, Migration and Asylum in the EU, Routledge, 2006, p.51
[20] Didier Bigo, "Security and Immigration: Toward a Critique of the Governmentality of Unease", **Alternatives**, Vol. 27, Special Issue, 2002, pp.63-92, p.73

new technologies of surveillance") are both creating the fear towards migration and successfully manage this fear, hence and making security 'their' object.[21]

In the 2010s, Europe continued to be a major destination for refugees. Approximately 74% of asylum claims submitted in industrialized countries in 2012 were European countries.[22] Starting with 2011, the Arab Spring impelled significant migration movements to Europe. This movement is what many refer to as the latest 'refugee crisis'. The crisis was initially felt in the so-called Central Mediterranean refugee route from North Africa to Italy, but with the acceleration of the civil war in Syria, the Eastern Mediterranean (through Turkey to Greece) became the major route. The Syrian Civil War caused more than 5,5 million Syrians to become refugees. Recently, more than two thirds (67%) of all refugees worldwide come from just five countries; Syria, Afghanistan, South Sudan, Myanmar and Somalia[23], indicating that this new migratory flow is due to conflict-induced migration. What lies at the heart of the latest refugee crisis is the blurring of concepts and categories, of who is a 'real' refugee fleeing persecution and who the others are moving to seek a better quality of life. In other words, the refugee crisis is a definitional crisis about the inseparability of voluntary and involuntary migrants.

Calling this latest migratory flow as 'refugee crisis' is much criticized in academia, though. Many scholars claim that this is a crisis of the Common European Asylum System, hence the crisis is not caused by the refugees themselves, but by the EU's responses to it.[24] Therefore, the section below will examine the EU's responses to this 'crisis' by briefly explaining the formation of the EU's common migration and asylum policy before going through a gender criticism of it.

### Formation of a European migration and asylum policy

The main problem any state faces in formulating its migration and asylum policies is, trying to keep the delicate balance between the political need to

---

[21] ibid., 75

[22] UNHCR Asylum Trends 2012: Levels and Trends in Industrialized Countries. https://www.unhcr. org/statistics/unhcrstats/5149b81e9/asylum-levels-trends-industrialized-countries-2012.html (Access: 20.11.2020)

[23] UNHCR, Global Trends, Forced displacement in 2018. https://www.unhcr.org/globaltrends2018/ (Access: 20.11.2020). This number is different in the 2019 report, however. Venezuela stands as the second country to have the largest refugee outflows in 2019, due to the political turmoil and political crisis in the country.

[24] See, for example, Neske Baerwaldt, "The European Refugee Crisis: Crisis for Whom?" https://www.law.ox.ac.uk/research-subject-groups/centre-criminology/centreborder-criminologies/blog/2018/03/european-refugee (Access: 12.11.2020) and Geoff Gilbert, Why Europe Does Not Have a Refugee Crisis. **International Journal of Refugee Law,** Vol.27, No.4, 2015, pp. 531–535.

be in control and the need to meet (or be seen to be meeting) humanitarian obligations.[25] The EU member states have additional problems. The fundamental paradox in the Europeanisation of refugee policies is between state sovereignty versus supranational governance and internal security versus human rights and human security.[26] Policies on migration, asylum, judicial and police matters have always been in the sole domain of sovereign states. As these areas indicate the state's sovereign power, it was not easy for the members of the EU to start cooperating on these issues and create a supranational asylum system. Cooperation in these fields firstly took place in the Council of Europe meetings (CoE), where officials from the CoE member states regularly met and discussed issues that would fall into judicial cooperation. Even though the CoE provides binding international human rights law that all the members of the EU are parties to, the CoE is an intergovernmental institution in which decision-making requires unanimity. It is difficult to combine the divergent interests of all 47 member states.

Albeit slow and difficult, two developments facilitated cooperation in these areas. The first one was related to concerns about the increasing cross-border movements between and among the member states. Member states were concerned about transnational crime, which could proliferate due to weakened border controls between themselves or lack of effective communication in justice and police matters among them.[27] The second reason was the signing of the Single European Act in 1986 and the commitment to the completion of a single market. Single market necessitated internal free movements and external control of the Community borders, hence European integration started to focus on cooperation in border controls, migration and asylum policies.

In 1975, the 'Trevi Group' was created as an ad-hoc organization to deal with cross-border terrorism and police cooperation among EC member states. Despite its ad-hoc character, Trevi was the first step towards further cooperation in justice and home affairs. In 1985, the Schengen Agreement was signed and some member states started to remove border controls between them[28]. The main aim was to remove the EC's internal borders so as to make a single market possible while developing common policies to be applied to the external borders. On asylum, the Schengen framework introduced a new system for reviewing asylum claims, in which only one member state could decide on the asylum application. It also introduced a

---

[25] Haddad, op.cit, p.173
[26] Sandra Lavenex, "The Europeanisation of Refugee Policies: Normative Challenges and Institutional Legacies", **Journal of Common Market Studies**, 2001, Vol. 39, No. 5, pp. 851-874,p. 852.
[27] Emek M. Uçarer, "Justice and Home Affairs", **European Union Politics**, Michelle Cini (Ed.), Oxford, Oxford University Press, 2004, p. 295
[28] https://eurlex.europa.eu/legalcontent/EN/TXT/HTML/?uri=CELEX:42000A0922(01)&from=EN (Access: 10.11.2020)

uniform visa policy and uniform visas, and cooperation on drug trafficking.

The 1990s witnessed the 'Europeanization' of migration. Asylum application process was further clarified in 1990, with the signing of the 'Convention determining the State responsible for examining applications for asylum lodged in one of the Member States of the European Communities' - Dublin Convention[29]. In signing the Dublin Convention, the Member States aimed at preventing an applicant from submitting multiple applications in more than one Member State. In the same year, the Convention Implementing the Schengen Agreement[30] was signed, creating the Schengen Information System, a database to store and share important information such as asylum applications or criminal records. These were the first steps in the harmonization of migration and asylum policies of European countries. The Maastricht Treaty (Treaty on the European Union) introduced the pillar system, in which Justice and Home Affairs constituted the third pillar of the EU. In its Article K.1, the Treaty puts forward the scope of the third pillar. It is stated that in order to achieve objectives of the Union, in particular the free movement of persons, the member states have identified several common interests: asylum policy; rules governing the crossing by persons of the external borders of the Member States and the exercise of controls thereon; immigration policy and policy regarding nationals of third countries (their entry and movement, conditions of residence, and unauthorized migration); combatting drug addiction; combatting fraud on an international scale; judicial cooperation in civil matters; judicial cooperation in criminal matters; customs cooperation; police cooperation for the purposes of preventing and combatting terrorism, unlawful drug trafficking and other serious forms of international crime. Even though these issues were Europeanized, meaning that there would be cooperation among EU member states on these issues, the third pillar had an intergovernmental structure where all decisions would be taken unanimously.

In 1999, the Amsterdam Treaty[31] came into force, transferring certain third pillar policy areas into European Community Law, thus *'communitarizing'* them. The aim was to harmonize all of the most important areas of refugee protection, such as reception conditions, procedures, criteria for eligibility, and rights to be granted.[32] The 1951Convention and the 1967 Protocol were

---

[29] https://eur-lex.europa.eu/legalcontent/EN/TXT/HTML/?uri=CELEX:41997A0819(01)&from= EN (Access: 10.11.2020)
[30] https://eur-lex.europa.eu/legal-content/EN/TXT/HTML/?uri=CELEX:42000A0922(02)&from= EN (Access: 10.11.2020)
[31] https://eur-lex.europa.eu/legal-content/EN/TXT/HTML/?uri=CELEX:11997D/TXT&from=EN (Access: 10.11.2020)
[32] Roland Bank, "Forced Migration in Europe", **The Oxford Handbook of Refugee and Forced Migration Studies,** Elena Fiddian-Qasmiyeh, Gil Loescher, Katy Long, and Nando Sigona (Eds.), Oxford, Oxford University Press, 2014, pp.691-700,p. 692-693

accepted as the measure for all refugee law instruments to be adopted in the EU framework (Article 73k), though elements of intergovernmental cooperation were maintained for a five-year transition period after the entry into force of the treaty. During these five years, member states retained full control of the contents of legal instruments adopted, because unanimity was required in the Council, and the European Parliament was excluded from co-decision in decision-making process. With an additional protocol to the Amsterdam Treaty, the Schengen Agreement was transferred into the EU acquis, hence the EU's external border controls were *communitarized*. In 2004, Frontex (European Agency for the Management of Operational Cooperation at the External Borders) was created to assist the member states in managing the Schengen Area external borders.

At the 1999 Tampere Summit, the EU member states committed themselves to creating a Common European Asylum System (CEAS) that would include specific rules to determine which EU state would be responsible for reviewing an asylum claim, common standards for reviewing claims, common minimum conditions for the reception of asylum seekers as they await the outcome of their applications, and approximate rules for refugee recognition. It was expected that in the longer term, Community rules should lead to a common asylum procedure and a uniform status for those who are granted asylum throughout the Union. The Tampere Summit called for the need for a comprehensive approach to asylum and migration policies "addressing political, human rights and development issues in countries and regions of origin and transit. This requires combating poverty, improving living conditions and job opportunities, preventing conflicts and consolidating democratic states and ensuring respect for human rights."[33]

The extension of policy-making in asylum and immigration beyond the borders of the EU is a major attitude change in the EU refugee policy. It enables the EU to use external policy tools to combat refugee crises. This process of externalization has two aspects. The first aspect is related to the countries of transit that are on the borders of the EU. Here, the EU attempts to use tools of migration control, including border control measures to try to combat illegal migration and smuggling and trafficking in human beings; capacity-building of immigration and asylum systems in transit countries; and readmission agreements to facilitating the return of illegal migrants and asylum-seekers whose claims have failed. This first aspect extends the logic of asylum and migration management beyond the EU's borders. The second external aspect tries to address the fundamental causes of forced migration and provide protection in the refugee-producing countries. While such an approach can reduce refugee overflows into Europe, it also appeals to state

---

[33] Tampere European Council Presidency Conclusions, Articles 13-17, https://www.europarl.europa.eu/summits/tam_en.htm (Access: 12.10.2020)

actors, who would be willing to be seen working hard for the prevention of international crises and human rights.[34]

The 2007 Lisbon Treaty abolished the pillar structure and supranationalized all policy areas on the previous third pillar, creating an Area of Freedom, Security and Justice.[35] The European Parliament gained a say in formulating the policies on migration, refugee, and asylum; the Council changed to majority voting in matters related to these issues, and the Court of Justice of the EU now had competence over conflicts related to them. The EU Charter of Fundamental Rights gained legal force with the Lisbon Treaty, so the right to seek asylum, which is protected in Article 18 of the Charter, became binding for the EU member states. Lisbon Treaty is a turning point in the formation of a European migration and asylum system.

Right after the Lisbon Treaty entered into force, the EU confronted a major refugee movement to test its supranationalized migration policy.

## Looking at the EU's responses to the refugee crisis through a gender lens

Even though a late-comer in migration studies, gender is widely studied after it was accepted as a factor impacting the whole migratory journey. It is accepted now that gender, in interaction with other social categories like nationality, age or sexual orientation influences all phases of the migration process.[36] Before the introduction of gender as a category of analysis, women's experiences in migration were not studied, and migration was thought of as a male-dominated process. Women and children were bundled up in one category – *womenandchildren* – and were considered as passive actors, dependent on the male migrant. There could be several reasons for the lack of studies in analysing women's migration. Firstly, during the initial phases of migration studies in the 19th and early 20th centuries, the dominant gender code was such that focusing on men was natural and it would be men, as natural bread-winners, who would initiate migration. Secondly, academic studies were male-dominated, hence there were no female researchers who would question women's experiences. Third, migrant women's work was ignored by scholars who regarded 'work' as waged work, taking place in the public sphere. Migrant women's work usually took place in the private sphere, as maids, nannies or care-givers, and hence subordinated to 'real work'. The majority of women participating in mass migration movements were rather

---

[34] Christina Boswell, "The 'External Dimension' of EU Immigration and Asylum Policy", **International Affairs**, Vol. 79, No.3 2003, pp.619-638, p.622–626.

[35] https://eur-lex.europa.eu/legal-content/EN/TXT/HTML/?uri=CELEX:12007L/TXT&from=EN (Access: 12.11.2020)

[36] Helma Lutz, "Gender in the Migratory Process", Draft Conference Paper, https://www.migrationinstitute.org/files/events/lutz.pdf (Access: 10.10.2020)

recruited for domestic work in occupational areas located rather in the re-productive than in the productive sphere.[37]

Two main developments in forced migration studies were helpful in studying women as a category in migration: the first was the 'Women in Forced Migration' paradigm[38] that gained importance in the mid-1980s and throughout the 1990s. This was mainly a criticism towards the 1951 Geneva Convention, pointing out the male characteristics of the international refugee system. The 1951 Geneva Convention Article I(A)2 defines a refugee as a person, who:

> ... owing to well-founded fear of being persecuted for reasons of race, religion, nationality, membership of a particular social group or political opinion, is outside the country of his nationality and is unable or, owing to such fear, is unwilling to avail himself of the protection of that country; or who, not having a nationality and being outside the country of his former habitual residence as a result of such events, is unable or, owing to such fear, is unwilling to return to it.

In her study titled 'Gendering the International Asylum and Refugee Debate',[39] Jane Freedman points out the problems of this definition. She states that a 'well-founded fear of being persecuted' or the term 'persecution' itself is subjective. It is up to the immigration officials and judges of the state assessing the asylum claim to decide if that person is really in danger of persecution. This ambiguity will lead to a subjective evaluation. For example, the Geneva Convention pictures a typical asylum seeker as a man escaping a prison sentence that might result in his death or torture. When that is the case, there will be no difficulty in granting him asylum. On the other hand, Freedman points out that a woman who is a victim of domestic violence or who is under the threat of forced marriage, genital mutilation, honour crimes, or who is refusing to adhere to certain dress codes is usually not regarded in the same category. Her 'fear of persecution' is usually justified within the framework of 'the right to privacy' and the inability of the liberal state to interfere in family matters, or sometimes by cultural relativism.

Sexual violence can be considered within the same line of analysis. Even though there is a huge body of international law criminalising sexual violence in armed conflicts as a crime against humanity and a war crime[40], Freedman

---

[37] ibid., p.5-6.
[38] Doreen Marie Indra, "Not a 'Room of One's Own': Engendering Forced Migration and Practice". In D.M. Indra (Ed.), **Engendering Forced Migration: Theory and Practice**. Oxford: Berghahn Books, 1999, pp. 1–22.
[39] Jane Freedman, Gendering the Gendering the International Asylum and Refugee Debate, Palgrave Macmillan, 2007
[40] The 1990s witnessed humanitarian crises and the development of a body of rules regarding sexual violence. International Criminal Tribunal for the former Yugoslavia (ICTY) and the International

provides cases of women who were not granted asylum because rape is not considered by immigration officials as persecution. In those cases, judges and state officials deciding on the issue agreed that rape was an act of sexual gratification or the result of combatant men's lust.[41] Further, the ways under which rape victims are interviewed for the evaluation of their asylum applications may not be suitable for them to talk freely and describe the events. Simply, the existence of family/community members in the same room and the shame attached to rape might discourage women to talk about the events.

Further, Freedman claims that the ways in which women engage in political activity are numerous. In comparison with a typical man, who is persecuted for being a member of a political party, guerrilla activity, or supporter of an anti-government group, women may engage in supportive roles. They may be providing shelter, food, medical care, or hiding people, carrying messages, or involving in protests regarding body-control policies of the government. However, none of these political activities are considered political enough to be granted asylum or considered as a refugee under Geneva Conventions.[42]

To sum up, the first efforts to include women in forced migration studies claimed that the refugee definition must be rewritten to include gender as a basis (of fear) of persecution. 'Persecution' itself be must also be "redefined in order to recognize the political nature of female resistance to systems of oppression and violence within both the public and private spheres."[43]

The second effort in including women in forced migration studies starts with the 1990s when the UNHCR adopted a new approach in their reports, highlighting 'special protection needs of women and girls' (UNHCR 1991). While this was an improvement, the reports also implied that women were exceptions to the norm that required special guidelines distinct from the normal refugee. Special efforts to protect children (UNHCR 1994), and LGBTI asylum seekers (UNHCR 2012) were recognized, demonstrating that the "so-called 'gender neutral' Convention was developed with adult, male,

---

Criminal Tribunal for Rwanda (ICTR) both criminalised sexual violence and considered sexual violence within armed conflict as a crime against humanity. The ICTR went a step further, claiming that rape 'constitute[s] genocide in the same way as any other act as long as they were committed with the specific intent to destroy, in whole or in part, a particular group [. . .]' (Akayesu Trial Chamber Judgement, ICTR-96-4-T, par.731). In 2002, the International Criminal Court came into force. Its statute criminalises a broad spectrum of sexual acts and defines systematic rape as constituting genocide, crime against humanity, and a war crime.

[41] ibid., pp.79-80
[42] ibid., pp.80-82.
[43] Elena Fiddian-Qasmiyeh, "Gender and Forced Migration", **The Oxford Handbook of Refugee and Forced Migration Studies,** Elena Fiddian-Qasmiyeh, Gil Loescher, Katy Long, and Nando Sigona (Eds.), Oxford, Oxford University Press, 2014 pp. 396-408, p. 398-399.

heterosexual asylum applicants in mind".[44]

After these initial stages of incorporating women in migration studies, it is accepted today that studying gender in migration means not only focusing on women's experiences and vulnerabilities, but it also requires looking into the interaction of gender with other social categories like nationality, age or sexual orientation and how these interactions shape the migratory experience. This newer paradigm insists on seeing that gender is socially constructed and opportunities and expectations attributed to its characteristics can change over time and depending on social change, including conflict and displacement. Studies adopting this perspective do not focus merely on women but they also highlight gender-specific violence and persecution committed against men, boys and the LGBTI. The incorporation of gender to the study of migration would reveal how power relations affect the whole migratory process and how patriarchy is "altered or reconstituted after migration"[45].

Gender influences all phases of the migration process. Refugee policies can create, highlight or weaken gendered inequalities. The way refugee policies refer to gender can be influential on who may leave their home countries and who may get recognized as a refugee. The first initiative for incorporating gender in the field of refugee policies came from the European Parliament (EP). In its Resolution of 13 April 1984[46], it demanded a gender-sensitive interpretation of the 1951 Refugee Convention. This decision was later reflected in subsequent UNHCR conclusions and guidelines. The EP resolution was non-binding and its implementation was not uniform, but it is a turning point for many EU member states to start adopting their own gender guidelines in their refugee policies.

The Amsterdam Treaty was an important turning point in two ways; first, by committing the EU to gender mainstreaming and second, by granting the EU institutions power to develop legislation in the 'third pillar' issues. After the Tampere Council of 1999 when the EU member states committed themselves to creating a Common European Asylum System, the EU developed the Asylum Procedures Directive, the Reception Conditions Directive, the Qualification Directive, and the Dublin Regulation and the EURODAC (European Asylum Dactyloscopy Database) Regulation. Despite some limitations, these documents adopted a gender-sensitive approach. In May 2015, the European Commission presented a

---

[44] ibid., p.400

[45] Monica Boyd and Elizabeth Grieco, "Women and Migration: Incorporating Gender into International Migration Theory", Migration Policy Institute Web Page. https://www.migrationpolicy.org/article/women-and-migration-incorporating-gender-international-migration-theory (Access: 01.10.2020).

[46] EP resolution of 13 April 1984 on the application of the Geneva Convention relating to the status of refugees, OJ C 127, 14.5.1984

comprehensive European Agenda on Migration[47] as a response to the refugee overflow triggered by the Syrian Civil War. Pressured into developing a more sophisticated refugee policy, the Agenda aimed to address immediate challenges and equip the EU with the tools to better manage problems related to irregular migration, borders, asylum and legal migration. It includes immediate, medium term and long term actions.

The Agenda has no direct references to gender. In its immediate actions, the Agenda proposes the setting up of 'hotspots' in order to help 'frontline Member States', where the European Asylum Support Office, Frontex and Europol will work on the ground with frontline Member States to swiftly identify, register and fingerprint incoming migrants and channel those claiming asylum into an asylum procedure where their claims will be assessed as quickly as possible[48]. In its 2017 Staff Working Document that explains the hotspot procedures[49], the European Commission takes a gender-sensitive approach. In deploying experts to work at hotspots, the Commission highlights that a minimum gender balance should be foreseen, in particular, to deal with certain vulnerable groups, such as victims of gender-based violence. This is a very progressive approach, highlighting that the EU is considering gender-based violence as persecution. In trying to find out who the vulnerable groups are, it is possible to refer to the EU's 2013 Directive laying down standards for the reception of applicants for international protection.[50] This Directive provides an inclusive list of vulnerable persons, who are defined as minors, unaccompanied minors, disabled people, elderly people, pregnant women, single parents with minor children, victims of human trafficking, persons with serious illnesses, persons with mental disorders and persons who have been subjected to torture, rape or other serious forms of psychological, physical or sexual violence, such as victims of female genital mutilation. So, even though the Agenda does not have a direct reference to gender, the detailed implementation guidelines embrace gender-sensitivity.

In 2016, the European Parliament Committee on Women's Rights and

---

[47] European Commission, A European Agenda on Migration. Communication from the Commission to the European Parliament, the Council, the European Economic and Social Committee and the Committee of the Regions. Brussels, 2015. https://ec.europa.eu/antitrafficking/sites/antitrafficking/files/communication_on_the_european_agenda_on_migration_en.pdf (Access: 17.11.2020)

[48] ibid., p.6

[49] European Commission, Commission Staff Working Document: Best Practices on the Implementation of the Hotspot Approach Accompanying the Documents Report from the Commission to the European Parliament, the European Council and the Council Progress Report on the Agenda on Migration. Brussels, 2017 https://eurlex.europa.eu/legalcontent/EN/TXT/HTML/?uri=CELEX:52017SC0372&from=EN(Access: 22.11.2020)

[50] Directive 2013/33/EU of The European Parliament and of the Council of 26 June 2013 laying down standards for the reception of applicants for international protection (recast), https://eur-lex.europa.eu/legal-content/EN/TXT/HTML/?uri=CELEX:32013L0033&from=EN#d1e39-96-1 (Access: 22.11.2020)

Gender Equality prepared a report, on the situation of women refugees and asylum seekers in the EU (2015/2325(INI)).[51] This Report is very comprehensive, stressing the gendered differences in the refugee movements. It stresses that women and LGBTI are subject to specific forms of gender-based persecution, which is still too often not recognised in asylum procedures. It points out to the gender dimension of refugee status, needs of women in asylum procedures, gender factors in reception and detention, social inclusion and integration, calling for policy initiatives in all these aspects. The Report indicates that, despite the creation of the Common European Asylum System, there is a noticeable gap in the protection provided to women seeking asylum in the EU. It is more likely for single men who reach the EU to seek international protection than women and children.

As well as being a key driver behind women's decisions to flee, gender-based violence is a common feature throughout journeys to and within the EU. In the gender dimension of refugee status determination, the Report claims that harms perpetrated against women seeking asylum are often at the hands of non-state actors, including family members. Persecution takes place when the state is unable or unwilling to provide protective measures to women in such cases. Hence, persecution must be thought in a wider perspective. The Report further highlights that violence against LGBTI individuals is common in reception facilities and that there is a need for LGBTI-sensitive reception facilities across all Member States. Women may be less likely to show evidence to support their asylum claims and may be reluctant to disclose relevant information due to their cultural reservations. This leads to a 'culture of disbelief' by the decision-makers towards women who are too slow to reveal their experiences or only sustain oral testimony. Therefore, the Report suggests that a new, comprehensive set of EU-wide gender guidelines should be adopted as part of wider reforms to migration and asylum policy. It puts forward that gender-related claims for asylum are often complex and may require additional legal work. With regards to trafficking, smuggling and sexual violence, the Report urges the Commission and member states to guarantee full access to sexual and reproductive health and rights, including access to safe abortion. To improve the security and safety of refugee women, safe and legal routes to the EU must be made available for those fleeing conflict and persecution. On reception and detention, the Report urges the EU and Member States to sign and ratify the Council of Europe Convention on preventing and combating violence against women (Istanbul Convention), which asserts that states shall take the necessary legislative or other measures to develop gender-sensitive reception procedures and support services for asylum seekers (Article 60 (3)). Detention should be used only as a last resort and vulnerable people should

---

not be detained. The needs of pregnant women, women with young children, and survivors of sexual violence are more appropriately accommodated through alternatives to detention, such as the surrender of travel documents or reporting obligations. Lastly, on social inclusion and integration, the report claims that women refugees face a number of specific integration challenges and experience multiple and intersectional discrimination based on characteristics including gender and minority ethnicity which puts them at an even higher risk of social exclusion, violence and poverty. To overcome these inequalities, member states should make greater use of funds to promote integration into the labour market and provide childcare which is critical in enabling the participation of women refugees in society.

In 2016, the CEAS went through a period of reformation. On September 23, 2020, the European Commission presented the new European Pact on Migration and Asylum. European Union Vice President Margaritis Schinas explained that the new Pact was like a building with three floors. It is comprised of an external dimension that is centred around strengthened partnerships with countries of origin and transit, a robust management of external borders, and firm but fair internal rules.[52] Certain criticisms can easily be levelled at this new Pact. Firstly, the New Pact introduces a "return sponsorship" and "balancing out competing interests", meaning that member states can now choose to opt-out from participating in the relocation of asylum seekers and refugees within the EU, and instead provide administrative and financial support to other member states. Secondly, the second floor – a robust management of external borders – is composed of mandatory screening of fingerprints, security, health and identity check at all borders of all arrivals. Those claiming asylum will be directed to the right procedure quickly, and those unlikely to get asylum will be channelled to quick and effective returns. For this purpose, the post of a new a new EU Coordinator on Returns and Frontex will be established. It seems once again that border security is prioritized over access to asylum, fortifying Fortress Europe. Lastly, the first floor - external dimension centred around strengthened partnerships with countries of origin and transit – is not new. Here, the EU aims to stop migration in the origin countries by addressing the root causes of irregular migration. Through external funding, the EU and member states will use a wide range of policy and financing tools, 'tailor-made' to each partner country's specific situation, interests and needs. These interests and needs may be in a wide range; from development cooperation, investment and trade, to employment, visa policy, education and research. What is new here is that the EU now proposes to "make use of the Visa Code to incentivise and improve cooperation to facilitate return and

---

[52] https://ec.europa.eu/commission/presscorner/detail/en/speech_20_1736 (Access: 29.11.2020)

readmission"[53]. The European Commission suggests using the visa policy strategically, by introducing a link between cooperation on readmission and visa issuance:

> Based on information provided by Member States, the Commission will assess at least once a year the level of cooperation of third countries on readmission, and report to the Council. Any Member State can also notify the Commission if it is confronted with substantial and persistent practical problems in the cooperation with a third country on readmission, triggering an ad hoc assessment. Following an assessment, the Commission can propose to apply restrictive visa measures, or in case of good cooperation, propose favourable visa measures.[54]

Visa policy is also proposed to be used to curb unfounded asylum applications from visa-free countries and ultimately result in the removal of third countries from the visa-free list.

In terms of gender, the New Pact on Migration does not offer any of the previous sensitivity. There is no reference to any of the factors explained in detail in the 2016 European Parliament Report, nor any mention of sexual orientation or the LGBTI. Under the category of the 'vulnerable', the Pact speaks only of children, and points out broader initiatives to promote the rights and interests of children, such as the Strategy on the Rights of the Child, in line both with international law on rights of refugees and children and with the EU Charter of Fundamental Rights. Women are only mentioned with reference to the risk for women and girls of becoming victims of trafficking for sexual exploitation or other forms of gender-based violence. Another 2020 Document, the EU's Security Union Strategy[55] also points out trafficking and women. Without going into detail, it puts forward that particular efforts are required when it comes to minorities and the most vulnerable victims, such as children or women trafficked for sexual exploitation or exposed to domestic violence. It claims that the Commission will present a new EU strategy on the eradication of trafficking in human beings. It also claims that all efforts should be made to reinforce gender mainstreaming and strengthen women's participation in law enforcement.

The European Commission has a brief reference to refugee women in its 2020 Communication on A Union of Equality: Gender Equality Strategy

---

[53] European Commission, Communication from the Commission on a New Pact on Migration and Asylum, 2020, https://eur-lex.europa.eu/legal-content/EN/TXT/HTML/?uri=CELEX:52020DC0609 &from=EN (Access: 29.11.2020)

[54] ibid., par. 6.5

[55] European Commission, **the EU Security Union Strategy**, 2020,https://ec.europa.eu/info/sites/info/ files/communication-eu-security-union-strategy.pdf (Access: 29.11.2020)

2020-2025. It is stated in this Communication that particular attention needs to be paid to women and girls in the asylum and migration area. Through the Asylum and Migration Fund, the Commission promises to encourage the Member States to target actions that support the specific needs of women in the asylum procedure, as well as actions that support the integration of women in the new society. Furthermore, the fund will enable the stepping up of protection of vulnerable groups, including women victims of gender-based violence in asylum and migration contexts.[56]

Compared to the previous CEAS documents, references on gender and gendered vulnerabilities are weak in the new Pact. It remains to be seen how the upcoming Directives, Working Documents, or European Parliament Resolutions will take up the issue.

So far, this section has examined the EU's references to gender in its internal responses to the latest refugee crisis. As mentioned above, a bigger part of the EU's response to the refugee crisis is external action. The EU-Turkey Statement of 18 March 2016[57], for example, is a striking external policy response. With this Statement, Turkey commits itself to readmission of irregular migrants crossing from Turkey into the EU borders and stricter controls on both land and sea borders. In return, the EU promises to activate a Voluntary Humanitarian Admission Scheme in which the EU Member States will contribute on a voluntary basis, financial assistance for projects benefitting Syrian refugees in Turkey, visa liberalizations for Turkish nationals, upgrading the Customs Union and the re-energizing the accession process. It is stated that the EU and its Member States will work to cooperate with Turkey in order to improve humanitarian conditions inside Syria, especially in certain areas near the Turkish border which would allow for the local population and refugees to live in a safer environment.

The 2016 EU-Turkey Statement has no references to a gender-sensitive refugee policy. However, in the reports on the progress made in the implementation of the EU-Turkey Statement, the European Commission refers to gender in certain ways. While pointing out vulnerability, the Commission refers to the UN vulnerability criteria, listing women and girls at risk; survivors of violence and/or torture; refugees with legal and/or physical protection needs; refugees with medical needs or disabilities; children and adolescents at risk as vulnerable. The Report lists 'child protection, women's health, and education in emergencies' as areas that shall benefit from EU humanitarian assistance in Turkey.[58] The June 2017 Report

---

[56] European Commission, A Union of Equality: Gender Equality Strategy 2020-2025
[57] European Council, EU-Turkey Statement, 18 March 2016. https://www.consilium.europa.eu/en/press/press-releases/2016/03/18/eu-turkey-statement/ (Access: 30.11.2020).
[58] European Commission, First Report on the Progress Made in the Implementation of the EU-Turkey Statement, 2016. https://ec.europa.eu/home-affairs/sites/homeaffairs/files/what-we-do/policies/

refers to the EU's funding of projects that aim to strengthen access to specialised services for conflict-affected refugees and provide lifesaving healthcare, physical rehabilitation, mental health(care), as well as support and protection for vulnerable refugees including victims of gender-based violence.[59] The Report in September 2017 refers to the importance attached to the services provided by the EU prioritizing the empowerment of women and girls, gender equality, rights of children, and human rights.[60]

These references, though very basic, may indicate the gender-sensitive approach of the EU in its external response to the latest refugee crisis. Still, only 3 out of 57 EU projects under the Facility for Refugees in Turkey explicitly mention a gender-related focus, amounting to only €18,000,000 out of €2.9 billion[61]. It can be inferred that the EU is using gender considerations as a conditionality of benefits for third countries[62]. This way, the EU externalizes not only its border controls but it also exports its normative gender mainstreaming policies to third countries.

## Conclusion

This article has shown that Europe's history is full of migratory movements and 'refugee crises'. After the havoc brought about by the post-Second World War refugees was settled, European countries managed refugees effectively in line with the 1951 Convention. The refugees throughout the Cold War, who were mainly fleeing from Eastern Europe or the communist states were mostly welcome due to political reasons and their numbers did not amount to a 'crisis'. Again, the EU member states managed the 'crisis' after the dissolution of the Soviet Union and Yugoslavia fairly well. The problem seems to be with the non-European migrants; those who flee from the Global South due to wars, political or economic reasons. Against the 'white, male, anti-communist' refugees of the previous period, the ones coming from the developing world are non-European and, in increasing numbers, women. The vast number of refugees and their non-European

---

european-agenda-migration/proposal-implementation-package/docs/20160420/report_implementation_eu-turkey_agreement_nr_01_en.pdf (Access: 30.11.2020)

[59] European Commission, Sixth Report on the Progress Made in the Implementation of the EU-Turkey Statement, 2017 https://ec.europa.eu/neighbourhood-enlargement/sites/near/files/170613_6th_report _on_the_progress_made_in_the_implementation_of_the_eu-turkey_statement_en.pdf (Access: 30.11. 2020)

[60] European Commission, Seventh Report on the Progress Made in the Implementation of the EU-Turkey Statement, 2017 https://ec.europa.eu/neighbourhood-enlargement/sites/near/files/20170906_seventh _report_on_the_progress in the_implementation_of_the_eu-turkey_statement_en.pdf (Access: 30.11. 2020)

[61] Natalie Welfens, Protecting Refugees Inside, Protecting Borders Abroad? Gender in the EU's Responses to the 'Refugee Crisis', Political Studies Review, 2019, pp.1-15, p. 10

[62] ibid., p.11

characteristics strengthened a security rhetoric and a securitized refugee policy. Migration was referred to as a perilous phenomenon that was threatening the economic and societal characteristics of European countries. The more the borders were strengthened, the more there was a division between insiders and outsiders. On the inside, the EU committed itself to gender equality and gender mainstreaming, whereas outside the borders, the EU's sensitivity on gender decreased visibly.

Still, it can be said that, with the incentive put forward by the Amsterdam Treaty towards gender mainstreaming, the previous CEAS contained elements of gender-awareness. The New Pact on Migration and Asylum, however, prioritizes security over asylum and focuses more on utilizing external policy tools. Externally, the EU can only inspire third/transit countries for gender equality by using funds. As a brief analysis on Turkey-EU Statement has shown, the EU can only mention that it will provide humanitarian assistance or funding based on gendered vulnerabilities. If the third/transit country does not wish to comply, the EU has no mechanism to push the country towards gender-sensitive policies. How the EU is going to attach gender mainstreaming to its newly styled migration and asylum policy remains to be seen.

A possible solution could be the EU's finalization of its accession to the Istanbul Convention. The Convention requires state parties to interpret the 1951 Refugee Convention in a gender-sensitive way and to provide gender-sensitive reception conditions, support services and asylum procedures. The EU signed the Convention in 2017, but it has not acceded to it yet. Concluding its accession to the Convention must be a key priority for the EU in achieving gender-sensitive refugee and asylum policies.

The magnitude of the humanitarian crisis facing Europe is a serious concern. Unequal gender relations thrive in times of such crises. But this may be the right time to see that crises also provide an opportunity to come up with better solutions. The EU has the economic and social capacity to come up with better gender regulations; what is needed is, perhaps, political motivation.

# CHAPTER 5

# RE-BORDERING EUROPE?: REFUGEES AND 'TEMPORARY' INTERNAL BORDER CONTROLS

N. Aslı Şirin* and Ebru Dalğakıran**

## Introduction: Debates on bordering Europe

European integration, in general, and the development of the Schengen regime, in particular, have transformed the nature of national borders, their role and function, as well as meanings and perceptions regarding them.[1] Rather than the traditionalists' definition of borders as fixed lines separating states' territories, critical border scholars theorize them by dwelling on their (re)construction, re-spatialization and re-allocation as dispersed, deterritorialized and mobile.[2] Another significant point critics elaborate on is how the bordering process creates an *Other* that always changes depending on *"who they are, where they are coming from and going to"*.[3]

The traditional meaning of borders changed in the Schengen Convention with the introduction of two new categories: internal and external borders. Internal borders were classified as *"the common land borders of the Contracting Parties, their airports for internal flights and their sea ports for regular ferry connections exclusively from or to other ports within the territories of the Contracting Parties and not calling at any ports outside those territories"*.[4] External borders were defined as *"the Contracting Parties' land and sea borders and their airports and sea ports, provided that they are not internal borders"*.[5] In such a border regime, it is neutral to make a distinction between internal and external borders. However, the problem is

---

* Asst. Prof. Dr. Marmara University, Institute of European Studies
** Research Assistant, Marmara University, Institute of European Studies
[1] Anssi Paasi "Boundaries as Social Practice and Discourse: The Finnish-Russian Border", **Regional Studies**, Vol. 33, No. 7, 1999, pp. 669-680; Chris Rumford, "Introduction: Citizens and Borderwork in Europe", **Space and Polity**, Vol. 12, No. 1, 2008, pp. 1-12; Étienne Balibar, **Politics and the Other Scene**, London: Verso, 2002; William Walters, "The frontiers of the European Union: A geostrategic perspective", **Geopolitics**, Vol. 9, No. 3, 2004, pp. 674–698.
[2] Balibar, op.cit; Chris Rumford, "Global Borders: An Introduction to the Special Issue", **Environment and Planning D: Society and Space**, Vol. 28, No. 6, 2010, pp. 951-956; David Newman, "Borders and bordering: Towards an interdisciplinary dialogue", **European Journal of Social Theory**, Vol. 9, No. 2, 2006, pp. 171-186; Luiza Bialasiewicz, "The uncertain state(s) of Europe?", **European Urban and Regional Studies**, Vol. 15, No.1, 2008, pp. 71-82; Walters, op.cit.
[3] Nick Vaughan-Williams, **Border Politics: The Limits of Sovereign Power**, Edinburg University Press: Edinburg, 2009, p.14.
[4] Convention Implementing the Schengen Agreement of 14 June 1985, Article 1, https://eur-lex.europa.eu/legal-content/EN/TXT/PDF/?uri=CELEX:42000A0922(02)&from=EN Access 20.06.2018
[5] ibid.

that they are still accepted as national borders. Although this distinction did not lead to a redrawing of borders in Europe, the Schengen regime did create a new way to conceptualize European borders.

The external borders marked the territory of all Schengen Member-States. While the borders were national before the Schengen regime, the latter borders gained unique features when national borders became simultaneously the Schengen borders. The border gained a collective meaning since the external borders belong to all countries in the Schengen area.

Recently the increase in mobility flows, diversification of terrorist attacks, and the COVID-19 pandemic in the EU have also put pressure on border-related issues. The rhetoric equating migration and threat has resulted in securitization of migration and reconceptualization of borders through change in border policies regarding migration.[6] Re-bordering processes have translated into new border management technologies as a means to restrict mobility and regulate borders both in internal and external terms. Thus, re-bordering through security concerns leads us to refer to "the EU as a global border machine".[7]

Although the EU's bordering practices along and beyond its borders are criticized, recently headlines appear such as: "The end of Schengen? Restrictions by Denmark and Sweden are 'threatening Europe's passport-free zone'",[8] "Is the Schengen dream of Europe without borders becoming a thing of the past?",[9] "Border checks are undermining Schengen",[10] and "Border Checks in EU Countries challenge Schengen Agreement".[11]

What do these headlines about internal border controls tell us about mobility and borders in Europe? As a result of the Arab Uprisings and particularly the so-called "migration crisis" of 2015, internal border controls that had been abolished with the signing of the Schengen Agreement, became a topic of discussion among the EU Member-States. Moreover, some of the Schengen Member-States reintroduced internal border controls and are allowed to prolong them. Although several Member States have used the

---

[6] Didier Bigo and Elspeth Guild, "Introduction: Policing in the Name of Freedom", **Controlling Frontiers: Free Movement Into and Within Europe**, Didier Bigo, Elspeth Guild (eds.), Ashgate Publishing, England and USA, 2003, pp. 1-13.

[7] Henk van Houtum, "Human Blacklisting: The Global Apartheid of the EU's External Border Regime", **Environment and Planning D: Society and Space**, Vol. 28, No. 6, 2010, pp 957-976.

[8] **Independent**, 04.01.2016, https://www.independent.co.uk/news/world/europe/the-end-of-schengen-restrictions-by-denmark-and-sweden-are-threatening-europes-passport-free-zone-a6796696.html Access 11.11.2019

[9] **The Guardian**, 05.01.2016, https://www.theguardian.com/world/2016/jan/05/is-the-schengen-dream-of-europe-without-borders-becoming-a-thing-of-the-past Access 12.11.2019

[10] **The Economist**, 27.10.2018, https://www.economist.com/europe/2018/10/27/border-checks-are-undermining-schengen Access 13.11.2019.

[11] **Deutsche Welle,** 12.11.2019, https://www.dw.com/en/border-checks-in-eu-countries-challenge-schengen-agreement/a-51033603 Access 13.11.2019

safeguarding mechanism in the past, due to the uniqueness of the geographical and temporal scale of the current restriction of mobility, some analysts portrayed this recent evolution as the 'dislocation', 'dismantling' or even the 'death' of the Schengen Area.[12]

Against this background, this article analyses the reintroduction of internal border controls as a re-bordering process to control, contain and filter mobility. We argue that with hardening of internal borders through the introduction of border controls and new security measures, the Schengen border regime does not promote a *borderless* mobility even within among the Members, it rather facilitates mobility within the internal borders compared to external borders. This article is composed of two parts. The first is centred on the historical evolution of the Schengen border regime while the second elaborates on the reintroduction of internal border controls mainly following the Arab Uprisings.

### History of the Schengen border regime

The 1980s witnessed an important development in terms of at least some of the borders in Europe. It was significant for the European Community (EC) which had a goal to create *"an area with no internal borders and in which there is free movement of goods, persons, services and capital"*. [13] [14] However, because there was no consensus in the Council on the concept of free movement of persons, the Benelux countries, in addition to France and Germany,[15] decided to establish an area without internal border controls. According to them, it was essential for Europe's internal market to ensure the free movement of goods as well as people. So, in June 1985, they signed the Schengen Agreement according to which they abolished border controls. This intergovernmental cooperation in the area of border management gained more political support and the Convention implementing the Schengen Agreement[16] (Schengen Convention) was signed in 1990. As it came into

---

[12] **Sénat**, "Rapport d'information fait au nom de la commission des affaires européennes sur la réforme de l'espace Schengen et la crise des réfugiés", Session ordinaire 2015-2016, p. 3 quoted by Estelle Evrard, Birte Nienaber, Adolfo Sommaribas, "The Temporary Reintroduction of Border Controls Inside the Schengen Area: Towards a Spatial Perspective", **Journal of Borderlands Studies**, DOI: 10.1080/08865655.2017.1415164, 2018, pp.1-2.

[13] This goal was actually envisaged in the Art. 2 and Art 3 (c) of the Treaty of Rome.

[14] **Single European Act**, Official Journal of the European Communities No 169/1, 1987.

[15] Germany was Federal Republic of Germany at that time.

[16] The Convention Implementing the Schengen Agreement is regarded as the basis of several acts that make up the Schengen acquis. "The elements making up the acquis, setting out the corresponding legal basis for each of them in EU law by Council Decisions 1999/435/EC and 1999/436/EC of 20 May 1999". Francesca Ferraro, "Schengen governance after the Lisbon Treaty", Library Briefing, **Library of the European Parliament**, 2013, https://www.europarl.europa.eu/ RegData/bibliotheque/briefing/2013/130358/LDM_BRI(2013)130358_REV1_EN.pdf Access 18.09.2018.

effect in March 1995, the "Schengen Area"[17] was created and internal border controls were effectively abolished. Additionally, a common external border where controls would be carried out according to a set of rules and operational instructions and procedures, was established.[18]

After its entry into law in 1995, it was signed by a further six countries - Austria, Denmark, Finland, Sweden - and the non-EU states of Norway and Iceland. The incorporation of the Schengen Agreement into the legal and institutional framework of the EU came with a Protocol attached to the Treaty of Amsterdam signed in 1997 and put into effect in May 1999. As known, a number of Justice and Home Affairs (JHA) and JHA-related policy areas were transferred to the European Community pillar (First Pillar) under Title IV: Visas, Asylum, Immigration and Other Policies Related to Free Movement of Persons. *"The main purpose of this was to facilitate, within a period of five years after the entry into force of the Treaty, the adoption of measures that would result in the progressive establishment of 'an area of freedom, security and justice'[19] in which there would be free movement of persons behind a common external border"*.[20] Regarding border control, the EU would be ensuring the absence of border controls as well as framing a common policy on asylum, immigration and external border control.[21] The policy issues, which were transferred to the First Pillar, included visas, asylum, immigration, refugees and displaced persons, and

---

[17] "The Schengen area gradually expanded to include nearly every Member State. Italy signed the agreements on 27 November 1990, Spain and Portugal joined on 25 June 1991, Greece followed on 6 November 1992, then Austria on 28 April 1995 and Denmark, Finland and Sweden on 19 December 1996. The Czech Republic, Estonia, Latvia, Lithuania, Hungary, Malta, Poland, Slovenia and Slovakia joined on 21 December 2007 and the associated country Switzerland on 12 December 2008. Bulgaria, Cyprus and Romania are not yet fully-fledged members of the Schengen area; border controls between them and the Schengen area are maintained until the EU Council decides that the conditions for abolishing internal border controls have been met". **Schengen Area**, https://novaric.co/malta/entry-to-malta/schengen-area/#:~:text=The%20Schengen%20area%20gradually%20expanded,Sweden %20on%2019%20December%201996  Access 18.09.2020. As regards the situation of Denmark, it should be noted that although Denmark did not take part in any of the policies under Title IV: Visas, Asylum, Immigration and Other Policies Related to Free Movement of Persons it was legally bound by certain measures related to the common visa policy. The United Kingdom and Ireland, on the other hand, would only participate in police and judicial cooperation in criminal matters, the fight against drugs and the Schengen Information System.

[18] Border surveillance and controls were also enhanced by the introduction of an information system called the Schengen Information System that would help exchange data on specific categories of people, and on lost or stolen goods. The main purpose was to secure more cooperation on external borders with the principle of facilitating the free movement of people as well as guaranteeing more security. See Stefano Bertozzi, "Schengen: Achievements and Challenges in Managing an Area Encompassing 3.6 Million Km²", **CEPS Working Document**, No. 284, 2008, pp. 4-5, http://dx.doi.org/10.2139/ssrn.1337624.

[19] **European Union Consolidated Versions of The Treaty on European Union and of The Treaty Establishing The European Community**, Article 61, 2002, https://eur-lex.europa.eu/legal-content/EN/TXT/PDF/?uri=CELEX:12002E/TXT&from=EN.

[20] Neill Nugent, **The Government and Politics of the European Union**, Macmillan: The UK, 4. Edition, 1999, pp.83-84.

[21] **Consolidated Version of The Treaty on The Functioning of The European Union**, Article 67, 2012, https://eur-lex.europa.eu/LexUriServ/LexUriServ.do?uri=CELEX:12012E/TXT:en:PDF

judicial cooperation in civil matters. With this transfer, the Third Pillar of the Treaty on European Union (TEU) changed in character.[22]

Apart from the Treaty of Amsterdam's entry into force, the year 1999 saw another development. A special European Council was held on 15-16 October in Tampere to discuss migration and migration-related issues. Protecting the EU's borders was on the agenda and the Tampere European Council called for more cooperation on border management to develop a more effective migration policy.[23] It was decided to establish a common area of freedom, security and justice in the EU and the Tampere Programme (1999-2004) adopted accordingly focused on strengthening surveillance and control of the external borders.

Since the Tampere European Council the protection of borders has been one of the political priorities of the EU, and effective border control has been emphasised recurrently in several Presidency Conclusions of the European Council including the Laeken European Council of December 2001 which asked *"the Council and the Commission to work out arrangements for cooperation between services responsible for external border control and to examine the conditions in which a mechanism or common services to control external borders could be created"*.[24]

Shortly after the Laeken European Council, the European Commission came up with a proposal on how to improve the Union's border management. The Communication of May 2002 entitled "Towards integrated management of the external borders of the member states of the European Union" was a proposal for closer cooperation in practical terms and developing a common policy on managing the EU's external borders.[25] This

---

[22] Under its new title, 'Provisions on Police and Judicial Cooperation in Criminal Matters', it now focused on providing citizens 'with a high level of safety within an area of freedom, security and justice by developing common action among the Member States in the fields of police and judicial cooperation in criminal matters and by preventing and combating racism and xenophobia'. see Nugent, op.cit., p.84.
[23] Bertozzi, op.cit., p.6.
The Tampere European Council "… requires the Union to develop common policies on asylum and immigration, while taking into account the need for a consistent control of external borders to stop illegal immigration and to combat those who organise it and commit related international crimes. …" see ibid. The basis for cooperation on border management is Art. 66 of the EC Treaty: "… the Council shall take measures to ensure cooperation between the relevant departments of the administrations of the member states in the areas covered by this title, as well as between those departments and the Commission".
[24] This statement covers two turning points. First of all, there is definitely a political jump in terms of developing an area of justice, freedom and security because for the first time Member-States realised that their attempts to tighten controls at their own borders were not sufficient to cope with the need to jointly manage the Union's external borders. Secondly, this decision signalled the readiness and willingness *"to abandon the old idea of borders as a mere demarcation of their sovereign territory in exchange for enhanced capacity to prevent terrorism and stop the smuggling of people, or drugs and weapons from slipping across borders"*. see ibid, p.8.
[25] The common policy would comprise five components, namely a common body of legislation, coordinated operational mechanisms, common integrated risk analyses, staff trained in European matters and financial and other burden- sharing between member states. see **Communication Towards integrated management of the external borders of the member states of the European Union,**

Communication[26] was important in the sense that it arranged the scene for the Presidency Conclusions of the Seville European Council of June 2002, which produced the first detailed plan on the Union's border management. The political foundations for the future Frontex[27] were laid down and there was more belief in the idea of integrated management of external borders. Thus the efforts bore fruit and the first seeds of the EU's border control model were sown.

In June 2003, The European Commission adopted a Communication on developing a common policy on illegal immigration, smuggling and trafficking in human beings, external borders and the return of illegal residents. The concluding remarks of the Communication emphasised that the EU's involvement in border management was significant because only if all of the member-states were convinced to cooperate and work together through common rules and standards, Europe would be able to deal more effectively with the problem of "illegal immigration". The Communication was reflected in the Presidency Conclusions of the Thessaloniki European Council which made linkages between different areas of a common migration policy, particularly border management, return, visa and cooperation with third countries.

A couple of months after the Thessaloniki European Council, another European Council was held in Brussels. This time the main themes were an Intergovernmental Conference on the EU's institutions and the Common Foreign and Security Policy and ways to relaunch the European economy. However migration-related issues were discussed, too. The Brussels European Council agreed on the following:

*"Recalling the conclusions of its Thessaloniki meeting, the European Council welcomes the Commission's intention to pursue rapidly the examination of the allocation of EUR 140 million envisaged for the period 2004-2006, in order to cover the most pressing needs in this area, especially in supporting the management of external borders, …. The European Council underlines the importance of full implementation of the Plan for the management of external borders … The European Council welcomes the Commission's intention to submit a proposal for the creation of a Border Management Agency, in order to enhance operational cooperation for the management of external borders..."[28]*

---

European Commission, COM (2002) 233 final, Brussels, 2002, p.12, https://eur-lex.europa.eu/legal-content/EN/TXT/PDF/?uri=CELEX:52002DC0233 &from =EN Access 22.10.2019.

[26] The Commission recommended the creation of an External borders practitioners common unit. This common unit was a group comprising members of the Strategic Committee on Immigration, Frontiers and Asylum (SCIFA) and heads of national border control services. ibid, p.13.

[27] Frontex stands for the European Agency for the Management of Operational Co-operation at the External Borders.

[28] Presidency Conclusions Brussels European Council 16/17 October 2003, https://ec.europa.eu/commission/ presscorner/detail/en/DOC_03_4 Access 12.10.2019.

As an essential element of the EU's integrated border management, Frontex was established with the Regulation (EC) 2007/2004 of 26 October 2004.[29] *"To help identify migratory patterns as well as trends in cross-border criminal activities, Frontex analyses data related to the situation at and beyond EU's external borders. It monitors the situation at the borders and helps border authorities to share information with Member States. … Frontex coordinates and organises joint operations and rapid border interventions to assist Member States at the external borders, including in humanitarian emergencies and rescue at sea. … Frontex supports the cooperation between law enforcement authorities, EU agencies and customs at sea borders. … Frontex focuses on preventing smuggling, human trafficking and terrorism as well as many other cross-border crimes."*[30]

Not long after the creation of Frontex, the European Council endorsed the Hague Programme that set the priorities for an area of freedom, security and justice in the 2005-2009 period. The major objective was to improve the ability of both the EU and the member-states to a) guarantee fundamental rights, procedural safeguards, and access to justice, b) fight organized crime, c) repress the threat of terrorism, d) provide protection to refugees, and e) regulate migration flows and control the external borders of the Union. [31] The focus was mainly on three areas: borders, biometrics, and visas. The primary aim was to fully abolish internal borders while providing the maximum security and orderly passage at external borders.[32]

The year 2006 witnessed a crucial development in terms of the Schengen border regime. On March 15, Regulation (EC) No 562/2006 establishing a Community Code on the rules governing the movement of persons across borders (Schengen Borders Code - SBC) was adopted. The aim was to *"to improve the legislative part of the integrated border management European Union policy by setting out the rules on the border control of persons crossing EU external borders and on the temporary reintroduction of border control at internal borders"*.[33] The Union's internal and external borders were defined in relation to each other by the SBC.[34]

---

[29] The aim of establishing Frontex was to improve procedures and working methods of the Common Unit that had been created in 2002.

[30] **Origin and Tasks**, Frontex, 2019, https://frontex.europa.eu/about-frontex/origin-tasks/ Access 24.11.2019.

[31] Joanne van Selm, "The Hague Program Reflects New European Realities", **Migration Policy Institute**, Feature, 2005, https://www.migrationpolicy.org/article/hague-program-reflects-new-european-realities
Access 14.09.2018.

[32] van Selm, op.cit.

[33] Regulation (EC) No 562/2006 of the European Parliament and of the Council of 15 March 2006 establishing a Community Code on the rules governing the movement of persons across borders (Schengen Borders Code), European Parliament and Council, 2006, https://eur-lex.europa.eu/legal-content/EN/TXT/PDF/?uri=CELEX:32006R0562&from=EN Access 18.09.2018.

[34] According to the SBC, the "internal borders" are (a) the common land borders, including river and lake

According to the SBC, EU citizens and other persons enjoying the right of free movement (like the family members of a Union citizen), go through a minimum check when they cross an external border. This minimum check is done to give authorization on the basis of their travel documents. Crossing internal borders is, on the other hand, free of checks. However, in case of a serious threat to public policy or internal security, the Schengen countries may, as an exception, reintroduce border controls at its internal borders for a period which cannot exceed 30 days or for the foreseeable duration of serious threat (Art. 23 (1)). According to Art. 25 (1), in case of a serious threat to public policy or internal security, a Member State may, as an exception, reintroduce border control at its internal borders immediately.

In short, the SBC is important since it codified most of the Schengen rules regarding the controls at the Union's external borders, both the removal and temporary re-introduction of controls at the internal borders, and the police controls of the area behind the internal border. Thus, it may be regarded as the main building block of the Schengen *acquis*.

The last noteworthy development concerning the Schengen border regime recently occurred with the Treaty of Lisbon, which amended the Treaty on European Union (TEU) and the Treaty establishing the European Community (TEC), that was renamed Treaty on the Functioning of the European Union (TFEU). The Schengen *acquis* was integrated with a Protocol into the EU's framework. The provisions were annexed to the TEU and TFEU. By abolishing the Union's pillar structure, the Treaty of Lisbon brought together the policies on JHA which had been dispersed with the Treaty of Amsterdam, under one heading named Area of Freedom, Security and Justice (AFSJ). As Takle notes, the policies on border control, as well asylum, immigration, judicial cooperation and police cooperation were combined in a thorough approach to border control.[35]

In the light of this brief background, the following pages examine critically the internal border controls introduced by some Schengen Member-States after the Arab Uprisings.

---

borders, of the member states; (b) the airports of the member states for internal flights; and (c) sea, river and lake ports of the member states for regular ferry connections. The "external borders" are the member states' land borders, including river and lake borders, sea borders and their airports, river ports, sea ports and lake ports, provided that they are not internal borders. see ibid.

[35] Marianne Takle, "The Treaty of Lisbon and the European Border Control Regime", **Journal of Contemporary European Research**, Vol. 8, No. 3, 2012, p. 289.

With the Treaty of Lisbon, Schengen cooperation was attached importance as regards making the EU an area of freedom, security and justice. The Stockholm Programme of 2010-2014, witnessing the entry into force of the Treaty of Lisbon, included the EU's integrated border management. Underlining the relevance of its policies for the people of Europe, the Stockholm Programme included the areas— among which is external border management and visa policy—that were dealt with separately. In short, the Treaty of Lisbon and the political and operational guidelines stated in the Stockholm Programme set up the framework for further development of the Schengen border regime. Takle, op.cit, pp.290-291.

## Is Schengen border regime under threat?: the reintroduction of internal border controls

The Arab Uprisings, which began at the end of 2010, unsettled the precarious balance on which the Schengen border regime had been built over the years and the regime was faced with a political crisis *"triggered by the collapse of political institutions in North African countries and by the widening of the web of bilateral agreements and diplomatic relations that for years have allowed a strict policing of migratory routes in the Mediterranean"*.[36] The emergence of misunderstandings between the Schengen Member-States about interpreting the rules on internal border control following the start of the Arab Spring was an indicator, in that sense, and the Franco-Italian affair constituted a specific example.

At the beginning of April 2011, Italian authorities started issuing temporary residence permits to many undocumented Tunisian migrants who had arrived in Italy via the island of Lampedusa.[37] With those permits they were granted an automatic right to move freely within the Schengen territory. As a response to this move, "France introduced internal border checks between the two countries, which have resulted in pushing back hundreds of immigrants holding these permits during the last three weeks [in April 2011] and the blocking of trains from Ventimiglia, the last Italian town before the French border, carrying some 300 migrants and NGO representatives on 17 April 2011". [38] France's response resulted in a row between the two governments and *"a confrontation with the European Commission on the matters of restricting migration and the legality of reinstated border controls"*.[39]

The Franco-Italian affair raised several legal and political questions which need to be critically assessed both in terms of the legal commitments France and Italy have under the EU's migration policy/border law and the political legitimacy of the Schengen border regime within and outside Europe. The first question is related to the legality of the Italian measures and French border practices in light of European legislation. Since both countries are members of the Schengen border regime they are bound by the rules set out in the Schengen *acquis* in managing the Union's external borders and guaranteeing the free movement of persons within their internal territories. The second is about the effects of the affair on the general principles of law

---

[36] Giuseppe Campesi, "The Arab Spring and the Crisis of the European Border Regime: Manufacturing Emergency in the Lampedusa Crisis", **EUI Working Papers**, RSCAS 2011/59, 2011, p.1.

[37] This was a part of the national state of emergency Italy had declared upon the arrival of big numbers of North African migrants.

[38] Sergio Carrera, Elspeth Guild, Massimo Merlino, Joanna Parkin, "A Race against Solidarity The Schengen Regime and the Franco-Italian Affair", **Centre for European Policy Studies (CEPS)**, 2011, p.1.

[39] Kiran K. Phull,, John B. Sutcliffe, "Crossroads of Integration? The Future of Schengen in the Wake of the Arab Spring", **The EU and the Eurozone Crisis-Policy Challenges and Strategic Choices**, Finn Laursen (ed.), [First published 2013 by Ashgate Publishing], USA: Routledge, 2016, p. 177.

at the foundations of the Schengen system as a whole: namely, principles of solidarity and burden-sharing, genuine cooperation, as well as respect of the fundamental human rights of persons on the move.[40]

Apart from raising the above-mentioned issues, the Franco-Italian affair opened a discussion on reforming the Schengen border regime in which many Member-States demanded greater freedom to decide on imposing controls on internal borders. Accordingly, in September 2011, the European Commission presented its first communication entitled "Schengen Governance – Strengthening the Area without Internal Border Control". The Communication comprised an evaluation mechanism as well as rules for reintroducing internal border controls. The Member-States were opposed to the Communication so the European Commission had to prepare a compromise proposal where the division of power between the Commission and the Member States was in favour of states. This time, the European Parliament showed opposition because the Council would unilaterally decide to accept the Schengen amendments so the EP would be excluded from the whole procedure. As a result, further changes were made to the proposal.

The outcome of the two-year-long discussion on reforming the Schengen regime was the Schengen Governance Reform Package, which came into effect in November 2013. Regulation (EU) No 610/2013 amended the Convention implementing the Schengen Agreement, Regulation (EC) No 562/2006 (SBC). The provisions about reintroducing border controls were in the new Regulation (Article 25-8). Internal border controls could be reintroduced (a) for a maximum period of six months (Art. 25) in cases of foreseeable events (e.g. political events) or (b) for a maximum period of two months (Art. 28) in cases requiring immediate action (unforeseen circumstances). Additionally, a specific procedure was introduced for cases where the overall functioning of the area without internal border control was put at risk by exceptional circumstances.[41]

The reform of the Schengen regime was put to test by the so-called "migration crisis" of 2015. The result of the conflicts in Iraq, Afghanistan and Syria was a bulge in the number of people seeking asylum in the EU.[42]

---

[40] Carrera, Guild, Merlino, Parkin, op.cit.
[41] This procedure is set as a provision (Article 29) in the codified SBC (Regulation (EU) 2016/399 of the European Parliament and of the Council of 9 March 2016 on a Union Code on the rules governing the movement of persons across borders).
[42] **The Implementation of the Common European Asylum System**, European Parliament, Policy Department for Citizen's Rights and Constitutional Affairs, Directorate General for Internal Policies Policy Department C: Citizens' Rights and Constitutional Affairs, 2016, https://www.europarl.europa.eu/RegData/etudes/STUD/2016/556953/IPOL_STU(2016)556953_EN.pdf Access 08.09.2018. EUROSTAT reported that, in 2015, 1.2 million people applied for asylum in the EU. The majority of the asylum-seekers came from Syria, Iraq and Afghanistan respectively. see **Asylum Statistics**, EUROSTAT, 2016, http://ec.europa.eu/eurostat/statistics-explained/index.php/Asylum_statistics Access 06.10.2018.

As a reaction to the number of asylum-seekers, internal border controls were reintroduced by several Schengen countries, namely Germany, Austria, Slovenia,[43] Hungary, Sweden, Norway, Denmark and Belgium.[44] The reason was an alleged "big influx of persons seeking international protection" or "unexpected migratory flow"[45]. Except Hungary,[46] those countries put the procedure into effect under Art. 28 of SBC at the beginning.

Article 27 of the SBC, which allows a Member-State to prevent foreseeable threats, was applied by Germany, Austria, Sweden, Denmark and Norway. France and Malta followed suit and "initiated border controls due to important international events (COP 21 – Paris Climate Conference and the Valletta Summit, respectively) and associated these events with a terrorist threat".[47]

The reintroduction of internal border controls by the Schengen Member-States brought criticisms with it. In its communication entitled "Back to Schengen-A Roadmap" of March 2016, the European Commission criticised the measure as follows: *"The conflict and crisis in Syria and elsewhere in the region have triggered record numbers of refugees and migrants arriving in the European Union, which in turn has revealed serious deficiencies at parts of the Union's external borders and resulted in a wave-through approach applied by some Member States. This has led to the creation of a route across the Western Balkans which sees migrants travelling swiftly north. In reaction, several Member States have resorted to reintroducing temporary internal border controls, placing in question the proper functioning of the Schengen area of free movement and its benefits to European citizens and the European economy.[48]*

---

[43] Slovenia "notified the Council about its internal border controls in mid-September 2015 and revoked its internal border controls as soon as mid-October 2015". see **The Implementation of the Common European Asylum System**, op.cit., p.16.

[44] As the last country to re-introduce internal border controls due to the fear of the arrival of refugees from the Calais refugee camp in France, Belgium did not prolong the controls after April 2016.

[45] Communication from the Commission to the European Parliament and the Council, Eighth biannual report on the functioning of the Schengen area 1 May-10 December 2015, European Commission, COM (2015) 675 final, Strasbourg, 2015, http://www.europarl.europa.eu/RegData/docs_autres_institutions/commission_europeenne/com/2015/0675/COM_COM%282015%290675_EN.pdf Access 06.10.2018. Member States' notifications of the temporary reintroduction of border control at internal borders pursuant to Article 23 *et seq.* of the Schengen Borders Code, European Commission, 2016, http://ec.europa.eu/dgs/home-affairs/what-we-do/policies/borders-and-visas/schengen/reintroductionbordercontrol/docs/ms_notifications__reintroduction_of_border_control_en.pdf Access 06.10.2018.

[46] Hungary began installing a barbed-wire fence on its internal Schengen border with Slovenia at the end of September 2015, but construction works were quickly stopped as the issue was settled with an agreement between the two. Yet Hungary was able to build the fence on its external Schengen border with Serbia and Schengen accession country Croatia. see European Commission, op.cit.

[47] "Nevertheless, France, from January 1 2016, has continued its border controls after the Paris attacks due to the subsequent 'state of emergency' and big sporting events, such as the Tour de France and the European Football Championship". see ibid.

[48] **Back to Schengen-A roadmap**, ANNEX 1 to the Communication from the Commission to the European Parliament, the European Council and the Council, , COM(2016) 120, European Commission, Brussels, 2016, p.2, https://eur-lex.europa.eu/legal-

Yet the Commission did not refrain from referring to the possibility of invoking Art. 29 of the SBC allowing the reintroduction and prolongation of internal border controls in exceptional circumstances where the overall functioning of the area without internal border control is put at risk as a result of persistent serious deficiencies relating to external border control as referred to in Article 21,[49] and insofar as those circumstances constitute a serious threat to public policy or internal security". Moreover, based on a Council Implementing Decision of 12 May 2016,[50] Germany, Austria, Sweden, Denmark and Norway obtained the permission to prolong their internal border controls for another six months.

The basis of the Council Decision was the existence of serious and persistent deficiencies at the Greek external borders. It was criticised because instead of deficiencies in external border management, it was actually the deficiencies in the Greek asylum system which caused the refugee flows. As Peers notes, both the European Court of Human Rights and the Court of Justice of European Union (CJEU) had already mentioned the difficulty of sending asylum-seekers back to Greece due to the collapse of its asylum system.[51]

After the first Implementing Decision, the initial reintroduction of internal border control was subsequently extended three times by the Council. The extension was done under the Art. 29. Thus Germany, Austria, Denmark, Norway and Sweden were allowed to maintain internal border controls up until 11 November 2017.[52] That was the maximum period of time

---

content/en/TXT/?uri=celex:52016DC0120 Access 06.10.2018.

[49] Art 21 (1) is as follows: "Where serious deficiencies in the carrying out of external border control are identified in an evaluation report drawn up pursuant to Article 14 of Regulation (EU) No 1053/2013, and with a view to ensuring compliance with the recommendations referred to in Article 15 of that Regulation, the Commission may recommend, by means of an implementing act, that the evaluated Member State take certain specific measures…"

[50] Council Implementing Decision setting out a Recommendation for temporary internal border control in an exceptional circumstances putting the overall functioning of the Schengen area at risk, 8835/16.

[51] Steve Peers, "Can Schengen be suspended because of Greece? Should it be?", **EU Law Analysis: Expert insight into EU law developments**, 2015, http://eulawanalysis.blogspot.com/2015/12/can-schengen-be-suspended-because-of.html Access 07.10.2018.

[52] In the meantime, on September 27, the Commission presented "a communication on preserving and strengthening Schengen, which was accompanied by a proposal for amending the Schengen Border Code, as well as by a recommendation on the implementation of the current Schengen border code provisions on internal border controls". The objective of the proposal was two-fold: (a) to ensure that the time limits applicable to the temporary border controls at internal borders enable Member States to take, when necessary, measures needed to respond to a serious threats to internal security or public policy; (b) to introduce better procedural safeguards in order to ensure that the decision on temporary border controls at internal borders or their prolongation is based on a proper risk assessment and is taken in cooperation with the other Member States concerned. See European Commission, "Communication from the Commission to the European Parliament and the Council on preserving and strengthening Schengen", COM(2017) 570 final, 27.09.2017, https://eur-lex.europa.eu/legal-content/EN/TXT/PDF/?uri=CELEX:52017DC0570&from=EN Access 11.06.2018The European Parliament was opposed to the proposal and it was not adopted in the end.

allowed under Art 29, i.e. 2 years.[53] When the deadline expired in November, these countries made a request and the Council once more allowed them to continue their border controls until May 2018. This time they resorted back to Art. 25 since Art. 29 makes it possible to be applied cumulatively to Art. 25, as different rationales are addressed in the Articles for reintroducing internal border controls.[54] As mentioned above, France, also relying on Art. 25 and making reference to a 'persistent terrorist threat' as a reason, kept border controls in place. When generally considered, those reasons may qualify as threats to public policy or internal security. Yet, what is more important is the fact that the Commission did not question whether or not the reasons were valid.

Thus, even if threats to public policy or internal security exist, it is still problematic. The countries cannot ask for prolongation because Art. 25 does not allow them to do so beyond six months. The wording of Art. 25 (4) is clear: "*The total period during which border control is reintroduced at internal borders, including any prolongation provided for under paragraph 3[55] of this Article, shall not exceed six months*".[56] Despite expiration in May, Austria, Germany, Denmark, Norway and Sweden once again reinstated internal border controls until November 2018. Moreover, while the reinstatement in May 2018 was already open to question both in terms of legality and legitimacy, new reinstatements followed. Relying on Art. 25, the same countries reintroduced border controls once more in November 2018, May 2019 and recently in mid-November 2019. The last reinstatement is supposed to end in May 2020, but further reintroductions are quite possible.

Indeed, even before the expiration in May 2020, we have come across another reintroduction of internal border controls. This time it has been a part of policy responses to the outbreak of Coronavirus disease 2019 (Covid-19)[57] in Europe in late February and early March. The policy responses to the

---

[53] Jakup Jasiewicz, "A not-so-temporary reinstatement of internal border controls?", **Leiden Law Blog**, 2018, https://leidenlawblog.nl/articles/a-not-so-temporary-reinstatement-of-internal-border-controls Access 11.06.2018.

[54] Jasiewicz, op.cit.

[55] Art 25 (3) is as follows: "If the serious threat to public policy or internal security in the Member State concerned persists beyond the period provided for in paragraph 1 of this Article [30 days], that Member State may prolong border control at its internal borders, taking account of the criteria referred to in Article 26 and in accordance with Article 27, on the same grounds as those referred to in paragraph 1 of this Article and, taking into account any new elements, for renewable periods of up to 30 days".

[56] https://www.europarl.europa.eu/doceo/document/TA-8-2018-0472_EN.html

[57] "The Coronavirus disease 2019 (COVID-19) is caused by the severe acute respiratory syndrome coronavirus 2 (SARS-CoV-2). It was first reported in China towards the end of December 2019 and early January 2020, and the first cases reached Europe towards the end of January 2020. On 13 March 2020 the WHO reported that Europe had become the epicentre of the coronavirus pandemic." Sergio Carrera, Ngo Chun Luk, "In the Name of COVID-19: An Assessment of the Schengen Internal Border Controls and Travel Restrictions in the EU", Study Requested by the European Parliament, LIBE Committee, September 2020, https://www.ceps.eu/download/publication/?id=30535&pdf=IPOL_STU202065950

Covid-19 pandemic have been mainly restrictions on international and intra-EU mobility. Accordingly, as Carrera and Luk note, in early March, came the reinstatement of internal border controls in the Schengen area pursuant to the SBC, the restrictions on intra-EU travel through entry bans and the shutting down of international passenger transport.[58] Shortly after, coordination actions have been taken at the EU level, as well. In March, the European Commission issued a set of guidelines with the aim of facilitating coordination among the EU Member States in terms of implementing the containment measures. What came to the fore were the Guidelines for border management measures to protect health and ensure the availability of goods and essential services[59] and the Guidance on the implementation of the temporary restriction on non-essential travel to the EU.[60] In mid-April, as a response to the European Council's call in late March, the Joint European Roadmap was issued by the Commission and the European Council. Including a coordinated approach necessary for the restoration of the freedom of movement and the lifting of internal border controls, the Roadmap described how the containment measures introduced because of Covid-19 would be phased out in the EU. The EU travel ban was initially introduced for 30 days, but the Commission recommended its extension in April, May, and June 2020. In the meantime, on 13 May, another package of guidelines for the progressively abolishing the travel restrictions was presented by the European Commission. The package included the Communication "COVID-19: Towards a phased and coordinated approach for restoring freedom of movement and lifting internal border controls".[61]

At that stage of the Covid-19 pandemic, we come across two justifications when the Member-States notified the European Commission of reinstatement of temporary internal border controls. One of them concerns cases requiring immediate action (Art. 28 of SBC) and the other concerns cases in which the overall functioning of the Schengen area is put at risk due to exceptional circumstances (Art. 29 of SBC). Accordingly, the Covid-19 pandemic threat has been invoked by almost all of the Schengen States.[62]

---

6_EN.pdf Access 20.10.2020

[58] Carrera, Luk, op cit. p.14.

[59] COVID-19: Guidelines for border management measures to protect health and ensure the availability of goods and essential services, European Commission, C (2020) 1753 final, Brussels, 16.3.2020, Access 16.10.2020.

[60] COVID-19: Guidance on the implementation of the temporary restriction on non-essential travel to the EU, on the facilitation of transit arrangements for the repatriation of EU citizens, and on the effects on visa policy, European Commission, C (2020) 2050 final, Brussels, 30.3.2020, Access 16.10.2020.

[61] Anna Doliwa-Klepacka, Mieczysława Zdanowicz, "The European Union Current Asylum Policy: Selected Problems in the Shadow of COVID-19", **International Journal for the Semiotics of Law**, July 2020, p.8.

[62] Sweden and Norway are exceptions since they have invoked the terrorist threat. Doliwa Klepacka and Zdanowicz. op.cit. p. 11.

As of 13 November, four Schengen countries still have temporarily introduced internal border controls in place due to the Covid-19 pandemic: Hungary, Denmark, Norway and Finland. Hungary has extended its 'existing' temporary internal border controls until 28 November 2020. Having extended its temporary internal border controls until 11 May 2021, Denmark expects to lift them and all other restrictions as soon as the situation allows. In addition, on 12 November, Denmark has reintroduced temporary border controls in the context of the terrorist threat.[63] Finland has lifted the internal border controls due to the pandemic but has reintroduced them for a short time period (11-22 November 2020). Norway extended its temporary internal border controls until 9 February 2021.[64] On the other hand, along with Denmark, Austria, Germany, Sweden and France reinstated temporary internal border controls due to the terrorist threat and situation at the external borders in the period 12 November-11 May 2021.[65]

As a last remark, it may be underlined that despite the fact that crossing the Schengen borders is already difficult for migrants, joined with the multi-faceted restrictions of Covid-19 pandemic, the widespread threat of an "invisible enemy" has made life even harder for them, especially the refugees. For example, everyday life has become more brutal in the refugee camps in Greece. As Doliwa-Klepacka and Zdanowicz note, the media are reporting about how the densely populated camps turn into a real war zones due to a constant struggle for survival, food, and health services.[66] Hate speech, as a part of racism and xenophobia, has been increasing during the Covid-19 pandemic and refugees are the main target.[67] This is mainly because of the fear and uncertainty caused by the pandemic. Those feelings have turned into hostility showing itself in hate speech directed towards migrants, particularly refugees. So the lives of refugees, which have already been full of hardships, are more difficult in the times of pandemic.

### Conclusion

Besides the free movement of goods, services, and capital, the free movement of people is accepted as one of the most fundamental values of

---

[63] ibid.
[64] For more on the temporary reintroduction of border controls see **Temporary Reintroduction of Border Control**, European Commission, 2020, https://ec.europa.eu/home-affairs/what-we-do/policies/borders-and-visas/schengen/reintroduction-border-control_en#:~:text=The%20Schengen%20Borders%20Code%20provides ,internal%20security%20has%20been%20established Access 13.11.2020.
[65] France's temporary internal border control is supposed to expire on 30 April 2021. see European Commission, op.cit.
[66] Doliwa-Klepacka, Zdanowicz, op.cit.
[67] An expert NGO named 'Association "Never Again"' has published a report showing acts of racism, xenophobia and discrimination which took place in the context of Covid-19 pandemic in Poland. see ibid.

European integration. Accordingly, internal borders were gradually abolished to expand these freedoms. The Schengen border regime dismantles internal border controls while reinforcing the protection of external borders. Although the rights related to free movement of persons differ according to different categories of people like workers, tourists, and etc., people can travel from one Schengen Member-State to another without being subject to border controls once they enter the Schengen area. Thus, when the Schengen Convention was implemented in 1995, "*Schengenland, a politically constructed …* *common space, both of inclusion and exclusion, where mobility is either free or restricted*" was established.[68] Nevertheless, the Schengen's evolution, which began three decades ago, has not been straightforward. Dramatic geopolitical developments like the fall of Berlin Wall, enlargements, and threats to peace and security led by terrorism tested the idea of creating an area of free movement across Europe.

Since the Arab Uprisings, Member-States have been questioning the borderless area between the Schengen members. Due to the lack of trust among themselves and the fear of an increase in the number of refugees, some Member-States started using the SBC, which was amended in 2013, to reinstate temporary border controls. As discussed above, Member-States are able to use this in the case of a serious threat to public policy or internal security.

The Schengen zone means a borderless area in technical terms, yet the recent implementations show that internal controls have never disappeared. The reintroduction of internal border controls after the summer of 2015 and recently with the Covid-19 outbreak reveals that states are still one of the main actors of the Schengen border regime, however not in the same way as they were in the past. Although the role of EU institutions, especially the European Commission, is limited and on the level of consultation, no individual Schengen Member-State holds exclusive rights and the means to control mobility on its territory since the Schengen *acquis* is integrated into the EU law. Yet, although the Schengen Member-States seem to replace traditional border controls by diffusing controls through *ad hoc* police controls to check mobility within the Schengen area, they are actually acting between international and supranational contexts. Thus, it seems that the Schengen Member-States are reformulating national notions of sovereignty and territoriality. However, it is a fact that these internal border controls might be more significant than the external controls since this re-bordering does not overlap with the idea of borderless movement.

---

[68] Maria de Fátima Amante, "Performing Borders: Exceptions, Security and Symbolism in Portuguese Borders Control", **Journal of Borderlands Studies**, Vol. 34, No. 1, 2019, pp-17-30.

Consequently, the Schengen area became a restricted space for mobility and may be perceived as an example of new type of border controls making movements inside easier but not from the outside. The current Schengen border regime allows the Member-States to redefine their authority nationally and internationally. Through high-tech surveillance systems, control mechanisms are more sophisticated, and security is used as an excuse by the Member-States to show their authority on their multiple borders.

# CHAPTER 6

## SECURITIZATION OF REFUGEE PROBLEM WITHIN EUROPEAN UNION

Mesut Şöhret[*]

### Introduction

Securitization is a complex set of processes in which political and social relations are evaluated within the framework of security. In this context, the issue of migration has become one of the most important areas where securitization is applied today. By the end of the Cold War, migration and security phenomena has started to be associated with each other and has gained new dimensions in the meantime. In this process, many different concepts, including social security, internal security, and human security, are on the agenda. The issue of migration ranks high on the national and international agenda, which are within the scope of quite different views and goals. Therefore, at the intersection of policy objectives and public interests in two important areas, various consequences for states and individuals (immigrants and citizens) emerge.

The mass migration movements occurring in the world are not a newly emerged phenomenon. In general, migration movements that started in the 1500s played an important role in colonialism, industrialization, the emergence of nation-states and the development of the capitalist world market. However, international migration has never been so widespread or socio-economically and politically distinct until today. Political actors have never before given priority to migration issues in this way. International migration has never been associated with conflict and disorder to this degree, neither with national security nor with global conflict.[1]

The refugee flows, which was considered as an issue requiring humanitarian intervention until the 1990s, is now seen as a problem to be overcome by European countries. With the inclusion of immigration in the field of security since the 1990s, the continuing effect of the September 11 incidents and the subsequent terrorist incidents have progressed by the EU countries with practices aimed at securitizing migration. With the effect of

[*] Assist. Prof. Dr. Gaziantep University, Faculty of Economics and Administrative Sciences, Global Politics and International Relations, sohretmesut@yahoo.com, ORCID No: 0000-0003-4052-9286
[1] Stephen Castles and Mark J. Miller, **Göçler Çağı: Modern Dünyada Uluslararası Göç Hareketleri**, Çev. Bülent Uğur Bal and İbrahim Akbulut, İstanbul, İstanbul Bilgi Üniversitesi Yayınları, 2008, p.405

the uprisings in Middle Eastern countries in 2011, the severity of the migration towards the EU has increased. Looking at the general picture in Europe, the phenomenon of immigration and the tendency to cast an increasing role to immigrants with security concerns in recent years draws attention. Local, national and international actors involved in the construction of this role are not just policies towards immigrants; they also play an active role in determining the image of immigrants in the eyes of European Union citizens.[2]

The increasing intensity and effects of international migration has made the issue of migration an important agenda item for today's societies and states. The enormous increase in irregular immigration movements in recent years has highlighted the security aspect of the problem. Besides terrorism, radicalization, extremism and criminal crimes, the issue of immigration has become one of the most important agenda items of European security, especially in the context of border security.[3] Even for the members of the European Union, the problem of refugee and immigration is no longer a national issue, and it has started to be seen as a threat to the future of the union. In this context, there is a "securitization" or "framing with security" in the issues of immigration and asylum in the process of integration of the Union. In this context, the issue of migration in Europe; it has become one of the biggest security areas for 21st century Europe as a result of mutual interaction and communication between the media, the public and the addressees of immigration.[4]

### The European Union and securitization of immigration

By the end of the Cold War, it is seen that all structures, actors and roles that can be considered as a part of security have entered a transformation process. Therefore, during this period, threats and security objects were also included in a simultaneous transformation process. As a result of this transformation, the adequacy of the state-centered perspective based on the perspective of traditional security studies and the military definition of security began to be questioned, and the questions of security studies faced with a change in size and scope.[5] The Copenhagen, Aberystwyth and Paris schools played a major role in developing new approaches to security and

---

[2]Nazif Mandacı and Gökay Özerim, "Uluslararası Göçlerin Bir Güvenlik Konusuna Dönüşümü: Avrupa'da Radikal Sağ Partiler ve Göçün Güvenlikleştirilmesi", Uluslararası İlişkiler Dergisi, Vol. 10, No. 39, p.106, pp.105-130.
[3] Sarah Leonard, "EU Border Security and Migration into the European Union: FRONTEX and Securitisation through Practices", **European Security,** Vol. 19, No. 2, 2010, p. 231.
[4] Alessandra Buonfino, "Between Unity and Plurality: the Politicization and Securitization of the Discourse of Immigration in Europe", **New Political Science,** Vol. 26, No.1, 2004, p.23-24, pp.23-49.
[5] Şevket Ovalı, "Ütopya ile Pratik Arasında: Uluslararası İlişkilerde İnsan Güvenliği Kavramsallaştırması", **Uluslararası İlişkiler Dergisi**, Vol.10, No.3 2006, p.4.

transforming the definition of security. Among them, the Copenhagen School and its pioneers Buzan, Waever and Wilde, who gave a new perspective to security studies based on the constructionist approach, created the literature on securitization as of the 1990s. The securitization approach offered a different perspective by positioning and defining security as a discursive and political force, beyond being an objective situation.[6]

In fact, immigrants or asylum-seekers were seen as positive and desired people until the 1973 Oil Crisis in terms of eliminating the labor deficit in parallel with the economic growth experienced in Europe in the post-World War II period. However, when the crisis caused many Europeans to lose their jobs, after this date, the view of the local people and governments in Europe on immigrants started to be negative and these people started to be seen as a burden for the economies that exploit the social systems of the countries and as "others" in social life. "In the 1980s migration increasingly was a subject of policy debates about the protection of public order and the preservation of domestic stability. These debates also represented migration as a challenge to the welfare state and to the cultural composition of the nation. A key theme running through these debates was that migration was a danger to domestic society."[7] In other words, security discourses and technologies penetrated the Europeanization of migration policy. The development of security discourses and policies in the area of migration was often presented as an inevitable policy response to the challenges for public order and domestic stability of the increases in the number of (illegal) immigrants and asylum-seekers.

The policy is an instrument to protect the state, its society and the internal market against the dangers related to an invasion of (illegal) immigrants and asylum-seekers. In other words, the problem comes first and the policy is an instrumental reaction to it. Accordingly, primarily migration and immigrants were seen as threats to the welfare of states and the cultural harmony of the people, and then new discourses and policies were developed against this threat. This point corresponds to an approach that expresses the concept of securitization. Immigration, which has become both an important agenda item and an important securitization issue in today's Europe, is also one of the securitization issues given as an example by the Copenhagen School.

---

[6] Mandacı and Özerim, Ibid., p.107
[7] Didier Bigo, "The European Internal Security Field: Stakes and Rivalries in a Newly Developing Area of Police Intervention" **Policing Across National Boundaries**, M. Anderson and Monica Den Boer (Ed.), Pinter Publications, 1994, pp.161-173.

## Politicization or securitization of immigration

According to Copenhagen School, security refers to the presence of a security threat and the situation where certain measures are taken against this threat. On the other hand, insecurity refers to a situation where there is a security problem but adequate precautions are not taken or an answer is not given.[8] According to this approach, if there is no threat, there is no concept of security. In other words, the occurrence of a security concept depends on the occurrence of a threat. In their joint study of 1991, Barry Buzan and Ole Waever defined security in two categories:

✓ National security that puts sovereignty at the center (traditional approach)

✓ Social security that centers identity and continuity of society (constructivist approach)

The concept of social security has shifted the focus of security from the state to the society and sees both security and threat as a structured structure. In this approach, threats to identity are now accepted as primary threats.[9] From this point of view, the Copenhagen School defines itself in the middle between traditional state-based security studies and post-structuralism security studies. On the one hand, this approach argues that the concept should not be limited to state-based military security; on the other hand, it warns that everything that threatens the existence and condition of people cannot be considered as a security problem.[10] The concept of social security has shifted the focus of security from the state to the society and sees both security and threat as a structured structure. In this approach, threats to identity are now accepted as primary threats.[11] Social security is important as one of the innovative concepts of securitization. This approach defines security as a "speech-act" product and sees security issues as "a political outcome of the actual forces of security agencies." In addition, the securitization approach positions and defines security as a discursive and political force beyond being an objective situation. According to the Copenhagen School's approach, security is seen as a speech-act. Moreover, issues can be presented as security problems through word-acts and this is referred to as "securitization."[12]Advocating this approach, Barry Buzan and

---

[8] Ole Waever, "Securitization and Desecuritization", **On Security**, Ronnie D. Lipschutz (Ed.),New York, Columbia University Press, 1995, p.7.

[9] Gökay Özerim, Supranationalisation of the Migration Policies in Europe and Transformation into A Security Issue: A New Phase in History of European Migration" Ege Strategic Research Journal, Vol. 5, No.1, 2014, p. 14, pp.11-48

[10] Sinem Akgül Açıkmeşe, "Algı mı Söylem mi? Kopenhag Okulu ve Yeni-Klasik Gerçekçilikte Güvenlik Tehditleri", Uluslararası İlişkiler, Vol. 8, No. 30, 2011, p.66, pp.43-73

[11] Özerim, Ibid., p.14

[12] Barry Buzan and Lane Hansen, **The Evolution of International Security Studies**, Cambridge, Cambridge University Press, 2009, p.213

other scholars explain securitization using a spectrum as follows.[13]

Not politicized ◄——————— Politicized ———————► Securitized

On the other hand, "What makes something a security issue?" or, in other words, "What does the concept of security mean?" questions are still at the center of security studies.[14] Different actors construct the definition of security, create or introduce threats in this construction process, but ultimately use it as a tool of power.[15] At this point, Security literally evokes a concept that "sets political priorities and legitimates the use of force, intensifies executive powers, the claim of privacy rights and other extreme measures."[16] Based on the definition of safety and security, the Copenhagen School defines securitization as follows:

> "Securitization is theact of takingpoliciesbeyondtheestablishedrules of thegame, framing an issue as a particulartype of policyorsupra-policy. Thussecuritization can be seen as an extremeversion of politicization. Theoretically, anyissue in thepubliceye can be positioned on a spectrumrangingfrom "unpoliticized" to "politicized" to "securitized"[17]

The use of the word security by national politicians or political elites creates an image of an emergency, in a way, by making a problem a priority issue and requiring the state to mobilize with all means. That makes "upset the political order of the state"[18] In addition to all these, the Copenhagen School defined security as a process in which threats are built by the elites. In this process, a securitizing actor securitizes by emphasizing that a reference object is under threat and trying to convince the audience to do so.[19] In other words, considering every issue as a security issue within the broad security agenda understanding will create a constant alarm and "paranoia" situation that requires the state to take immediate measures that it does not implement within normal political processes. Under these alarm conditions, civil society will be suppressed, the state will follow interventionist and repressive policies, and the economy will have negative effects.[20]

Speech-act, reference object and securitizing actors can be defined as important components of the securitization process. The reference object is

---

[13] Buzan, Waever and Wilde, Ibid., p.23-24; Başar Baysal and Çağla Lüleci, Copenhagen School and Securitization Theory, **Güvenlik Stratejileri Dergisi**, Vol. 11, No. 22, p.75, pp.61-96
[14] Waever, Ibid., p.54
[15] Özerim, Ibid., p.14
[16] Barry Buzan, Ole Waever and Jaap de Wilde, **Security: A New Framework for Analysis**, Boulder, Lynne Rienner Publishers, 1998, p.208
[17] Buzan, Waever and Wilde, Ibid., p.23
[18] Waever, Ibid., p.54-55
[19] Özerim, Ibid., p.15
[20] Buzan, Waever and Wilde, Ibid., p.208

the subject or elements that have been shown under threat. It can be described as something that is seen under threat from the outside and a legitimate right to continue their existence. Securitizing actors are actors who create the perception that these reference objects are threatened or try to justify this argument. Political leaders, bureaucracy, governments, lobbyists and pressure groups can be counted as the most common securitizing actors.[21] In general, when an issue is to be securitized, a state representative puts a certain development in a private sphere by translating the concept of security and demands the right to use all the means necessary to prevent this development.[22]

In the light of this information, it is possible to say that it is not very difficult to securitize the migration problem in the European Union. Discourses against immigration and anti-refugees, which started to increase especially in the 1980s, the actual situation that emerged after the Cold War in the 1990s quickly brought the issue of migration to the agenda of governments and European societies in the European Union. It is possible to say that the anti-immigration political rhetoric and actions that increased in this period actually peaked after the terrorist attacks of September 11. Especially the terrorist attacks of September 11 and the terrorist attacks carried out in some countries of Europe such as France and Belgium, England and Spain have united the peoples and politicians of Europe under an anti-terrorism understanding. National security can be regarded as one of the most widely used and well-known themes in the anti-immigration discourses of radical right parties. In other words, the issue of immigration has been quickly turned into a national security issue by radical right-wing parties, populist parties or xenophobic and racist parties in the European Union member countries. It also seems quite interesting that the securitization process in question occurred through the stages specified by the Copenhagen School.

The radical right parties have successfully integrated national security into the anti-immigration discourse through their election campaigns, manifestos, local and national election programs, slogans and speeches of party leaders. The acceptance of asylum requests, the granting of the right of residence and citizenship, work permits and related quotas, registration procedures and requirements for foreigners are actually presented as national security threats that need to be rearranged and limited.[23]

---

[21] Matt McDonald, Securitization and the Construction of Security, **European Journal of International Relations**, Vol. 14, No.4, 2008, p.571-572, pp.563-587

[22] Waever, Ibid., p.55

[23] Bilal Karabulut, "Migration and Immigration in International Relations: The Case of European Union" **Uluslararası Kriz ve Siyaset Araştırmaları Dergisi**, Vol.3, No 2, 2019, p.92, pp.80-102.

## The shaping of refugees as a security threat

Defense of a society against a perceived threat to its identity is called as social security. At this stage, the essential point is to ensure the continuity of that social structure in case of an actual or possible threat against the elements that bring together the social structure. In other words, the existence of elements that keep society together such as culture, language, religion, togetherness, national identity, values and traditions can continue. If we consider the dimension of the relationship with migration, immigrants, asylum seekers, refugees and especially irregular migrants are securitized as possible threats by the securitizing actor, considering that they may harm the unifying character of the society.[24] From this point of view, it is not difficult for governments or political parties to convince the society in European Union countries, which have had a negative attitude towards irregular migrants such as immigrants, asylum seekers and refugees for many years.

"Migration is identified as being one of the main factors weakening national tradition and societal homogeneity. It is reified as an internal and external danger for the survival of the national community or western civilization. This discourse excludes migrants from the normal fabric of society, not just as aliens but as aliens who are dangerous to the reproduction of the social fabric. The discourse frames the key question about the future of the political community as one of a choice for or against migration. But it is not a free choice because a choice for migration is represented as a choice against (the survival of) the political community. The discourse reproduces the political myth that a homogenous national community or western civilization existed in the past and can be re-established today through the exclusion of those migrants who are identified as cultural aliens."[25]

According to the Copenhagen School, an issue shows itself as a security problem with discursive policies regarding security. In this framework, discourse has a central "intermediary" role in the securitization approach. From this point on, the securitization as a process that pursues argumentative practices in order to convince a certain "target audience" to accept it, claiming that a particular development creates a threat enough to deserve a restraining policy.[26] In this context, the current conditions of the social structure, which is one of the most basic elements in activating the securitization process and defined as audience, also constitute an effective ground for the transformation of migration into a security problem. Terrorist attacks in

---

[24] Ela Gökalp Aras, "Biyopolitik Bir Nüfus Politikası Olarak Avrupa Birliği'nin Düzensiz Göç Rejimi ve Sınırlarda Ölüm Siyaseti" **Turkish Journal of Population Studies**, No. 36, 2014, p.72 pp.67-102.

[25] Jef Huysmans, "The European Union and the Securitization of Migration", **Journal of Common Market Studies**, Vol. 38, No. 5, 2000, p.758, pp. 751–777

[26] Thierry Balzacq, "Constructivism and Securitization Studies", **Handbook of Security Studies**, London, Routledge, 2002, p.9.

Europe or crimes involving immigrants are very effective tools in persuading the target audience. In addition to that, the cultural values, beliefs, dressing styles and even their mere presence of immigrants play an important role in persuading the target audience and getting their support.

Most of the time, this situation can be turned into an "opportunity" by politicians. This opportunity, which is generally used by far-right or populist parties, is sometimes used by left parties or social democratic parties with more humanistic and universal values to persuade the voters (target audience). Namely, unwanted changes that occur or may occur in the cultural structure of the host country can be presented as a result of the phenomenon of immigration, and the idea that these immigrants may dominate the society of the host country is tried to be instilled. In this way, a society is formed that adopts the idea that its own values will be assimilated, and thus the migration-securitization process is shaped by many reasons.[27]

"One may be tempted to reduce the securitization of migration to the critical action of a few agencies, such as extreme right parties in some European countries. However, the process has included multiple actors such as national governments, grassroots, European transnational police networks, the media, etc. The securitization of migration is a structural effect of a multiplicity of practices. If one wishes to interpret how this structural effect has been produced by the political, Professional and social factors involved, one has to focus on the relation between the positions of these actors and the practices they perform."[28]

Actors and agencies are the most important components of this migration-securitization process; because securitization is shaped in an actor-driven perspective as a process. Speech act, referent object and securitizing actors are defined as other important components of the securitization process. The reference object is the subject or element that has been shown under threat. Securitizing actors who create the perception that these reference objects are threatened or try to justify this argument.[29] Securitization frames something or as a security issue, and this framing process is accomplished through verbal action. The concept of speech act borrowed from the conceptualization of linguist Austin, with its simplest definition, brings a different perspective to the function of the word, unlike the concept of discourse, and that the word does not contain only negative or positive judgments; claims that it can also include performative

---

[27] Sevinç Çetinkaya, AB Göç Politikalarının Güvenlikleştirme Ekseninde İncelenmesi, (UnpublishedPhD Dissertation), Bolu, Bolu Abant İzzet Baysal Üniversitesi Sosyal Bilimler Enstitüsü, 2018, p.83
[28] Huysmans, "The European Union and the Securitization of Migration, p.758
[29] Mandacı and Özerim, Ibid., p.108

expressions in its content.[30]

Migration has been defined by the Copenhagen School as one of the most general issues on the social security agenda. It is also presented as an interesting example of the place of different issues in social security discourse. In this context, the formulation of immigration in the security discourse mostly occurs within the following pattern.[31]

> "The people of X are being invade dor weakened by the raids of the people Y. Society X will not be abletostay as it is; because others will redesign society. Identity X will differ with the change in the composition of the population."[32]

Looking at these discourses, it can be seen that elements such as "invasion", "others", "identity" are often emphasized by various actors in the current anti-immigration discourse. In fact, it is possible to hear such discourses on immigration from European politicians. For example, regarding what happened after the Arab Spring by the former Minister of Greece, Nikos Denias; "The country is about to perish. We are currently facing a complete invasion… I wake up every morning and ask: What happened in Syria today? Because if something happens in Syria, thousands of people will flow to Greece. Illegal immigrants have already become a huge problem for us. We are already taking great steps to prevent illegal immigrants from coming to the country. Imagine that the current numbers have increased ten times… "supports this idea.[33]

However, it cannot be denied that many actors in Europe, especially anti-immigration parties, are now creating a discourse that goes beyond these stereotypes while securing migration. However, securitization frames the migration in two consecutive interrelated processes:[34]

1. Migration is transformed into existential events and developments that endanger the independent identity and functional autonomy of a political unit.

2. The securitization process became an autonomous political claims that it endangers the society as a whole.[35]

In the anti-immigration discourse, this process explanation that

---

[30] Rita Taureck, "Securitisation Theory–The Story so far: Theoretical Inheritance and What it Means to be a Post-structural Realist", **4th Annual CEEISA Convention, University of Tartu**, 25-27 June 2006, p.6

[31] Özerim, Ibid., p.16

[32] Buzan, Waever and Wilde, Ibid., p.121

[33] Çetinkaya, Ibid, p.84

[34] Jef Huysmans, The Politics of Insecurity: Fear, Migration and Asylum in the EU, London, Routledge, 2006, p.51

[35] Huysmans, Ibid, p.51

Huysmanhas set up is actively used by the actors who secure migration. Until the 1990s in the European Union member countries, the issue of migration was generally interpreted as an issue that would require humanitarian intervention. The Copenhagen School actually positions security as the opposite of the politicization process. Therefore, when we look at it from this perspective, the security-oriented approach of migration also represents an attempt to go beyond normal political borders and measures. The legitimating reasons for this initiative may be national identity, sovereignty or national unity, as well as individual reasons such as employment and social security. Therefore, the effects of the individual-oriented approach in the definition of security are also seen in the discourse that secures migration.[36]

### Refugees as threats to presence of European identity

The concept of "threats to presence" included in the security speech is related to Carl Schmitt's political concept defined on the basis of friendship and hostility. To understand this relationship, one should first look at how Schmitt defines his political concept:

> "The free political distinction that can be used to explain political actions and motives is the distinction between friends and enemies ...Any concrete opposition approaching the most extreme opposition to friend and enemy becomes more politicized. The political enemy does not have to be morally bad, aesthetically ugly, or economically rival, and it may even seem advantageous to do business with the political enemy. The important thing is that the political enemy is the other, foreign. It is sufficient for the political enemy to be another be ingandalien in its most existential sense."[37]

Policies to securitize the phenomenon of international migration progress through three important rhetorical processes. In the first stage, while a subject is included in the extraordinary political agenda as an external threat through speech act. In the second stage, the request for authorization is brought to the agenda in order to take extraordinary measures in the fight against this external threat in order to maintain the existence of the securitized reference object. At this point, the administrative detention of immigrants, their expulsion without procedural guarantees, irregular push back, disproportionate force and the extreme risk of death or direct death are within the scope of the irregular measures encountered. In the last process, in order to protect the element whose existence is shown under threat, these illegal measures listed above are legitimized.

Thus, while the subject has become a routine that is constantly on the

---

[36] Özerim, Ibid., p.17
[37] Açıkmeşe, Ibid., 60-61

agenda; the violation of rules that normally bind the securitizing actor (such as international human rights law or refugee law) is legitimized. In this context, the Copenhagen School presents an important approach that explains the EU's securing of illegal and irregular immigration and its institutional structure with the conceptual framework mentioned above.[38]

In the securitization process, a problem is marginalized by presenting it as a threat to existence, thus transforming into a "political" speech act. In this case, otherness appears as a criterion of politicization. In other words, the other, defined as the enemy, is a deliberate threat to existence in the securitization process; therefore, the security speech act is a political speech act. In other words, the securitization move is related to the preference of the securitizing actor. Although the success of securitization does not depend solely on the securitizing actor, the securitizing actor makes the decision whether an issue should be securitized or not. This election called as a political act[39]

In the second stage, the request for authorization comes to the fore in order to take extraordinary measures in the fight against this external threat in order to maintain the existence of the securitized reference object. This demand ensures that the measures to be taken or the policies to be implemented are justified by the decision of the state or government bodies or state officials, which are the dominant authority. At this point, the administrative detention of immigrants, their expulsion without procedural guarantees, irregular push back, disproportionate force and the extreme risk of death or direct death are within the scope of the irregular measures encountered. For example; "although the United Nations' refugee agency is urging Greece to stamp out migrant abuse and investigate multiple accusations of push backs at the country's sea and land borders with neighboring Turkey. Forcing migrants to turn around is a serious breach of international law, violating asylum-seekers' right to safe passage and protection. Croatia, France, Spain and Italy—all of which face similar migration challenges—also have been accused of engaging in unlawful, sometimes violent push backs."[40]

In case of danger or threat the statesman makes an assessment of the situation and determines the existence of a threat. In other words, after any situation passes the filter of the mind of the statesman, it turns into a policy-

---

[38] Bülent Şener, "Soğuk Savaş Sonrası Dönemde Uluslararası Göç Olgusu ve Ulusal Güvenlik Üzerindeki Etkileri Üzerine Bir Değerlendirme", **Güvenlik Bilimleri Dergisi**, Vol. 6, No.1, 2017, p.16, pp. 1-31.

[39] Pınar Bilgin, "Güvenlik Çalışmalarında Yeni Açılımlar: Yeni Güvenlik Çalışmaları", **SAREM Journal of Strategic Studies**, Vol. 8, No. 14, 2010, p. 82, pp.69-96

[40] Anthee Carassava, UNHCR, EU Slam Greece Over Migrant Pushbacks, Abuse, November 21, 2020 https://www.voanews.com/europe/unhcr-eu-slam-greece-over-migrant-pushbacks-abuse (12.01.2021)

generated threat. This subjective understanding prevails in neoclassical realism; in other words, the existence of the security threat will subjectively decide authoritatively in the direction of the statesman mind. The parallelism of these views with Schmitt's understanding of politics is obvious. However, it does not require the relevant mass approval on whether there is a threat to take action against the statesman in accordance with either Schmitt's views or the new-classical understanding. The consent of the relevant population to the measures to be taken will only give legitimacy to the actions.[41]

In the third and last stage, in order to protect the element whose existence is threatened, these extraordinary measures listed above are legitimized. Thus, while the subject has become a routine that is constantly on the agenda; the violation of rules that normally bind the securitizing actor (such as international human rights law or refugee law) is legitimized. In this context, the Copenhagen School presents an important approach that explains the institutional structure and securing the illegal and irregular immigration of the EU with the above-mentioned conceptual framework.[42]

### Reasons for the securitization of refugees in the European Union

Most of the refugees, who come to the European Union irregularly or illegally, come from Asia and Africa. For this reason, these people are primarily marginalized due to ethnic reasons, namely their differences in skin color, slanting eye structure, hair colour and other racial differences, and then they are presented as enemies to European societies by far-right parties and populist parties. In addition, reasons such as religious beliefs, dressing styles and different ways of worship are presented as a potential danger for European societies.

Economic reasons also play a key role in seeing refugees as a potential threat to Europeansocieties. Unemployed local people see refugees and immigrants as the reason for this, and tend to see their countries as enemies when their living standards fall because immigrants are an economic threat, by taking away jobs or depressing wages, that the nation's culture wasundermined by foreigners or that there should be restrictive policies toward refugees.43 In other words, many of the EU member countries workers are responding to feelings of economic threat that are induced by insecure prospects and the fear of wage pressures because of immigration; they are driven more strongly by feelings of cultural threat and the view that immigration threatens national identity; or they are socially alienated therefore the people express their dissatisfaction with established political

---

[41] Açıkmeşe, Ibid., 63

[42] Şener, Ibid., p.16

[43] Pippa Norris, **Radical Right: Voters and Parties in the Electoral Market**, Cambridge, Cambridge University Press, 2005, p. 260

channels.44 As a result, the people fear that immigrants will take their jobs, and as a result, a "closure" situation occurs.

Unwanted changes in the cultural structure of the host country can be introduced as a result of the phenomenon of migration and the idea that these immigrants may dominate the society of the host country is tried to be instilled. In this way, a society is formed that adopts the idea that its own values will be assimilated, and thus the migration-securitization process is shaped by many reasons. For instance, "nativism 'which holds that states should be inhabited exclusively by members of the native group ("the nation") and that non-native elements (persons and ideas) are fundamentally threatening to the homogeneous nation-state"[45]

More importantly, immigrants are seen as threats to European liberal values and the democratic structure of Europe. For example, the comments and discourses made by Geert Wilders, the leader of the far-right Freedom Party of the Netherlands, about Islam and Muslims draw attention at this point.

"Most Muslims are moderate, but the ideology of Islam is dangerous. The moderates are the prisoners of the barbaric system of Islamo-fascism. Despite the many moderate Muslims, the growing Islamization is causing huge problems. Europe's Islam lobby is increasingly assertive. It has successfully managed to push European politicians to implement pro-Islamic policies and to limit freedom of speech as well. All this under the pretext that the expression of truthful statements about Islam is a form of hate speech and is therefore criminal. Instead of expediting the assimilation of immigrants into our countries, ourgovernments support the creation of an Islamic paralel society — a Trojan horse inside ourborders. Since there is no suchthing at all as a moderate Islam, theIslamisation of our society is a dangerous threat. This Islamisation is mainly propelled by immigration from Islamic countries. Muhammad himself conquered Medina with the help of immigration; or Hijra, as it is called. On this basis we must stop immigration from Islamic countries. Allow noone to tell you that Islam respects freedom. Freedom and Islam are not compatible. Allow noone to tell you that Islam is a religion of peace. Islam is an ideology of violence. Allow noone to tell you that the in tolerant must be tolerated. We have to show our colors. We have to draw a redline. We have to call for the following: Firstly, no more mosques; secondly, no

---

[44] Daniel Oesch, "Explaining Workers' Support for Right-Wing Populist Parties in Western Europe: Evidence from Austria, Belgium, France, Norway and Switzerland", **International Political Science Review**, Vol. 29, No.3, 2008 p.370, pp. 349–373

[45] Cas Mudde, 'The Populist Radical Right: A Pathological Normalcy', West European Politics, Vol. 33, No. 6, pp. 1167–1186.

more Islamic schools; and thirdly, all criminal immigrants with double citizenship must be deported!"[46]

In fact, this and similar views and hate speech are frequently expressed in the party programs and election discourses of many political parties in Europe and thus all immigrants coming from outside Europe, especially Muslim refugees, are actually demonized in the eyes of European societies (target audience). By this way Muslims are framed as a distinct cultural threat to European societies, and as subscribing to values that are incompatible with Western liberal democracy.

In addition, factors such as homosexual rights, women's rights, freedom of dress, freedom of religion are positioned as elements that constitute the modern western line, and it is presented to the public that immigrants 'others' will have trouble internalizing and accepting these values and pose a threat to these elements. The reason why the problem is evaluated in such a pattern is religious differences. In this respect, threats originating from religion are an important part of the cultural security-themed discourse.[47]

### Securitization of International Migration and Refugees as National Security Problems for European Union Member

We can analyze the "securitization" of the phenomenon of international migration as a national security problem in European Union countries on four factors:[48]These are respectively are as follows:

**Socio-economic Factors:** Illegal immigration is accepted as a threat that negatively affects the unemployment level in EU member countries and a negative stance is displayed by the native people. The cheap labor force provided by illegal immigrants, who are accepted as the main source of the problem, changes the balances significantly. On the other hand, the reasons for the economic anxiety of the indigenous people are that the idea that immigrants pose a threat to the employment market, the state structure based on welfare and social security, direct tax practices, and contributing to social security is widely established. In addition, issues such as the expenses made by states for immigrants, aid to immigrants, education and reintegration of immigrant children are financial issues that attract public reaction. Likewise, considering the increase in the birth rates of immigrants in the social sense,

---

[46] Geert Wilders, Geert Wilders' Speech in Bonn, February 6, 2013, https://www.parlementairemonitor.nl/9353000/1/j9vvij5epmj1ey0/vj6xcz568lxd?ctx=vg09llkg6xvb&start_tab0=20 (12.01.2021)

[47] Matthew Goodwin, "**Right Response: Understanding and Countering Populist Extremism in Europe**". Catham House Report, The Royal Institute of International Affairs, 2011, p.11

[48] Reyhan Atasu Topçuoğlu, Reyhan, "Düzensiz Göç: Küreselleşmede Kısıtlanan İnsan Hareketliliği". Küreselleşme Çağında Göç: Kavramlar, Tartışmalar. **Küreselleşme Çağında Göç: Kavramlar, Tartışmalar**, Suna Gülfer Ihlamur Öner and Aslı Şirin Öner, (Ed.) İstanbul: İletişim Yayınları, 2016, p.507, pp.501-509.

the fact that it is more than the main population makes the public believe that the existing culture can be "invaded" and will disappear over time. When these anxiety fluctuations occurring at rates that affect each other, combined with the discourses of the political powers, they constitute the most effective arguments that cause the securitization of migration within the European Union.[49] "As a result of successive economic recessions and the rise in unemployment since the early 1970s, the struggle over the distribution of social goods such as housing, health care, unemployment benefits, jobs and other social services has become more competitive. Scarcity makes immigrants and asylum seekers rivals to national citizens in the labour market and competitors in the distribution of social goods. This has resulted in an increasingly explicit assertion of welfare chauvinism, or the privileging of national citizens in the distribution of social goods."[50] "Recent political conflicts around social rights of immigrants have often been based on the claim that the willingness to share social goods distributed by the welfare state needs a basis of common feeling. It is thus not surprising that those political actors opposed to (further) immigration, and/or to granting certain social rights to immigrants, have tended to refer to the alleged threat immigrants pose not only as economic competitors in the labour market and for social policies ('they take away our jobs and our benefits') but also as a threat to the cultural homogeneity of the national state."[51]

**Security Related Factors:** Political elites (especially radical right-wing and populist parties and political groups) impersonating international immigrants as criminals with their discourse create an atmosphere of insecurity and unrest in the society and they can point to immigrants as the reason for this. However, there is no statistical data consisting of direct links between organized crimes and immigrants. The increase in the number of illegal immigrants in Europe has brought along an increase in the need for a security environment. This rising environment of insecurity is among the reasons why political leaders representing the right-wing have high success in the elections.[52] The use of terminology regarding illegal immigration within the framework of a security-oriented approach has an extremely important effect on the perception of any individual coming from outside the Union as a suspect and not to be trusted. From this point of view, it constantly reveals a suspicious approach and a culture of insecurity towards third country citizens and irregular migrants. This culture of insecurity is also strengthened

---

[49] Çetinkaya, Ibid, p.91
[50] Huysmans, "The European Union and the Securitization of Migration, p.767
[51] Thomas Faist,"Boundaries of Welfare States: Immigrants and Social Rights on the National and Supranational Level", **Migration and European Integration: the Dynamics of Inclusion and Exclusion,** Miles, R. and Thränhardt, D. (Ed.) London, Pinter Publishers, 1995, p.189, pp. 177–195.
[52] Hilal Zorba, "AB'nin Göçmenlere Yönelik Politikalarını Etkileyen Faktörler" **Barış Araştırmaları ve Çatışma Çözümleri Dergisi**, Vol. 4, No. 1, 2016, p.12, pp.1-17

by the development of EU immigration policies because these policies also secure immigration and do not take the human rights dimension into account too much in this context.[53]

**Identity Related Factors:** The perception of immigrants as a threat in areas such as language, education, religion, and daily life that are important in terms of national identity reveals that migration is a securitization problem in the cultural and social field besides only economic or political fields. In this context, immigrants are perceived as "the other" by the society they live in. For this reason, the phenomenon of migration is defined as a social security threat that corrupts national values and culture and points out the necessity of an urgent and comprehensive anti-migration policy. On the issue of securitizing immigration as a threat to social security, it is also necessary to discuss the discourses of the populist right social and political groups that campaigned for Britain's exit from the European Union (EU) membership in 2016. These groups, which carried out pro-Brexit campaigns, carried out propaganda that the increasing EU integration of Britain increased immigration from Eastern European countries, especially Hungary and Poland, to British lands and this situation eroded the British identity. The argument that individuals who settled in England by immigration carry a social security risk that will destroy their British identity in time can be discussed within the framework of securitizing thephenomenon of immigration.54

**Political Factors:** International migrations play a role in the production of identity politics in the separation of "us" and "them", on the other hand, settled immigrants and their culture threaten and erode the duality of "us" and "them". This dialectical process turns international migration into an identity bargaining ground, politicizes and securitizes migration and immigrants rapidly. A wide variety of policies are implemented for the integration or exclusion of this massive migration wave towards EU countries. In this context, factors such as the common or different points of immigrants with the local population, the time they live with the local people, their economic and social income levels are important factors in determining these policies. Three main models stand out within the scope of policies implemented for non-EU citizens. The first of these, the "Assimilation Model", includes the policies implemented to "quickly" adapt the elements such as language, culture and social character that immigrants have and have to carry with them whether they want to or not. In order to create a suitable

---

[53] Ryszard Cholewinski, "The Criminalisation of Migration in EU Law and Policy". **Whose Freedom, Security and Justice**, Anneliese Baldaccini, Elspeth Guild and Helen Toner (Ed.) Portland, Hart Publishing, 2007, p.301-302, pp.301-336.
[54] Christopher S. Browning, "Brexit, existential anxiety and ontological (in)security", **European Security**, Vol. 27 No.3, 2018, pp. 336-355.

basis for the implementation of this idea, it is possible to give citizenship to all immigrants who have the right to reside and to implement policies to ensure assimilation in this way. In the second model, the "Multicultural Model", immigrants are given equal economic, social and political rights with the indigenous people without waiting for them to lose their language, culture and social differences and without resorting to such a practice. Finally, in the "Exclusion Model", governments and indigenous people do not accept immigrants as members of their own nation. In addition, migrants' economic, social, cultural and political rights are restricted. The models in question play a role in both countries' determination of policies towards immigrants and especially in regulations on granting citizenship rights to non-EU immigrants. However, with the increasing efforts of the EU in determining a common immigration policy, the change of policies with the changing governments in the countries and the effect of globalization, all countries are moving away from the above systems, which can be classified clearly.[55]

Immigration and immigrants have always been seen as a problem and a source of threat by the people living within the borders of the European Union. Terrorist incidents that developed as a result of this have taken their place as a very effective input in terms of securitizing migration.

## Conclusion

Although commemorating immigration with security is not a new approach, the expansion of security from military-centered problems to problems expressed as "low politics" was born out of the criticism of realism, which was the dominant view in international relations in the 1980s. Although the Copenhagen School opened security to a state-centered intellectual debate, security and the expansion of the area of threat have given the school an innovative perspective. The regional security complex, sectoral approach and securitization theories put forward by the Copenhagen School do not go beyond a state-centered security understanding, but also criticize the restriction of security to the military field.

It is alleged that immigrants in member states of the European Union damage the sovereignty of the state, the identity of the society and / or the social security system. Refugees who flee from conflict or persecution in their countries by illegally crossing the borders are constructed as a threat because they threaten the integrity of states and border security. It is also alleged that societies that were hitherto presumed homogeneous risk losing their identity because of immigrants.[56] The actors who securitize the immigrants also cite

---

[55] Uğur Özgöker and Ferhat G. Batı, "Avrupa Birliği Hukukunda Göç Sorunu Parametreleri Ekonomi", **İstanbul Arel Üniversitesi Yönetim ve Sosyal Araştırmalar Dergisi** Vol. 1, No. 2, pp.1-10.
[56] Deniz Genç,(2010). "A Paradox in EU Migration Management", **SEER Journal for Labour and Social Affairs in Eastern Europe**, Vol.13, No. 2, p.189, pp.181-192

the weakening of the social welfare system of the country because of the refugees.

The most important securitization discourse on immigration policy is the threat to the internal security of the state. Policymakers on immigration, while putting their solutions to migration problems into a rationale, can use "burden", "bogus asylum seeker", "boat people", "the boat is full" or "uses certain security-related terms such as "organized crime". This discourse presents migration as a social and cultural threat as well as a military threat.[57] After the September 11 incidents, the security discourse on immigration has become more dominant in politicians and media and thus in the public opinion.[58] Immigrants, who are seen as "other" and "foreigners", are seen as threats to the jobs and homes of the country's citizens, the borders of the countries, security, moral values, collective identities and cultural homogeneity. These threatening discourses take place not only in the press, but also in studies in demography and political science. Thus, this association, also known as the migration-security link has increased.[59]

"The migration policy developed in the EU is ambivalent in the way it deals with this fear. On the one hand, the Europeanization of migration policy indirectly sustains nationalist, racist and xenophobic reactions to immigrants. It portrays immigrants and asylum-seekers primarily in negative terms. They are presented as an acute problem challenging societal and political stability and the effective working of the internal market. In doing so, the EU feeds the idea that migrants do not belong to the European communities, that they are a serious burden for European societies, and, therefore, that they should be kept at a distance. It is a policy that confirms nationalist and xenophobic positions and to that extent undermines the initiatives for the institutionalization of a more inclusive multicultural Europe which would provide extensive political, economic and social rights to immigrants."[60]

While expressing the securitization process of the phenomenon of immigration and refugees, the effects of the events that occurred especially after the Arab Spring on the securitization of migration are experienced on a wide scale. In Europe, migration is perceived as a problem to be overcome, and it turns into a resource that emerging political parties use to increase their

[57] Agnieszka Weinar, The Polish Experiences of Visa Policy in the Context of Securitization, 2006, http://www.libertysecurity.org/IMG/doc/The_Polish_experiences_of_visa_policy_in_the_context_of_securitization-1.doc, p.2 (13.01.2021).
[58] Alessandra Buonfino, "Between Unity and Plurality: The Politicization and Securitization of the Discourse of Immigration in Europe", **New Political Science**, Vol. 26, No. 1, 2004, p. 1.
[59] Thomas Faist, "Göç-Güvenlik Bağı: 11 Eylül Öncesi ve Sonrası Uluslararası Göç ve Güvenlik", **Kökler ve Yollar: Türkiye'de Göç Süreçleri**, Ayhan Kaya ve Bahar Şahin (Ed.), İstanbul Bilgi Üniversitesi Yayınları, İstanbul, 2007, s. 21
[60] Huysmans, "The European Union and the Securitization of Migration, p.766

voting potential. Political parties or leaders constantly keep the issue of immigration on the agenda through discourses and try to get approval from the reference group for unusual methods to solve this issue. However, one of the important points to be emphasized here is that the phenomenon of immigration is not a temporary or postponable problem, and it is a problem that concerns and affects every sector in terms of both Europe and migration-based countries. The perception that the phenomenon of migration in the European Union poses a threat to every sector, including military, economic, political, social and environmental, in the form of fluctuations, shortens the process of persuasion of the reference object in the securitization phase of migration.[61]

It seems that immigration and immigration issues will be one of the issues that especially politicians will "securitize" the most and use them as a tool to increase their voting potential. Problems related to immigration and refugees have become the "most sensitive" of the European Union. In many areas from security to economy, from cultural structure to other social processes, the reality of immigration is expected to be one of the issues that will affect the European Union the most in the short and medium term.

---

[61] Çetinkaya, Ibid, p.85

# CHAPTER 7

# NORMATIVE ELUSIVENESS OF EUROPE IN TERMS OF REFUGEE CRISIS

## Sinem Bal[*]

## Introduction

What makes the EU different from other actors is its use of a catalogue of values and principles that are shaped, shared, and diffused by Europe around the world. By expanding these values beyond Europe, the EU constitutes its self-identification and reflects a particular kind of actorness in international affairs. These performances have ontologically been designated within specific role conceptualizations, such as a 'civilian power'[1], 'structural power'[2], 'normative area'[3], and 'normative power'.[4] Among these scholars, Ian Manners, in most of his works[5], coins the concept of Normative Power Europe (NPE) and describes the EU as a norm promoter that conditions universal norms to third countries in order to consolidate the moral consciousness in international politics. Although this approach of Manners was ground-breaking approximatively two decades ago, the EU has yet continued to include universal values as criteria in its external relations or in its constitutive documents and makes the scholars to elaborate the NPE role conception through case studies. However, the EU's stance on refugee crisis

[*] Dr. University of Nottingham, Postdoctoral Research Fellow at School of Politics and International Relations, sinem.bal@nottingham.ac.uk.
[1] François Duchene, "Europe's Role in World Peace", **Europe Tomorrow": Sixteen Europeans Look Ahead**, Richard Mayne (Ed.) London, Fontana, 1972.
[2] Stephen Keukeleire, "The European Union as a Diplomatic Actor: Internal, Traditional and Structural Diplomacy". **Diplomacy and Statecraft**, Vol. 14, No. 3, 2003, pp. 31-56.
[3] Göran Therborn, "Europe – Superpower or Scandinavia of the World", **European Union and New Regionalism, Regional Actors and Global Governance in a Post-Hegemonic Era,** Mario Telo (Ed.), England, Ashgate, 2001
[4] Ian Manners, "Normative power Europe: A Contradiction in Terms?" **JCMS: Journal of Common Market Studies,** Vol. 40, No. 2, 2002, pp. 235-258.
[5] Ian Manners, "The European Union as a Normative Power: A Response to Thomas Diez". **Millennium-Journal of International Studies**, Vol. 35, No. 1, 2006, pp. 167-180; Ian Manners, "The Constitutive Nature of Values, Images and Principles in the European Union", **Values and Principles in European Union Foreign Policy**, Sonia Lucarelli and Ian Manners, (Ed.), New York, Routledge, 2006; Ian Manners, "The Symbolic Manifestation of the EU's Normative Role in World Politics", **The European Union's Roles in International Politics: Concepts and Analysis,** Ole Elgström, Michael Smith (Ed.), New York, Routledge, 2006; Ian Manners, "European Union, Normative Power and Ethical Foreign Policy", **Rethinking Ethical Foreign Policy: Pitfalls, Possibilities and Paradoxes,** David Chandler , Volker Heins (Ed.), London, Routledge, 2006; Ian Manners, "The Normative Power of the European Union in a Globalized World", **European Union Foreign Policy in a Globalized World: Normative Power and Social Preferences**, Zaki Laïdi (Ed.), London, Routledge, 2008.

manifests itself with noncompliant practices that cause myriad political challenges; such as the rise of nationalist parties in member states' parliaments, breaking of the Dublin Regime, the lack of coordination between nation states and failure in the common protection policies for refugees, all of which undermine the NPE image and unravel the fact that the EU pulls between human right norm promoter and security dichotomy.

Taking the recent challenges into account, this chapter strives to provide answer to whether the EU itself has socialized and internalized universal norms inside its borders and if so, to what extend? Hereby, the NPE role conception is re-evaluated by questioning how the Responsibility to Protect (RtoP[6]) principle of the UN, which is another universal norm, has been applied by the EU in refugee crisis. RtoP matters because it is a moral commitment within the context of cosmopolitan law and is directly related with the EU's core values: human rights and solidarity. It is argued in this chapter that before designating the EU as a normative power and the related meta-narratives, it is significant to ask whether the EU acts in compliance with the universal norms and with its own founding principles that shape its political-normative identity. The unlawful practices of the member states and of the EU's refugee policies demonstrate the fact that when hit by human rights and solidarity issues, the normative power role conception of the EU has become elusive and contradictory.

The vast majority of the literature focuses on the EU's performance as a normative power and its implementation in practice. Scholars have scrutinized the 'responsibility' concept in line with the EU's lack of role in military force within the operationalization of the RtoP framework[7], even though the EU member states are believed to have the ability of using coercive military power.[8] The criticisms target the EU's unwillingness and slow exertion of responsibility on the emergence of new atrocities[9], such as not making an effort in the programmatic, bureaucratic and operational

---

[6] In this paper, RtoP and R2P abbreviations are used interchangeable

[7] Carla Barqueiro, Kate Seaman, and Katherine Teresa Towey, "Regional Organizations and Responsibility to Protect: Normative Reframing or Normative Change?" **Politics and Governance** Vol. 4, No. 3, 2016, pp. 37-49; Laura Steenbrink, **Responsibility to Protect at Stake: R2P in Relation to the US, NATO and the EU: The Case of Syria.** (Master Thesis), Utrecht University, 2017; Dan Bulley, "Shame on EU? Europe, RtoP and the Politics of Refugee Protection", **Ethics & International Affairs**, Vol. 31, No. 1, 2017, pp. 51-70; Cristina G. Stefan, Edward Newman, "Europe's Progress and the Road Ahead at R2P's 15th Anniversary", **Global Responsibility to Protect**, Vol. 12, No. 4, 2020, pp. 369-371.

[8] Darina Dvornichenko, Vadym Barskyy, "The EU and Responsibility to Protect: Case Studies on the EU's Response to Mass Atrocities in Libya, South Sudan and Myanmar", **InterEULawEast: Journal for the International and European Law, Economics and Market Integrations** Vol. 7, No. 1, 2020 pp. 117 138.

[9] David Chandler, "Unravelling the Paradox of The Responsibility to Protect", **Irish Studies in International Affairs**, Vol. 20, 2009, pp. 27-39; Jan Wouters, Philip de Man, "**The Responsibility to Protect and Regional Organisations: The Example of the European Union,**" Leuven Centre for Global Governance Studies Working Paper No. 101, 2013, pp. 4-27.

implementation of the RtoP norm[10], or only acting in a pragmatically principled way.[11] However the literature falls short in addressing the EU's human rights breach while protecting the refugees, since the RtoP is a norm in which the international community[12] has to respond when there is a risk of genocide and mass atrocities. In order to analyze RtoP norm's socialization in light with the EU's response to refugee flow from Syria, this chapter puts the concept of NPE in a constructivist modelling. From norm's life cycle theoretical approach, the chapter analyzes how the RtoP norm emerged in the universal level, was accepted-cascaded by the EU, and internalized (if any) by the member states and EU institutions.

## On the Constructivist Modelling of Normative Form of Power Europe

After laying the economic foundations for integration on substantial grounds, the European Economic Community (EEC) has changed its outlook towards a deeper union, through the Treaty of Maastricht in 1992, the Copenhagen Summit and its membership criteria in 1993, the Treaty of Amsterdam in 1997 and the Lisbon Treaty in 2009, along with several directives and declarations. All these binding and non-binding agreements are noteworthy due to their intensified political dimensions and contribution to the EU's self-representation. Particularly, the Treaty of Lisbon and its agenda gave rise to external actions and has become one of the key aspects of the normative identity of the EU. These universal norms are the constituents of the EU's external relations, especially when enlargements and relations with neighboring countries are concerned. Hence, researchers, especially those who work on Europeanization, have tended to investigate how these norms penetrate, are activated and adjusted to the third countries' domestic laws and institutional settings. In a similar vein, their researches focus on whether the EU norms are internalized by the non-member states and create an ideational change in the given society. If concrete sustainability and ideational change occur after the norm diffusion, then EU conditions have reflected a credibility and a degree of 'power' that includes a 'normative' character.

This distinct political entity of the EU does not "closely resemble those of a state (whether unitary or federal) or those of an international

---

[10] Sarah Brockmeier, Gerrit Kurtz and Julian Junk, "Emerging Norm and Rhetorical Tool: Europe and a Responsibility to Protect". **Conflict, Security and Development,** Vol. 14, No. 4, 2014, pp. 429–60; Chiara De Franco, Christoph O. Meyer and Karen E. Smith, "Living by Example? The European Union and the Implementation of the Responsibility to Protect (R2P)", **JCMS: Journal of Common Market Studies** Vol. 53, No. 5, 2015, pp. 994-1009.

[11] Karen Smith, "**The EU and Responsibility to Protect in an Illiberal Era**", Dahrendorf Forum IV, Working Paper No. 3, pp. 1-28

[12] In this paper, 'international community' and 'international society' concepts are used interchangeably.

organization (whether regional or global)".[13] According to Manners and Whitman, the EU is a novel kind of actor with a hybrid international entity based on civilian, military, and normative roles[14], which make the EU "a political system with multiple perspectives to its polity"[15]. Amongst several designations for the EU's actorness, unlike conventional powers of conceptualizations, the normative form of power described by Manners has a mission to establish normatively sustainable relations between the EU and others. According to him, what distinguishes the EU from rest of the international actors is that the EU constitutes nine substantive major and minor normative values, which are sustainable peace, freedom, democracy, human rights, rule of law, equality, social solidarity, sustainable development, and good governance, and promotes them in its relations.

Manners stresses that the EU is a normative power in threefold: first, the EU promotes norms in the international system because it has an ontological quality to it. It is because of the "way in which its policies shape our understandings of the EU and the way in which the EU is a political and social agent embedded in and employing political and social institutions".[16] Second it has "'a positivist quantity' to it that the EU acts to change norms in the international system; and lastly it has 'a normative quality' to it, where the EU 'should' act to extend its norms into the international system".[17] By pointing 'should' modality, he refers the self-reflexivity of the normative power conceptualization and argues that "if the EU displays reflexivity in its external policies, it can be considered as both normative and powerful".[18]

Manners theorizes the NPE argument by using normative theory, which is derived from the distinction between cosmopolitanism and communitarianism. According to communitarianism, communities themselves define the limits between proper conduct and universal moral codes because their own morality arises from the culture that underpins the basis of their community. It is the community's responsibility to determine which morals are privileged: the community's moral code or the universal moral code. Cosmopolitanism, on the other hand, stems from a universal moral standard to which all actors should adhere. If an actor violates the rights of an individual or the humanity, then cosmopolitan intervention is

---

[13] Ian Manners, Richard Whitman, "The Difference Engine: Constructing and Representing the International Identity of the European Union", **Journal of European Public Policy**, Vol. 10, No. 3, 2003, p. 384.

[14] Manners and Whitman, ibid.

[15] Ibid, p. 387.

[16] Sonia Lucarelli, "Introduction: Values, Principles, Identity and European Union Foreign Policy", **Values and Principles in European Foreign Policy**, Sonia Lucarelli and Ian Manners (Ed.), London and New York, Routledge, 2006, p. 12.

[17] Manners, Normative power Europe: A Contradiction in Terms, p. 252.

[18] Ian Manners, **'The European Union as a Normative Power in the Global Polity'**, Paper presented to the PSA Annual Conference, Leeds, 4–7 April 2005, p. 10.

needed to restore justice, because there should be a universal moral standard by which every community must abide. On this point, Manners contends that NPE emphasizes the moral code of cosmopolitan law and acts ethically by including "universal norms at the center of its relations with its member states and the world"[19]. The EU's foreign policy is mostly formed by member states (communitarian), the supranational EU (semi-communitarian; semi-cosmopolitan), and cosmopolitical world society"[20], which means there is an allowance for member state autonomy, yet they should not be completely self-determining and free from moral obligations to the rest of the international community.

As Manners asserts, all international relations are normative and designed by cosmopolitan law, where normative judgements show us what ought to be done. This encompasses actors with their moral cases, directing societies towards the normal, which is an extension of the norm. According to him, another mission of the concept of NPE is the gradual transference of the EU from a normative heading to the ideal type of actor in world politics, as it intentionally or unintentionally legitimizes 'normal' and creates an 'ideational change' in third parties. The ultimate aim is to normalize the cosmopolitan world to a more just environment.[21] He also grounds NPE on normative justification, which is embodied by principles that appear through actions, and actions have impacts that cause for a change and all this cycle produce an on-going mutual constitutiveness[22]. Considering this normative justification, he defines 'power' in terms of EU actions and their effects.

Likewise, Manners' normative theory and ideational change, norm's life cycle modelled constructivist theory also suggests employing the power of ideas and norms at the center of international relations. Although the EU's international identity and its norm promotion role link with several theoretical debates in international relations (IR), the importance of ideas, norms, and identity concepts in foreign policy analysis deserve more investigation from the perspective of how norms are owned by a actors. While theorizing NPE, most studies have not overtly identified the stages of the process although phasing is crucial for ascertaining the EU's shortcomings and neglected acts not only in its external relations but also inside the Union. That is, these absences can unravel where the EU should

[19] Manners, Normative power Europe: A Contradiction in Terms, p. 241.
[20] Richard G. Whitman, **"Normative Power Europe: Empirical and Theoretical Perspectives"**. London, Palgrave Macmillan, 2011, p. 5.
[21] Manners, **The Normative Ethics of the European Union**, p. 67; Ian Manners, "The European Union's Normative Power: Critical Perspectives and Perspectives on the Critical", **Normative Power Europe: Empirical and Theoretical Perspectives,** Richard G Whitman, (Ed.), London, Palgrave Macmillan, 2011.
[22] Ian Manners, "The European Union in Global Politics: Normative Power and Longitudinal Interpretation", **Research Methods in European Union Studies,** Kennett Lynggaard, Ian Manners, Karl Löfgren (Ed.) UK, Palgrave Macmillan, 2015.

readjust in its foreign policy self-image even inside its borders.

With respect to the EU's human rights norm promoter role and its normative power on 'others', Manners suggests a three-stage analysis for normative justification comprising an action-impact-change cycle. Albeit it does not directly overlap, Finnemore and Sikkink's[23] three-staged constructivist norm's life cycle (norm emergence, norm acceptance/cascade, and norm internalization) has similarities with Manners' in understanding the process. In terms of crystallizing NPE concept, Finnemore and Sikkink's categorization of norm diffusion can help to detect not what the EU is or does do but 'should do'. Hence, Manners' insistence on reflexive monitoring for a more normative Union, which is defined by using a 'should' modality, is similar to Finnemore and Sikkink's counterpart modality 'oughtness' as an advice for shaping the 'normal'. Although Finnemore and Sikkink do not directly suggest shaping the 'normal' in their arguments, both approaches reach the same conclusions and a life cycle model probe the normative and ideational performance of the EU as a norm practitioner as well as promoter.

These three stages of the norm's life cycle are designed to theorize the effect of norms on other actors' behavior. First, the idea finds grounds through norm entrepreneurs, who look for suitable opportunities to spread this agreed norm. These norm entrepreneurs "attempt to convince a critical mass of states, without which the achievement of the substantive norm goal is compromised".[24] After norm is emerged in a proper kind of standard, between the first and second phases, there is a threshold called tipping point that defines the success of the acceptance of the norm and the succeeding moves. Soaring beyond the tipping point refers "enough states and critical states endorse the new norm".[25] In the following, the new norm becomes a subject of state socialization, which decides whether the society can localize the norm or not, as there is no guarantee that every nation or locality would accept and internalize the norm. Once the life cycle of any norm has been completed, it can be asserted that the norm is internalized, bureaucratized, and institutionalized. This means that both the society and its political leaders have accepted and habituated the norm. If the transmitted norm has not explicitly completed its life cycle, then this ill-completed norm will certainly face with non-conformity in its arrival.

In terms of human rights and solidarity norms such as RtoP, in which international society is expected to respond to the problem of genocide and mass atrocities[26], norm emergence was completed at the universal level

[23] Martha Finnemore, Kathryn Sikkink, "International Norm Dynamics and Political Change". **International Organization**, Vol. 52, No. 4, 1998, pp. 887–917.
[24] Ibid, p. 901.
[25] Ibid, p. 902.
[26] Alex Bellamy, "The Responsibility to Protect Turns Ten", **Ethics & International Affairs**, Vol. 29,

before being issued by the EU during the acceptance process, then through policies and legal arrangements the EU socializes it inside it borders. Internalization of the norm, as a sequel and longitudinal step, turns human rights norm into an EU identity. This is because it is assumed that at both EU and member state levels, 'benign' universal norms are acknowledged as the components of the Union's self-image. Thus, these common principles are should be practiced by both EU institutions and member states, given that the norm originated from the EU and are exported to the 'others' as the essential part of normative Europe.

### Emergence of responsibility to protect norm at universal level

Establishing universal standards for refugees and asylums under international protection came to be regarded as a responsibility of the League of Nations after the World War I. However, it came to be a subject of an international law mainly developed after 1950, "with the regulations that referred to the international protection of human rights and the creation of a procedural framework for the inspection of state practices".[27] During the interwar years, the states were responsible for the actions of the individual that fell under their protection. According to Skran, in these years, refugees represented a fundamental challenge for the state sovereignty because international actors had forced states to tackle refugee issue in terms of ethical principles and fundamental human rights, which were part of their international obligations, over the interests of sovereign states.[28] However, after the Second World War (WWII) new legal instruments regarding refugees and asylum-seekers had been re-shaped as a result of -particularly- European emigration to all around the world or conversely due to the move from the ex-colonies to Europe. Until 1951 Geneva Convention, which is the main international mechanism of protection, none of the instruments had clearly defined that refugees might be subject to repatriation, unless there was a valid objection to their specific circumstance.[29] The Geneva Convention, which was also amended in 1967 with an additional protocol, enlarged the scope of the Refugee Law and comprehensively regulated the admission, residence, and personal legal status based on individual cases, and access to court, education and employment.

The crucial point in the refugee crisis is how the international society is "responsible to intervene when a given state is not capable to protect its

---

No. 2, 2015, p. 182.
[27] Katya Pestrova, "The Evolution of International Refugee Law: A Review of Provisions and Implementation." **Cambridge Review of International Affairs**, Vol. 9, No. 2, 1995, p. 36.
[28] Claudena M. Skran, "**Refugees in Inter-war Europe: The Emergence of a Regime**", Oxford, Oxford University Press, 1995.
[29] Pestrova, ibid.

people".[30] The Geneva Convention includes specific principles, and guides states regarding how to protect asylum seekers and refugees. Even though the responsibility to protect individuals requires the full implementation of international refugee law (the 1951 Convention on the Protection of Refugees, the 1967 Protocol, and especially the principle of 'non-refoulement', which forbids the return of those seeking asylum to their place of persecution), there still more needs to be done in the face of specific atrocities.[31] Hereby, humanitarian intervention, as a part of the international responsibility of the society, refers to the measures that shall be taken by the international authorities as well as the frames of the duties[32] that have arisen above the right of sovereignty of individual states. A paradigm shift from 'humanitarian intervention' to 'Responsibility to Protect' (RtoP)[33] at the beginning of the new millennium aimed to emphasize the victims instead of the interveners in response to failed or absent humanitarian interventions.[34]

United Nations General Assembly unanimously adopted the RtoP under paragraphs 138 and 139 of the 2005 World Summit Outcome Document[35], which was first introduced in 2001 by the International Commission on Intervention and State Sovereignty (ICISS).[36] The ICISS is financed by the Canadian government "in the aftermath of NATO's intervention in Kosovo and the world's well-documented lack of response (or inefficacy) in Rwanda and the former Yugoslavia".[37] RtoP has been put forward "as a frame for how international society thinks about, argues over, and responds to, genocide and mass atrocities"[38], because ICISS initiative "sought to provide an answer to the question of how to deal with grave humanitarian concerns within the context of the UN Charter and limitations with the UN system".[39]

---

[30] Gareth Evans and Mohamed Sahnoun, "The Responsibility to Protect", **Foreign Affairs,** Vol. 81, No. 6, 2002, p. 101.
[31] Alex J. Bellamy, "Safe Passage and Asylum Key to Fulfilling Responsibility to Protect" **Global Observatory,**
September 8, 2015, www.theglobalobservatory.org/2015/09/syria-refugees-unhcr-aylan-kurdi/ (Access: 20.11.2020).
[32] James Pattison, "Whose Responsibility to Protect? The Duties of Humanitarian Intervention", **Journal of Military Ethics**, Vol. 7, No. 4, 2008, pp. 262-283.
[33] Ibid, p. 264.
[34] Steenbrick, ibid.
[35] UN General Assembly, "60/1. 2005 World Summit Outcome",
https://www.un.org/en/development/desa/population/migration/generalassembly/docs/globalcompact/A_RES_60_1.pdf (Access: 24.11.2020).
[36] International Commission on Intervention and State Sovereignty (ICISS), **"The Responsibility to Protect: Report of the International Commission on Intervention and State Sovereignty"**,
International Development Research Centre, 2005, https://idl-bnc-idrc.dspacedirect.org/bitstream/handle/10625/18432/IDL-18432.pdf?sequence=6&isAllowed=y (Access: 24.11.2020).
[37] Barbara J. Falk, Sara M. Skinner, "The Responsibility to Protect: A Normative Shift from Words to Action?" **International Peacekeeping**, Vol. 23, No. 3, 2016, p. 493.
[38] Alex J. Bellamy and Tim Dunne, "The Oxford Handbook of the Responsibility to Protect", Oxford, Oxford University Press, 2016, p. 12.
[39] Falk and Skinner, ibid, p. 493.

RtoP stipulates three pillars of responsibility that forms states' sovereignty and entails the responsibility with a set of duties.[40] The first pillar indicates that states are responsible to protect their populations from genocide, war crimes, ethnic cleansing and crimes against humanity, and from their incitement; the second pillar outlines the international community's responsibility to help and encourage states to fulfill their own responsibility; whereas the third pillar expresses the collective responsibility of the international community to use appropriate diplomatic, humanitarian and other means to protect population from those crimes and violation.[41] In RtoP, in terms of solidarity and human rights the third pillar is salient, as it is "a fully-fledged normative aspiration"[42] and calls on states for collective action to protect populations when their states manifestly fail to do so.[43] Hence, sovereign states are assigned as the main duty holder that should offer security and protection for those who "moved from the individual state to the international community".[44]

RtoP is about political will[45], yet it is the "only fundamental normative innovation agreed upon by the member states during this round of UN reform".[46] It has emerged as a universal norm that sets standard of appropriate behavior by indicating what states 'ought' to do.[47] The evolution of responsibility to protect 'from idea to norm' "provides a unique opportunity to analyze the changing global order in a way that focuses on fundamental conflicts over sovereignty and responsibility, universalism and exceptionalism, hypocrisy and selectivity".[48] According to Bellamy, RtoP is an emerging norm because "there are 'shared expectations' within the international society that (1) governments and international organizations do, in fact, exercise this responsibility; and (2) they recognize both a limited duty and a right to do so; and (3) failure to fulfil this duty should attract criticism".[49] Such norms "are intended to provide a framework of standards by which a state or group of states' behaviors will be judged"[50], because resistance against the implementation to such norms means rejecting 'moral

---

[40] Ibid., p. 995.

[41] UN Responsibility to Protect https://www.un.org/en/genocideprevention/secretary-general.shtml, (Access: 24.11.2020).

[42] Jason Ralph, James Souter, "Is R2P a Fully-Fledged International Norm?", **Politics and Governance**, Vol. 3, No. 4, 2015, pp. 68-71.

[43] Ibid., p. 68.

[44] ICISS, ibid., p. 7.

[45] Ralph and Souter, ibid.

[46] Jutta Brunnée, Stephen Toope, "Norms, Institutions and UN reform: The Responsibility to Protect", **Journal of International Law and International Relations**, Vol. 2, No. 1, 2005, pp. 121-140.

[47] De Franco, et al., ibid.

[48] Philipp Rotmann, Gerrit Kurtz, and Sarah Brockmeier. "Major Powers and the Contested Evolution of a Responsibility to Protect" **Conflict, Security & Development**, Vol. 14, No. 4, 2014, pp. 355-377.

[49] Bellamy, The Responsibility to Protect Turns Ten, p. 163.

[50] Barqueiro, et al., ibid., p. 40.

cosmopolitanism', which would then be assumed as illegitimate.[51]

## The EU's Acceptance and Socialization of the RtoP norm

Since the RtoP emerged as a norm at the universal level, the EU "appears a fitting candidate for the role"[52], as it has made "considerable progress in affirming its role as an international actor willing to act in mass atrocity cases".[53] In terms of the Union's constitutive values that include human rights, justice and solidarity, which are sought upon in its international activities, "there is a close normative and political fit between the EU and RtoP."[54] Before RtoP became an issue, in 2003, in response to mass atrocities and conflicts, the Council of the European Union agreed on the 'European Security Strategy' (ESS), which clearly indicated that threats would not be addressed solely by military means but also by preventive engagement with more coherent policies and instruments such as aid and trade.[55] In a similar vein, in the 2004 Barcelona report, which is called 'A Human Security Doctrine for Europe', the EU again stressed its concern on protecting human security at the core of its foreign policy. However, specific indication on how the EU would protect civilians in case of mass atrocities or role the EU could play in such situations to save the affected population had not been mentioned clearly.[56] Hence, in 2006, as a manifestation of the 'acceptance of the RtoP' and passing the life cycle's threshold, the EU expressed its willingness to support the norm by declaring 'European Consensus on Development' strategy. It is highlighted in the common framework that the EU cannot stand by genocide, war crimes, ethnic cleansing or other gross violations as the international humanitarian law and human rights are committed by the Union.[57] Both the EU institutions and EU member states have "endorsed R2P and participated in supportive diplomacy at the UN level"[58] and " been among the most fervent advocates of the concept of RtoP, all the while being careful to place it firmly within the limits of the United

---

[51] Amitav Acharya, "How Ideas Spread: Whose Norms Matter? Norm Localization and Institutional Change in Asian Regionalism". **International Organization**, Vol. 58, No. 2, 2004, pp. 239-275.
[52] Brockmeier, et al., ibid., p. 340.
[53] Dvornichenko and Barskyy, ibid. p. 119.
[54] Tonny Brems Knudsen, "The Responsibility to Protect: European Contributions in a Changing World Order", **Handbook on the European Union and International Institutions: Performance, Policy, Power**, Knud Erik Jørgensen, Katie Verlin Laatikainen (Ed.), London, Routledge, 2013, p. 475.
[55] European Security Strategy (Access: 24.11.2020).
https://data.consilium.europa.eu/doc/document/ST-15895-2003-INIT/en/pdf
[56] Dvornichenko and Barskyy, ibid.
[57] European Parliament, Council and Commission, "Joint statement by the Council and the representatives of the governments of the Member States meeting within the Council, the European Parliament and the Commission on European Union Development Policy: 'The European Consensus'", 2006, (Access: 23.11.2020).
https://eur-lex.europa.eu/legal-content/EN/TXT/?uri=CELEX%3A42006X0224%2801%29
[58] De Franco et al., ibid., p. 996.

Nations."[59]

In terms of cascading the norm inside its borders, the EU has started to socialize it through specific instruments. With a rather timid backing[60], most EU documents that refer RtoP are country-specific resolutions of the European Parliament and statements of the EU Presidency stressing the need for collective action through the UNSC.[61] In 2008, in order to implement ESS more comprehensively the EU issued the strategy report 'Providing Security in a Changing World', which identified the strategic objectives against key threats. In the document, it is indicated that all states need to "take responsibility for the consequences of their actions and hold a shared responsibility to protect populations from genocide, war crimes, ethnic cleansing and crimes against humanity".[62] According to Barqueiro et al., the 2004 Barcelona Report had an influence on the ways in which human security ideas were more incorporated into the ESS document and "included responses to human trafficking, and nuclear non-proliferation".[63] A year later, the Treaty of Lisbon was ratified by the EU member states and it clearly underlined that one of the Union's central aims is to promote universal values, both at home and in its relations with the outside world by contributing to peace, security, solidarity and mutual respect among peoples. Following the Treaty of Lisbon's expression of cosmopolitan solidarity with non-Europeans,[64] the Commission's Global Approach to Migration and Mobility (GAMM) expressed an overarching framework that emphasized the need to "enhance solidarity with refugees and displaced persons"[65] by putting human rights as a cross-cutting priority".[66]

However, the EU's socialization of the RtoP norm was challenged and reframed by the Arab Spring, which erupted in 2011 and influenced the European countries greatly because of its geographical proximity to the region. The Arab Spring also revealed the necessity of materializing what ought to be done about the conflict and the populations affected by the atrocities, instead of manifesting the EU's willingness to implement the RtoP with supportive documents. Especially the Libyan and Syrian cases could be

---

[59] Wouters and De Man, ibid. p. 17.

[60] Smith, ibid.

[61] Wouters and De Man, ibid.

[62] Council Report on the Implementation of the European Security Strategy, "Providing Security in a Changing World", Brussels, 2008, (Access: 23.11.2020).
https://www.consilium.europa.eu/ueDocs/cms_Data/docs/pressdata/EN/reports/104630.pdf

[63] Barqueiro et al., ibid., p. 40-41.

[64] Bulley, ibid.

[65] European Commission, "The Global Approach to Migration and Mobility," Communication from the Commission to the European Parliament, the Council, the European Economic and Social Committee and the Committee of the Regions, COM (2011) 743 final, Brussels, November 18 2011, p. 17.

[66] Yalçın Diker, "**International Migration and Asylum in the European Union: Recent Developments and Policy Reactions**", Norman Paterson School of International Affairs First Student-Run Conference, Ottawa, Carleton University, 2015.

considered the testing ground for the implementation of RtoP as a global norm, not only for the EU but also for all international actors. In the case of Libya, the RtoP norm has been successfully applied by the norm entrepreneurs, predominantly from Western countries,[67] and the intervention might have tied RtoP more closely to the UN Security Council than was the case previously.[68] Unlike Libya, the Syrian crisis is a first, "in which non-Western powers are taking the lead, discarding any move that could be construed as legitimizing intervention, and standing firm in support of state sovereignty".[69] In addition to the resilience of the Assad regime, the violence of radical groups, such as Daesh (Islamic State in Iraq and Syria or ISIS), unpacks a reality that democratic alternatives lie further beyond expectations of peace in the near future. As Tocci notes, while Libya intervention is the final flames of a liberal Western order; the Syrian conflict is the incipient signs of a post-liberal polycentric world.[70] Moreover, the atrocities inside and at the border of the Syria "have caused the flow of the citizens outside the state",[71] and "intensified the humanitarian crisis".[72] Not only those inside of the Syria but also the victims who escaped from the onslaught of the human rights violations of the Daesh have taken refuge elsewhere, because RtoP's third pillar and Geneva Convention guarantee a form of asylum where "the international community has a responsibility to assist these people and to protect them".[73]

With regards to the EU's response to the Syrian crisis by using its RtoP norm, Smith argues that "the EU has enormous capacity to assist states and societies to build resilience, a wide range of appropriate policy instruments that can be used in response to mass atrocities, and credibility and legitimacy in the areas of conflict prevention and human rights protection".[74] However, the decision-making process has taken a long time, because of the member states' different approaches. On the other hand, despite the wide consensus among the member states in confirming the attitude of 'never again' in relation to mass atrocities, which was indicated at the 2018 debate on the RtoP at the UN General Assembly by the EU ambassador[75], there is a lack

[67] Alex J. Bellamy, "Libya and the Responsibility to Protect: The Exception and the Norm", **Ethics & International Affairs**, Vol. 25, No. 3, 2011, pp. 263-269.
[68] Jennifer Welsh, "Civilian Protection in Libya: Putting Coercion and Controversy Back into RtoP", **Ethics & International Affairs**, Vol. 25, No. 3, 2011, p. 255.
[69] Nathalie Tocci, "On Power and Norms: Libya, Syria and the Responsibility to Protect", **Global Responsibility to Protect**, Vol. 8, No. 1, 2016, p. 53.
[70] Ibid., p. 52.
[71] Ralph and Souter, ibid., p. 69.
[72] Barqueiro et al., ibid., p. 42.
[73] Ibid., p. 69.
[74] Smith, ibid., p. 1.
[75] Statement on behalf of the EU and its Member States by Ambassador Joanne Adamson, Deputy Head of Delegation at the UN General Assembly Debate on **The Responsibility to Protect and the Prevention of Genocide, War Crimes, Ethnic Cleansing and Crimes against Humanity**, https://eeas.europa.eu/headquarters/headquarters-homepage/47293/debate-responsibility-protect-and-

of "political will and preparedness to actually take the responsibility to act on the emergence of new mass atrocities as in Syria"[76]. Even though the "RtoP seems a substantial normative innovation in international society"[77], what the refugee crisis demonstrates that states act deeply conservative. Nevertheless, significant attempts have been made by EU institutions in accepting some of the refugees because the "politics of protection underlying both RtoP and the EU's migration and asylum policy primarily entail a solidarity with, and a bolstering of, the sovereign capacity of the modern state".[78]

De Franco et al. argue that the main benchmark to understand how the EU has socialized the RtoP norm can be found in EU leaders' speeches, institutional documents and statements; in bureaucratic structures and procedures; in the existing policies and allocated resources.[79] For example, it can be investigated since 2013, when the European Parliament[80] called for member states and EU institutions to agree on a European Consensus on RtoP. This initiative aimed to consolidate the EU's support for an international responsibility and "reflected a number of important features which provide an insight into the EU's attempts to form an international political role".[81] In the following years, in 2015 the EU appointed a RtoP contact point as a Deputy Secretary-General of the European External Action Service (EEAS) [82], and the Commission prepared a European Agenda on Migration, which indicates that Common European Asylum System (CEAS) as an enactment of its 'duty to protect' guides for the lives and fundamental rights of asylum seekers.[83]

One of the important documents that directly -but briefly- related to the implementation of RtoP to Syrian refugees is the European Council's 'Global Strategy for the European Union's Foreign and Security Policy', which was adopted in 2016. Although the title of the strategy seems to provide responses for humanitarian crisis, the document only included a short statement that 'the EU will promote the responsibility to protect in order to prevent or end

---

prevention-genocide-war-crimes-ethnic-cleansing-and-crimes_en, (Access: 22.11.2020).

[76] Chandler, ibid., p. 28.

[77] Bulley, ibid., p. 52.

[78] Ibid., p. 52.

[79] De Franco et al., ibid.

[80] European Parliament (2013), 'European Parliament Recommendation to the Council of 18 April 2013 on the UN principle of the **"Responsibility to Protect"** ('R2P'), P7_TA (2013)0180.

[81] Edward Newman, Cristina G. Stefan, "Normative Power Europe? The EU's Embrace of the Responsibility to Protect in a Transitional International Order", **JCMS: Journal of Common Market Studies** Vol. 58, No. 2, 2020, p. 472.

[82] Information about the EU's R2P contact point is unavailable on the European External Action Service (EEAS) website. Only by reading the press releases regarding the annual meetings of the Global Network of R2P Contact Points is it possible to confirm that there is indeed an R2P contact point in the EEAS. http://www.globalr2p.org/our_work/global_network_of_r2p_focal_points, (Access: 22.11.2020).

[83] European Commission, **"A European Agenda on Migration,"** COM (2015) 240 final, Brussels, May 13, 2015, section III.3.

mass atrocities'[84], which is vague and provides "no concrete commitment as to how the EU will do so",[85] and "without any reference to further explanation on how the EU will accomplish this support for the concept"[86] staying in solidarity with refugees. The 'Toolkit for Atrocity Prevention', on the other hand, was officially launched by the European External Action Service in January 2019. It aims to coordinate European responses to atrocities in a proactive and coherent manner, and seems to be taken place "in parallel with broader efforts on the part of European foreign policy elites to project a more active global role for the EU in conflict resolution, security and normative leadership".[87]

## Limits of cascading and incomplete life cycle of RtoP norm

Despite the EU officials' and institutions' expressing statements in the international level on their pledge to actualize their responsibility to protect refugees, the Union's response to Syrian refugees, who fled from a mass atrocity, explicitly shows the gap between the EU rhetoric and practice. The gap was due to the fact that the "overt support for and actual implementation of the RtoP notion has been slow to emerge within the Union itself".[88] The flow of Syrian Refugee makes one to question the duty of international community to act on behalf of the afflicted people's inevitably arise and fueled convoluted debates[89] about RtoP. The RtoP norm has not been clearly referred by government officials, practitioners and diplomats during the refugee crisis[90] because the commitment of the EU institutions to the protection of human rights seemed to be shaky.[91] The European solutions towards solidarity and the implementation of RtoP can somehow be seen in some "[i]nitiatives such as asylum-seekers' relocation within EU members in order to lessen the burden of the 'frontline' states overwhelmed by refugee arrivals (i.e. Greece and Italy)"[92] because of the principles of Dublin Regulations. However, on the other hand, since the EU released its Global Strategy in 2016, not only the UK decided to leave the EU, but also "deep divisions between its members that were triggered by refugee inflows and the

---

[84] European Union, "Shared Vision, Common Action: A Stronger Europe. A Global Strategy for the European Union Foreign and Security Policy", Luxembourg, 2016, http://europa.eu/globalstrategy/sites/globalstrategy/files/regions/files/eugs_review_web_0.pdf, (Access: 22.11.2020).

[85] Smith, ibid., p. 3.

[86] Steenbrink, ibid., p. 40.

[87] Newman and Stefan, ibid., p. 472.

[88] Wouters and De Man, ibid., p. 17.

[89] Stefania Panebianco, Iole Fontana. "When Responsibility to Protect 'hits home': The Refugee Crisis and the EU Response", **Third World Quarterly**, Vol. 39, No. 1, 2018, pp. 1-17.

[90] Newman and Stefan, ibid.

[91] Smith, ibid.

[92] Ibid, p. 1.

rise of populist nationalist parties"[93] have hampered the habituation of the RtoP. Hence, the Strategy shifted the EU's normative or ethical self-image to a "'principled pragmatism' in which the EU's principles derive not just from 'idealism' but from "a realistic assessment of the current strategic context".[94]

Indeed, the refugee crisis turned from being a debate about a humanitarian crisis to a security concern in Europe, when committed Daesh/ISIS terrorists entered the process. In the meantime, keeping RtoP alive as an international form of human rights and solidarity within the borders of the EU became very much of a debatable thing for the Union. Even though the CEAS has aimed to create "Europe as an 'area of protection' based on shared values and solidarity"[95], it contains no responsibility to welcome Syrian refugees and asylum seekers. In a similar vein, none of the EU institutions has made serious commitment to socialize the norm by assigning it to a specific body,[96] but laid on the external dimension remaining external and opt for outsourcing its protection of the responsibility elsewhere beyond the EU member states.[97] The EU's overwhelming focus on its external relations curves to strengthening the sovereignty capabilities of third countries through financing them with specific funds, such as Madad Trust Fund and the Regional Development and Protection Programme, for the use of both refugees and host communities. Nevertheless, the EU's sponsoring UNHCR and NGO projects in these countries to both build protection capacity in these affected regions and promote durable solutions in the regions that produce and transit refugees[98] means that the Union has "sought to increase the financial aid to the region rather than to share the need to provide protection to these refugees".[99]

In terms of the member states' attitude towards the refugees and conforming with the RtoP, national political elites' pragmatism on human rights problematizes the contradiction between human rights norms and political interests that pave the way for the debate on the normative interest of the EU versus the material interests of the member states.[100] The arrival of the refugees has led to a situation where a "number of nationalist political parties – such as the French Front National, and the UK Independence Party

---

[93] Newman and Stefan, ibid., p. 484.
[94] Smith, ibid., p. 2.
[95] Bulley, ibid. p. 53.
[96] Brockmeier, et al., ibid.
[97] Thomas Gammeltoft-H., "Outsourcing Asylum: The Advent of Protection Lite," **Europe in the World: EU Geopolitics and the Making of European Space**, Luiza Bialasiewicz, (Ed.), Surrey, Ashgate, 2011.
[98] Bulley, ibid.
[99] Roxana Barbulescu, "Still a Beacon of Human Rights? Considerations on the EU Response to the Refugee Crisis in the Mediterranean" **Mediterranean Politics,** Vol. 22, No. 2, 2017, p. 305.
[100] Newman and Stefan, ibid.

– have benefitted from and promoted this narrative and have in turn risen in popularity."[101] The greatest example of problem of solidarity and burden-sharing among the member states emerged in quotas and control of national borders. For instance, in terms of quotas while France, Germany and Spain claimed that they have been already sharing the burden, Central and Eastern Europe countries argued they are not preferred of being a destination for asylum seeker and put reservations on admitting refugees[102]. Hence it becomes clear that outsourcing the solidarity came about due to the conflict among the member states, particularly the Visegrad states that led the opposition to find a solidaristic solution in terms of the relocation and resettlement of the refugees inside the EU borders.[103]

The Visegrad countries Hungary, Slovakia, Czech Republic and Poland had reservations about admitting Syrian refugees by putting the Muslim faith forward as a pretext. They released a joint statement that says "any [EU] proposal leading to [the] introduction of mandatory and permanent quota for solidarity measures would be unacceptable."[104] Hungary, as one of the aggressive opponents of the idea of accepting refugees from Syria, framed Syrian refugees as "bringing threats of Muslim terror into Europe"[105], which was later consolidated by the following statement of Prime Minister Viktor Orban: 'Europe needs to encourage its citizens to have more children instead of welcoming refugees, because the survival of Western Civilization is at stake'.[106] Slovakia even proposed to "select only Christian asylum seekers by introducing mandatory quotas,"[107] whereas the Czech President Milos Zeman claimed that it is "practically impossible" to integrate Muslim communities into the European society.[108] In a similar vein, according to the European Social Survey, 34.3 % of Polish nationals, a strong Catholic majority, had said that no Muslims should be allowed to come to Poland even

---

[101] Edward Newman, "The Limits of Liberal Humanitarianism in Europe: The 'Responsibility to Protect' and Forced Migration", **European Review of International Studies** Vol. 4.2, No. 3, 2017, pp. 59-77.

[102] Barbulescu, ibid., p. 305.

[103] Beken Saatçioğlu, "The EU's response to the Syrian refugee crisis: a battleground among many Europes", **European Politics and Society**, 2020, pp: 1-17, https://doi.org/10.1080/23745118.2020.18 42693, (Access: 22.11.2020).

[104] Bart Bachman, "Diminishing Solidarity: Polish Attitudes toward the European Migration and Refugee Crisis",https://www.migrationpolicy.org/article/diminishing-solidarity-polish-attitudes-toward-european-migration-and-refugee-crisis, (Access: 22.11.2020).

[105] Amelia Hadfield, Andrej Zwitter. "Analysing the EU Refugee Crisis: Humanity, Heritage and Responsibility to Protect", **Politics and Governance**, Vol. 3, No. 2, 2015, pp. 129-135.

[106] The Washington Post, 'European Union Predicts 3 Million More Migrants by End of Next Year', 5 November 2015, https://www.washingtonpost.com/world/european-union-predicts-3-million-more-migrants-by-end-of-next-year/2015/11/05/d70aff6c-e521-4280-a7b6-e05cf0b0f8ee_story.html, (Access: 21.11.2020).

[107] Barbulescu, ibid., p. 305.

[108] The Guardian, 'Integrating Muslims into Europe is 'impossible', says Czech president. 18 January 2016, https://www.theguardian.com/world/2016/jan/18/integrating-muslims-into-europe-is-impossible-says-czech-president, (Access: 21.11.2020).

before the refugees' arrival.[109] Probably not as tough as those, but the Mediterranean and Aegean member states also have struggled to accept the refugees and eliminated the ships that arrived at their coasts by blocking the sea routes for the asylum seekers who have the right to access Europe not only under the international protection of law but also as part of the protection of the EU. On the other side, the UK has acknowledged the issue as a potential burden on its welfare system, while France and Germany, which are familiar with Muslim peoples and the phenomenon of migration, "have asserted that refugees contribute greatly to the welfare and economic systems"[110] since they entered their countries.

It is clear that instead of establishing solidarity in terms of willingness to find a common solution to the problem and internalizing the RtoP through policies and laws, the EU has been prioritizing 'security', 'societal (religion-based) cohesion' and 'burden sharing' over humanitarian obligations and "most European states are therefore arguably failing to live up to their own demanding cosmopolitan commitments".[111] The problem does not seem to be solved as the member states refused to grant the EU right to do so; however, there is also a paradox in that because the same nationalist states would criticize the EU for its insufficient response to the 'crisis'.[112] Yet, the refugee crisis unpacks that there is a "collective EU ambivalence towards RtoP ever since the norm was established, and this makes one to distinguish the EU from its member states."[113]

RtoP has not been internalized inside the EU borders and seems like never will be, unless "a proper engagement with this evolving norm has the potential to help EU states navigate their moral, political, and legal responsibilities with regard to refugees."[114] The European ethos on RtoP and the EU's normative power in terms of solidarity and human rights metanarratives are blurred by the failure of the modern states, in terms of refugees. The EU does not only come across as being either unwilling or incapable to implement the norm, but also some member states' religious attitudes demonstrate that the EU still has a lot to do inside its borders in terms of human rights before diffusing it as a norm to 'others'. The human rights and solidarity norms such as RtoP require localization and resonance inside the given society, hence human rights abuses against refugees through religion and violence then mean that the norm has never been socialized properly. At this point, Newman argues, the European responses to the

---

[109] Bachman, ibid.
[110] Hadfield and Zwitter, ibid., p, 129.
[111] Newman, ibid., p. 59
[112] Maurice Stierl, "Reimagining EUrope through the Governance of Migration", **International Political Sociology**, Vol. 14, 2020, pp: 252–269.
[113] Newman and Stefan, ibid. p. 473.
[114] Bulley, ibid., p. 51.

refugee crisis is a test of the credibility of European states' humanitarianism more broadly, where their "response to refugees have reflected a collective action mentality geared towards sharing the 'burden' of this crisis, rather than moral commitments to people fleeing danger."[115]

## Conclusion

The EU's human rights norm promotion in terms of Normative Power Europe conceptualization has been tested by several case studies with regards to the EU's normative role on 'others'. On the contrary, since the Arab Spring and the Syrian refugee flow erupted, scholarly researches have been questioning how fragile the member states' human rights and solidarity commitments in humanitarian crises are and whether the EU machinery itself and the member states internalize these norms inside their borders. The refugees' arrival has triggered even more existential problems, such as the Brexit process, the rise of nationalist parties in member states and the EU's failure in its implementation of international norms of protection properly. The RtoP norm requires legitimacy and credibility whereas the EU reflect an elusive power framed by the contradiction between what statements have to offer and what practices really show. The EU is at the center of most academic debates not only because it draws upon a role of regional normative authority and the expectations from the EU are high, but also the member states have taken slow steps in establishing collective actions towards the refugee crisis given that refugee protection under the Responsibility to Protect is the core norm of international human rights regime.

The EU could not easily response to the sudden refugee crisis. The poor record of the EU's refugee policy, which is masked by rhetoric, and inefficient consensus among the member states manifest that most member states still favor status quo over further cosmopolitanism. The EU's response to the refugee crisis has arguably called into question its credibility and capacity to overcome intra-conflicts on humanitarian challenges relevant to RtoP, because of the EU lacks effective mechanisms for responsibility-sharing. Hence it can be argued that the EU foreign policy and its self-image alternate security, state sovereignty to narratives of promoting human rights norms, which illustrates an elusive stance in the world politics.

---

[115] Newman, ibid., p. 66.

# CHAPTER 8

# REFUGEE POLICIES OF THE BALTIC COUNTRIES

Burulkan Abdibaitova Pala*

## Introduction

The international community, and particularly wealthy nations, fail to share the responsibility to protect people fleeing their homes in search of safety. In other words, they cannot agree and support a fair and predictable system to protect people who are forced to leave everything behind because of violence and persecution. The European Commission has designed a quota system to distribute refugees among member states, using criteria such as population size, GDP, unemployment rates and the number of asylum applications received in the past. The mandatory quota proposal has strained relations between Western, Eastern and Central European member states. This was due to some countries bearing a disproportionate burden. Western European states, such as Germany, accept large numbers of refugees while Eastern European states are reluctant to share the burden.

The mandatory quota strategy continues to be met with great resistance in the Baltic countries. Estonia, Latvia and Lithuania are among the loudest opponents of refugee admission quotas. The governments of the Baltic countries initially declared that they would accept refugees of their own accord. However, as the refugee problem became more serious, the adoption of additional quotas imposed by the European Commission was problematic. In addition, Latvia resists these the most. Two of the three government coalition parties opposed a compromise on the European Commission's proposal. This prevented the government from developing its political stance. Although the governments of Lithuania, Estonia and Latvia decided to accept an additional amount of refugees at one time as part of EU solidarity, these countries do not want a permanent quota mechanism. They also want to preserve the possibility of choosing which people are allowed in their country.

Since the collapse of the USSR, Russian-speaking people, a large minority group in the Baltic countries, did not integrate with the society of the respective countries after independence. This situation posed a major political and social problem in the relevant countries. Nationalist circles in

* PhD in International Relations, Postdoctoral Researcher. burulkanapala@gmail.com

Estonia and Latvia claim that they have 'immigrants' who have been in their countries since the collapse of the Soviet Union and used this as evidence against quotas. The acceptance of new minority groups will strengthen nationalist tendencies and social tension. This is also a challenge to the policy towards minorities adopted by these countries. It has been criticized both at home and abroad for its failure in this matter. Government coalitions in Latvia and Estonia include nationalist groups who fear an influx of refugees given unfavorable demographic trends and high levels of immigration from the Baltic countries, and this can intensify the social fragmentation that already exists. This makes it difficult to make political decisions on the refugee debate. In line with these explanations, the aim of this article will be to investigate the reasons why the Baltic countries refrain from accepting refugees. For this purpose, the first part of the article will focus on Russian minorities in the Baltic countries. The second chapter will examine the reasons behind the countries who are against taking in refugees. The third chapter will focus on the process of harmonizing refugee laws in the European Union membership process. Lastly, the forth chapter will focus on the views of refugees in the Baltic countries.

## Baltic states and Russian minorities

Lithuania, Latvia and Estonia, known as the "Baltic States", are the countries located on the eastern coast of the Baltic Sea. They are also small countries in terms of geographical area and population. They are overshadowed by their great Russian neighbors in the East. The Soviet government dominated all three countries from World War II to independence in the early 1990s. Soviet administration forced these countries to renounce their sovereignty and submit to Soviet forces. During this period, Russians were encouraged to migrate to these countries for work. During this migration process, the number of Russian citizens in these countries also increased rapidly.[1]

Immediately after regaining their independence in 1991, the Baltic States became parliamentary democracies with a common strategy to quickly integrate with Western Europe, joining as many Western organizations as possible. This was done to ensure the survival of their independence. The first problem with immigration in the newly independent countries was with the Russian minorities. In Latvia and Estonia, citizenship was not automatically granted to all residents after independence. For this reason, those who settled in the Soviet era had to apply for citizenship, where basic competence in the national language was the main criterion. As a result, most residents of Estonia and Latvia chose Russian citizenship or remained

---

[1] Marina Best, "The Ethnic Russian Minority: A Problematic Issue in the Baltic States", **Verges: Germanic & Slavic Studies in Review (GSSR)**, Vol. 2, No. 1, 2013, p. 34.

stateless. Although Lithuania had given citizenship to all its inhabitants, the Russian minority is not significant and ethnic Lithuanians make up 80% of the population.[2]

Unlike Lithuania, Estonia and Latvia can be described as "multi-legal". The legal framework for the existence of predominantly Russian-speaking minorities, which make up 30-40% of their population, is complex. Some of the countries' permanent residents who belong to minorities have citizenship status, while others are divided into various categories. For example, Estonia's current legislation treats the latter as "aliens". This category of persons includes citizens of the Russian Federation (Belarus, Ukraine, etc.) and stateless former citizens of the Soviet Union, implicitly labeled by the Estonian authorities as "persons with unidentified nationality".[3] In the process of regaining their independence in 1991, descendants of those who were citizens of Estonia or Latvia before 1940 automatically acquired new citizenship. However, those who came to these Soviet republics after the Second World War found themselves as non-citizens. The status of a non-citizen also extends to third-generation descendants born in the Baltic lands.[4] Latvia first introduced the term "non-Latvian national" for Soviet residents in international practice. These residents are recognized by local legislation as legal residents. However, it places serious restrictions on civil and political rights.[5]

Since gaining independence, the number of ethnic Russians has decreased in all three provinces. This decline is mostly due to immigration and naturalization. At the beginning of the twenty-first century, the percentage of Russians in these countries changed as follows: 25.6% of the total population in Estonia, 28.8% in Latvia and 6.4% in Lithuania. Although all three countries are parliamentary republics, they deal with the large Russian minorities in quite a different way since regaining their sovereignty. Both Latvia and Estonia perceive the Russian population as a reminder of their unhappy past. Despite the Russians who have lived in these countries for years and generations, they do not accept these people into their society. On the contrary, Lithuania deals with this minority group in a very different way. It does not perceive the Russian minority as a threat and honors their culture and history as an enriching part of their multicultural society.[6]

In the hope of joining the European Union, Estonia and Latvia had to

---

[2] Egle Macijauskaite, **The Baltic States As Countries of Asylum,** (Master's thesis), Copenhagen, Aalborg University, 2014, p. 18.

[3] Julia Kovalenko, **New Immigrants in Estonia, Latvia and Lithuania,** Legal Information Centre for Human Rights, Estonia Peter Mensah, AFROLAT, Latvia, Tallin, 2010, p. 4.

[4] Konstantin Ranks, "Pochemu Pribaltika buntuet protiv novoj migracionnoj politiki ES", https://carnegie.ru/commentary/60255, (Accessed on: 3.10.2020).

[5] Julia Kovalenko, op.cit., p. 4.

[6] Marina Best, op.cit., p. 34.

meet the minority policies of the Copenhagen criteria to be considered valid candidates. This meant that these two countries had to significantly reduce the number of stateless people. In the mid-1990s, Estonia and Latvia started working on integration methods to reduce statelessness. After granting some citizenship to some people and joining the European Union, the two countries started to slow the process once again. The number of stateless individuals in these two countries is still alarming, as 18% is Latvia and 13% of the total population of Estonia. Lithuania is more liberal in this naturalization area as the number of stateless persons is only 0.3%.[7]

Access to citizenship and nationality laws of the three Baltic States reflects immigration issues. Both Estonia and Latvia follow the jus sanguinis (blood tie criterion / basis) principle or the "right to blood" principle. This means that citizenship is determined by the parents' nationality, not by place of birth. Therefore, children born in Latvia or Estonia to Russian or stateless parents will not be able to acquire the national citizenship of the country in which they were born. In contrast, Lithuania has moved towards the jus soli (birthplace criterion) principle of citizenship or the principle of "land right". Therefore, Lithuanian citizenship is granted to anyone born in the country ("Republic of Lithuania: Citizenship Law"). Thus, the differences in nationality laws show that the ethnic Russian minority in Lithuania is not as segregated as in Estonia or Latvia. The Lithuanian government has taken the initiative to make its residents feel good and integrated into society, and they are very successful with this liberal citizenship law.[8]

The number of new immigrants is relatively small and has not played an important role in the local minority discourse dominated by traditional and former immigrant groups. This makes it difficult for national governments to demand comprehensive policies to meet the specific needs of new immigrants and promote their integration. The marked declines in the ethnic population resulting from the Soviet occupation made the ethnic populations of the Baltic States, especially Estonians and Latvians, feel as minorities in their own state. Accordingly, these fears were reflected in the newly prepared citizenship laws after the states declared their independence from the Soviet Union. The history of the Baltic states serves as a starting point in understanding contemporary cooperation, unity, and a sense of nationalism.[9]

Estonia and Latvia were based on exclusion policies rather than inclusion-based citizenship laws. Nationalism in the two countries was "nationalism, based on ethnic or principled ties and emphasizing the ecclesiastical and symbiotic (related to common life) relationship between the core nation,

---

[7] Ibid, p. 35
[8] Ibid.
[9] Egle Macijauskaite, op.cit., p. 18.

promising and citizenship". In fact, many Latvian residents were so scared of "national destruction" that Latvian politicians supported the introduction of quotas designed to deter migration. Estonian citizenship law suggests similar discontent for immigrants.[10]

In contrast, Lithuania did not experience a huge influx of immigrants during the Soviet occupation. Therefore, citizenship laws were based on a policy of inclusion rather than an exclusion policy. Lithuanian law based its citizenship conditions on regional factors rather than primitive factors. This is designed to foster a sense of national self-determination. Their experience with migration can no longer be considered the historical relics of a bygone era; it continues to influence the Baltic States and has undoubtedly played at least some role in the formation of current migration and asylum policies.[11]

Here, it is possible to show the above explanations as the main reasons why the Baltic states oppose the quota application that the EU allocates to the member states. In addition, most of the citizens of the Baltic states, especially the part which contains the young and educated, immigrated to other EU member states within the framework of free movement after joining the EU. As a result, the ethnic population of the Baltic states has decreased. Immigrants and refugees coming to these states pose a security threat to these states. That is, it creates a sense of risk of disappearing the Baltic ethnic population.

## Immigration from the Baltic States

On the eve of the collapse of the Soviet Union, the three states of the Baltic region - Latvia, Lithuania and Estonia - were seen on the European continent as a showcase of the economic, social and cultural achievements of the people of these countries. These states had the opportunity to become one of Europe's most promising, thriving regions. However, these hopes did not come true. After a quarter of a century of independent development, the socio-economic and demographic situation in the mentioned countries of the Baltic region were characterized by economic stagnation, decline and aging of the population, and mass migration from the region of the indigenous population.[12] The key aspects of assessing the change in socio-economic and demographic situations in the Baltic region are reflected in a series of EU political documents, namely, the European Union's Baltic Sea Region Strategy, the Council of the Baltic Sea States, "Baltic 21", and in other documents. The analysis of these sources makes it possible to understand the

---

[10] Amy Elson, "Baltic State Membership in the European Union: Developing a Common Asylum and Immigration Policy", **Indiana Journal of Global Legal Studies**, Vol. 5, No. 1, Article 15, 1997, p. 333.

[11] Ibid, p. 333.

[12] Yury Krasnov, "Migracionnye Processy v Pribaltike", **Migracionnoe pravo**, 2017, No. 1, p. 2.

scale of the demographic and immigration crisis in the region.[13]

**Table 1.** Baltic states population by years

| GEO/TIME | 2010 | 2011 | 2012 | 2013 | 2014 |
|----------|------|------|------|------|------|
| Estonia | 1.333.290 | 1.329.660 | 1.325.217 | 1.320.174 | 1.315.819 |
| Latvia | 2.120.504 | 2.074.605 | 2.044.813 | 2.023.825 | 2.001.468 |
| Lithuania | 3.141.976 | 3.052.588 | 3.003.641 | 2.971.905 | 2.943.472 |
| | **2015** | **2016** | **2017** | **2018** | **2019** |
| Estonia | 1.314.870 | 1.315.944 | 1.315.635 | 1.319.133 | 1.324.820 |
| Latvia | 1.986.096 | 1.968.957 | 1.950.116 | 1.934.379 | 1.919.968 |
| Lithuania | 2.921.262 | 2.888.558 | 2.847.904 | 2.808.901 | 2.794.184 |

Source: http://appsso.eurostat.ec.europa.eu/nui/show.do?dataset=demo_pjan&lang=en, (Accessed on: 20.10.2020).

The region is one of the fastest depopulation regions in the world. According to the estimates of the United Nations, by 2050, Latvia's population may decrease by 22 percent, Lithuania by 23 percent and Estonia by 10-20 percent.[14] During the Nazi and Soviet occupations, the sparsely populated Baltic region suffered an enormous loss of the population. After the collapse of the Soviet Union and the opening of the borders to the West, the Baltics experienced a significant migration. Later, when all three Baltic states joined the European Union in 2004, free movement within the bloc encouraged immigration. Triggered by the 2009 global financial crisis, the region lost even more of its population. Lithuania, the largest Baltic country, hosted 2.8 million people as of 2019, while Latvia had 1.9 million and Estonia 1.3 million.[15]

Migration in the Baltic States is closely associated with economic decline and rising unemployment, as the majority of immigrants are young graduates and middle-aged working class. The lowering of fertility rates and immigration and the increasing number of retirees will pose serious political and economic challenges in the near future. States will face the need to attract foreign workers while at the same time seeking to preserve their identity and cultural customs, which is an important issue for the Baltic States. Of particular interest is the impact of ethnic processes on the demographic situation in the Baltic region. The problem is that the increase in illegal immigration will result in a change in the ethnic composition of immigrant receiving countries. That is, this combination can lead to the replacement of the existing population with a population of immigrants or their descendants,

---

[13] Ibid, p. 3.

[14] https://population.un.org/wpp/Publications/Files/WPP2019_Highlights.pdf, (Accessed on: 4.11.2020).

[15] "Can Return Migration Revitalize the Baltics? Estonia, Latvia, and Lithuania Engage Their Diasporas, with Mixed Results", https://www.migrationpolicy.org/article/can-return-migration-revitalize-baltics-estonia-latvia-and-lithuania-engage-their-diasporas, (Accessed on: 4.11.2020).

or a population of mixed origin.[16] The Baltic states are regularly included in the list of European Union leaders in terms of migration of the working-age population, low fertility and high mortality rates. Young people are actively leaving the Baltics in search for a better life as they are unable to find a decent job and salary. As a result, the population is aging and declining rapidly. It should not be forgotten that the migration of the young working-age population to other countries brings about a crisis in the pension system.[17]

According to the demographic situation forecast in Europe, for the period up to 2060 published by the European Commission, Lithuania and Latvia will be leaders in population decline among EU countries in the next 50 years. The number of inhabitants in the Baltic republics will decrease by 38% and 30% respectively. Thus, the population of Latvia, which refuses to support the European initiative to introduce quotas for the admission of refugees, will drop to 1.4 million people by 2060. In contrast, in Lithuania, which decided to follow the example of its neighbor in transforming the country into an ethnographic museum and stopped accepting immigrants from Ukraine, the number of residents will drop to 1.8 million. The greatest population decline among the Baltic republics will be seen in Estonia, whose population will drop to 1.1 million. For Latvia, Lithuania and Estonia, the most important issue regarding demographic challenges is the need for social security. Even today, the budgets of the Baltic republics are unable to cope with the increase in obligations due to their residents, and the ruling elites refuse to allocate additional funds for indexing health care and pensions. At the same time, the International Monetary Fund and the European Commission recommend that Latvia and Lithuania choose the way to increase taxation in order to continue social payments. So far, only Estonia has followed the advice of European auditors, whose new government has increased indirect taxes since 2016. It canceled benefits, including hobby training, and increased excise taxes on alcohol, tobacco products and car fuel.[18]

Experts point out that none of the peripheral European countries have yet been able to offer an effective solution to demographic problems and a way to stop their population from moving to more developed EU countries. Numerous youth employment programs, re-migration plans and other projects have failed to deliver the desired results. The only way out of this situation, contrary to the Baltic elites who want to turn their republic into the ethnic reserves of Lithuanians, Estonians and Latvians, is the forced admission of refugees from third-world countries.[19] As a result of the

---

[16] Yury Krasnov, ibid, p. 6.

[17] Ibid, p. 4.

[18] Ibid, p. 8.

[19] "Demograficheskij krizis ES: Chislennost' naselenija Pribaltiki sokratitsja na tret'", https://www.rubaltic.ru/article/ekonomika-i-biznes/18052015-demografia/, (Accessed on: 2.10.2020).

increasing demographic problems, the countries concerned will have to accept refugees, which will inevitably lead to a change in the cultural sphere of the Baltic peoples.

**Figure 1.** The Emigration and Immigration Indicator in Lithuania

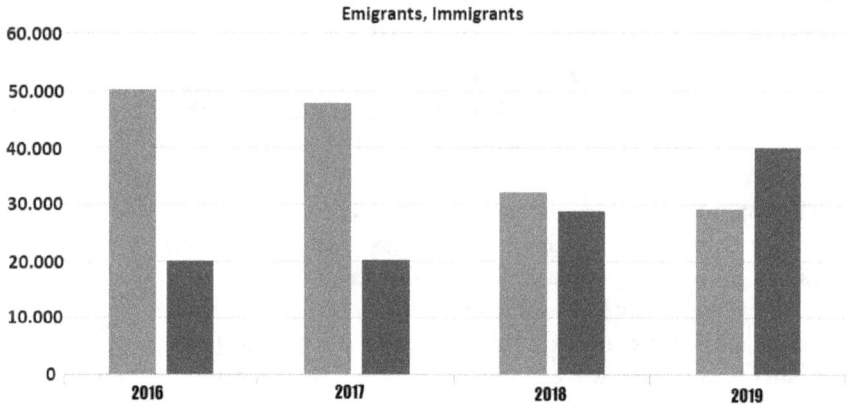

Source: https://osp.stat.gov.lt/

In general, the problems arising in Latvia, Lithuania, Estonia and other surrounding EU countries as a result of the demographic crisis are a red flag for aging Western Europe. The changes in the population structure announced in the European Commission's estimate show that young people entering working age will no longer live as well as their fathers and grandparents, not only in the suburbs, but also in developed European countries. With the failure of the European bureaucracy to solve demographic problems, Europeans will inevitably be disappointed in the EU as a "welfare state" and consequently intensify the process of the European Union's disintegration. First of all, these phenomena will be observed in the periphery of the EU - countries that have failed to find themselves in the European project, including the Baltic states.[20]

### Reasons for the Baltic States not to accept refugees

The three Baltic countries, which regained their independence as a result of the dissolution of the Soviet Union, associated the security of the region with the EU and NATO. The relevant countries have seen these memberships as the main guarantee against possible threats from Russia. Almost all major security threats have been associated with their Eastern neighbors. For thirty years, international cooperation and integration has

---

[20] Ibid, p. 10.

provided these countries with an effective "protection" from Russia's pressure on the former USSR independent states. However, in light of the current refugee crisis and the Baltic states' opposition to mandatory EU immigration quotas, this concept of security has been challenged. Although Estonia, Latvia and Lithuania, together with the Visegrád countries, have fulfilled their obligations under the EU Treaties, they have been criticized by Germany and France for not being prepared to share the burden of the growing refugee influx to Europe.[21]

The Baltic countries like to talk about the importance of solidarity between EU countries and the need to act as a united front against the threats posed by Russia. However, as soon as Brussels propose a mutual solution to a new and urgent problem, the Baltic states have shown that their solidarity cannot be trusted. For example, the resettlement of several hundred refugees from Africa and the Middle East. When Brussels decided to distribute refugees among EU countries according to quotas calculated according to a number of parameters, Latvia and Estonia immediately declared that they did not agree with this idea. The reason is that they were not ready to host people of a different culture, religion or skin color. Also, the population of the Baltic states is too small to accept different people. However, the Baltic states do not perceive refugees as a threat to their national identity solely. However, they do this when associating refugees with Russian speakers who have not successfully integrated into their community.[22] In other words, it is understood that refugees are perceived as a threat to their national identity because of the small population of these states.

According to Latvian "politician" Dainis Liepiņš, the Baltic states are concerned that the influx of refugees from Africa and the Middle East contain Islamic terrorists who pose a threat to their security. In response to this statement, Alex Cowles said:

"Politicians cannot be too stupid to understand that the growing number of refugees (not "economic refugees") is a direct result of European powers (and the US) military and political intervention in the Middle East and North Africa. Have we forgotten the Iraq war, the bombing of Libya, the civil wars in Syria, Yemen and elsewhere, or the arming of Islamist groups by Western powers and their regional allies? We drive people out of their homes but refuse to allow them to move. And the injustice is that these refugees, drowning in the Mediterranean

---

[21] Viljar Veebel, Raul Markus, "Europe´s refugee crisis in 2015 and security threats from the Baltic perspective", **Journal of Politics and Law**, Vol. 8, No. 4, 2015, p. 1
[22] Elina Malasenko, Views On Immigration In Latvia. An Exploration of Opinions and Some Possible Causes, (Master Thesis), Holland, Leiden University, 2016, p. 71 and 82.

or living in uncertainty on the borders of Europe, are used as justification for further EU military intervention. Really scary stuff ".[23]

The citizens of the countries concerned are reacting to the opposition of the Baltic states' governments to the mandatory quotas and agree that such a move is not correct. On this issue, Alex Cowles said:

> "We are happy to accept NATO support when we are under threat and to call the EU for extra cash when it is up to our agenda. But when the EU asks us to help in exchange for all the benefits we get, the xenophobic government is doing more than opposing a mandatory quota rather than helping people in need". "About 250 thousand Latvians and indeed many others from the rest of the Baltic countries were once themselves refugees, forced to seek refuge in the Western world by World War II and the second Soviet occupation. Perhaps you are all so blinded by your Soviet-era hangover that you fail to see the irony in this".[24]

However, there is the impression that the political order of the Baltic states fears that the incoming refugees may be an unexpected test that will show the rest of the European Union how xenophobia, nationalism and latent racism actually stand. At the same time, the Russian-speaking minority in Estonia and Latvia, on the contrary, support the idea of hosting refugees, hoping that the emergence of immigrants from Africa and the Middle East in the Baltic States will inevitably bring Latvians, Estonians and Russians closer together. So far, at least in Latvia, there is a point of view that not all Russian-speaking residents are fully integrated into Latvian society. While the Russian-speaking residents of Latvia and even Latvian residents who can speak the Latvian language fluently and have long held Latvian citizenship are often referred to as poorly integrated, this is the main argument in favor of not entering the country of new immigrants.

It is precisely these categories of citizens and non-citizens that allow Latvia and Estonia to claim that the Baltic states should not participate in receiving refugees, as they have yet to cope with the assimilation of their Russian-speaking residents. As a result, when the President of the European Commission Jean-Claude Juncker made a proposal for the co-housing of refugees from Africa and the Middle East, [25] the Latvian Prime Minister Laimdota Straujuma had announced that Latvia's decision not to support the

---

[23] "Why Is Latvia Whining About Refugees?", https://lifeinriga.com/why-is-latvia-whining-about-refugees/, (Accessed on: 12.10.2020).

[24] Ibid.

[25] Jean-Claude Juncker, "State of the Union 2015: Time for Honesty, Unity and Solidarity", https://ec.europa.eu/commission/presscorner/detail/en/SPEECH_15_5614, (Accessed on: 10.10.2020).

introduction of refugee quotas in the EU.[26] Estonia's perspective was also supported by the Estonian Interior Minister Hanno Pevkur who emphasized that Estonia advocates a voluntary approach to the reception of refugees. In fact, he stressed that the country of origin should be dealt with and people should be helped where they have problems. Rather than redistributing people, he stated that this problem should be solved more effectively.[27]

At the same time, there was no mention of massive refugee flows that could drastically change the demographic or ethnic composition of the Baltic population. According to the decision of the European Commission, Estonia should accept only 326 people, and Latvia 220 people.[28] Overall, this is a drop in the ocean among the tens of thousands of refugees the European Union is planning to distribute among its 28 member states. That is, it is not about the actual participation of the Baltic States in solving the EU immigration problem, but a purely symbolic manifestation of pan-European solidarity. However, for the leaders of Latvia and Estonia, even the symbolic steps seemed so unacceptable that some of their representatives called Brussels on the European Union to stop admitting refugees altogether. For example, "the white race is in danger" was written on Facebook by Kristiina Ojuland, Estonian Foreign Minister and a former member of the European Parliament.[29]

On the other hand, the idea of relocating refugees from Africa and the Middle East to the Baltic States has been met with active support from the Russian-speaking community. Russian-speaking residents truly believe that the emergence of representatives of other cultures and religions will show Europe the true face of the Latvian and Estonian national elite, which is tolerant of words and strives for multiculturalism, but actually follows a strict assimilation policy and greatly influences the rights of local residents. In addition, Russian speakers are hoping for Africans and Arabs as a new starting point, so that Latvians will understand how close they and Russians are to each other.[30]

There are also those who believe that the European Union has long been aware of the state's discrimination policy against the Russian-speaking

---

[26] "Majority of Latvian politicians against European Commission's refugee quotas", https://www.baltictimes.com/majority_of_latvian_politicians_against_european_commission_s_refugee_quotas/, (Accessed on: 17.10.2020).
[27] "Minister of Internal Affairs Pevkur explained the Estonian refugee policy at Question Time", https://www.riigikogu.ee/en/press-releases/others/minister-of-internal-affairs-pevkur-explained-the-estonian-refugee-policy-at-question-time/, (Accessed on: 10.10.2020).
[28] "Why Is Latvia Whining About Refugees?", https://lifeinriga.com/why-is-latvia-whining-about-refugees/, (Accessed on: 12.10.2020).
[29] "Former liberal MEP Ojuland calls African refugees 'threat to white race'", https://news.err.ee/115949/former-liberal-mep-ojuland-calls-african-refugees-threat-to-white-race, (Accessed on: 3.10.2020).
[30] Konstantin Ranks, op.cit.

minority in the Baltic countries. However, they condone this, justifying everything with the old grievances of the Soviet era. However, these people also support the idea of resettling refugees because they believe that hidden racism will quickly provoke incoming refugees and complaints to European structures and human rights activists will arise. This will force the Brussels to tackle the Baltic xenophobia problem that Europeans prefer to keep quiet on. If we dig a little deeper, however, it becomes clear that the Russian-speaking community of the Baltic states is no less prone to racism and xenophobia than "native nations" and is also unhappy with the prospect of refugees from distant countries. Thus, if the Estonian and Latvian authorities approach with great care to the feelings and needs of non-Russian-speaking citizens, then the Russian-speaking community will be in solidarity with the titled nations in the fight against the cosmopolitanism of Brussels.[31]

### The Baltic States' harmonization process with the EU acquis

The Baltic States had to give legal and political responses to the increasing transit migration of asylum seekers from the East aiming to reach Western Europe. Moreover, Soviet-era legislation had to be modernized and the EU acquis had to be implemented, as it sought membership in the EU. A refugee policy has emerged as an increasingly important area of cooperation as it deals with broader issues of security and external border control. In 1997, clear requirements were set for states that applied for EU membership, including the Baltic States. It consisted of the adoption of the Geneva Convention and its necessary enforcement mechanism and the Dublin Convention, as well as the adoption of relevant measures in the EU acquis to approximate asylum measures. Lithuania was the first Baltic State to join the international refugee regime. It ratified the Geneva Convention and the New York Protocol on January 21, 1997.[32] This was followed by the adoption of the Lithuanian Refugee Act. Thus, on 27 July 1997, the Convention and the Refugee Law came into force. In 2004, the Law on the Legal Status of Foreigners of the Republic of Lithuania was passed to bring the law in line with EU standards. Lithuanian experts noted that the restrictions adopted in the new Aliens Law were mainly due to the restrictions adopted in Western Europe, such as "safe third country", "safe country of origin" and "clearly baseless claims". However, there was a social difference between the Western countries and the newly independent Baltic States. Therefore, the same restrictions applied may have different consequences.[33]

Estonia became the second country to ratify the Geneva Convention and

---

[31] Ibid.
[32] UNHCR 1997, https://www.unhcr.org/news/press/1997/2/3ae6b81342/unhcr-welcomes-baltic-states-acceding-international-refugee-convention.html, (Accessed on: 10.10.2020).
[33] Egle Macijauskaite, op.cit., p. 18-19.

the New York Protocol on 19 February 1997.[34] The area of asylum was regulated by the Law on International Protection of Foreigners, adopted in 2006, and contained principles derived from both the Geneva Convention and the EU directives. Some amendments were adopted following the European Commissions' comments on limited progress in the area of asylum. However, the call for Estonia to strengthen its administrative capacity to deal with asylum seekers and to define the role of the border police continued.[35]

Asylum seekers enjoyed international assistance and protection offered by the Estonian Illuka Reception Center. Today, there is no program for immigrants. The only document was an Integration Strategy, the first in 2000, the second in 2008 and the third from 2014 to 2010. The aim of the strategies was to highlight the areas of social integration while they considered the social, economic and political context. Currently, state support in the field of education is the most visible. Students who do not speak Estonian are given a language aid to better participate in the education process and deepen the process of integration into society. In addition, special projects are run by the Migration Foundation, but there is still a problem for employers to learn about the legal employment of shelters and asylum seekers.[36]

Latvia was the last of the three countries to join the Geneva Convention and the New York Protocol on 19 June 1997. The road to membership faced initial opposition. Latvian officials explained their reluctance to join the regime due to two arguments: Latvia's attractiveness for asylum seekers and its desire to avoid the risk of becoming a "buffer" zone for those traveling to the West. However, shortly after the ratification of the Geneva Convention, the Asylum Seekers and Refugees Law was adopted in the Republic of Latvia, which regulates all matters relating to asylum seekers and refugees in Latvia.[37]

Despite the initial shortcomings of the newly created asylum regimes, participation in the EU process has encouraged significant advances in refugee protection. The transposition process of the EU asylum acquis has introduced asylum determination systems and basic safeguards based on Western European practice in the jurisdiction of the Baltic States. Finally, on 1 May 2004, all three Baltic States became EU Member States. Moreover, asylum systems are now part of the CEAS (Common European Asylum System). This means that they are at least officially in line with the EU acquis and are constantly improving.[38]

---

[34] UNHCR 1997, op.cit.
[35] Egle Macijauskaite, op.cit., p. 19
[36] Agata Włodarska-Frykowska, "Migration processes in the Baltic States – the dynamic of change", **Eastern Review**, 2017, T. 6, p. 147.
[37] European Parliament 1999, Migration and asylum in Central and Eastern Europe: Lithuania, https://www.europarl.europa.eu/workingpapers/libe/104/lithuania_en.htm, (Accessed on: 10.10.2020).
[38] Egle Macijauskaite, op.cit., p. 20.

**Asylum application procedure and refugee rights in the Baltic countries**

The European Union in 2015 took into consideration the conflict in Syria and the increasing flow of refugees who could not cope with the outbreak of the Middle East alone, thereafter, they decided to help Southern Europe and Turkey. As a result of long disputes (despite some countries, including the Baltic states, being reluctant to admit refugees initially) two programs have been developed:

1. Regarding the movement of refugees to other EU countries who have already entered the EU via Italy or Greece.

2. Refugees from Turkey about the placement of the EU.

Under these programs, Lithuania pledged to accept 1077 people, Latvia - 776 people and Estonia - 550 people. Both programs were launched in 2015, extended several times and ended in October 2019. During this period, Lithuania received 490 people, Latvia - 374 people and Estonia - 213 people. Most of the refugees who came to the Baltic countries were citizens of Syria, Eritrea and Iraq. At the same time, some of them had already been in the Baltic countries and took asylum then migrated to other EU countries, for example Germany or France. Thus, 350 people left Lithuania and 89 people left Estonia. The number of refugees who left Latvia is unknown.[39]

In each of the three countries, the decision to grant asylum is made by the Office of Migration in accordance with the rules of the Geneva Convention on the Status of Refugees. According to the Geneva Convention, the Baltic States are obliged to provide protection to immigrants who have left their states due to war. The types of asylum are different, usually there are three that are distinguished from each other. The first is the refugee status, which allows for permanent resident status, and the second is secondary protection, which is usually granted for two years, after which it can be extended. The third is temporary protection, this form can be given in case of mass influx of newcomers.[40] According to the convention, a refugee is a person who fled his/her country because of "justified fear of being persecuted on the basis of race, religion, nationality, membership of a particular social group or political opinion". The asylum procedure is almost the same in all three countries. Initially, incoming refugees are housed in temporary detention centers for

[39] Yana Leshkovish, Daniil Krivko, Maria Epifanova, "Bezhency v stranah Baltii: cifry i fakty", http://novayagazeta.ee/articles/28617, (Accessed on: 12.09.2020). Also see: https://www.pmlp.gov lv/en/home/services/asylum-seeking/the-procedure-of-granting-asylum.html, "Integration of refugees in Lithuania Participation and Empowerment, Understanding Integration in Lithuania through an age, gender and diversity based participatory approach", October – November 2013, UNHCR 2014.
[40] Agata Włodarska-Frykowska, op.cit., p. 150.

several months. During this time, the police and border guards check the refugee's information: they identify the person, check the path he/she came from, and evaluate the risks of leaving his/her country. If a person has enough money, he/she can live outside the center during the examination of documents with the permission of the police.[41]

The documents are then transferred to the Immigration Agency, which decides whether applicant(s) are qualified for asylum. In all three countries, one asylum-seeker can receive the following from a state:

- a place in an interim center of detention

- required clothing and medical care

- food

- translation services

They are also entitled to monthly benefits which vary based on the country. In Estonia, the monthly benefits include 130 Euros per month for an adult or child and 104 Euros for each subsequent adult family member. In Latvia, the monthly allowance per adult or child is 90 Euros. In Lithuania, it is 85 euros a month for an adult or a child, plus a one-time allowance of 244 euros for an adult, 122 euros for a child, and 1342 euros for an unaccompanied child. The decision to grant asylum is made within 6 months. In the case of rejection, the applicant has the right to appeal.[42]

If the applicant is approved, he/she receives official refugee status. Each country has developed its own refugee support programs. With the shelter, a person receives a work permit, the opportunity to attend free language courses and cash benefits. Refugees in Lithuania receive 244 Euros per person for 6 months. In Latvia, the allowance is 139 Euros per adult and 97 Euros per child. They can get this money within 10 months. In addition, there is a one-off payment immediately following the granting of refugee status - 278 Euros for an adult and 194 Euros for a child. Estonia does not provide special assistance to refugees. However, a person who has taken asylum in Estonia has the right to claim the same benefits from the state as a resident in Estonia: unemployment benefits, family benefits, social benefits and state pension. By granting asylum and paying social benefits, the state actually fulfills part of its duty as finding jobs and further integration is already the refugee's task. In each of the three countries, there are a number of non-profit and voluntary organizations that assist refugees, for example, they offer legal advice, additional language courses, assistance with employment or

---

[41] Yana Leshkovish, Daniil Krivko, Maria Epifanova, op.cit.
[42] Ibid.

housing.[43]

### Views on refugees

According to the European Commission's plan for the distribution of refugees, the Baltic states have to accept a certain number of asylum seekers in the EU. At the end of May, Brussels presented a plan providing a quota system for the distribution of asylum seekers in Europe between EU countries. First of all, residents of African countries who find themselves illegally in the territory of the European Union are addressed. Under this plan, five EU countries - France, Germany, Sweden, Italy and Hungary - should receive 75 percent of all asylum seekers. According to the proposal of the European Commission, the 23 countries of the European Union, based on the quota system, will host 40,000 migrants within two years, most of them in Italy and Greece. Moreover, Brussels insists on accepting another 20,000 refugees from countries affected by the conflict of the community countries.[44] Vilnius, Riga and Tallinn find it difficult to accept the number of refugees mentioned by the European Union. Although Lithuanians, Latvians and Estonians understand the need to show solidarity, the quota system worries them.

According to the Brussels plan, Latvia will have to accept 737 refugees, most of them from Syria and Eritrea.[45] According to official data, 1,531 people have applied for asylum in the country since 1998 while 65 applicants received refugee status and 127 persons received temporary status. Ilmar Mezs, a Latvian demographer and expert on immigration issues, explained the reasons for refusing to accept refugees as follows:

"Latvia has been isolated from the rest of the world for generations, and until the 90s, the inhabitants of another continent were something unprecedented and strange for most Latvians. Moreover, the refugee candidates will come from countries we know almost nothing (Syria and Eritrea). Most of us cannot sympathize with the pain these people suffer because we really do not know about it. I think if the top 500 refugees come from closer and more understandable countries, Ukraine for example, people will have a more sympathetic attitude. In this case, the attitude will be more positive. In addition, negative information about refugees is dominant in the Latvian media, and there

[43] Ibid.
[44] "COM (2015) 286 final, Proposal for a Council Decision establishing provisional measures in the area of international protection for the benefit of Italy and Greece," European Commission, May 27, 2015, https://eur-lex.europa.eu/resource.html?uri=cellar:7a15efe3-053d-11e5-8817-01aa75ed71a1.0001.02/DOC_1&format=PDF, (Accessed on: 2.10.2020).
[45] Dalia Grybauskaite calls European Commission's refugee quota "discriminatory", **The Baltic Times**, https://www.baltictimes.com/dalia_grybauskaite_calls_european_commission_s_refugee_quota__discriminatory_/, (Accessed on: 2.10.2020).

is almost no positive information. I think after the first hundred refugees arrive, Latvians will make sure they are organized and they will think positively".[46]

In the public domain, refugees are usually compared with Soviet-era immigrants. Sovietization has an indirect effect on the Latvian society's reception of asylum seekers. In this regard, Ilmar Merzs said:

"In the Soviet era, all forms of immigration were very negative - both mass migration to Latvia and the deportation of Latvia to Siberia. Therefore, all types of migration still have a negative rating. In addition, Latvia has not been able to solve the integration of immigrants in the Soviet era and the solution of this problem will take a lot of time. Also, there is still no mechanism for the adaptation of migrants and refugees in Latvia. Therefore, it is difficult to be optimistic that the new immigrant volume integration process will be implemented with much better results this time around. On the other hand, the number of immigrants in the USSR era is not seen as an argument as to why the Latvian quota will be smaller. Because there are no employment and income differences between Latvians and Soviet-era immigrants, they are economically well integrated".[47]

To Lithuania, another Baltic republic, Brussels has offered to accept 710 refugees, mostly from Syria. Lithuanian Prime Minister Algirdas Butkevicius stated that Lithuania is ready to accept only 30 to 40 refugees, not as much as the European Commission suggests.[48] According to the data of the Immigration Department, 17 people were given refugee status and 69 people were given secondary protection in 2015.[49] Andrzej Pukšto, head of the Department of Political Science at Vytautas University, told DW that *"Lithuania has not had any major problems with immigrants so far, negative statements from politicians likely mean they are trying to show to Brussels that more money is needed to accommodate refugees in the country"*.[50] That is, a selection of the conservative society in the country is not psychologically prepared for the emergence of a multitude of immigrants.

The European Commission has offered Estonia to admit 1064 refugees.[51]

---

[46] Elina Malasenko, op.cit., p. 109.
[47] Ibid, p. 110.
[48] "Prime minister says Lithuania could accept only up to 40 refugees", https://lithuaniatribune. com/prime-minister-says-lithuania-could-accept-only-up-to-40-refugees/, (Accessed on: 2.10.2020).
[49] Statistical data extracted from UNHCR statistical reports made available by the Ministry of Interior of Lithuania in 2015 and the UNHCR Population Statistics, Database, available at http://popstats.unhcr.org.
[50] "Strany Baltii: kvoty ES po bezhencam - povod dlja trevogi?", https://www.dw.com/ru, (12.10.2020).
[51] "European Commission proposes Estonia to adopt 1,064 refugees, ministers oppose the quota", https://news.err.ee/115932/european-commission-proposes-estonia-to-adopt-1-064-refugees-ministers-oppose-the-quota, (Accessed on: 12.10.2020).

Although Estonians understand the need for solidarity with Europe, they believe it is too much for their country. Between 1997 and 2019, Estonia granted 280 refugee status and 251 subsidiary protection. In these 20 years, most refugees in Estonia are from Syria (192), Ukraine (93), Iraq (41) and Russia (40).[52] According to Estonian Political Scientist Leonid Karabeshkin, there is a strong belief in Estonian society that the flow of refugees will continue. Everyone shares such concerns among Estonian politicians. Karabeshkin believes that it is recommended not to talk about integration in the immigrants, rather than the harmonization of life in Estonia. *"The unemployment benefit is about 125 Euro, which covers only modest food costs. In some regions, actual unemployment is high and more than 100,000 work abroad. It is doubtful that refugees will enjoy low-wage jobs with difficult working conditions"*.[53]

Kristina Kallas, a board member of the Estonian Refugee Council, warned that large numbers of immigrants could lead to increased tensions in the country and a social explosion with large numbers of immigrants. However, according to the interlocutors, some of the refugees will prefer to leave because of the difficulties of adaptation and low wages compared to the richer European countries.[54] According to Kristina Kallas,

"Refugees who come to Estonia, after applying for refugee status, pass to Finland and Sweden, where they already have their communities. It is true that Estonia will remain as a transit point. Persons who legally obtain refugee status in Estonia only have the right to work in Estonia. Actually, this is a wrong practice. Therefore, employment and employment opportunities are limited in other EU countries. If they are to place refugees from one part of Europe to another, they should be given the opportunity to look for work where this job is. That is, they should not be forced to live in countries where they cannot find a new place. Most refugees are generally low skilled workers. Although there are doctors and professors among them, many of them have low qualifications. They will occupy a niche in the labor market with very low wages in Estonia; minimum wage, hard work, etc. For this reason, most refugees will have a very difficult time in Estonia. Therefore, a significant number of refugees - they think they cannot live in Estonia, go on their way".[55] This situation is also valid for the other 2 countries.

---

[52] "Bezhency v Jestonii", https://www.pagulasabi.ee/ru/bezhency-v-estonii, (Accessed on: 8.10.2020).
[53] "Strany Baltii: kvoty ES po bezhencam - povod dlja trevogi?".
[34] Ibid.
[55] "Kristina Kallas: nel'zja zastavljat' bezhencev zhit' v Jestonii, esli oni ne smogut najti zdes' rabotu", https://rus.err.ee/212058/kristina-kallas-nelzja-zastavljat-bezhencev-zhit-v-jestonii-esli-oni-ne-smogut-najti-zdes-rabotu, (Accessed on: 5.10.2020).

## Conclusion

Developments in recent years - the conflict between Russia and Ukraine, and the economic and political instability of Greece - have disturbed Europe's peace. However, previous crises have not challenged the sovereignty, solidarity and responsibility of the EU's member states as much as the refugee influx crisis in 2015. The EU fails to share its responsibility to protect people fleeing their homes in search of safety. In other words, it cannot agree on a fair and predictable system to protect people who are forced to leave everything behind because of violence and persecution. The European Commission has designed a quota system to distribute refugees among member states through the use of criteria which includes population size, GDP, unemployment rates and the number of asylum applications received in the past. The mandatory quota proposal strained relations between western, eastern and central European member states, especially since some countries faced a disproportionate burden. Western European states such as Germany accepted large numbers of refugees, Eastern European states avoided sharing the burden. The current refugee crisis has shown that the EU has no control over its external border. It has not been able to fulfill the obligations of some EU member states, right or not. It has made it clear that it tends to protect its own interests. Rather than focusing on joint efforts to strengthen Schengen beyond borders, member states have focused on reestablishing internal border controls.

Among the EU countries, the countries that refugees want to reach the most are Germany, France and Spain. However, the Baltic countries that are the least preferred by the refugees are the countries with the lowest asylum demand and the lowest number of refugees in the EU. According to UNHCR, this is a result of governments' strict migration policy and lack of alternative strategies for the reception of refugees. Asylum claims are restrictive but very competent. Since the Baltic states associate their security with the EU and NATO, they think that they should not oppose the EU immigration quotas so that the countries are not isolated from the international community, the EU subsidies do not decrease, the NATO security network is not lost, and Russia is not exposed to security threats. Not accepting these quotas means "an existential security threat" for the countries concerned.

The Russians, a large minority group in the Baltic states, did not integrate with the rest of the society in the respective countries after independence. This has been a major political and social problem. Nationalist circles, especially in Estonia and Latvia, claim that there are "immigrants" left in their countries since the collapse of the USSR and put forward this as an evidence against quotas. Government coalitions in Latvia and Estonia include nationalist groups that fear an influx of refugees. Given the unfavorable demographic trends and high levels of immigration from the Baltic countries, it makes it difficult to make political decisions on the refugee issue.

On the other hand, the countries concerned do not have sufficient financial resources to support vulnerable groups among permanent residents in their territories. In addition, the uncertain economic situation regarding the resolution of the refugee crisis is one of the reasons why public opinion in the Baltic States often tends to oppose EU-wide refugee quotas. However, the Baltic States lack the experience and "best practices" of integrating the ethnic groups that dominate the current refugee flows in Europe, such as Syrians, Afghans, Albanians and Iraqis. This raises the corresponding concern that they may not be successful in integrating "new" immigrants into their society. The Baltic States' previous unsuccessful experience of integrating "old" immigrants from the Soviet era is highly discouraged. Finally, the pressure of asylum seekers on the Baltic States has been relatively modest in the past, compared to other EU member states, particularly Estonia's Scandinavian neighbors or Germany, Hungary and Austria. This may be the reason why there is hardly any public debate regarding national refugee policy in Baltic societies.

# CHAPTER 9

## A HISTORICAL AND CONTEMPORARY ANALYSIS OF THE BRITISH IMMIGRATION POLICIES AND THEIR IMPLICATIONS FOR SETTLEMENT AND INTEGRATION: THE CASE OF TURKISH IMMIGRANTS IN THE UNITED KINGDOM

Serkan Baykuşoglu [*]

### Introduction

It is generally argued that not all members of the society are being treated equally in the UK because some people face various barriers in accessing vital public services and lack opportunities. Although there are many people having such disadvantages, some migrants, refugees, and asylum seekers are being left further behind because they face certain barriers, and they do not benefit from equal opportunities in the society. This study has focused on the experience of Turkish Immigrants, who are a diverse group whose members have experienced a range of problems and inequalities due to their immigration status and complex and tough immigration policies, over the last five decades. However, not much is known about Turkish immigrants and their immigration patterns[1], and thus equally little is known about their integration into the British society and their contribution to social, economic and political life.

This small-scale research study is based on the relevant literature review, research reports, national and international statistics, and my professional working experience as an Immigration caseworker. It includes the latest findings and the outcome of the previous academic studies from 1970s onwards.

[*] Serkan Baykusoglu, BA, CertEd (PCET), BA (Hons), PgCert, CELTA, MA, PgCert, PgCert (TEL), MA (Ed), Researcher, University of Eastern Finland, Finland; former Immigration Caseworker.
[1] Pinar Enneli, Tariq Modood, Harriett Bradley, **Young Turks and Kurds. A set of 'invisible' disadvantaged groups,** York: Joseph Rountree Foundation, 2005. Aydin Mehmet Ali, "Why are we wasted?", **Multi-Ethnic Education Review**, Vol. 4, No. 1, 1985, pp. 7-12. Mark Thomson, **Immigration to the UK: the case of Turks,** Brighton: Sussex Centre for Migration Research, 2006. http://www.eliamep.gr/eliamep/content/Folder.aspx?d=11&rd=5565300&f=1368&Rf =2036318440 &m=1&rm=0&l=1 (Access 07.07.2020).

## Background of the Turkish community in the UK

This is an extensive overview of when, how and why the Turkish Community came to the UK. Three different groups with varying connections, such as national, religious, ethnic and linguistic make up the Turkish community; It is a very diverse community comprising Turkish Cypriots, Turks from mainland Turkey and Kurdish people[2]. There is a broad term used to define them: "Turkish Speakers". They came from different historical and social backgrounds, for different reasons and migrated to the UK at different periods. Turkish Cypriots were the first settlers arriving in the 1930s. However, their actual migration to the UK began at the end of the World War II, mainly as a result of the conflict in Cyprus in the 1950s. The migration of Cypriots to Britain could be considered as part of the widespread influx of immigration from the New Commonwealth countries to Britain that happened during the post-war period[3]. Cyprus was a British colony from 1878 until 1960, and thus the British influence made the UK their main destination country. The labour recruitment policy of the British government also encouraged them to migrate in the 1960s[4]. This was mainly an economic migration due to the withdrawal of British forces and thus the loss of jobs with high income linked to the British colonial presence in Cyprus. Therefore, this was also seen as a good opportunity to "make good money"[5] in Britain. This was followed by further migration which took place during the 1970s and 1980s following the political separation of the Northern Cyprus from the island in 1974. Cyprus was a former British Colony with historical relationship, and so the Turkish Cypriots' first destination country.

Turkish people-from mainland Turkey began to migrate in the late 1960s and early 1970s. They were "single men *who were joined by their wives and children later in the decade*"[6]. They were skilled workers who came to work in the textile industry. The majority of Turkish (except Turkish Cypriots) and Kurdish people settled under asylum and refugee status. The term 'asylum seeker' is used for those who have applied for asylum and are waiting for a decision on their applications as well as those whose applications are refused. This term is also used for those whose asylum applications are refused but they have

---

[2] Inge R. Strüder, Do concepts of ethnic economies explain existing minority enterprises? The Turkish speaking economies in London, London School of Economics, 2003.

[3] Robin Oakley, "Family, kinship and patronage: The Cypriot Migration to Britain", V. S. Khan (Eds.), **Studies in Ethnicity: Minority Famzlzes In Brztazn. Support and Stress**, London: Macmillan Press, 1979, pp. 13-34.

[4] Mehmet Ali, op.cit

[5] Sarah Ladbury, "The Turkish Cypriots: Ethnic Relations in London and Cyprus", **Between Two Cultures: Migrants and Minorities in Britain**, J.L. Watson (ed.), Oxford, Basil Blackwell, 1977, pp. 301-331.

[6] Russell King, Mark Thomson, Nicola Mai, Yilmaz Keles, "Turks' in London Shades of Invisibility and the Shifting Relevance of Policy in the Migration Process", **Sussex Centre for Migration Research**, Working Paper No. 51, 2008. http://www.sussex.ac.uk/migration/documents/mwp51.pdf

appealed in the court. The term 'refugee' is used for those who applied for asylum and their applications have been approved, and thus they have been recognised as refugee. It also includes those who have been granted exceptional leave to remain in the terms humanitarian protection or indefinite leave to remain.

The other main reasons for migrating to the UK were political and economic. The military coup in Turkey in 1980 led other Turkish people to flee and apply for asylum in the UK. According to the Organisation for Economic Co-operation and Development (OECD) data, 2,045 Turkish asylum seekers entered UK in 1994, and this figure increased to 3,990 in 2000 and then reduced by around 15% to 1,760 in 2003. In total, 23,880 Turkish people applied for Asylum during this 10-year period (Table 1). Another report published in 2008 shows trends in immigration of Turkish people (including all groups; Turkish Cypriots, Turks, and Kurds from mainland Turkey) for over 60 years from 1945 to 2005. This phase of immigration reached to its peak in 1975s for Turks from Cyprus and Turkey. Turkish Kurdish peoples' migration goes back to the 1980s and continued until 1990s due to security issues and instability in South East Turkey, but the phase of immigration for Kurds from Turkey reached its peak in 2005 and stayed steady until 2010[7]. The Refugee Council report in 2002 and Home Office report in 2007 also show there was an increase in asylum applications from Turkey and its neighbouring countries since 1985.

## Population

The number of Turkish pupils in the UK fluctuates according to the various resources. It is estimated that the current population of Turkish immigrants is around 150,000. This figure comes from an official source, the General Consulate for Turkey in London declaring that estimated number of Turkish nationals living in the UK (students, au pairs, illegal immigrants included) is around 150,000. According to the Home Office, "there are approximately 150,000 Turkish nationals in the UK at present, of a total of about 500,000 people of Turkish origin in the UK, including Cypriot Turks (about 300,000) and Turks with Bulgarian or Romanian citizenship"[8].

This figure is disputed by different sources as about 200,000[9], 51,000

---

[7] Tozun Issa, Kimberley Allen, and Alistair Ross, Young People's Educational Attainment in London's Turkish, Turkish Kurdish and Turkish Cypriot Communities: A report for the Mayor of London's Office, Institute of Policy Studies in Education, London Metropolitan University, 2008.

[8] Implications for the Justice and Home Affairs area of the accession of Turkey to the European Union, House of Commons Home Affairs Committee, Tenth Report of Session, 2010-12, 2011, p. 38.

[9] Asu Aksoy, "Some 'Muslims' Within: Watching Television in Britain After September 11", MunshiShoma, Peter VanDer Veer, Media, **War and Terrorism: Responses from the Middle East and Asia**, Routledge: London and New York, 2004.

(foreign-born and without UK nationality)[10], 60-90,000 (only the Turkish Cypriots and British citizens of Turkish Cypriot origin[11], 80-120,000 Turks and Kurds, and about the same number of Turkish Cypriots[12],40,000 in the mid-1970s (only the Turkish Cypriot community)[13], 120,000 (only the Turkish Cypriots-Cyprus-born plus second and third generations)[14], and over 400,000 in total. An annual report[15] shows that 2,011 Turks were settled in Britain in 1973 and the figure raised to 79,000 in 2003.

The 2001 UK Census[16] showed that almost 60,000 Turkish-born people were resident, although the total number of Turks including those born in Cyprus and those born in the UK with Turkish roots is unknown. The same census included the proportion of Turkish groups born outside UK (varied from 58% to 85.5%); population numbers by country of birth (total of 92,021); age group by country of birth (over 65% is aged 25 and over); population by gender & ethnic group (between 50.2% and 54.3% is male and between 45.7% and 49.8% is female); population by gender & country of birth (51.7% male and 48.3% female); and age group by ethnic group (majority is adults including young adults over 16 with around 75%).

According to another research the estimated number of Turkish people living in the UK was between 180,000 and 250,000[17]. This figure is disputed with different sources showing over 400,000. The Annual Report of the Turkish Ministry of Employment and Social Security shows that there were 70,000 Turkish people living in Britain in 2003, increasing from 2,011 in 1973. According to the Turkish Studies Centre (StiftungZentrum fur Turkeistudien) in Essen, there were 70,000 Turkish people living in Britain in 2002[18].

The latest annual population survey in 2010 shows UK residents by country of birth. This data gives a very close figure, 72,000[19], to the above statistics.

The following figures also give similar numbers to above statistics

[10] John Salt, International Migration and the United Kingdom: Report of the United Kingdom SOPEMI Correspondent to the OECD 2004, London: UCL Migration Research Unit, 2004.
[11] Gilles Bertrand, "Cypriots in Britain: Diaspora(s) Committed to Peace?", **Turkish Studies**, Vol. 5, No. 2, 2004, pp. 93-110.
[12] Y. Cicek, TSBCS. **Turkish speaking business counselling service**, Presentation at the EQUAL meeting in Bremen, 6.-8.4.2003.
[13] Ladbury, op.cit.
[14] Enneli et.al., op.cit
[15] **SOPEMI,** Beauftragte der Bundesregierung fur die Belange der Auslander (Federal Government's Office for Foreigners), 1995.
[16] **Office for National Statistics,** 2001 Census: Special Migration Statistics (United Kingdom)
[17] Ibrahim Sirkeci, Neli Esipova, "Turkish migration in Europe and desire to migrate to and from Turkey", **Border Crossing**, Vol. 1, 2013, pp. 1-13.
[18] **Eurostat**, Federal Office of Statistics & Centre for Studies on Turkey, Essen 2002
[19] **UK Data Archive**, Annual Population Survey, 2010, Economic and Social Data Service

showing number of Turkish nationals in main European countries. According to the OECD[20] report in 2004, while there were 31,000 Turkish nationals in the UK in 1993, this number almost doubled, nine years later in 2002, making 52,000 and 67,000 respectively in 2003. However, according to the Turkish Ministry of Employment and Social Security report in 2003, there were 63,220 with either Turkish Nationality or dual nationality in Great Britain. The total presence of Turkish nationals in Great Britain was given as 52,000 and 100,000[21]. It is therefore claimed that "The UK is one of the least popular destinations among Turkish migrants. Half of the Turkish migrants in the UK originate from Cyprus, so there is a colonial Cypriot link. Some of them have mixed marriages, Greek-Turkish, so it is very difficult to categorise. Maybe as much as half of the people in the UK in the Turkish group are actually Cypriots"[22].

## Geographical distribution of the Turkish Community

Turkish speaking people are not spread out throughout the UK, but they are mostly in London where over 80% of them live; they became resident in specific North London boroughs (Hackney, Haringey, Enfield, Waltham Forest and Islington) and in South London (Southwark and Lewisham) turning into an invisible community within the majority white population of Londoners[23.] The first settlers of the Turkish community, Turkish Cypriots, initially settled slightly to the east of London areas, namely Camden and Islington[24]. They also located south of London. This trend later changed for second and third generations, *"as they have been able to afford better housing conditions"*[25] towards the north, the Haringey axis to Enfield, and to Croydon in the south. They were successful in establishing themselves in their new urban location[26]. A short survey published in 1981 described Turkish Cypriots as *"an already well-adjusted community"* and *"on the whole, there is a success story"*[27].

According to the latest data, Turkish communities are found in ten areas in London. The largest number lives in Tower Hamlets and the smallest in

[20] Trends in International Migration, OECD, SOPeMI, 2004.
[21] **The Turkish Ministry of Employment and Social Security**, General Directorate of Services for the Workers Abroad Publications, 2003, Year 3, Volume 4), Reports, Ankara, (2003, 2004)
[22] House of Commons Home Affairs Committee, op.cit, p. 38.
[23] Centre of Expertise on Ethnic Minority Businesses, **Turkish Speaking Communities in London**, London, Business Link for London, 1999.
[24] Ladbury, op.cit.
[25] Kevin Robins, Asu Aksoy, "From Spaces of Identity to Mental Spaces: Lessons from Turkish Cypriot Cultural Experience in Britain", **Journal of Ethnic and Migration Studies**, Vol. 27, No. 4, 2001, p. 690, pp. 685-712.
[26] Salahi R. Sonyel, The Silent Minority: Turkish Muslim Children in British Schools, Cambridge: The Islamic Academy, 1988.
[27] F.M. Bhatti, "Turkish Cypriots in Britain, Research Papers", **Muslims in Europe**, Vol. 11, London: Centre for the Study of Islam and Christian-Muslim Relations, p. 1 & p. 19, 1981.

Camden (Table 2). Greater London was the popular city for the community and thus became the main area for settlement. Turks living in London had 15th place among 20 nationals by country of birth in 2001 (Table 3).

### British immigration policies from 1970s to 2020s

Britain has been a country of net emigration until the 1990s. Since then, there has been increasing net immigration to Britain. 'British citizen' label was once referred to a wide range of people from the mainland UK to the colonies, but the changing political atmosphere brought a need to restrict this definition and added further exclusivity to the right to residence in the United Kingdom. Whilst Commonwealth rights decreased, rights of entry for citizens from the European Community –now the European Union – increased after Britain's entry into the EC in 1973.

Prior to the 1993 Act, asylum seekers had access to local authority housing, were able to claim cash benefits and were occasionally permitted to work. From the implementation of the 1993 Act, it is clear that the main aim was to reduce the number of asylum seekers settling through restriction of their rights in accessing state benefits rather than implementing effective and fair immigration policy. This Act removed the right to access permanent local authority housing for asylum seekers, so social housing became inadequate[28]. In 2012, the local authorities' responsibilities for housing asylum seekers were abolished, and new contracts to provide asylum seekers housing were awarded to private contractors by the Conservative and Liberal Democratic coalition government. The benefit entitlement for asylum seekers was limited to 90% of the standard rate given to British citizens. The following 1996 Immigration Act further reduced this benefit to 70%, and the responsibility for supporting asylum seekers was transferred to local authorities. A sudden fall in the number of asylum applications was witnessed in 1996 following these restrictions on rights declared in these two immigration acts. This fall therefore was in response to what is called as the emergence of the *"restrictionist regime"[29]*.

British immigration policy has moved from 'zero immigration' in the 1970s and 1980s to 'managed migration' as claimed under New Labour government from 1997–2010, the pace of migration increased to a level beyond historical pattern. In fact, between 2001 and 2018 the foreign-born population doubled from 4.6 million to more than nine million in Britain. The main reason for this huge expansion in migration is that under the

---

[20] Peter Dwyer, David Brown, "Accommodating 'others'?: housing dispersed, forced migrants in the UK", **Journal of Social Welfare & Family Law**, Vol. 30, No. 3, 2008, pp. 203 218.

[29] Roger Zetter, Pearl Martyn, "The minority within the minority: refugee community-based organizations in the UK and the impact of restrictionism on asylum-seekers", **Journal of Ethnic and Migration Studies**, Vol. 26, No. 4, 2000, pp. 675-697.

Labour Government of 1997-2010 immigration controls were eased immensely. In 2004, when the EU was expanded to include seven nations from the Eastern Block including Hungary, Poland and Czech Republic (now Chechia), the UK put no temporary restrictions on entering UK from these new member states. The Labour government argued that the economy was growing so a larger labour force was needed. It was predicted by the labour government that EU enlargement would increase net immigration to UK up to 13,000 people a year. However, more than a million people from these countries arrived and settled during the next 10 years until and even after the government changed. This was one of the biggest arrivals in British immigration history.

Over that period, net foreign migration totalled 3.6 million. This was the result of intentional policy changes rather than changing patterns of migration or globalisation. The massive increase in the level of migration after 1997 is totally unprecedented in the country's immigration history, shadowing the size of anything that used to be[30]. This policy then changed to 'good immigration, not mass immigration' with the creation of an 'unreceptive environment' for 'unwanted immigrants' under the Conservative – Liberal Democrat Coalition government 2010–15 and finally Conservative government after 2015. Opinion polling data which has always been exaggerated by the media highlighted immigration as one of the top three most important issues facing the country, and thus anxieties were rising in the society. As a response, a points-based system for migration has been implemented to convince the public that immigration is under control to meet labour market needs.

### Gaps in evidence for implications of British immigration policies

There are number of major gaps in the evidence for implications of the immigration policies on asylum seekers and refugees in Britain; these arise mainly from lack of or poor data collections systems or lack of central data reporting system. The official data which are collected clearly indicate the urgent needs of government in controlling asylum seekers through the various tracking and administrative processes. The data being collected provide information on applicants' identity, asylum decisions, court appeal outcomes, deportation and removals, but very limited comprehensive data on important areas such as work conditions for those who are given the right to work, education, academic or vocational training, and health status of asylum seekers and refugees. Once asylum seekers are given settled status, though they are recognised as refugees, they are classified as ordinary residents in the country, and they are under no further obligation to declare

---

[30] **Immigration under Labour**, Migration Watch UK, Briefing Paper 11.36, 2015.

their refugee status. Therefore, almost all knowledge and information about the circumstances of asylum seekers and refugees are based on limited research findings, limited and incomplete data. They are largely invisible in central administrative data collection systems as well as in the society; and while it could be claimed that refugees and asylum seekers are among the most socially and emotionally disadvantaged members of society in the UK today, there is little empirical evidence to confirm this. In addition, there are large numbers of migrants who enter the country illegally who do not formally undergo the asylum-seeking process. They are not officially known by the state and the government's estimations are no more than indicative. One of the outcomes of these disparities and exclusions is that it is impossible to provide the actual number of migrants including these non-asylum seekers and those whose claims have failed but who disappeared from administrative systems prior to removal as well as asylum seekers who were granted refugee status and thus settled in the country at any one time. The UK censuses are decennial – consisting of data from the last ten years rather than population registers. The censuses do not count asylum seekers and refugees. Questions are asked on ethnic group and country of birth but their migrant status is not further taken into account. This means significant data is neither recorded nor evaluated.

The term 'migrant' is defined as those who enter the UK expecting to stay over a year. When those migrants are granted entry with visa on a set of conditions they are classified as regular migrants. Those who evade formal migration control or present false papers to enter are classified as illegal entrants. And those regular migrants who remain despite not being able to regularise their stay by the end of the permitted period become illegal migrants. These included failed asylum seekers who continued to stay in the country despite exhausting even their asylum appeals; overstayers whose permitted residence visa has expired without renewal and have not been given right of appeal due to being illegal as well as children born in the UK to these irregular migrants. It is estimated that there are between 310,000 and 570,000 irregular migrants in the UK as of 2001[31]. Total of irregular migrants changed since then mainly due to losing control on immigration. The number of asylum seekers remaining after refusal appears to have increased further by 220,000 after 2001. In 2007, the government introduced new legislation – case resolution scheme to clear the backlog of asylum decisions through regularisation of their status or otherwise deporting. However, the number of irregular migrants reached to the range of 373,000 – 719,000 by the end of 2007 as estimated[32]. This means that these irregular migrants remained in the

---

[31] Jo Woodbridge, Sizing the unauthorised (illegal) migrant population in the United Kingdom in 2001, Home Office Online Report 29/05, 2005.
[32] Ian Gordon, Kathleen Scanlon, Tony Travers, Christine Whitehead, Economic impact on the London and UK economy of an earned regularisation of irregular migrants to the UK, London: LSE, 2009.

country for at least five years without having heard from the Home Office. They had no access to any benefit and housing. They had no right to work either upon they lost all appeals and became overstayer.

### The impact of British Labour Governments immigration policies on immigrants in UK.

The immigration policies introduced under Tony Blair's Labour government were welcomed by asylum seekers, temporary immigrants such as students and temporary workers. Britain's immigration policy changed from a highly restrictive approach to one of the most expansive in Europe. The government expanded existing worker schemes for low and high-skilled migrant workers; work permit criteria were relaxed; the number of international students was doubled; and finally, citizens of eight countries that were about the join European Union were given the right to work in Britain. These decisions resulted in one of the largest migration flows in the British history.

The labour government was in power between 1997 and 2010. Despite the revisions of the 1996 Immigration Act, by which the government aimed to speed up the asylum decision making process, it was declared that the asylum process was still slow and inefficient. It rejected asylum seekers who remained in the UK for years while their case was heard through appeals, and thus a new Asylum and Immigration Act was introduced in 1999. The new Act included policies to place asylum seekers across the country to prevent any specific region from being overburdened by the cost of supporting asylum seekers. This was aimed at reducing the intensity of asylum seekers in certain cities.

I argue that, as a result, the government lost control on immigration. Asylum cases rose out of control. Asylum rights allowed asylum seekers to enter the UK border without initial assessment or checks on their authenticity. Bogus asylum trafficking increased between UK and Europe. Asylum seekers came from various countries including Middle East countries and Turkey through Europe.

British immigration policies assessed asylum seekers at the point of entry to the country where some nationals were deported while others were not noticed. Thus, asylum seekers' lives were put in danger by forbidding them to work[33]. There is a system of civic stratification which provides newcomers with distinct level of rights. They had various rights on paper but when it came to claiming these rights, not everyone had the same access to them.

---

[33] Don Flynn, An historical note on labour migration policy in the UK Labour Migration and Employment Rights, London: Institute of Employment Rights, 2005.
Lydia Morris, Managing Migration: Civic stratification and migrants' rights, London: Routledge, 2002.

They had certain difficulties in fulfilling some of the conditions to access to such rights.

## The impact of immigration policy on Turkish immigrants

The immigration status of Turkish people includes having a work permit, self-employed/business visa (through Ankara Agreement route), au pair (in 2008, the au pair visa was scrapped and replaced by a tiered immigration system), students, family reunification and asylum seekers.

According to the Home Office records there were 36,569 Turkish nationals applying for asylum in the UK between 1986 and 2005. 5 percent of total applications received in 2000 were from Turkish nationals representing a small share of the total asylum applications to the UK. However, the National Asylum Support Service provided accommodation and/or maintenance support to only 4,750 asylum seekers and their dependents of Turkish nationals in Britain[34].

Turkish nationals have faced difficulties in every aspects of life due to their immigration status and British immigration policies as discussed throughout. Three main areas namely housing, work conditions and legal status were explored here due to nature of this study. None of them has priority or more importance than the others, but they are all linked to each other, and neither are issues that impact Turkish peoples' lives only limited to these areas. However, I argue all relevant issues and problems are connected with poor housing and working conditions and most importantly lack of legal status.

## Housing

Turkish-speaking families are often found to be living in overcrowded conditions. This is partly due to the fact that traditionally, families from Turkey live in extended family groups. They continue to live in the UK much the same way as they lived in Turkey. Recent arrivals also stay with their close relatives until they are provided with their own accommodation. It appears that the children of those families have been adversely affected by overcrowding and unsuitable housing. The children usually shared their rooms with their younger sisters and brothers who disturbed them. Lack of space at home with unsuitable conditions badly affected the children's achievement, as stated by many Turkish parents. This is because *"Turkish*

---

[34] Home Office Asylum Statistics: 4th Quarter 2005 United Kingdom. Surrey: Immigration Statistics and Research Service, **Home Office Research Development and Statistics Directorate**, 2005.
http://webarchive.nationalarchives.gov.uk/20130128103514/http://www.homeoffice.gov.uk/rds/pdfs 06/asylumq405.pdf(Access 18.09.2020).

*families are often not suitably re-housed. Many are housed in temporary accommodation in which they continue to live for two or three years"[35]* such as hostels which offer a single room with other facilities shared. In 2006, widespread complaints were reported regarding the condition of housing and the behaviour of housing staff including inappropriate accommodation for people with disabilities, mixed sex accommodation and other *"problems ranged from poor furnishing, heating and cooking facilities to leaking ceilings, damp, infestation and lack of privacy"[36]*. In 2006 and 2007, 3,170 asylum seekers who were eligible for Home Office's asylum support, could not be provided any support as a result of delays and error in the Home Office's administration of asylum support[37]. The quality of housing became a concern and, in some circumstances, appeared to conflict with the respect for family and home life required by Article 8 of the European Convention of Human Rights (ECHR) and the Human Rights Act (HRA).

## Work conditions

Right to work and access to employment became a major concern for migrant workers who were mostly vulnerable to exploitation because of not having the same economic rights as ordinary citizens workers and lack of awareness of their rights. They were likely to be concentrated in low-wage, low-skill jobs in poorly managed sectors and they found themselves open to discrimination at work.

The public opinion on Turkish immigrants in the UK varies. During the late 1970s and early 1980s, Turkish immigrants were often classified as illegal workers[38]. The majority of early arrivals of Turkish people prior to 1990s worked as labourers in the textile industries. They then established shops with their savings after the industry collapsed and moved out to other developing countries.

Turkish immigrants – mainly asylum seekers experienced problems with unemployment, psychological distress and poverty[39]:

---

[35] Academic Achievement and Entitlement to Free School Meals, National Statistics, 2004. http://www.wales.gov.uk/keypubstatisticsforwales/content/publication/schools-teach/2005/sb15-2005/sb15-2005.pdf(Access on 12.08.2020)

[36] Refugee Media Action Group, **Seeking asylum: a report on the living conditions of asylum seekers in London**, London: Migrants Resource Centre, 2006, p. 4.

[37] **The Treatment of Asylum Seekers. Tenth Report of Session 2006-07**, Joint Committee on Human Rights, Vol. 1, 2007. http://www.publications.parliament.uk/pa/jt200607/jtselect/jtrights/jtrights.htm (Access 10.09.2020).

[38] Nony Ardill, Nigel Cross, **Undocumented lives - Britain's unauthorised migrant workers**, London: Runnymede Trust, 1987. T. Esward, B. Duzgun, "Turks in North East London", **Race Today**, Vol. 15, No. 1, 1983, pp. 13-15.

[39] Bill Jordan, Franck Düvell, **Irregular migration: the dilemmas of transnational mobility**, Cheltenham: Edward Elgar, 2002, p. 136.

*"This was despite the fact that the majority, as asylum seekers, had eventually gained permission to work legally. It seems that, although they had the support of their communities and organisations, their positions in UK society, and in those communities, trapped them in disadvantage, in comparison to their mobile (and, perhaps most important, white European) Poles".*

Turkish migrants who were either temporary or permanent workers with high level of skills worked in the food industry at low wage for long hours. The other sectors included restaurants, grocers, and supermarkets. Their employment and work-related activities are "largely shaped by the structure of ethnic enclave economy and their position in the labour market"[40]. Temporary Turkish migrants who were usually students had the right to work for 20 hours when the Labour government was in power. However, in most cases, they worked over 70 hours a week for 6 days. Their studies were mostly interrupted due to heavy work conditions. Their intention to come to UK for purpose of studying changed in time, so they wanted to find better jobs or establish business to stay permanently. They could not improve their English skills without which it was not possible to enter a profession even with higher academic or vocational skills from their country of origin. According to Migration Advisory Committee[41], 2.1 million foreign-born migrants were in low-skilled occupations regardless of skill level. The other survey records show that 41.1 per cent of Turkish-born immigrants in London worked in elementary employment which includes administrative, sales and basic jobs in 2004 and 2005[42].

Restriction to work on the other hand was the main problem for many asylum seekers. As previously stated, the Labour government lost control on immigration and so could not establish an effective immigration system to allow only real asylum seekers coming to UK, and then to process asylum applications within a reasonable time scale. As a result, the number of asylum seekers increased immensely after 2000. They were allowed to enter UK and asked to wait to be called for asylum interviews. The number increased continuously and even the call for first initial interview took a few years for some asylum seekers. Until 2015, asylum seekers had to wait for 12 months to be granted access to the labour market. After this date, this period was reduced to 9 months. This pushed them into an irregular work life. They

---

[40] Ibrahim Sirkeci, Tuncay Bilecen, Yakup Costu, Saniye Dedeoglu, Mehmet Rauf Kesici, Betul Dilara Seker, Fethiye Tilbe, Kadir Onur Unutulmaz, **Little Turkey in Great Britain**, Transnational Press London, 2016, p.168.

[41] **Annual Report 2014/15**, Migration Advisory Committee, 2014. https://assets.publishing.service.gov.uk/government/uploads/system/uploads/attachment_data/file/480386/mac_annual__report_2014_15.pdf (Access on 03.09.2020).

[42] Lorna Spence, Country of Birth and Labour Market Outcomes in London: An Analysis of Labour Force Survey and Census Data, London: Data Management and Analysis Group, Greater London Authority, 2005.

mostly preferred to work within the Turkish community while waiting for their cases to be assessed in order to avoid losing legal status and thus deportation. Those with professional qualifications lost their skills either their qualifications in the UK were not equivalent to UK degree or they had to wait for too long for their refugee status to be approved.

In the meantime, not everyone was provided appropriate accommodation and mostly placed in temporary places, namely hostels on conditions that there was no permission to leave their accommodation after certain hours at nights. They were not allowed to work at all until their case was being dealt with. They were provided with coupons for food. However, a majority of asylum seekers were economic migrants and had no political or criminal issue within their country of origin which was mainland Turkey in this case for Turkish asylum seekers. Turkish asylum seekers had contacts in UK before arriving and these contacts were either their close family or relatives, and also friends in some cases. They used their contacts to find jobs either in their business or in the ones recommended by them. They worked illegally without right to work for years during the day until they were called to give statement for asylum applications. They had to be back at the hostels where they were accommodated before midnight, otherwise they would risk losing their accommodation which was maintained by the private sector and cost was covered by the government. Those who came as a family were also placed in hostels. Their children suffered from unhealthy hostel accommodation, as the whole family had to stay together in one room with shared bathroom use with other occupants.

## Legal status and rights

It seems to me that the UK governments – mainly the Labour government failed to implement and comply with fully efficient, effective, and fair immigration system. Turkish asylum seekers were highly affected as well as other asylum seekers. The immigration rose out of control: asylum seekers were allowed in without proper checks and records at the borders; in country asylum rights were given to those who had connection in the country; no sufficient accommodation was provided to asylum seekers; no permission to work was given to asylum seekers but they were informally allowed to work; it often took many years for many asylum seekers to hear from the Home Office about their cases. Many established their lives in the UK while their cases were being assessed. In addition, the children born to asylum seeking families were not given any status and were even asked to leave when their parents' cases were turned down. These children started schooling and integrated into the society much better than their parents, but their circumstances were not separately assessed. They were classified as overstayer when their parents became overstayer too. There were cases that a child born to such parents reached the age of 7, but their parents were already overstayer. The legislation allowed the child to remain, but their parents were asked to leave. When it was realised that it was unjustified and the breach of the human rights, the Government changed the law by giving further right to those in this category a new application to regularise their status on the basis that their child had reached that age. Even this new application took years and during all these years asylum seekers were left alone without any support and right to work in most cases. All these have created a hostile environment for the migrants in the UK.

### Invisibility of the Turkish community

The Turkish community became an "invisible population" soon after their first arrivals in the UK[43]. Their presence and significance as a trans-national community in the cultural life of Britain was not acknowledged. There has been very limited study and research about the Turkish community; *"the conditions for their experience are left absent and the historical circumstances of their arrival in Britain are left unaccounted for"*[44]; they have never been counted as "Turkish" in neither surveys nor in census; their diverse needs were not considered; and, for example, *"Turkish Cypriots did not think it appropriate to assert or to make an issue of their cultural presence and difference"*[45]. As census data does not clearly identify and distinguish Turkish speakers, it is difficult to calculate the actual number[46]. It is argued that *"(…) where their 'minority' presence was relatively invisible, Turks did not feel the need to become engaged in identity politics – unlike South Asian and Afro-Caribbean migrants, say, particularly, whose presence was more numerous and symbolic"*[47]. It is also argued that Turkish-speaking communities in the UK are a 'silenced minority' due to the number of racial attacks on them which have not been reported[48]. Another factor contributing to their 'invisibility' is the perception that they are a highly self-sufficient group, for example because many find employment in the 'ethnic economy' in labour-market niches such as coffee-shops and kebab houses[49].

Also discussed is the invisibility of Turkish Cypriots in the other Turkish Communities as well as in the British society. It was claimed that there were various factors for this external and internal invisibility:

---

[43] Andy Teague, "Ethnic Group: First Results from the 1991 Census", **Population Trends**, Summer, 1993, pp. 12-17.

[44] John Solomos, Stephen Woodhams, "The Politics of Cypriot Migration to Britain", **Immigrants and Minorities**, Vol. 14, No. 3, 1995, p. 233, pp. 231-256.

[45] K. Robins, A. Aksoy, op.cit. p. 686.

[46] Talip, Kucukcan, Politics of Ethnicity, Identity and Religion: Turkish Muslims in Britain, Aldershot, Ashgate, 1999.

[47] Aksoy, op.cit. p. 235.

[48] Mehmet Ali, op.cit.

[49] King et al., op.cit, p. 7.

*"First, in the overall context of a multicultural Britain, Turkish Cypriots have been overshadowed by the larger, and far more high-profile, Black and Asian communities. Second, and more particularly, their presence has been somewhat eclipsed by the later and more prominent and demonstrative migrations of Turks and Kurds from 'mainland' Turkey. Third, in the context of these latter migrations from Anatolia, Turkish Cypriots have tended to emphasise what they regard as their own qualities of being both more 'progressive' (that is, more 'European') and also more 'integrated' into the British way of life"[50].*

## Conclusion and recommendations

The UK asylum policy has had great impact on asylum seekers, regular and irregular immigrants, including Turkish and all other nationals. Their rights have declined since the early 1990s. The policies continue to restrict the ability of asylum seekers to integrate in the UK. This study presented here refers mainly to Turkish Asylum seekers but also shows that all other asylum seekers and refugees have experienced a range of distinct problems, restrictions, and inequalities as a result of harsh immigration policies of Britain. Such policies continue to have the greatest impact on the day to day lives of migrants including Turkish migrants in Britain. As a result of complex, tough and constantly changing immigration policies, the arrival of asylum seekers continued; the clearance of the backlog of asylum cases took long years; further illegal migrants entered the country; further migrants overstayed their permission; and the regularisation of previously irregular migrants was delayed.

In the UK, the governments have not looked into the root cause of non regularised immigration. Instead, they attempted to reduce such migration by making life as difficult as possible for those who fall in this category as described throughout in this study. In 2012, for example, the government requested banks, landlords, employers, and public service providers that they refuse to provide services to anyone without evidence of immigration status. The government also asked them to share information about and report non-regularised migrants to the immigration enforcement authorities. This approach to those migrants remains in place and is directly affecting them in large numbers. This tight legislation itself is evidence that the immigration policy has not been structured for achieving smooth settlement and integration of Turkish and other migrants into the British society.

The British immigration policy needs a transformation and improvements in a number of areas for asylum seekers, regularised and non-irregularised immigrants as the UK governments' approach has served to undermine trust in the system for decades. The UK needs a fair, principled and effective

---

[50] K. Robins, A. Aksoy, op.cit. p. 686.

immigration policy. There is a lack of trust in official data and administration which do not account for all nationals. As shown above, some Turkish speaking people have never been counted as "Turkish", and as a result they became invisible. In such circumstances their needs could not be assessed so they were non existent. The Home Office needs to act to reduce errors and to speed up accurate decision making. There should be a much greater focus on early enforcement at the borders for full control of entries to the country.

It could be argued that if someone enters any country without having been permitted or overstaying their visa, they should not expect any support and regularisation of their status at the end. This should be the sole responsibility of that person who put themselves in that situation. However, I argue that it is governments' responsibilities to control their borders; to introduce effective and fair immigration system; to allow only those who are real asylum seekers to enter; to have a good administration system for recording; to provide sufficient accommodation during asylum cases are being dealt with; to provide sufficient financial support for basic needs such as foods and clothing without need to work; to assess asylum cases favourably, efficiently in good time and to allow those whose cases are real to stay on with indefinite leave to remain settlement visa, and remove those who fail immediately. They should also provide free legal aid for all court appeals and free legal aid until all appeal rights including judicial reviews are exhausted. Free education to the children of asylum seekers should be a right while their cases are being assessed. Rules should be simplified and underpinned by clear principles and fair rules including effective management and better decision making, enforcement and control. All immigrants should be treated as the same and allowed open debate in the public for continued improvement in the policy. Better coordination is needed between immigration policy, social services, the labour market and economic policies for the mutual benefits of the UK and all members of the society. Appropriate investment in housing and public services needs to be made. Integration is highly important and should be embedded in immigration policy. In order to achieve all these targets, the government can take first step to regularise irregular immigrants who have been living in the country for years without any rights, and this would be a good sign of tangible forthcoming fair immigration policy.

# Figures

**Figure 1.** Entry of Turkish Asylum-seekers into a Number of OECD Countries

| Country | 1994 | 1995 | 1996 | 1997 | 1998 | 1999 | 2000 | 2001 | 2002 | 2003 |
|---|---|---|---|---|---|---|---|---|---|---|
| Austria | 362 | 509 | 477 | 340 | 210 | 335 | 592 | 1.868 | 3.561 | 2.839 |
| Belgium | 601 | 581 | 713 | 436 | 403 | 518 | 838 | 900 | 970 | 618 |
| France | 1.282 | 1.653 | 1.205 | 1.548 | 1.621 | 2.219 | 3.735 | 5.347 | 6.582 | 6.143 |
| Germany | 19.118 | 33.750 | 31.732 | 25.937 | 11.754 | 9.065 | 8.968 | 10.869 | 9.575 | 6.235 |
| Greece | - | - | - | - | - | 195 | 591 | 800 | 211 | - |
| Norway | 30 | 35 | 24 | 44 | 129 | 279 | 164 | 204 | 257 | 240 |
| Sweden | 305 | 269 | 186 | 208 | 280 | 220 | 229 | 458 | 696 | 733 |
| Sweden | 1.068 | 1.293 | 1.317 | 1.395 | 1.565 | 1.453 | 1.431 | 1.960 | 1.940 | 1.661 |
| Switzerland | 1.068 | 1.293 | 1.317 | 1.395 | 1.565 | 1.453 | 1.431 | 1.960 | 1.940 | 1.661 |
| UK | 2.045 | 1.820 | 1.420 | 1.445 | 2.015 | 2.850 | 3.990 | 3.700 | 2.835 | 1.760 |

(Source: OECD, Trends in International Migration, SOPeMI 2004, complied on the basis of the tables in the appendix; in the case of Greece: country notes).

**Figure 2.** Trends in Immigration between the Turks over 60 Years

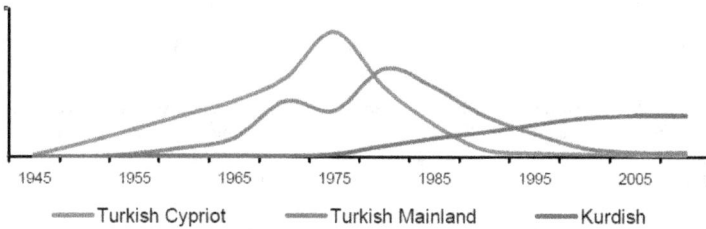

Schematic representation of phases of primary immigration

Source: (Issa et al 2008), Young People's Educational Attainment in London's Turkish, Turkish Kurdish and Turkish Cypriot Communities, A Report for the Mayor of London's Office, London Metropolitan University.

**Figure 3.** The numbers of people from Turkey and its two neighbour countries applied for asylum in the UK between 1985 and 2007. (The figure includes main applicants and excludes any dependents).

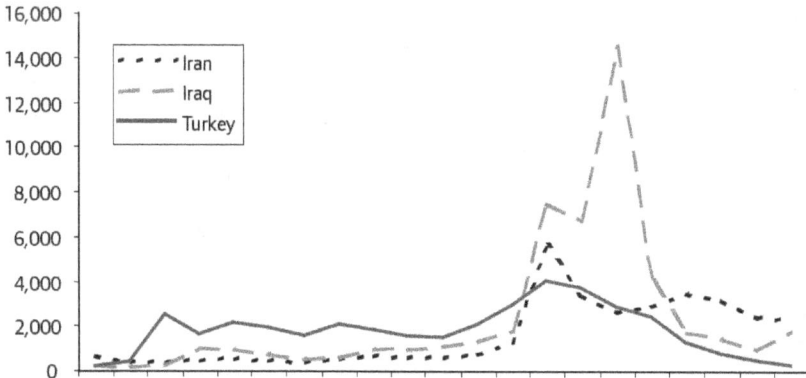

Source: Analysis of numbers of asylum seekers from 1985 to 2000, Refugee Council (February 2002); and Figures for 2001 to 2007, Home Office.

**Figure 4.** Turks in Selected European Countries

| Country | 1973 | 1984 | 1995 | 2003 |
|---|---|---|---|---|
| Germany | 615.827 | 1.552.328 | 1.965.577 | 2.053.600 |
| France | 33.892 | 144.790 | 254.000 | 311.356 |
| Netherlands | 30.091 | 154.201 | 252.450 | 299.909 |
| Austria | 30.527 | 75.000 | 150.000 | 134.229 |
| Belgium | 14.029 | 63.587 | 90.425 | 70.701 |
| Denmark | 6.250 | 17.240 | 34.700 | 35.232 |
| Britain | 2.011 | 28.480 | 65.000 | 79.000 |
| Norway | - | 3.086 | 5.577 | 10.000 |
| Sweden | 5.061 | 20.900 | 36.001 | 38.844 |
| Switzerland | 19.710 | 48.485 | 76.662 | 79.476 |
| Italy | - | - | - | 10.000 |
| Spain | - | - | - | 1.000 |
| Finland | - | - | - | 3.325 |
| Liechtenstein | - | - | - | 809 |
| Luxemburg | - | - | - | 210 |
| Total Turks | 777.727 | 2.108.097 | 2.930.392 | 3.127.691 |

Sources: SOPEMI, 1995; Beauftragte der Bundesregierung fur die Belange der Auslander (Federal Government's Office for Foreigners), 1995; Annual Report, Turkish Ministry of Employment and Social Security, 1984, 1992, 1993, 2003; Statistics on Turkish Migrant: Report of the Turkish Ministry of Employment and Social Security, available online at *www.calisma.gov.tr*

**Figure 5.** Proportion of ethnic group born outside the UK

| Ethnic group | % born outside UK |
|---|---|
| Cypriot (part not stated) | 65.5 |
| Kurdish | 85.5 |
| Turkish | 76.3 |
| Turkish Cypriot | 58.0 |
| All London residents | 27.1 |

Source: Census 2001

**Figure 6.** Population numbers by country of birth

| Country | Greater London | England and Wales total | % Living in London |
|---|---|---|---|
| Cyprus | 45.888 | 75.763 | 60.6 |
| Iran | 20.398 | 40.767 | 50.0 |
| Iraq | 17.294 | 30.815 | 56.1 |
| Syrian Arab Republic | 2.066 | 3.975 | 52.0 |
| Turkey | 39.128 | 52.893 | 74.0 |

Source: Census 2001

Figure 7 - Age group by country of birth

| Age in years | Cyprus | Iran | Iraq | Syrian Arab Republic | Turkey | All London residents |
|---|---|---|---|---|---|---|
| | % | % | % | % | % | % |
| 0 to 4 | 0.3 | 0.9 | 1.4 | 1.9 | 2.0 | 6.7 |
| 5 to 15 | 2.3 | 6.8 | 11.4 | 9.1 | 12.0 | 13.5 |
| 16 to 24 | 4.2 | 11.0 | 11.6 | 12.9 | 18.0 | 12.1 |
| 25 to 44 | 25.4 | 44.3 | 41.6 | 42.5 | 50.0 | 35.3 |
| 45 to 59 | 33.6 | 24.3 | 21.1 | 23.6 | 13.7 | 16.1 |
| 60 to 64 | 11.6 | 3.8 | 4.0 | 4.1 | 1.6 | 3.9 |
| 65 to 74 | 15.8 | 5.2 | 6.0 | 3.8 | 1.6 | 6.5 |
| 75 and over | 6.9 | 3.5 | 2.9 | 2.6 | 1.1 | 5.9 |
| All ages | 100.0 | 100.0 | 100.0 | 100.0 | 100.0 | 100.0 |

Source: Census 2001

**Figure 8.** Proportion of population by gender, by ethnic group

| Gender | Cyprus (part not stated) | Kurdish | Turkish | Turkish Cypriot | All London residents |
|---|---|---|---|---|---|
| | % | % | % | % | % |
| Female | 47.6 | 45.7 | 49.8 | 49.8 | 51.6 |
| Male | 52.4 | 54.3 | 50.2 | 50.2 | 48.4 |

Source: Census 2001

**Figure 9.** Proportion of population by gender, by country of birth

| Gender | Cyprus | Iran | Iraq | Syrian Arab Republic | Turkey | All London residents |
|---|---|---|---|---|---|---|
| | % | % | % | % | % | % |
| Female | 50.5 | 48.6 | 44.7 | 44.1 | 48.3 | 51.6 |
| Male | 49.5 | 51.4 | 55.3 | 55.9 | 51.7 | 48.4 |

Source: Census 2001

**Figure 10.** Age group by ethnic group

| Age group | Cypriot (part not stated) | Kurdish | Turkish | Turkish Cypriot | All London residents |
|---|---|---|---|---|---|
| | % | % | % | % | % |
| 0-15 | 12.4 | 31.3 | 24.7 | 19.9 | 20.2 |
| 16-39 | 35.0 | 50.9 | 49.8 | 37.8 | 40.3 |
| 40-59/64* | 34.5 | 15.6 | 21.8 | 30.7 | 25.1 |
| 60/65-74* | 13.3 | 1.7 | 2.9 | 9.3 | 8.6 |
| 75 and over | 4.7 | 0.5 | 0.8 | 2.4 | 5.9 |
| All ages | 100.0 | 100.0 | 100.0 | 100.0 | 100.0 |

Source: Census 2001(*The Census table broke down the age groups for women as 40-59 and 60-74 and for men as 40-64 and 65-74)

**Figure 11.** Turkish Population and Naturalised Turks in the EU in 1000's (2002)

| Countries | Naturalised Turks | | Turkish EU Citizens | |
|---|---|---|---|---|
| | Total Population | Turkish Citizens | Citizen of the Country of Residence | Proportion of those Naturalised (%) |
| Belgium | 110 | 67 | 43 | 39.1 |
| Denmark | 53 | 39 | 14 | 26.4 |
| Germany | 2,637 | 1,907 | 730 | 27.7 |
| France | 370 | 196 | 174 | 47.0 |
| The Netherlands | 270 | 96 | 174 | 64.4 |
| Austria | 200 | 94 | 106 | 53.0 |
| Sweden | 37 | 14 | 23 | 62.2 |
| United Kingdom | 70 | 37 | 33 | 47.1 |
| Other EU countries | 20 | 19 | 1 | 5.0 |
| EU Total | 3,767 | 2,469 | 1,298 | 34.5 |

Source: Eurostat; Federal Office of Statistics & Centre for Studies on Turkey, Essen 2002.

**Figure 12.** UK Residents by Country of Birth (2010)

| No | Origin | Thousands | % |
|---|---|---|---|
| | UK born | 54.215 | 88.36 |
| | Non-UK born | 7.139 | 11.64 |
| 1 | India | 693 | 1.13 |
| 2 | Poland | 532 | 0.87 |
| 3 | Pakistan | 431 | 0.70 |
| 4 | Republic of Ireland | 405 | 0.66 |
| 5 | Germany | 296 | 0.48 |
| 6 | South Africa | 236 | 0.38 |
| 7 | Bangladeshi | 220 | 0.36 |
| 8 | USA | 200 | 0.33 |
| 9 | Nigeria | 151 | 0.25 |
| 10 | Kenya | 128 | 0.21 |
| 27 | Turkey | 72 | 0.12 |
| | Others | 3.775 | 6.15 |
| | All people | 61.354 | 100.00 |

Source: UK Data Archive, Annual Population Survey, 2010, Economic and Social Data Service

**Figure 13.** Turkish Nationals Present in a Number of OECD countries (data in thousands) (*) 67.000 in 2003, (**) 12.400 in 2003.

| Country | 1993 | 1994 | 1995 | 1996 | 1997 | 1998 | 1999 | 2000 | 2001 | 2002 |
|---|---|---|---|---|---|---|---|---|---|---|
| Germany | 1918.4 | 1965.6 | 2014.3 | 2049.1 | 2107.4 | 2110.2 | 2053.6 | 1998.5 | 1947.9 | 1912.2 |
| Austria | - | - | 311.2 | 314.2 | 314.4 | 315.8 | 319.9 | 322.2 | 322.0 | 320.9 |
| Belgium | 88.3 | 86.0 | 81.7 | 78.5 | 72.8 | 70.7 | 69.2 | 56.2 | 45.9 | 42.6 |
| Denmark | 34.7 | 35.0 | 35.7 | 36.8 | 37.5 | 38.1 | 36.6 | 35.2 | 33.4 | 31.9 |
| Finland | 1.0 | 1.2 | 1.3 | 1.5 | 1.7 | 1.7 | 1.7 | 1.8 | 2.0 | 2.1 |
| France | - | - | - | - | - | - | 208.0 | - | - | - |
| Netherlands | 202.6 | 182.1 | 154.3 | 127.0 | 114.7 | 102.0 | 100.7 | 100.8 | 100.3 | 100.3 |
| UK | 31 | 44 | 29 | 42 | 56 | 63 | 41 | 38 | 58 | 52* |
| Sweden | - | 22.0 | 20.3 | 18.9 | 18.4 | 17.4 | 16.4 | 15.8 | 13.9 | 12.6** |
| Switzerland | 75.6 | 77.1 | 78.6 | 79.4 | 79.6 | 79.5 | 79.9 | 79.5 | 79.5 | 78.8 |

Source: OECD, Trends in International Migration, SOPeMI 2004.

Figure 14 – Immigrant Populations in the Main European Countries of Immigration who have either Turkish Nationality or Dual Nationality through Acquiring the Nationality of their Country of Residence.

| Country | Turkish Population (2003) [*] | Nationals of Turkish Origin or Total Number of Naturalisations [***] | Total Presence |
|---|---|---|---|
| Germany | 1.912.169 | 546.576 [1972-2003] | 2.458.745 |
| France | (314.438) | 44.596 [1991-2003] | 359.034 |
| Netherlands | (117.366) | 224.034 [1946-2002] | 341.400 |
| Belgium | 45.866 | 83.933 [1985-2003] | 129.799 |
| Austria | (41.969) | 88.734 [1983-2003] | 130.703 |
| Sweden | 33.094 | 26.056 [1990-2003] | 59.150 |
| Switzerland | 78.256 | 26.328 [1990-2003] | 105.584 |
| Denmark | 30.450 | 19.386 [1980-2002] | 49.836 |
| United Kingdom | (63.220) | 36.780 [1989-2002] | 100.000 |
| Total | (2.573.608) | 1.135.611 [2003] | (3.709.219) |

Source: The Turkish Ministry of Employment and Social Security, General Directorate of Services for the Workers Abroad Publications, 2003, Year 3, Volume 4), Reports (2003, 2004), Ankara.

**Figure 15.** LAs with the Highest Percentages of Bangladeshi, Somali and Turkish Pupils living in London.

| Bangladeshi LA | % | Somali LA | % | Turkish LA | % |
|---|---|---|---|---|---|
| Tower Hamlets | 58.2 | Ealing | 7.6 | Haringey | 11.5 |
| City of London | 30.7 | Brent | 6.9 | Enfield | 11.4 |
| Newham | 15.8 | Camden | 5.8 | Hackney | 9.8 |
| Camden | 14.3 | Haringey | 4.9 | Islington | 7.7 |
| Oldham | 10.8 | Islington | 4.9 | Waltham | 3.2 |
| Westminster | 10.3 | Leicester | 3.9 | Lewisham | 1.8 |
| Luton | 8.7 | Newham | 3.9 | Barnet | 1.5 |
| Islington | 7 | Hounslow | 3.9 | Southwark | 1.4 |
| Hackney | 5.5 | Wandsworth | 3.5 | Greenwich | 1.3 |
| Redbridge | 5.5 | Hillingdon | 3.2 | Camden | 1.2 |

Source: *PLASC 2007*.

**Figure 16.** London Residents by Country of Birth Outside the UK 2001

| Rank | Country | Number |
|------|---------|--------|
| 1 | India | 172.162 |
| 2 | Ireland | 157.285 |
| 3 | Bangladeshi | 84.565 |
| 4 | Jamaica | 80.319 |
| 5 | Nigeria | 68.907 |
| 6 | Pakistan | 66.658 |
| 7 | Kenya | 66.311 |
| 8 | Sri Lanka | 49.932 |
| 9 | Ghana | 46.513 |
| 10 | Cyprus | 45.888 |
| 11 | South Africa | 45.506 |
| 12 | USA | 44.602 |
| 13 | Australia | 41.488 |
| 14 | Germany | 39.818 |
| 15 | Turkey | 39.128 |
| 16 | Italy | 38.694 |
| 17 | France | 38.130 |
| 18 | Somalia | 33.831 |
| 19 | Uganda | 32.082 |
| 20 | New Zealand | 27.494 |

Source: (GLA (2005) London – The World in a City: An Analysis of the 2001 Census, London: GLA Briefing 2005/6).

**Figure 17.** Resident Population by Ethnic Group in Great Britain 1991

| Ethnic Group | Numbers (thousand) | % of Total Population |
|--------------|--------------------|-----------------------|
| All groups | 54.889 | 100.0 |
| White | 51.874 | 94.5 |
| Other Groups | 3.015 | 5.5 |
| Black Caribbean | 500 | 0.9 |
| Black African | 212 | 0.4 |
| Black Other | 178 | 0.3 |
| Black Total | 891 | 1.6 |
| Indian | 840 | 1.5 |
| Pakistani | 477 | 0.9 |
| Bangladeshi | 163 | 0.3 |
| Chinese | 157 | 0.3 |
| Other Groups | | |
| Asian | 198 | 0.4 |
| Other (non-Asian) | 290 | 0.5 |

Source: TEAGUE, A. (1993), "Ethnic Group: First Results from the 1991 Census", Population Trends, Summer, 1993, pp.12-17.

174

# CHAPTER 10

# MIGRATION POLICY OF SPAIN

Ferda Özer[1]

## Introduction

The movement of migration has existed throughout of the Earth in the course of the history. Spain as a member of the EU (European Union) countries is always alluring especially for people living in Latin America and MENA (Middle East and North Africa) Region. The migrants which want to migrate the Europe Continent use three ways of migration. That is why three countries have key importance among the migration routes, which are Greece, Italy and the last but not the least Spain. But, Spain is more different than Italy and Greece. Spain shows more tolerance than others. Also, in the matter of diversity of integration policies and the issue of acquisition of citizenship Spain is better than other EU countries. The study tries to examine the migration policy of Spain. By doing this, it is separated two main titles. First of all, general framework of migration definition is drawn, then the migration movements towards Spain are presented. Finally, migration policies of Spain are dealt with details.

The notion of migration is one of the most crucial and elaborated phenomena related to not only the national size but also international scope.[2] Although the notion of migration has a lot of attentive definition, these meet on a common ground that change of location. This common ground includes short-term or long-term, interstate or intrastate.[3] International Organization of Migration defines to migration that *"The movement of persons away from their place of usual residence, either across an international border or within a State."*[4] On this perspective, this phenomenon refers that for the change of location one to another for short-term or long-term for the purpose of political, cultural and economic reasons. In a nutshell, migration is the movement from original location to destination where migrants want to desire.[5] By the way, when irregular migration comes from being highlighted legal perspective. The type

---

[1] Kocaeli University, Institute of Social Sciences, Master's Student of The Department of the European Union Politics and International Relations, ferdaaozerr@gmail.com.
[2] Ministerio De Asuntos Exteriores Y De Cooperacion, Spain's Perspective on Migration & Development: Migration Policies", p. 1.
[3] Mehlika Özlem Ultan, **Avrupa Birliği'nde Yasa Dışı Göç ve Ülke Uygulamaları**, Ankara, Nobel Academic Publication, 2016, p. 8.
[4] https://www.iom.int/key-migration-terms , (Access 20.11.2020).
[5] Ultan, op.cit, p. 8.

of migration has not been exactly defined universally. Irregular migration is defined as *"Movement of persons that takes place outside the laws, regulations, or international agreements governing the entry into or exit from the State of origin, transit or destination."*[6]

## Migration to Spain

Within the scope of this title, the pros and cons of migration in Spain are presented. Then, Spain's statistical data is tried to be interpreted to some extent.

### The pros and cons of migration in Spain

In this part, firstly pros and cons of migration are tried to be analysed. International migration affects both receiving country and also sending country. Whereas receiving country improved with regard to labour force to great extent, sending country has disadvantage with respect to labour force. The country which managing effectively the movement of migration establishes good system that supporting economic development, ensuring and preserving public safety and human rights. However, if irregular migrant movements soar, some negative effects such as deterioration of public safety and security or violation of human right are observed.[7] First of all, that is overcrowded. This issue triggers soaring cost of services such as health care and education. Furthermore, cultural side is that disagreement between different cultures,[8] increasing language barriers and racial conflict. On the political perspective, migration leads to escalating crime rates, security issues, besides inefficaciousness of planning and policy enhancement.[9]

Sometimes individuals take a decision whether they move, however sometimes they are constrained to move. The consequences individuals leave a place are named the push factors about migration. The reasons individuals are attracted to new locations to reside are named the pull factors.[10] Immigration brings about both advantages and also disadvantages for not only host country but also country losing people. For host country, there are lots of advantages with respect to political, economic and cultural notions. Economic advantages are reduced labour force, workforce dynasty, business expansion, increased competitiveness and so on. In the political framework, advantages of migration are that improving the foreign relations and standing in the international community. In addition, that multiculturalism and

---

[6] https://www.iom.int/key-migration-terms (Access 20.11.2020).

[7] Ultan, op.cit, p 69.

[8] https://www.bbc.co.uk/bitesize/guides/zkg82hv/revision/5 (Access 22.11.2020).

[9] Dina Jaccob, "Euro-Mediterranean Security and Cooperation: Immigration Policies and Implications.", **SSRN Electric Journal,** 2013, p. 4.

[10] https://www.bbc.co.uk/bitesize/guides/zkg82hv/revision/5 (Access 22.11.2020).

cultural, lingual diversity are remarked about cultural perspective.[11]

On the other hand, migration has considerable number of disadvantages in terms of economic, social and political aspects. Firstly, migration affects short-run inflationary pressures, employee resistance, legal issues, short-term deterioration of the trade balance, the increasing urban-rural gap, soaring skilled labour relative wages due to inflow of unskilled labour and so on. Also, migration influences adversely in respect to security problems and crime concern. The effects of migration with respect to culture are that it can create language barriers and racial conflict.[12]

Moreover, immigration phenomena within the context of the European Union, some regulations are encountered. Thanks to Single European Acts, within the border of the European Communities (EC), the four basic freedoms that are people, capital, goods and services have been ensured legally.[13] As a result this regulation has created that migrants have moved to Communities territory without restriction. This situation is deeply affected the member countries. When analysing socio-economic effects, political rights and the right to education are influenced. By the way, constructing single type of policy is not likelihood on the other hand it is suggested that these needs are changed person to person. Since some political issues occurred in 1990s, the EC has attitudinized to South European Countries. The oppression of employment has led to soaring xenophobia[14] which refers to *"Attitudes, prejudices and behaviour that reject, exclude and often vilify persons, based on the perception that they are outsiders or foreigners to the community, society or national identity."*[15] Thus the phenomenon of migration has become politicized and the EU has tried making common policies to overcoming this issue. Whereas the European Union has tried to restrict the arrival of immigrants with legal status whereby the precautions it takes, it has tackled difficulties in controlling illegal immigrants. Escalating adverse thought about migration is based on increasing number of migration movement.[16] But, migration is not assessed in neither positive nor negative manner. It would be more appropriate to consider it as a reaction to the economic developments, the transportation and communication systems of the countries, political pressures and individual motives. However, the most appropriate explanation on migration

---

[11] Dina Jaccob, op.cit, p. 3-4.

[12] Ibid, pp. 3-4.

[13] Jacques Delors Institute, "The Four Freedoms in the EU: Are they inseperable?" https://institutdelors.eu/wpcontent/uploads/2018/01/171024jdigrundfreiheitenenwebeinzelseitena4.pdf, (Access 25.11.2020).

[14] Enver Bozkurt, Mehmet Özcan ve Arif Köktaş, Avrupa Birliği Hukuku, Ankara, Asil Publisher, 2011, pp. 338.

[15] https://ec.europa.eu/home-affairs/what-we-do/networks/european_migration_network/glossary_search/xenophobia.en, (Access 24.11.2020).

[16] Hakan Samur, "Avrupa Birliği'nde Göçe Yönelik Global Yaklaşım", **Uluslararası İnsan Bilimleri Dergisi,** 2008, Vol. 5, No. 2, p. 1.

is that it has economic, political and social impacts on all societies with which it is related.[17]

### Migration statistics on immigration in Spain

Spain receives more immigrants from Latin American countries on account of historical backgrounds, speaking same language and having some political privileges.[18] The official institutions for migrants is Dirección General de Migraciones, Secretaría General de Inmigración y Emigración, Ministerio de Empleo y Seguridad Social.[19] Looking at some statistical data, firstly foreign migration movement is dealt via Table 1. This data source is Spanish Statistical Office (Instituto Nacional de Estadística). According to this table, it obvious that Spain is receiving country for foreigners. In other saying, Spain would receive the number of 664,554 migrants. Also 219,970 foreigners would emigrate in Spain. When the Spanish are compared to foreigners, it is investigated that the Spanish migrants are less than foreigners.[20]

**Table 1.** Foreign Migration Movements in 2019 (provisional)

|  | Immigration | Emigration | Migration Balance |
|---|---|---|---|
| Total | 748,759 | 297,368 | 451,391 |
| Spanish | 84,202 | 77,398 | 6,804 |
| Foreigners | 664,557 | 219,970 | 444,587 |

Source: https://www.ine.es/dyngs/INEbase/es/operacion.htm?c=Estadistica_C&cid= 1254736177 000&idp=1254735573002&menu=ultiDatos (Access 28.11.2020).

Spain has received migrant from many different countries, especially from south American countries. When looked at Table 2, the top three location are Colombia (South America), Morocco (North Africa) and within a sharp decreasing, Venezuela (South Africa). The following states are Italy as a member state of the EU also a part of Schengen area and the United Kingdom. These data are limited top twenty states. Additionally, Russia and the United States of America (USA) are included the first twenty.

Having looked at age distribution of migrants living in Spain, it is observed that they are mainly in the range of working age, which is between 25 and 44.[21] As far as Migration Policy Institute statistics are concerned, net immigration rate referring to *"net migration is the net total of migrants during the period, that is, the total number of immigrants less the annual number of emigrants,*

---

[17] Hal Kane, "Leaving Home", **Society,** Vol. 12, No. 4, 1995, ss. 1-4; Ultan, op.cit, p. 70.

[18] Ibid, p. 268.

[19] General Directorate of Migration, General Secretariat of Immigration and Emigration, Ministry of Employment and Social Security

[20] https://www.ine.es/dyngs/INEbase/es/operacion.htm?c=Estadistica_C&cid= 1254736177000&idp =125473557 3002&menu=ultiDatos, (Access 28.11.2020).

[21] https://www.iom.int/countries/spain (Access 28.11.2020).

*including both citizens and noncitizens. Data are five-year estimates.''*[22] in 2020 is estimated at 7 migrants' of 1000 population.[23] Allocated fund to migrants within the period of 2014-2020 is €257.101.877,00.[24]

**Table 2.** Number of immigrants into Spain in 2019, by nationality

| Nationality | Number of Immigrants | Nationality | Number of Immigrants |
|---|---|---|---|
| Colombia | 76,524 | Brazil | 16,538 |
| Morocco | 72,778 | Cuba | 14,101 |
| Venezuela | 57,700 | China | 12,213 |
| Italy | 33,312 | France | 12,092 |
| The UK | 29,290 | Paraguay | 11,947 |
| Honduras | 28,950 | Pakistan | 11,623 |
| Peru | 28,515 | Ecuador | 10,653 |
| Romania | 27.120 | Germany | 9,436 |
| Argentina | 17,877 | The USA | 9,114 |
| Nicaragua | 17,060 | Russia | 9.001 |

Showing entries from 1 to 20 (totally 20 entries)

Source: https://www.statista.com/statistics/446225/number-of-immigrants-into-spain-by-nationality/ (Access 28.11.2020).

### Spain's migration policy

Spain is the only European country that encourages the legalization of illegal immigrants and passes laws on this issue. In addition, the policies developed for legal immigration and the processes it applies to ensure the adaptation of immigrants are among the elements that differentiate Spain. It differs from other countries as it gives irregular migrants the right to free healthcare and education. Due to the fact that Spain is an EU country where different national minorities live together and receives heavy immigration, border and integration policies towards immigrants have almost always been important problems for Spanish governments. Although the Spanish state expresses its desire to build a multicultural society, it has difficulties in solving its political problems with national minorities and continues to develop strong border policies in order to control migration flows. Spain has moved from being a country of immigration to receiving country in the last two decades of the 20th century.[25]

### Historical background of migration in Spain

Immigration became a part of the Spanish political agenda in 1985,

---

[22] https://data.worldbank.org/indicator/SM.POP.NETM?start=2002 (Access 28.11.2020).

[23] https://www.migrationpolicy.org/country-resource/spain (Access 28.11.2020).

[24] https://ec.europa.eu/home-affairs/financing/fundings/mapping-funds/countries/spain_en (Access 28.11.2020).

[25] Ultan, op.cit, p. 270.

however it was not until the mid-1990s.[26] As of the beginning of the 1990s the government became conscious about the dimension and continuousness of the immigration flows, also set out the first checking precautions.[27]

When migration history of Spain is analysed, two turning points are remarked. First one is between the periods of 1880 and 1930; on account of the effects of WWI on the Europe Continent and some economic problems, a great deal of Spanish migrated to Venezuela, Mexica, Brazil, Argentina, Cuba and some other South American countries. Second of them, it is the period of within 1950-1970. In this period Spanish prefer to migrate mostly North European Countries. After the Oil Crisis, Spanish migrated less rather than previous period also the Spanish who had migrated turned back their own country. But it should be stated that at that time, the number of incoming migrants is low, both official and social tolerance was high, so restriction migration policies were not needed. Even so, between the years of 1970-1985, the number of migrants coming to Spain started to soar. The increase of both legal and illegal immigrants has required Spain to take precautions because these immigrants also want to join the workforce.[28]

**Migration policy specific to the European Union**

The European Continent and the EU Countries are exposed to quiet migration waves. So, they developed most of the migration programmes. Important reasons behind migration to Europe are high welfare level and liberal migrant policy that is implementing that is why, the continent has become receiving destination. The countries surrounding the EU are generally accepted transit countries. Especially three routes come into prominence. First of all, Hungary and Austria are transit countries for the illegal migrants coming from Croatia and Slovenia to reaching to the European territory. Second route is that Czechia and Slovakia are transit countries for the migrants coming from Middle East and Far East Countries. The last but not the least, third transit countries are Spain, Greece and Italy for the migrants from the countries which located in North African and Asia. [29] Also, Spain as a Mediterranean country and as a member state of the EU has conducted the most efficient and the comprehensive migration policy. One of the most crucial issue facing the European Union migration from outside of the territory to their land.[30] The EU apprehension about

---

[26] Nieves Ortega Pérez, "Spain: Forging an Immigration Policy", Migration Policy Institute, February 2003, p. 1.

[27] https://journals.openedition.org/belgeo/15770#tocto1n3 (Access 28.11.2020).

[28] Ultan, op.cit, p. 266.

[29] Mehlika Özlem Ultan, "Avrupa Birliği'nde Istenen Göçmen Profili Analizi: Ekonomik Göçmen Mi, Politik Göçmen Mi?", Süleyman Demirel Üniversitesi İktisadi ve İdari Bilimler Fakültesi, Göç Özel Sayısı, No. 22, 2017, p. 1444.

[30] Samur, op.cit, p. 1.

immigration soared particularly after the uprising movement of people – the named as Arab Spring - in the South Mediterranean states that led to new political context (European Commission, 2011c). This result the EU leaders to address both the short term and long-term challenges. The rebelling movements of people which resided in the countries that located in the MENA Regions has concluded in immense residents' dislocation in the region which generated a further difficulty for these countries that are located in the centre of a political tension.[31] The issue of immigration elicits important problem for the European Union. The Unions separated two sides on this issue as some countries have loose regulation, others have strict regulations such as promotes coming back their countries etc.[32]

Prior to Amsterdam Agreement, the migration policy of the EU based on four type recommendation policy. First of all, the normative definition of illegal migration and regulations that increase control against illegal migration such as limited residence, marriage of convenience etc. Second one is that arrangements to assist the operational aspects of expulsion via agreements or regulations. Third one includes approaches to third countries to facilitate readmission whereby agreements or laissez-passer and so on. The last one refers to exchange of information, directly linked to other policies. Additionally, Amsterdam Agreement included new title within the context of "Free Movement of People, Asylum and Migration". Legal and illegal migration were arranged. European Council held right to some regulation about visa, right to habitation for within the scope of marriage, illegal migration and illegal residence.[33]

## Spain's country specific migration policies

When comparing to the EU countries, Spain has distinct feature than others. Spain has not faced international migration gradually. Firstly, since the policies developed in the period after the dictatorship regime in the country did not take into account the phenomenon of international migration and this process coincided with a period in which immigration to Europe was very intense, Spanish immigration policies were put into effect very quickly and the institutions that would be the executors of these policies were the same. It had to institutionalize immediately.[34] Spain's first enterprise at immigration legislation was under the then the government of Socialist Party.[35] Additionally, the 1978 Constitution, which was made after the Franco regime in Spain, contains general provisions regarding foreigners, it is

---

[31] Jacoob, op.cit, p. 2.
[32] Enver Bozkurt, Mehmet Ozcan and Arif Koktas, **Avrupa Birligi Hukuku,** Ankara, Yetkin Publishing, 2012, p. 353.
[33] Ibid., p. 355-356.
[34] Ozturk, op.cit, pp. 112-113.
[35] Pérez, op.cit, p. 4.

thought that the main regulations should be made by law. In this direction, the migration policy of Spain is carried out with the newly enacted laws.

Furthermore, Spain joined the European Community in 1981 so, the new migration policies to be created by Spain has to be in accordance with the European Union standards and also to provide an effective solution to the immigration problem of the country. Spain was used as a transit country by migrants who came from Africa and South America until the 1990s, who were thinking of moving to other European countries.[36] The first immigration law enacted by the second democratic government of Felipe González in 1985 (Constitutional Article 7/1985 dated 1 July) 14 should also be considered in this context. This law cannot be considered independent of the laws that have been put into effect by the governments of other European countries and which provide the basis for the EU's strict border control. This immigration law, which caused criticism by human rights activists due to its many articles, ignored the social problems of migrants such as education, health and family reunification. The phenomenon of migration has been seen as only short-term labour migration. The Spanish state aimed to end the opposition of human rights activists by amending this law on immigration by issuing decree laws.[37] Voluntary return programs, which had been active within the period of 2003-2008, have been changed since 2008. Accordingly, decisions were taken to encourage unemployed third-country nationals to return to their countries.[38]

### Immigrant integration policy

In general, Spanish governments have also considered migrants only as workers, as they take into account the needs of the labour market when implementing migration policies. It has clearly shown itself in the transfer of the regulation of migration management and integration policies from the Ministry of Immigration and Employment to the Ministry of Social Affairs. This institutional approach clearly reveals how the social and political problems of immigration have been thrown into the background. The 1996 amendment to this first immigration law is important as it regulates permanent residence and work permits for immigrants living in the country, as well as family reunification. With a comprehensive law reform enacted in 2000, these rights have been more firmly secured. The Spanish immigration law, which took its current form with the law reforms no. 8/2000, 14/2003 and 2/2009, reveals the political attitudes of the governments governing the country towards the border and integration problems during this period. In

---

[36] Mehlika Özlem Ultan, "Ege Denizi'nde Yasa Dışı Göç Hareketlerini Önleme Çabaları ve Frontex Örneği", **Ege Jeopolitiği** 2. Cilt, Ankara, Nobel Yayıncılık, 2020, pp. 1541-1542.

[37] Ozturk, op.cit, pp. 112-113.

[38] Ultan, 2016, op.cit., p. 269.

Spain, both the immigration law and the changes made in this law and all other legal regulations cannot be considered separately from the European Union's regulations on external migration.[39] In 2001, another plan for the integration of immigrants was implemented. "The Integrated Program for the Regulation and Coordination of Foreigners and Immigrants in Spain", in short, the GRECO Plan, states that Spain needs migration because immigrants actively contribute to economic growth. For this reason, he stated that migration flows should be regulated and migration management should be activated.[40]

Spain started to reveal the general framework of integration policies in the country only in the 1990s. It was established the General Administration of Migration (Dirección General de Migracions) in 1991, established the first inter-ministerial migration commission in 1992, and in 1994 put into effect the first social integration plan for immigrants. Among these first institutional steps to ensure social integration are the establishment of the Coordinator for Integration (Foro para la Integración, n.d.) and another unit observing the phenomenon of migration (Observatorio Permanente de la Inmigración, n.d.). Organized around the phenomenon of immigration and integration, these public institutions have evolved into more institutional and established structures over time and formed the staff that can manage this process. A high commission for immigration policies (el Consejo Superior de Política de Inmigración) (Real Decreto por el que se crea el Consejo Superior), established outside the institutions mentioned above and under the Ministry of Labour and Immigration (1 Ministerio de Trabajo e Inmigración) de Política de Inmigración, 1985) and another working commission (la Comisión Laboral Tripartita17). In addition to these institutions, the four-year integration plans put into effect by the government's General Commissioner for Internal and External Migration (la Secretaría General de Inmigración y Emigración) are important for understanding Spain's roadmap for immigration and integration (Ministerio de Trabajo e Inmigración, 2011) (Ministerio de Trabajo e Inmigración, 2007). Although immigration and integration management has been institutionalized by central governments in this way, it would be correct to say that the institutions that directly work to facilitate the integration processes of immigrants are institutions affiliated to the autonomous region governments and local governments. In order to correctly evaluate the integration policies for immigrants and the work done in this field, the distribution of the political power in Spain between 17 autonomous regions and 2 autonomous cities should not be overlooked. Their autonomy status was guaranteed by the Spanish Constitution. Success

---

[39] Ozturk, op.cit, p. 113.
[40] Pérez,op.cit, p. 5.

in the integration of aliens is directly related to access to rights provided by the welfare state. Apart from that, being able to exercise other fundamental rights such as health and education services is important for the functioning of the welfare state. For this reason, laws are also applied to prevent social exclusion that prevents immigrants from using such services.[41]

## Citizenship

One of the issues on migration is citizenship in the European Union immigration policy. But Spain is differed from the others. In other words, Spain does not follow general tendency which egalitarian policy for all migrants. Indeed, migrants coming from Latin America countries which were colonies of Spain can obtain citizenship more easily, immigrants from Morocco and other African countries do not have similar rights.[42] Moreover, while immigrants from other countries acquire citizenship if they stay legally in the country for ten years; immigrants from Latin America if they stay in Spain for two years legally and entitle visa liberalization before the Schengen system can be counted among these privileges.[43] Additionally, due to the fact that the right to vote is depended on citizenship, migrants are limited on the issue of political participation.[44]

## Conclusion

The phenomenon of migration is problematic issue for Spain whose history of migration dates back a long period of time. It possesses plenty of advantages besides disadvantages for both sending country and receiving country. In terms of economic, political and cultural aspects, migration is mixed blessing. Additionally, Spain is one of the most immigrant countries. Lots of issue lead to receiving immigrants to Spain. Foremost among these reasons, Spain is a member country of the European Union. Others are the integration policies for migrants, acquisition of citizenship, and some regulations. But it is crucial to state that Spain is not only receiving or sending country but also a transit country. In other words, for migrants Spain plays critical role for the purpose of achieving other EU member countries. This means that Spain is a vital country for avoiding migrant flows to EU countries. All of them show that taken steps by Spanish government has critical importance for the EU's migration management.

---

[41] Ozturk, op.cit, p. 114.
[42] Ozturk, op.cit, p. 116.
[43] Ultan, 2016, op.cit, p. 268.
[44] Ozturk, op.cit, p. 116.

# CHAPTER 11

# POPULISM AND REFUGEE POLICIES OF AUSTRIA

Sinem Eray*

## Introduction

At the center of European politics, racist, anti-immigrant and especially anti-Muslim populist discourses are used extensively. Popular concerns about identity and welfare have become the basis of radical right populist discourse, concepts that have given the radical right great momentum. Anti-immigration, anti-Islam and anti-EU, which are the main arguments of the radical right, have reached a dangerous point with their growing development.

Although populism is not essentially a new concept and phenomenon, it has never historically been as widespread and popular as it has been in recent years. Populism is experiencing –almost– the most vibrant period in its history. Populism is one of the main concepts that characterize today's political changes, as well as one of the main phenomena that shape our day. So much so that political analyses and interpretations that characterize today's political changes and political atmosphere as the 'explosion of populism'[1] and depict the period in which we live in the form of the 'age of populism' are becoming increasingly common[2].

Populism has a wide range of uses that can qualify political positions that are at the two ends of a completely opposite line, one side of which is a fascist dictatorship and the other side is a real democracy. Those at one extreme can characterize populism as neo-fascism as the modern form of fascism adapted to the present day, while those at the other extreme can consider it as true democracy or 'democratization of democracy' and 'the true voice of democracy' that addresses the shortcomings of democracy[3].

Especially the right-wing form of populism, authoritarian, xenophobic, exclusionary and monoculturalist as nativism, openly violates even the most minimal principles of human rights by displaying nationalist and even racist

* PhD Candidate, Political Science and International Relations, Bahçeşehir Univesity.
[1] Ivan Krastev, "The Populist Moment", https://www.eurozine.com/the-populist-moment/. (Access Date: 15.11.2020)
[2] Salim Orhan, "Popülizm, Liberal Demokrasi ve Faşizm Denklemi." **Ankara Üniversitesi Hukuk Fakültesi Dergisi,** 68.4: p.796.
[3] Orhan ibid. , p.798.

attitudes in places[4].

The zenophobic and nationalistic attitude of right-wing populism is aimed at their origins rather than at the legal status of foreigners and immigrants. In other words, there is a policy that antagonizes immigrants because of their origin, even though they have come entirely by legal means. In addition, in right-wing populism, real and pure people also have ethnic and cultural dimensions, excluding some ethno-cultural groups and displaying a discriminatory attitude towards them[5].

Considering the common characteristics populism and fascism similar, or sometimes both combining to form a single whole and interpreted by, the populism of neo-authoritarianism and liberal democracy is asserted that the opposite of the dictatorship of fascism as is evaluated. John Bellamy Foster argues that organized neo-fascism today is formally presented as Democratic and populist, adhering to legal-constitutional structures, because explicit identification with classical fascism is considered taboo in today's mainstream politics[6].

A comparison of its basic elements and concepts shows that populism and fascism are ideologically –although they have similarities– two separate ideologies and styles of politics that have differences. In practice, this difference may be less than the difference at the theoretical level between them, and it is more possible for these two to resemble each other.

Fascism, which emerged as a nationalist political ideology against all ideologies after the World War I, has started to rise relentlessly in Europe for the last few years. Fascism continued as the official ideology in Italy during the reign of the Italian leader Mussolini in 1922. In a short time, it turned into a description describing the oppressive and authoritarian regime understanding in general and became a general name given by the people to all anti-democratic and authoritarian ideologies and administrative systems, especially national socialism.

In order for a regime to be considered fascist, the ideology of that regime must be nationalist and put the wealth and interests of the nation above all else. In this respect, it should also include populism and aim to ensure the welfare of not only the rich or the workers, but all members of the nation. In order to achieve this goal, it is among the policies of fascism to implement measures such as strict state control over the economy, ensuring that workers' wages are sufficient, preventing arbitrary layoffs, and applying price control

---

[4] Cas Mudde, "Fighting the system? Populist radical right parties and party system change", **Party Politics,** Vol. 20, Issue.2, 2014, p. 217-226.

[5] Ibid. p.824

[6] John Bellamy Foster, "This Is Not Populism", **Monthly Review**, Volume 69, Number 2, June 2017, p. 9.

to prevent cost of living.

After the World War I the rise of fascism under the leadership of Mussolini in Italy and Hitler in Germany caused the collapse of Europe. As a result of this fear in Europe after the World War II, the rise of far-right parties was feared and avoided. The rise of the far right in Europe can be considered as a process in which certain currents and political atmosphere were the catalysts in certain periods since the World War II. In this regard, leaving aside the dynamics of the World War II, the acceleration of the far right in Europe today can be seen as a reflection of the elements that have been going on since the 1970s. Historically, it should be noted that the rising right in Europe in the 1970s and 80s diverged from the extreme right in the 2000s and today. The new far-right, which has a wider community as its target audience, takes its place in the European political scene in a different dimension when it encounters new concepts of populism.

For the first time in Europe, nationalism has reached its present level since the strong nationalist movements of the pre-World War II period. In many places, from the Nordic countries where social democratic parties are strong to the countries of Central and Western Europe with strong democratic traditions, right-wing populists have left the elections with strength. Brexit in Britain, the Trump government in America, The Kurz-Strache coalition in Austria and the AfD, the party that emerged from the elections most strongly in Germany, show how strong populism has become a form of politics. The concept of populism is used consciously or unconsciously in many areas, especially politics. In order to get rid of this concept confusion, the framework of populism was drawn theoretically in the study. The construction of populist discourse was determined, and examples of history were also used in ensuring this determination.

In this study, the concept of populism, which is today's phenomenon, will be analyzed by looking at fascism in Europe from a historical perspective. The historical development of populism in Europe will be discussed, the phenomenon of right wing populism will be investigated and the rising right wing populist parties and voting rates in Europe will be shown. After the analysis of populism, how the right-wing parties and populism have risen on the basis of Austria will be revealed and the most important reasons of this rise, the refugee policies and crises, will be viewed. The rise of current Austrian right parties and the consequences of their discourse on refugees will be discussed.

## What is Populism?

Populism has become one of the most common ideas in politics today. With the global spread of populism, many different groups, movements, or leaders have become "populists" in many different geographies around the world, as if there were no distinction between them. The emergence of populism is frequently cited as an troubling trend in the media, academia and daily life. Although the rise of populism is viewed in several ways as a disturbing situation , the main emphasis is on its relationship with democracy and the extent of its harm to democracy.

Nowadays, the talk of populism, "one of the main political buzzwords of the 21st century[7] as a problematic political stance has almost become omnipresent. Although there is no consensus on the definition of populism, the definitions taken as criteria by certain approaches in the literature of populism studies can be mentioned. Various traditions attempt to understand populism on the basis of ideology, political style, political strategy and discursive approach.

Looking at the accumulated literature on populism, it is noticed that the concept is defined in very different forms and used in quite different contexts. Populism has been defined in various forms as a movement, a style of politics, an ideology, a discourse, a strategy, a political culture and a multi-purpose concept.[8] Although there is a fairly wide literature on the definition of the concept, a precise and acceptable definition does not yet exist.

The word populism was chosen by the Cambridge Dictionary as the word of the year in 2017[9]. In the literature, there is no clear definition of the concept of populism, and there are various debates about whether populism is an ideology, a phenomenon or a political discourse. Cass Mudde argues that populism is a weakly centered ideology. Mudde argues that populism can be easily articulated with other ideologies, as it does not have a deep intellectual accumulation[10].

Laclau states that despite the breadth in the use of the concept of populism, the common basis and reference in all of them is 'the people' as a similar source and basis. ' The people" is the main indicator of populist discourse. But not every discourse that emphasizes the public means a populist discourse. Because a populist discourse also divides the social space into two different areas, 'people' and 'power bloc'[11].

---

[7] Cas Mudde, Cristóbal Rovira Kaltwasser, **Populism: A Very Short Introduction**, New York, NY: Oxford University Press, 2017. p.1

[8] Takis S. Pappas, "Modern Populism: Research Advances, Conceptual and Methodological Pitfalls, and the Minimal Definition", **Politics Oxford Research Encyclopedia**, Oxford University Press, 2016, p. 18-19. https://www.pollux-fid.de/r/cr-10.1093/acrefore/9780190228637.013.17 (Access Date: 13.11.2020)

[9] https://www.cam.ac.uk/news/populism-revealed-as-2017-word-of-the year by-cambridge-university-press (Date of Access: 15.11.2020)

[10] Cas Mudde, The Populist Zeitgeist. **Government and Opposition**,39(4), 541-563.

[11] Ernesto Laclau, **Politics and Ideology in Marxist Theory**, New Left Books, London, 1977, p. 165.

Changing the theory of populism in his later work, Laclau states that populism does not mean much about the relationship between the 'people' and the 'elites', and instead is the product of the relationship on an antagonistic basis between the two entities.

Stating that there is no comprehensive theory of populism and that 'populism is not a written doctrine, but a set of obvious claims with a certain internal logic', Müller also states the two main features of populism as the opposition to elitism and pluralism. Müller notes that populism, which he believes is 'based on the conception of politics from a specific moralist point of view', deals with and understands politics through a distinction between the morally pure and integrated people and the morally inferior corrupt elites –ultimately in a fictional way. Being against the elite is a necessary but not enough trait to be a populist. "Populists, in addition to being anti-elite, are always anti-pluralism. They believe that they, and only themselves, represent the people. "Populists claim that anyone who is outside of them is immoral and is not part of the real people. They always integrate themselves with the people they describe as virtuous and moral, and describe their opponents as 'enemies of the people'. Such a policy is essentially a form of identity politics and treats the public as a homogeneous and monolithic structure12.

Margaret Canovan stated in her book "Populism" that she frequently encountered the word populism in many different fields of research, but the term still retains its ambiguous identity[13].

Hans-Jürgen Puhle in his work on the concept of populism, with different approaches to the explanation of the concept; It states that despite the classification efforts such as right-left, old-new populism, nobody has been able to develop a generally accepted definition. Puhle allegorically identifies the situation with Potter Stewart's "I know it when I see it" expression,[14] and this concept, which is used by many people from politicians to the media, from academics to ordinary citizens, is actually without a definite definition and without indicating the same situation. draws attention to its use.

Taggart provides an explanation for populism as follows: "That populism is a reaction to the ideas, institutions, and practices of representative politics, and that it implicitly or explicitly glorifies a homeland (heartland) in the face of a feeling of crisis; However, it can be said that it is chameleon-like, loaded with the qualities of its environment and is periodic in practice, since it lacks universal key values. Populism is the anti-political, heartless and chameleon-

[12] Jan-Werner Müller, **Populizm Nedir?**, İstanbul: İletişim Yayınları, 2019, p.14

[13] Margaret Canovan, **Populism**, New York: Harcourt Brace Jovanovich.1981, p.3

[14] Hans-Jürgen Puhle, Zwischen Protest und Politikstil: Populismus, **Neo-Populismus und Demokratie**. Werz, N. (Hrs.). Populismus Populisten in Übersee und Europa. Opladen, 2003, p.15.

like glorification of the homeland in the face of a crisis.[15]."

Expressing that populism defends the language of the people, in Taggart's point of view, populism always calls them using the rhetoric of the people. And because the language of the people covers the basis of democratic beliefs and popular rule, populists are constantly trying to take over[16].

Albertazzi and McDonnell define populism in "Twenty-First Century Populism: The Specter of Western European Democracy" as follows: "*Populism; We define virtuous and homogeneous people as an ideology that opposes those who describe the sovereign individuals as a group of elites or dangerous others who deprive or attempt to deprive them of their rights, values, well-being, identity, and voices* [17]."

Cas Mudde stated that populism cannot be regarded as an ideology in the strict sense, because it does not contain the basic criteria that an ideology should contain. Since populism stands on a slippery ground, it has been used in articulation with many different ideologies in the historical process, and because of this feature, it has been expressed as "weak-centered ideology"[18]. The definition of populism as a 'thin-centered ideology' means that populism becomes apparent by articulating it to other ideologies. So in the real world, populism appears along with quite different and sometimes contradictory ideologies and can take very different forms[19]. In other words, populism itself repeats itself with other ideologies as an eclectic ideology rather than a pure ideology that responds comprehensively and thoroughly to the problems produced by contemporary societies. That is, populism exists and survives by other concepts or ideologies rather than by pure existence. Because of this, both right and left politics and ideologies can carry populist elements. In different times and places, it is possible for populism to become apparent in various forms and axes according to socioeconomic and socio-political context[20].

Mudde and Kaltwasser emphasize that the definition of populism that they have developed will make sense not only by what they contain, but also by what they leave out, that is, by their opposite characteristics, and note that the direct opponents of populism are elitism and pluralism. The presented definition of populism and its stated features or opposing features make three basic concepts and/or elements important to populism in the form of

---

[15] Paul Taggart, **Populism**, Philadelphia: Open University Press.2000, p.6

[16] Paul Taggart, ibid., , p.95

[17] Daniele Albertazzi, Duncan McDonnell, **Twenty-First Century Populism**, New York: Palgrave Macmillan, 2008, p.3

[18] Cas Mudde, Populism: An Ideational Approach. K. R. Kaltwasser, P. Taggart, P. Ostiguy, & P. O. Espejo içinde, **The Oxford Handbook of Populism**, Oxford: Oxford University Press. 2017, p.30.

[19] Cas Mudde, Cristobal R. Kaltwasser, **Populizm: Kısa Bir Giris**, Tra. S. Erdem Türközü, Nika Yayınevi, Ankara, 2019, p. 17.

[20] ibid. p.806

'people', 'elites' and 'general will'[21].

Although it is difficult to determine an exact date as to when it was first used, it appears that it was used in the 1890s. This concept was used to qualify the American People's Party, founded in 1892, and subsequently became widespread[22].

The concept of populism was also used for the Narodnik movement in Russia, which emerged in the second half of the 19th century. While historically the Narodnik movement was some time earlier, it was characterized as populist after the concept of populism emerged with The Peoples Party of America. The people's Party of America and the Russian Narodnik movement, characterized as populist movements of the first period, differ in detail, but both tend to the idea of a virtuous 'people' at its core.

In fact, the spread of the concept of populism and the subject of academic interest coincides with the emergence of modern populism after the World War II. The concept of populism has hardly been used to refer to or refer to political movements or parties that existed in the period between the two World Wars. But after the World War II, the concept of populism began to be used with a different meaning and became increasingly common. The popular support of totalitarian movements such as fascism and Nazism, and the popularly endorsed policies of McCarty, revealed a new interpretation of populism. Now American experts have defined' populism 'as a form of opposition to liberal democracy and used it in a' vilifying" and pejorative sense against the past experience of ancient totalitarian regimes[23].

In this context, modern populism has often been tried to be defined through political movements in Latin America, and Peronism that emerged in Argentina has been considered the first modern populist regime [24]. One of the places where the concept of populism is most used –perhaps the most used– is political movements and actors in Latin America. 1960-1970's populist political movements in Latin America and the world, including many third countries be treated as actors in the political debate and the concept of populism and to get more space, and increased academic interest in this topic has intensified.

Looking at the wide literature on populism, it can be expressed that there is limited agreement that anti-elitism and anti-pluralism are the key

---

[21] Mudde, Kaltwasser, a.g.e. , p.17.

[22] Tim Houwen, The non-European roots of the concept of populism, Sussex European Institute, **Working Paper** No 120, Brighton, 2011, p. 7.

[23] Houwen, a.g.e., p.18

[24] Federico Finchelstein, **Faşizmden Populizme**, Tra. Ali Karatay, İletişim Yayınları, İstanbul, 2019, p. 14.

characteristics of populism, and that 'citizens',' elites' and 'common will' are the main elements and ideas that stand out in relation to these characteristics. The sense that these fundamental principles, which are divisive, reflect populism and the intent with which they correspond, must be understood. Since without knowing these principles that form the foundation of populism, it is difficult to understand populism itself.

### Populism and the reasons for the Far Right's rise in Europe

The first examples of populism are found in the USA and Russia at the end of the 19th century. Populism in the USA started to be seen in the period following the civil war. Populism emerged in the form of regional weak organizations in the process that started with the farmer revolts in the late 19th century in the USA. The poor people of this period were farmers, and the elites were politicians and bankers. The emergence of populism in Russia was on the axis of farmers as in the USA, but in the 19th century, it was in the form of rebellion against the feudal order.[25] This kind of populist movement has been observed from time to time in Eastern European countries. Especially in Europe, populism was seen together with fascism and communism. Hitler's Nazi party, which synthesizes fascism and socialism and contains populist rhetoric, can be cited as an example[26].

The history of Western European populism is not quite long. Since the 1950s, European countries, which had relatively homogeneous populations before World War II, have begun mobilizing ethnic and religious migrant movements and asylum applications from outside Europe. In Central and Eastern Europe, especially in the early 20th century, populist peasant movements, generally prone to fascism, were seen. Unlike the USA and Latin America, populism turned into a political movement in Western Europe only in the 1980s.

Fascist groups were thoroughly marginalized during the World War II and with a few exceptions, a declining presence on the fringes of parliamentarism persisted. Yet the contempt for authoritarian politics went deep and impeded the rise of populism. In the early 1980s, right-wing nationalist groups arose as a marginal movement. About one in a hundred European voters voted for a fascist or right-wing nationalist party. In the first half of the 1980s, such parties received only a few scattered votes.

While the extreme right movements generally gained the support of the people affected by the economic crisis in the 1930s, today they are mostly supported by those who are not able to benefit from the elements of the

---

[25] Pau Taggart, "New Populist Parties in Western Europe", **West European Politics.** 18(1):1995, p.34-51.
[26] Mudde, Kaltwasser, a.g.e, p.33.

globalization process, on the contrary, those who have been affected economically and socially from this process.[27] Unlike the 1930s, today's far-right movements have a they have no desire, but they have a desire to redefine it as an "ethnocracy"[28]. Among far-right parties, authoritarian, radical, populist, nationalist, and even racist tendencies prevail in some, and they are against globalization.

In Western Europe, 19 far-right parties were formed between 1965 and 1995. In Western Europe, the presence of far right parties has been rising since the 1980s. The fact that people feel vulnerable to the negative socio-economic consequences of globalization is one of the key reasons for the emergence of far-right parties. In strengthening the far right in Europe, socio-economic and political crises, such as the distribution crisis, the crisis of political representation and the crisis of identity, are successful. The emergence of the far right is hard to avoid without solving these crises. These parties often portray themselves as the representative of the "man in the street" or the "true voice of the people". They characterize the center right and left parties as elitist and claim that they represent only their economic interests.[29]

Increasing immigration after the wars in the former Yugoslavia and the enlargement of the EU to Eastern Europe and the end of the center parties' consensus on excluding the far right parties in many countries are also among the factors that have been effective in the rise of the far right parties..[30]

With the successful election results of The National Front in France in the mid-1980s, the Northern League in Italy in the mid-1990s and the Austrian Freedom Party in the early 2000s Right-wing populism has entered the political agenda of Europe. The shrinkage of Europe's welfare state, increasing migration waves, and the 2008 economic crisis are among the reasons for the rise of populism in Europe. In this context, the refugee crisis reflected in Europe after the Syrian crisis was also effective in the success of right-wing populist parties.

The main argument of right-wing populism is to restore the "people" to

---

[27] Emanuel Godin, David Hanley, "Introduction: No Enemies on the Right? Competition and Collusion between Conservatives, Moderates and Extreme Right Parties in Europe", **Journal of Contemporary European Studies**, 21(1), 2013, p.2.

[28] Roger Griffin, The Nature of Fascism, New York: St. Martin's Press, 1991. Trs: Michael Minkenberg, "From Pariah to Policy-Maker? The Radical Right in Europe, West and East: Between Margin and Mainstream", **Journal of Contemporary European Studies**, 21(1), 2013, p.10.

[29] Nora Langenbacher, Britta Schellenberg, "Introduction: An Anthology about the Manifestations and Development of the Radical Right in Europe", Nora Langenbacher ve Britta Schellenberg der., **Is Europe on the "Right" Path?: Right-wing Extremism and Right- wing Populism in Europe**, Forum Berlin, Friedrich Ebert Stiftung, 2011, p.12-15.

[30] Marc Morje Howard, " Can Populism be Suppressed in a Democracy?", **East European Politics and Societies**, 14(2), 2001, p. 21.

sovereignty. The central rhetoric of right-wing populism is therefore focused on the argument that what is right is given back to the people" whose authority has been usurped. Because, national sovereignty is reserved for the "people", "the real owners of the country". The mobilizing ability of the right-wing populists of Europe depends on unique regional and national features. Experts on the far right point out that in the regions or countries where they are based during crisis periods and at some times, right-wing populist parties are emerging and becoming stronger. It is also emphasized that without a leader who should be charismatic and powerful speaker, right-wing populists, who combine current problems with the biases of majority societies and take them into their discourse, will not be effective.

The rise of populist radical right parties was also noticed in the 2014 European Parliament (EP) elections. One of the most important common features of these parties has been European skepticism. For example, UKIP increased 16.09% of the votes it received in the 2009 EP elections to 26.77% in the 2014 EP elections. On the other hand, the upward trend of the populist radical right reflects not only on the election results, but also on its power to influence the agenda more and more and guide public opinion[31].

**Figure 1.** Aggregated Populist Votes 1980–2019[32]

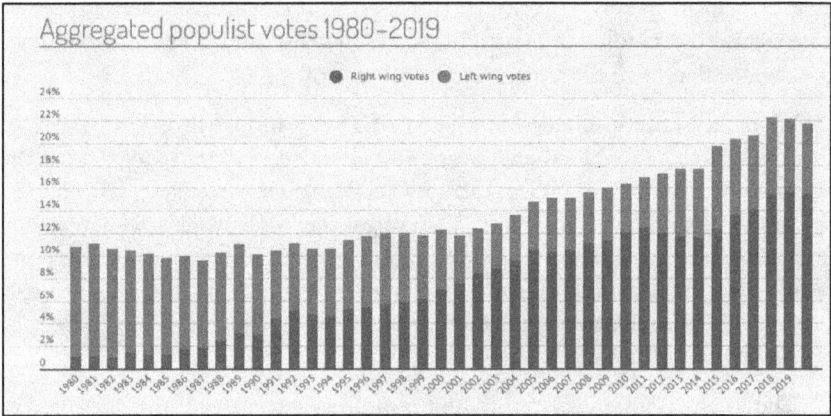

In Figure 1 ; The average voter support for authoritarian populists in the 33 countries included in TAP is 22 percent. However, since populist parties are more successful in populous countries the total voter support is 26 percent.

---

[31] Yavuz Yıldırım, Liberal Demokrasinin Krizi Baglamında Avrupa'da Sag Populizm ve Yukselen Aşırı-Sag. **Amme İdaresi Dergisi,** 50(2), 2017, p.62

[32] https://populismindex.com (Access Date: 20.10.2020)

**Figure 2.** Average Share Of Votes For Populist Parties 1980–2018[33]

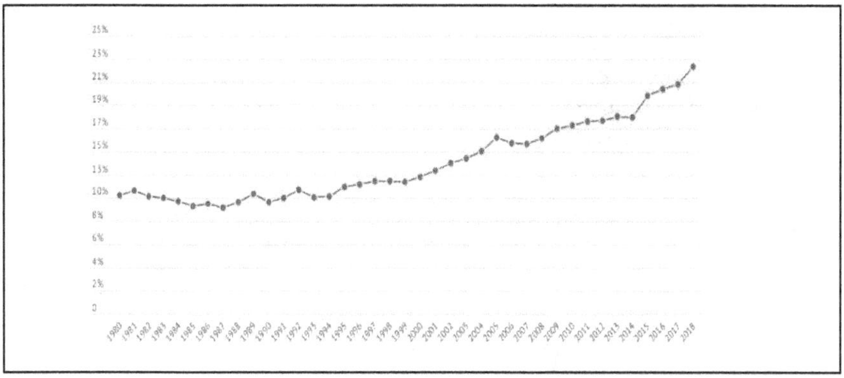

In Figure 2, we can see the increase in the voting rates of parties with populist rhetoric.

**Figure 3.** Percent of votes for populist parties 2008 and 2018[34]

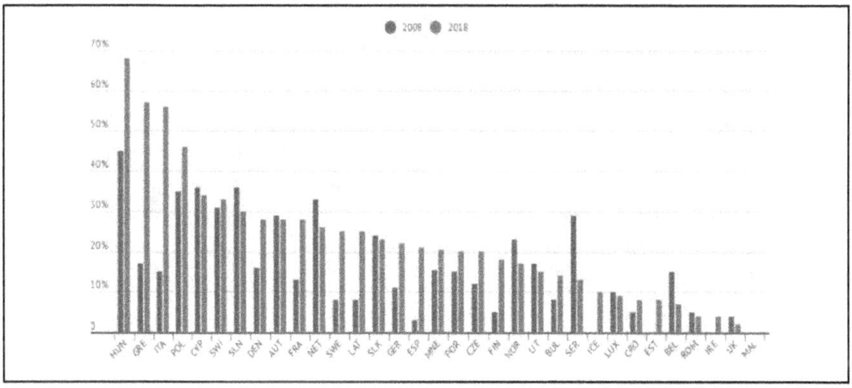

In Figure 3, the variance between countries is substantial. Populist parties in three countries amass more than half of the vote: Hungary, Greece, and Italy; share in four countries is higher than thirty per cent. Populist parties in four countries – Ro- mania, Ireland, UK, and Malta attract less than five per cent. Support for populism has risen across all of Europe over the last decade. Support is more than three percentage points higher in half of the countries than it was in 2008. Just six countries have seen a similar-scale decline.

When we look at figure 4, we can see right-wing populist parties stagnated in the first few years of the 2010s, but have expanded significantly since 2014. Their popularity dropped from 11.6 per cent in 2014 to 15.4 per cent in 2018.

---

[33] https://populismindex.com (Access Date: 20.10.2020)
[34] https://populismindex.com (Access Date: 20.10.2020)

Of course, these numbers depend on their concurrent success in many countries. Upport is highest in Hungary, Poland and Switzerland. Ireland is the only country that does not have a conservative right-wing faction. Spain has long been the only major counter-trial without right-wing populism, but Vox has risen significantly in the polls since the fall of 2018, collecting only 0.2 percent in the last election.

**Figure 4.** Average Electoral Support Right Wing Parties Europe 1980–2018[35]

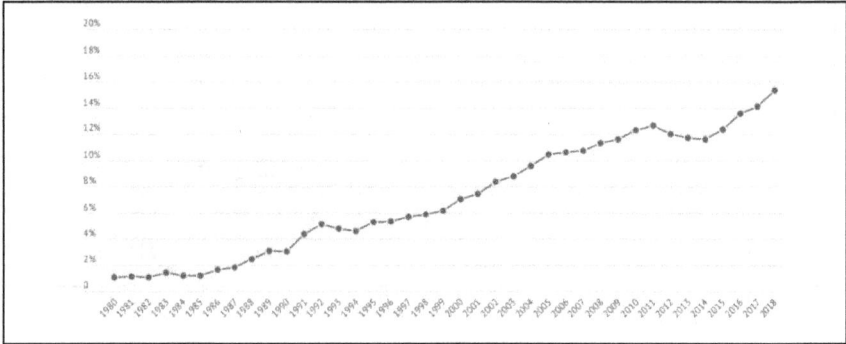

The support of the right-wing populist parties and movements in the majority societies of Europe enables them to use the thesis "we respond to the expectations of the people with our policies, we defend the views of the community center". Indeed, research in various European countries has shown that right-wing populist parties and movements are not merely short-term electoral alternatives chosen to "teach" politicians or protest governments, on the contrary, the right populists of a growing constituency have shown that right-wing populists are not just political life. It proves that they are seen as their usual part and as political formations that can become a government in the long run.

### The radical right in Austria

Located at the center of the multi-ethnic Habsburg Empire and at the crossroads of Europe, Austria has been the center of right-wing ideologies since the 19th century. After the fall of the Austro-Hungarian Empire by World War I, the first choice of the Austrian elites was not to become an independent state but to join Germany. The fact that the state established after the war is called the German-Austrian Republic is a proof of this. However, it became clear in the 1919 Saint-Germain Treaty that the Entente states did not agree. When we look at the demography of the Republic of

---

[35] https://populismindex.com (Access Date: 20.10.2020)

Austria established by this treaty, it is seen that although there are a limited number of minority groups, especially Hungarian, Croatian, Slovenian and Roma, the majority of the population consists of citizens whose native language is German.

Austria is one of the countries where it is possible to follow a reflection of trends and debates in Europe concerning the presence of immigrants. After the World War II, European countries choose from less developed societies and former colonies in Southern and Eastern Europe to fulfill the labor force needs of their increasingly increasing economies. Other European countries such as Austria primarily by a number of countries, including Turkey, "temporary workers" have made agreements, namely from the workers "temporary" thought it would be. Since the 1980s, the number of "foreigners" in Austria has rapidly increased due to the end of the Cold War, the fact that workers who are thought to be "temporary" prefer to stay by bringing their families and the increase in the number of political refugees and illegal immigrants.

The growing and increasingly visible immigrant population has led to significant changes in the political system. The most important of these changes is the weakening of the electoral base of traditional political parties, such as the Social Democratic Party of Austria (SPÖ) and the Austrian People's Party (CHP). in contrast, the influence of political parties such as the Freedom Party of Austria (FPÖ), which used the issue of immigrants to mobilize voters, began to grow.

The Freedom Party of Austria (FPÖ – Freiheitliche Partei Österreichs), one of the powerful branches of the rising far right in Europe, currently governs the Republic of Austria together with the Christian Democratic conservative-minded ÖVP (Austrian People's party)[36].

The FPÖ's effectiveness in Austrian politics dates back many years. FPÖ was founded on 7 April 1956 in Vienna. Founded in 1956, the FPÖ reached its most active years in the late 1990s, after more than 40 years. The FPÖ received only 6.5 percent of the vote in the 1956 elections. The FPÖ, whose directors are mostly former NSDAP members, received between 5.5 percent and 7 percent for a long time. Until the 1980s, there were administrative conflicts within the party between radical nationalists and economic liberals. As a matter of fact, the FPÖ became a government partner for the first time, joining the coalition led by social democrats, although it received a low rate of 5 percent in the 1983 elections after the liberals took over.

The party took a right-wing populist course after Haider was elected president in 1986. Haider broke the party's steering wheel in the anti-

---

[36] Farid Hafez, **"Avusturya Semboller Yasasının Hedefinde Ne Var?"**, SETA Perspektif, 2019, s. 1.

immigrant direction due to immigration and social incursions. Haider declared his opposition to immigration with the following statement:

"Existing immigration laws should not be softened. Every potential immigrant must prove that they can meet their job and accommodation needs. Identity requirements must be met to ensure the return of migrants, as in many industrial countries today. Legally, citizenship rights before 10 years must not be guaranteed to immigrants[37]."

Haider's right-wing populist and demagogic-actionist policies caused the party to get votes in traditional workers' circles. FPÖ became the country's second largest party and Europe's most successful right-wing populist party with 26.9 percent in the 1999 elections. Having formed a coalition with the conservative Austrian People's Party (ÖVP) in 2000, the FPÖ gathered it upon the reaction of the EU member states. [38]

The ÖVP-FPÖ coalition remained in power for only two years. In the elections held in the fall of 2002, the FPÖ was defeated with 10 percent. ÖVP formed a new coalition with the weakened FPÖ. The government partnership and the election defeat enraged the conflicts within the party. On April 4, 2005, Haider and his friends left the party and founded the party called the Austrian Future Union (BZÖ). ÖVP continued the coalition with the BZÖ, but the government's need for the FPÖ continued. [39]

The FPÖ, whose ideology turned into positive nationalism over time, adopted the mission of protecting the cultural heritage of its ancestors and passing them on to the new generations. So there was a strange dichotomy where secular and conservative values clashed. The xenophobic rhetoric of the FPÖ and the anti-immigrant feelings of the Austrian people fed each other, as a result, xenophobia and Islamophobia in the society reached disturbing levels.[40]

After Haider's death, the far-right "Austrian Identity Movement" organization emerged in 2012. This organization, which is still in existence, has also carried out some violent acts. This movement, which argues that the question of "identity" plays an important role, is an interesting way to identify its identity as an ethnographer. The organization believes that all nations should protect their identities and read the world on "us" and "the other".

---

[37] John Jack Malone, "**Examining the Rise of Right Wing Populist Parties in Western Europe**", Honors Thesis, College of Saint Benedict and Saint John's University, 2014, p. 30
[38] https://www.bundestag.de/resource/blob/189774/7c6dd629f4afff7bf4f962a45c110b5f/elections_weimar_republic-data.pdf (Access Date: 15.11.2020)
[39] Selcen Oner, Avrupa'da Yükselen Aşırı Sağ, Yeni 'Öteki'ler ve Türkiye'nin AB Üyeliği. Ankara **Avrupa Çalışmaları Dergisi**, 13(1), 2014 p.163-184
[40] Andre Zaslove, Closing the door? The ideology and impact of radical right populism on immigration policy in Austria and Italy. **Journal of Political Ideologies,** 9(1), 2004, p.99-118.

The organization that makes the distinction between" we "and" others " openly claims, however, that it is against racism and that its members only want to protect their own culture.[41] .

There are differences in the right-wing structure of the FPÖ between the Haider period 1986-2005 and the Heinz-Christian Strache period in 2005. Strache has been following a different strategy since 2005. Under the leadership of the Haider, the FPÖ acted in the form of a far-right party. In this period, the FPÖ had never broken its ties with both the national socialist background and anti-Semitism and never left its far-right direction.

Strache, known as Haider's greatest defender, has gradually become his biggest rival and has become the leader of the party. Strache modernized his party and discourse in order to get him to accept the idea of coming to power. He chose to address a wider segment by developing a more flexible discourse. Strache drew an executive elites to a wider segment, and placed his policies on the "Austrian patriotism" discourse instead of the far-right nationalist discourse of Haider. Here, the great German nation of the past and the others created against it were replaced by the "Austrian patriotism" and the other by immigrants and Muslims.

Despite its extreme right-wing nationalist structure, the FPÖ was able to reach wider sections by overcoming classical class divisions and sexist approaches both during the Haider period and during the Strache period. The fact that he was a coalition partner with the FPÖ center-right party between 2000 and 2005 drew the reaction of the EU and EU countries. They frozen their bilateral diplomatic relations with Austria for a while. After a while, they lifted the sanctions they imposed on the Austrian government, following some commitments from the coalition government. In recent years, the FPÖ has abandoned some of its extreme rhetoric and policies..[42]

The populist radical right discourse and all these policies that the FPÖ took a role in the implementation of the government as a partner show that there is a significant shift from democracy to ethnocracy and increasing authoritarianism in Austria. The government's tolerance of immigrants and asylum seekers has not only diminished, but the numerous anti-Jewish, neo-Nazi and asylum seekers and minorities that have eroded Austrian democracy since the FPÖ came to the government as a coalition partner in 2017, and the statement that attitudes encourage them to move away from democracy and applications have increased [43].

---

[41] Göç Vakfı, (2017). Avusturya'daki Aşırı Sağcı "AvusturyaKimlik Hareketi" Örgütü. http://gocvakfi. org/ avusturyadaki-asiri-sagci-avusturya-kimlik-hareketi-orgutu/. (Access Date: 12.11.2020)

[42] BBC. (2017, December 16). Austrian Far-right joins coalition led by PM Sebastian Kurz. https://www.bbc.com/news/ world-europe-42374693, (Access Date: 12.11.2020)

[43] Liam Hoare, "Praise for Hitler and calling refugees 'untermenschen' - the members of Austria's

As a result of the general elections held in Austria on 15 October 2017, the conservative Austrian People's Party (ÖVP), which received 31.5 percent of the votes and did not get the majority, formed a coalition in December 2017 with the FPÖ, which received 26 percent from the elections. Although this coalition government ended with a scandal in May 2019, the more moderate ÖVP came out as the first party in the September 2019 elections[44].

Today, the FPÖ has pioneered these issues by developing rhetoric strategies and tactics to impose on migrants, a common feature of far-right and populist movements across Europe. The FPÖ, which plays a major role in making Islam an existential threat to its European identity and values, has pioneered it not only in Austria but also in many European countries. During the foundation period, the FPÖ brought the people who had important duties under the Hitler regime to the party's management staff.

### Refugee politics and crises in Austria

European countries, which had relatively homogeneous societies until the World War II, have assumed an ethnically and religiously multicultural structure with migration movements and asylum requests from outside Europe since the 1950s. The increasingly multicultural societies have brought many discussions in terms of European countries.

One of the topics of discussion is the demands of these new groups, which have different cultures, religions and lifestyles, to live in the host countries according to their own cultural and religious values, provoked debates in areas such as secularism or freedom of thought. The other topic is How immigrants will adapt to European values has been discussed. It has been claimed that immigrants, who form a new subclass, increase the crime rate in the society and damage the social state.

Immigrants have been claimed to be loyal to their country of birth or religion, rather than the countries in which they reside, and their citizenship has been challenged. The presence of Muslim immigrants has been evaluated around a security problem, especially with the September 11 attacks in New York, the Madrid and London bombings, the assassination of Theo van Gogh in Amsterdam or the attacks in Paris.

Given the idea that democracies are more open to differences relative to other contemporary political systems, it is shown that existing societies in

---

governing Freedom Party," The JC Network, Mart 20, 2019,
https://www.thejc.com/news/world/praise-for-hitler-and-calling-refugees-untermenschen-the-members-of-austria-s-governing-freedom-1.466578, (Access Date. 12.11.2020)
[44] Hilary Clarke, Stephanie Halasz ve Judith Vonberg, "Coalition Government with far-right party takes power in Austria," CNN, Aralık 18, 2017, https://edition.cnn.com/2017/12/18/europe/austria-government-intl/index.html, (Access Date: 12.11.2020)

Europe have difficulties integrating the variations in the structure that come with immigrants. Although European societies seek to accommodate and incorporate differences in the structure within the context of democratic rights and freedoms, on the other hand, they are struggling to do so because of a number of financial, economic, cultural and political problems , especially for security reasons.

The discomfort stemming from the necessity of recognizing the rights and freedoms that democracy promises to individuals and groups and the extensive use of these rights and freedoms by foreigners is one of the dilemmas that European democracies are hotly debated today. On the one hand, there are those who claim that a multicultural society will enrich democracy, on the other hand, there are those who see the responsibility of non-European groups for not being adequately integrated into society and acts of violence taking place. [45]

The fear of immigrants has increased in Austria since the 1980s. In the 1990s, after the immigrants from Eastern Europe and the increasing refugee influx due to the Bosnian and Kosovo Wars, concerns about immigrants increased..[46]

After the World War II, Austria became a heavily immigrant country. The first period after the war is a migration period determined by the "guest worker" mobility. Especially since the early 1960s, Yugoslavia and with Turkey "guest workers" in this period, beginning on framework agreements they did not think the Austrian government on relations with the bulk of these workers did not develop any policy in this regard. Because in this period, which continued until the early 1970s, it was assumed that immigrants would return to their countries. The second period, which continued from the early 1970s to the 1990s, is the period when the immigrant population increased uncontrollably and this issue became the focus of political discussions. First of all, it has been understood that a significant part of the guest workers who are supposed to return will continue to remain and the integration of immigrants into society has become a priority issue due to the family reunification of these workers. A second phenomenon that marked this period is refugee mobility. In the Cold War environment, Austria became a transit or destination for refugees fleeing communist Eastern European countries. [47]

With the emergence of Islamophobia and anti-Islamism in the West after

---

[45] Edip Asaf Bekaroglu, Belonging through eveyday-life practices: the Dutch case. Kerry Gallagher (ed.) **Multiculturalism: Critical and Inter-Disciplinary Perspectives**, Oxford: Inter-Disciplinary Press, 2011, p.141-149

[46] Zaslove, ibid. p.99-118

[47] Albert Kraler, Karin Sohler, Austria. A. Triandafyllidou & R. Gropas (Der.) **European Immigration: A Sourcebook**, Hampshire: Ashgate. , 2017, p.19-31

9/11, rather than racist discourses and policies, populist extreme right-wing parties began to tend towards culturally exclusionary discourses and policies. Anti-Muslim immigration and refugee opposition have come to the fore in the rhetoric and policies of these parties in recent years. Despite EU countries' attempts to establish a common refugee policy, especially in the aftermath of the refugee crisis, these efforts have been inconclusive and the refugee crisis in EU countries has been growing.

One of the most important factors in Austria's uninterrupted arrival of the far-right movements is that they did not come to terms with their responsibilities during the Nazi period. This continuity does not allow him to get rid of this trauma. Thus, in fact, the far-right remnants of a kind of ashy past can easily emerge as a form of expression that is easily resurrected and blown to the extremes in any wind. In a broader sense, this disturbance and the weakness of the collective ego prepared the Austrians to be hostile to the "other". Today, the anxiety of losing identity has been replaced by the hostility towards the "other" and the "stranger".[48]

Until the 1990s, Austria's migration policy was completely shaped within the framework of the "rotation model", that is, economic concerns and the expectation of the return of "guest workers" to their country. In the 1990s, the necessity of abandoning the rotation model and building a new immigration and immigration policy was accepted by all actors in Austria. In this context, the first comprehensive law change was made in 1992. The main purpose of this law change, called the 1992 Residence Act, is to limit immigration. The most important innovation brought by this law is that it classifies migration types and brings a quota for each category. However, these quotas have affected the immigrants in the country as well as the immigrants who want to enter the country. Due to the conditions of obtaining a residence permit, immigrants who have been in Austria for a long time have lost their residence.[49]

The FPÖ pioneered these issues by developing rhetorical strategies and tactics of burdening immigrants, which are a common feature of far-right and populist movements across Europe today. Playing a major role in making Islam accepted as an existential threat to European identity and values, the FPÖ pioneered this not only in Austria but also in many European countries. The FPÖ also greatly influenced the rapid growth of Alternative für Deutschland (AfD) in Germany.[50]

---

[48] Cristen Karner, Negotiating National Identities: Between Globalization the Past and 'the Other'. Ashgate: Routledge, 2011, p.11

[49] Kraler, Sohler, ibid. , p-19-31.

[50] Matthew Karnitschnig,. Austria's right-wing insurgency. Politico, Mayıs 19, 2016, https://www. politico.eu/ article/austria-political-upheaval-not-just-flirting-with-far-right-werner-faymann-norbert-hofer-fpo/, (Access Date: 12.11.2020)

The platform of the FPÖ party gives a special position to indigenousism, which advocates for the country, heritage, language, values and culture, starting with the motto "first Austria," referring to the German-speaking cultural groups, their background and traditions. This also notes that Austria belongs to European society, and that Christianity forms this. Even the software stresses that Austria is not an refugee country.[51]

It is possible to see examples of indigenousism in Sabastian Kurz's policies against Muslims when he was Foreign Minister in 2015. At that time, Kurz supported the Draft Islamic Law on imams to preach in German, not in their own language. He stated that they do not want imams appointed by the governments of other countries in Austria. Again with the same law, it prohibited the funding of Islamic organizations, mosques and imams with foreign capital and mosques associated with political Islam were closed. However, it has shown that there is no equal treatment before the law, by not applying any sanctions for funding organizations belonging to other minority religions with foreign capital. These practices showed that the perception of immigrants as terrorists and the use of Islam and terrorism in similar meanings has become widespread and damaged pluralism.[52]

Foreign Minister Sabastian Kurz has reached an agreement with Austria's Balkan neighbors to close the borders to immigrants despite the EU and UN protests. With the closure of the border between Greece and Macedonia, tens of thousands of migrants were stranded. These anti-immigrant policies of Kurz were perceived by the Austrian people as protecting their country from external threats and were appreciated by a large part of the public. Kurz has been declared a hero of Austria as it closed the borders to immigrants.

Kurz took over the ÖVP in 2017 thanks to his anti-immigration policies and became Europe's youngest prime minister. He managed to win the support of Austrian right-wing voters by launching an anti-Islam campaign to control migration and the deportation of asylum seekers due to the 2015-2016 refugee crisis. They stated that they will not accept refugees seeking illegal asylum in Austria, they will only give temporary protection, they also plan to close Islamic schools and will work to prevent the creation of parallel societies.[53] Kurz, who was elected as the term presidency of the Council of the European Union in July 2018, said that ensuring security in Europe is

---

[51] Party Programme of the Freedom Party of Austria," https://www.fpoe.at/fileadmin/user_upload/www.fpoe.at/dokumente/2015/2011_graz_parteiprogramm_englisch_web.pd (Access Date: 12.11.2020)

[52] Shuster, Simon. "Austria's young Chancellor Sebastian Kurz is bringing the Far-Right into Mainstream." Time Kasım 29, 2018, http://time.com/5466497/sebastian-kurz/ (Access Date: 13.11.2020)

[53] Stephanies Halasz, Judithe Vonberg,Stephanie Clarke, , "Coalition Government with far-right party takes power in Austria". https://edition.cnn.com/2017/12/18/europe/austria-government-intl/index.html (Access Date: 15.11.2020)

their top priority and chose the slogan "Protect Europe" for the term presidency. With this slogan, he stated that Europe belongs to Europeans and Christians.

The fact that the far-right FPÖ became a coalition partner with ÖVP in 2000 had a great impact on migration and integration policies. In the far-right populist discourse, it is accepted that uncontrolled immigration policies have direct effects on the increase in crime rates, the emergence of situations that threaten national security and the degeneration of national culture, and immigration must be stopped or restricted.[54]

Indeed, extensive legislative changes were made three times on migration between 2000-2006. The first of these came in 2002. With this change, new immigrants who want to come to Austria and immigrants entering the country after 1998 are required to sign the "integration agreement" and take compulsory language lessons. On the other hand, it has initiated the practice of "residence certificate", which makes it safer for immigrants who meet certain conditions to stay and work in Austria. With this certificate, which is given to immigrants who have been living in the country for at least five years, unlimited working right has been gained. [55]

In 2005, a very comprehensive change was made in immigration law once again. With this law, the content of the "integration agreement" was expanded, the entry of new immigrants was made difficult and the authority of state institutions over immigrants was hardened. For example, it has been made difficult to obtain a residence permit from spouse status in order to prevent Austrian residency from fake marriages. Another change that concerns immigrants in 2005 was made in the Citizenship Law. [56]

On issues of Islamic radicalization and Islamophobia, the presence of Muslims in the country, which has been perceived as a security issue since the September 11 attacks, has constantly engaged the public, often handled in the media, it has been claimed that second and third generation young Muslim immigrants tend to radicalism and violence. Combined with the growing and visible population of Muslims in Austria and this security perspective, it is observed that Islamophobic approaches are proliferating. In the light of these controversies, the Islamic law was adopted in 2015.

At the beginning of 2020, it was claimed that "with the wave of migration in recent years, people who came to the country reject basic values such as democracy, there has been an increase in criminal incidents and antisemitic tendencies" and that a new center will be established for research, prevention

---

[54] Ibid., p.99-118
[55] Ibid., p.19-31
[56] Claus Hofhansel, Citizenship in Austira, Germany, and Switzerland: Courts, Legislators, and Administrations. **International Migration Review**, 42(1), 163-192, 2008, p.163.192

and enlightenment work and on the grounds of fighting political Islam. The" Center for Documentation of political Islam " was established as a federal fund, as in the case of the Austrian Integration Fund. The newly formed Central Government programme was planned to be set up under the title of Combating Antisemitism, racism and religiously motivated extremism. But the announcement that the government will only act on 'political Islam' and Muslims by the great partner of the ÖVP has caused a lot of reactions. In the future, we will follow the payoff of this very new anti-Islamic step in Austrian politics.

As we can see in Table 1, as a result of the interventions made after September 11, we can see that too many refugees from Syria, Afghanistan and Iraq came to Austria with the effect of the Arab Spring. We can say that many Muslims fleeing civil war, religious and political pressures took refuge in many European countries, especially Austria. At this point, we can observe the pursuit of democracy in line with the humane living conditions of these refugees. Although they seek democracy, they are exposed to a lot of pressure in the places they go, and they cannot feel that they belong anywhere.

**Table 1.** Refugees Recognised in Austria 2006-2016 By Citizenship[57]

| Citizenship | 2006 | 2007 | 2008 | 2009 | 2010 | 2011 | 2012 | 2013 | 2014 | 2015 | 2016 |
|---|---|---|---|---|---|---|---|---|---|---|---|
| Total | 4.063 | 5.197 | 3.753 | 3.247 | 2.977 | 3.572 | 3.680 | 4.133 | 8.734 | 14.413 | 22.307 |
| Syria | 47 | 86 | 68 | 51 | 117 | 360 | 542 | 838 | 3.604 | 8.114 | 15.528 |
| Afghanistan | 475 | 497 | 486 | 587 | 584 | 822 | 969 | 1.259 | 2.450 | 2.083 | 1.756 |
| Iraq | 92 | 215 | 240 | 177 | 81 | 202 | 161 | 121 | 211 | 637 | 1.328 |
| Somalia | 103 | 191 | 118 | 149 | 189 | 261 | 241 | 254 | 269 | 548 | 494 |
| Russian Federation | 2.090 | 2.636 | 1.557 | 1.398 | 1.082 | 1.016 | 839 | 673 | 775 | 667 | 460 |
| Iran | 211 | 318 | 198 | 153 | 222 | 275 | 442 | 520 | 422 | 436 | 439 |
| China Peoples Rep. | 25 | - | 18 | 38 | 29 | 48 | 42 | 61 | 65 | 54 | 57 |
| Eritrea | 3 | 6 | 4 | 10 | 15 | 12 | 11 | 15 | 23 | 39 | 56 |
| Tadjikistan | 2 | 6 | - | 7 | 6 | 4 | 10 | 9 | 12 | 10 | 54 |
| Bangladesch | 5 | 4 | 4 | 14 | 13 | 9 | 5 | 19 | 12 | 42 | 38 |
| Congo Dem. Rep. | 55 | 40 | 27 | 29 | 52 | 21 | 32 | 26 | 41 | 32 | 38 |
| Pakistan | 6 | 4 | 12 | 2 | 3 | 4 | 14 | 28 | 41 | 25 | 30 |
| Egypt | - | 9 | 3 | 4 | 2 | 9 | 15 | 9 | 31 | 16 | 29 |
| Sudan | 26 | 29 | 15 | 11 | 21 | 41 | 21 | 29 | 30 | 26 | 25 |
| Kazakhstan | 1 | 4 | 4 | 4 | 3 | 7 | 4 | 2 | 16 | 7 | 24 |
| Ukraine | 20 | 20 | 33 | 13 | 14 | 11 | 8 | 3 | 5 | 22 | 22 |
| Jemen | - | 3 | 1 | - | 1 | 1 | 2 | 2 | 1 | 12 | 21 |
| Cameroon | 16 | 32 | 29 | 30 | 18 | 18 | 21 | 26 | 14 | 25 | 16 |
| Guinea | 4 | 6 | 5 | 1 | 8 | 18 | 5 | 11 | 7 | 26 | 16 |
| Jordan | - | 3 | - | 1 | 1 | - | 1 | 3 | 2 | 13 | 16 |
| Nigeria | 11 | 20 | 12 | 16 | 15 | 15 | 13 | - | 20 | 12 | 16 |
| Ethiopia | 16 | 10 | 4 | 13 | 15 | 12 | 10 | 4 | 18 | 9 | 13 |
| Armenia | 100 | 135 | 105 | 44 | 22 | 30 | 19 | 12 | 16 | 22 | 12 |
| Azerbaijan | 31 | 73 | 59 | 24 | 46 | 13 | 8 | 14 | 10 | 11 | 12 |
| Congo | 10 | 13 | 10 | 15 | 11 | 21 | 11 | 9 | 7 | 8 | 12 |
| Kosovo[1]) | - | - | - | - | - | 18 | 19 | 14 | 13 | 10 | 12 |
| Lebanon | - | 18 | 1 | 2 | 2 | 6 | - | 4 | 3 | 10 | 12 |
| Gambia | 6 | 5 | 4 | 13 | 20 | 8 | 11 | 8 | 4 | 20 | 8 |
| Turkey | 113 | 195 | 246 | 93 | 112 | 64 | 33 | 35 | 23 | 9 | 8 |
| Kyrgyztan | 25 | 22 | 43 | 26 | 9 | 28 | 10 | 4 | 12 | 13 | 7 |
| Cote d'Ivoire | 1 | 7 | 5 | 3 | 3 | 2 | 4 | 1 | 5 | 1 | 6 |

---

[57]http://www.statistik.at/web_en/statistics/PeopleSociety/population/migration/asylum/index.html
(Access Date: 11.11.2020)

| Georgia | 38 | 56 | 61 | 62 | 25 | 11 | 27 | 4 | 11 | - | 4 |
|---|---|---|---|---|---|---|---|---|---|---|---|

| Citizenship | 2006 | 2007 | 2008 | 2009 | 2010 | 2011 | 2012 | 2013 | 2014 | 2015 | 2016 |
|---|---|---|---|---|---|---|---|---|---|---|---|
| Total | 4.063 | 5.197 | 3.753 | 3.247 | 2.977 | 3.572 | 3.680 | 4.133 | 8.734 | 14.413 | 22.307 |
| Libya | - | - | - | - | - | - | - | - | 2 | 13 | 4 |
| Serbia³) | 318 | 240 | 117 | 49 | 42 | 39 | 13 | 15 | 12 | 18 | 4 |
| Uganda | 4 | 2 | 1 | 1 | 2 | 1 | 1 | 2 | 1 | 1 | 4 |
| Algeria | 1 | 11 | 1 | 2 | 4 | 8 | 1 | 2 | 2 | - | 3 |
| Morocco | 3 | - | - | 1 | 1 | - | 1 | 1 | 2 | 2 | 3 |
| Sri Lanka | 1 | 4 | 4 | 12 | 4 | 2 | - | 2 | 3 | 3 | 3 |
| Albania | 16 | 9 | 5 | 7 | 11 | 5 | 5 | 1 | 3 | 1 | 2 |
| Angola | 17 | 22 | 9 | 12 | 11 | 7 | 6 | 5 | - | 7 | 2 |
| Belarus | 6 | 15 | 9 | 6 | 4 | 6 | 4 | 3 | 1 | - | 2 |
| Bosnia and Herzegovina | 17 | 11 | 11 | 8 | 5 | 3 | 1 | - | 8 | 11 | 2 |
| Guatemala | - | - | 5 | - | - | - | - | 1 | - | - | 2 |
| Philippines | - | - | - | - | 1 | 1 | 2 | - | - | - | 2 |
| Usbekistan | 13 | 14 | 39 | 11 | 6 | 8 | 3 | 4 | 4 | 3 | 2 |
| China Rep. (Taiwan) | - | 35 | 1 | 10 | 3 | 2 | 1 | 5 | 1 | - | 1 |
| Cuba | 1 | 7 | 2 | 3 | 1 | 2 | 2 | - | - | 1 | 1 |
| Indonesia | - | - | - | - | - | - | - | - | - | - | 1 |
| Kenya | 1 | 1 | 1 | 5 | 2 | 8 | 3 | 3 | - | 3 | 1 |
| Kuwait | - | - | - | - | - | 1 | 1 | - | - | - | 1 |
| Liberia | 3 | 2 | 1 | 2 | - | - | - | - | 1 | 2 | 1 |
| Mongolia | 2 | 23 | 20 | 6 | 3 | 3 | 4 | - | 4 | 4 | 1 |
| Rwanda | 3 | - | - | 8 | 3 | - | - | 1 | - | - | 1 |
| Senegal | - | - | - | - | - | - | 1 | - | 1 | - | 1 |
| Togo | 1 | 3 | 2 | 6 | - | 1 | - | - | - | - | 1 |
| Tunisia | 2 | - | 2 | - | - | - | - | - | 1 | - | 1 |
| United Arab Emirates | - | - | - | - | - | - | - | - | - | - | 1 |
| United States | - | - | - | - | - | - | - | - | 1 | - | 1 |

| Citizenship | 2006 | 2007 | 2008 | 2009 | 2010 | 2011 | 2012 | 2013 | 2014 | 2015 | 2016 |
|---|---|---|---|---|---|---|---|---|---|---|---|
| Benin | 2 | 1 | - | - | - | - | - | - | - | - | - |
| Bhutan | - | - | - | - | 1 | - | - | 1 | - | - | - |
| Bolivia | - | - | - | - | 9 | - | - | 1 | 1 | - | - |
| Bulgaria | - | - | - | - | - | - | - | - | - | - | - |
| Burkina Faso | 1 | 1 | 1 | - | 2 | 3 | 1 | 1 | - | 1 | - |
| Burundi | 2 | 2 | 2 | 4 | 2 | 1 | - | 1 | - | 4 | - |
| Cambodia | - | - | - | - | - | - | - | - | - | - | - |
| Canada | - | - | - | - | - | - | 1 | - | - | - | - |
| Central African Republic | - | - | 31 | 41 | 34 | - | - | - | - | - | - |
| Colombia | 8 | - | - | - | - | - | - | - | - | - | - |
| Croatia | 1 | - | - | - | - | - | - | - | - | - | - |
| Czech Rep. | - | - | - | - | - | - | - | - | - | - | - |
| Equatorial Guinea | - | - | - | - | - | - | - | - | - | 1 | - |
| Estonia | - | - | 3 | - | - | - | - | - | - | - | - |
| France | - | - | - | - | - | - | - | - | - | - | - |
| Gabon | - | - | - | - | - | - | - | - | - | 1 | - |
| Ghana | 4 | 1 | 5 | 1 | - | 1 | - | - | - | - | - |
| Guinea-Bissau | - | - | - | 1 | - | - | - | - | - | - | - |
| Haiti | - | - | - | - | - | - | - | - | - | 1 | - |
| Hungary | - | - | - | - | - | - | - | - | - | - | - |
| India | 2 | 2 | 3 | 3 | 2 | 1 | 1 | - | - | - | - |
| Israel | - | - | - | - | - | - | - | - | 8 | - | - |
| Korea, South | - | - | - | - | 1 | - | - | - | - | - | - |
| Laos | - | - | 1 | - | - | - | - | - | - | - | - |
| Latvia | - | 2 | - | - | - | - | - | - | - | - | - |
| Macedonia | 10 | 18 | 11 | 1 | - | - | 1 | - | 2 | - | - |
| Madagascar | - | - | - | - | - | 2 | 1 | - | - | - | - |
| Mali | - | - | - | - | - | - | 3 | 2 | - | 1 | - |
| Mauritania | 1 | - | - | - | - | - | 1 | - | - | - | - |
| Mauritius | - | - | - | - | - | - | - | 2 | - | - | - |
| Moldova - Republic of | 13 | 13 | 9 | 5 | 6 | - | 1 | 1 | 2 | 2 | - |
| Montenegro² | - | 1 | - | - | - | - | - | - | - | - | - |
| Myanmar | - | - | 4 | - | 1 | 2 | 5 | 9 | 4 | 4 | - |
| Nepal | 8 | 4 | 3 | 5 | 5 | - | 2 | 1 | 1 | 1 | - |

| Nicaragua | - | - | - | - | - | - | - | - | - | 1 | - |

| Citizenship | 2006 | 2007 | 2008 | 2009 | 2010 | 2011 | 2012 | 2013 | 2014 | 2015 | 2016 |
|---|---|---|---|---|---|---|---|---|---|---|---|
| Niger | 1 | - | - | - | - | - | - | 10 | - | - | - |
| Peru | - | - | - | - | - | - | - | - | - | - | - |
| Poland | - | - | - | - | - | - | - | - | - | - | - |
| Romania | 5 | 5 | 2 | 2 | 2 | - | 3 | - | - | - | - |
| Saudi Arabia | - | - | - | - | - | - | - | - | - | 3 | - |
| Sierra Leone | 1 | 3 | 3 | 2 | 2 | - | 2 | 2 | 1 | 2 | - |
| Slovakia | 1 | - | - | - | 1 | - | - | - | - | - | - |
| South Sudan | - | - | - | - | - | - | - | 2 | - | - | - |
| Turkmenistan | - | - | - | 2 | - | - | - | 3 | - | 1 | - |
| Vietnam | 3 | 8 | 6 | 2 | 1 | 2 | 2 | 1 | - | - | - |
| Zimbabwe | 1 | - | 5 | 2 | 5 | 4 | - | 1 | - | 1 | - |
| stateless | 41 | 50 | 55 | 34 | 49 | 83 | 48 | 32 | 458 | 1.333 | 1.690 |
| unsettled citizenship | 17 | 24 | 7 | 5 | 10 | 9 | 9 | 1 | 36 | 29 | - |

## Conclusion

Populism is now in a position that not as an ideology, but as a mode of action, dominates the political arena in almost every region of the world. Many politicians, regardless of right or left ideology, dominate the masses through their nationalist rhetoric and populist actions. Right-wing populism has risen in strength in Europe, especially in the period after the Arab Spring. In the process of increasing terrorist attacks and waves of immigration, right-wing conservative politicians have often taken a line that extends from time to time to bigotry in their rhetoric and suggestions. Immigration surges, terrorist attacks and jihadist groups that identify themselves as, as well as a crack in the country's Unity State and the economic downturn of the European Union, have triggered the sound of voices to intensify the elevation of conservative politicians in both countries. With the combination of different factors, the importance of the promises of nationalist politicians of a more introverted, closed frontier, free of outsiders, returning to traditional values, the nationalized economy has risen. It has been shown that right-wing populists, who carry out their propaganda through concepts that appeal to emotions like religion, language, ethnicity, and country, have used democracy several times by combining it with demagogy.

Populist radical right parties often claim a link between rising crime rates, rising immigration numbers, and immigration policies, and view immigrants as scapegoats. In the expressions of the FPÖ, "refugee influx", "foreign flood", etc. It is seen that he frequently uses expressions about migration. It is seen that the FPÖ is effective in creating the "we" and "others" distinction, as seen in other populist radical right-wing parties. [58]

The FPÖ advocates that asylum seekers should remain in isolated areas until all procedures are completed. It advocates for the inclusion of the abuse of the social welfare state in the criminal law as a crime and the urgent

---

[58] Ibid. p.99-118

removal of those who commit this crime from the country.[59]

FPÖ stated that Austria was never and will never be an immigrant country. According to them, citizens have the right to oppose, control and stop unlimited and uncontrolled immigration. He claims that excessive migration leads to unemployment, decreases in wages and negatively affects the utilization of welfare state opportunities for local people.[60]

Today in Austria, the center-right People's Party (ÖVP) and the Green Party government are preparing to document the certification center and institutions and organizations belonging to Muslims under the name of "struggle against political Islam". In the government program, the documentation center planned to be established under the heading "Combating anti-Semitism, racism and religious extremism" announced that the ÖVP, the main partner of the government, will work only for "political Islam". It caused the reaction of Muslims, non-governmental organizations and academicians, especially some members of parliament from the coalition partner Green Party.[61]

The political, economic , and cultural changes that occurred after 2000 can be said to have increased the problems found by Hentges. The debates focused more on immigrants' "integration issue" than on racism and xenophobia. Since the 2000s there have been numerous claims in both Germany and Austria that immigrants were unwilling to embrace or absolutely unwilling to integrate. With these statements, it was stated that immigrants do not want to adopt German or Austrian cultural values, for example they do not accept gender equality. Although these allegations seem to point more towards Turks and Muslims, it has been implied that larger immigrant groups actually resist integration. This discourse, in keeping with the neoliberal ideology, implied that immigrants were responsible for their own destiny and situation; In other words, the socio-economic, political, institutional and cultural problems that emerged with migration have been neglected, this has led to an increase in negative attitudes and discourses towards immigrants, and ultimately, the concept of integration has become a means of assimilationist expectations.

Austria is today the country that struggles least with the spatial segregation of migrants, unemployment and delinquency. Despite a long history of immigration, Austria has never declared itself an official immigration country like Germany. The fact that Muslims are seen as suspicious groups that

---

[59] Nazif Mandacı , Gökay Özerim, Uluslararası Göçlerin Bir Güvenlik Konusuna Dönüşümü: Avrupa'da Radikal Sağ Partiler Ve Göçün Güvenlikleştirilmesi. **Uluslararası İlişkiler**, 10(39), 2013, p.106-126

[60] Ibid.. p..99-118

[61] https://batiraporu.com/irkcilik/avusturya-siyasal-islam-bahanesiyle-muslumanlara-ait-kurumlari-fislemeye-hazirlaniyor/ (Access Date: 13.11.2020)

cannot be integrated and are prone to violence in European countries has made the lives of Muslims in general and Turks in particular. Due to the contraction in employment, unemployment and related poverty have become a serious problem among European Turks and other minorities.

Austrian Turks and Muslims, as in other European countries, have to take negative attitudes towards the country they live in, to feel excluded and alone. They started. Many people think that they are not treated as equal citizens in the country they live in, and they do not feel at home.

# CHAPTER 12

# BELGIUM'S IMMIGRATION ASYLUM POLICIES IN TIMES OF CRISIS

## Ebru Dalğakıran*

## Introduction

Since World War II, the idea of peace, liberty, and economic prosperity has driven European nations closer. As a result of political cooperation, the establishment of a common market with a free-travel zone, the European continent has turned into one of the favored places in the world to live. Besides that, liberal democracy, economic growth, stability, and social welfare facilities have made the continent an attractive destination for migrants. Belgium, an open economy and the capital of the EU, has been one of the attractive destinations in Europe for years for both EU citizens and others.

Belgium is one of the least populated countries after Luxembourg when compared to other founder members of the European Union (EU).[1] Despite its small population, Belgium is one of the most multicultural and multinational countries of the EU. It could be said that the main reason why Belgium has a highly multicultural and multinational population is that, similar to other European countries, immigration to Belgium has been continued under intra-EU mobility, international students, family reunions, refugees, and asylum seekers migration patterns since the end of the World War II. Thus, all patterns of migration have contributed to the diversification of the Belgian population. Today, the foreign resident population represents 12.4 percent (8.2 percent EU citizens, 4.2 percent non-EU citizens) of the total population of Belgium.[2]

Even though Belgium is a country of immigration, similar to other Western European countries, the increased influx of asylum seekers in mid-2015 has had a severe effect on Belgium's migration and asylum policies as well as socio-economic policies. This is because in high-income countries like

* Ph.D. Candidate and Research Assistant Marmara University Institute of European Studies, Istanbul, Turkey.

[1] According to the Eurostat data, on January 1, 2020, Belgium's population is 11.549.9 million. "Among the founding EU Member States, Germany has the largest population with 83.2 million, followed by France 67.1 million, Italy 60.2 million, Netherlands 17.4 million, and Luxembourg 626 thousand". *See* "Eurostat Newsrelease", https://tinyurl.com/y2nzewpt (Access 17.11.2020).

[2] National Bank of Belgium, "Resident population by nationality in Belgium, broken down by Region", https://tinyurl.com/yvx2p8u7 (Access 17.11.2020).

Belgium, the population has increased less than the number of migrants in the country. Thus, immigration became a source of fear in society and one of the major concerns of politicians.[3]

In addition to the reception crisis of 2015, Belgium has been under the effect of the economic crisis since 2007. At the same time, currently, Belgium has been dealt with a global health crisis: COVID-19. Thus, Belgium is amid multiple crises and has to respond to eliminate their effects. During crisis periods, the most vulnerable group is undoubtedly immigrants, especially asylum seekers.

In this chapter, I aim to find answers to the questions of whether the Belgian immigration and asylum policies have changed in times of crisis and, if so, how. My primary objective is to examine the conflated effects of the three global economic, humanitarian, and health crises (2008 financial crisis, 2015 refugee crisis, and 2020 COVID-19 pandemic) on Belgium's migration and asylum policy in the last decade. These are the most similar cases, as all three stem from exogenous or external events, so-called global crises. By examining and comparing the response of the Belgian government and the authorities[4], I intend to reveal the changes or continuities in Belgium's migration and asylum policies in crisis times. Accordingly, my response to these research questions has two main arguments. The first is that instead of dramatic policy changes, Belgium's federal government has simply made small changes that aim to pursue the restrictive migration and asylum policies in implementation since the 1970s. My second argument is that so-called global crises could be accepted as opportunities for politicians to justify their restrictive migration and asylum policies. Methodologically, the research builds on the analysis of primary and secondary resources.

In terms of structure, this chapter builds on four sections. The first offers an overview of Belgian's migration and asylum policies after World War II. The following three sections examine the Belgian government's response to three events in detail—the 2008 economic and financial crisis, the 2015 refugee crisis, and the 2020 COVID-19 pandemic—to examine the restrictive

---

[3] **Refugee and immigration crises: at what cost to Belgium?**, https://tinyurl.com/59tej9on (Access 15.10.2020)

[4] The Belgian state structure consists of three ethnolinguistic regions, and competences are divided between the federal level and the level of regions. The north of Belgium is called as Flanders region, and the community speaks Dutch. The French-speaking community is located in the south of Belgium where is called as Wallonia region. The German-speaking community is located in the northeast of the federal state. Although the issues of migration and asylum are discussed differently, it can be argued that the handling of the subject and approach to the subject is the same in the North and the South. The policy competences are multi-layered in Belgium. While immigration and asylum are a federal responsibility, linguistically defined communities are responsible for integration-related issues. In this paper, I will focus on federal policies, but when necessary, address the debates in the North and the South.

changes in asylum policy.

## An overview of Belgium's migration and asylum policy: from Liberalism to Restrictionism

Belgium's migration history has developed in parallel with its history of industrialization. During the nineteenth century, the foreign population in Belgium consisted of mostly foreign workers who were working in Belgian coal mines. After World War II, migration continued through bilateral recruitment agreements with Southern European countries. The bilateral agreements were signed with Italy in 1946, Spain in 1956, Greece in 1957. Later, with non-European countries such as Morocco and Turkey in 1964, Tunisia in 1969, Algeria and Yugoslavia in 1970, the bilateral agreements were signed.[5] Consequently, from 1960 to 1970, immigration to Belgium increased thanks to the official request of Belgium to recruit foreign labour.

Unlike neighbouring states -Germany, the Netherlands, and France- Belgium granted migrant workers the right to migrate with their families. This was to keep migrants' salaries within the Belgian economy.[6] Following the oil crisis and the economic recession in the 1970s, in 1974 the Belgian government took the decision not to recruit low-skilled workers from other countries. On December 15, 1980, the Belgian parliament adopted the Aliens Law which regulated the entry, settlement, and removal of foreigners. The aim was to limit new migration to Belgium and start the integration of those had already migrated and had been living there for almost two decades.[7] However, this decision did not put an end to migration to Belgium. After that time, according to Martiniello, migration to Belgium continued under five patterns: i) mobility of EU citizens, ii) family reunions, iii) residence permits, iv) asylum applications and v) specific categories of foreign workers.[8] Thus currently, approximately 1.4 million foreign nationals are living in Belgium.[9]

---

[5] Johan Wets, "The Turkish Community in Austria and Belgium: The Challenge of Integration", **Turkish Studies**, Vol. 7, No. 1, 2006, p. 93.

[6] Therese De Raedt, "Muslims in Belgium: A Case Study of Emerging Identities", **Journal of Muslim Affairs**, Vol. 24, No. 1, 2004, p. 15.

[7] Sonia Gsir, Jean-Michel Lafleur, Mikolaj Stanek, "Migration policy reforms in the context of economic and political crises: the case of Belgium", **Journal of Ethnic and Migration Studies**, 2016, Vol. 42, No. 10, p.1655.

"The law of 15 December 1980, on the entry on the territory, residence, settlement and removal of foreign nationals" is the fundamental law which regulates Belgium's immigration and asylum issues. It is widely known as the Immigration Act. The law also provides the procedure for the competences of the institutions dealing with migration and asylum. Until now, the royal decree and Immigration Act has been modified several times. In addition to that the law of 12 January 2007 regulates reception conditions for the international protection applicants. It is also known as Reception Act. The law of 30 April 1999 and the implementing decree of 9 June 1999 regulate the access to work of foreign nationals.

[8] Marco Martiniello, "Belgium's Immigration Policy", **International Migration Review**, Vol. 37, No. 1, 2003, pp. 226-227.

[9] **Population of Belgium from 2009 to 2020, by origin**, https://tinyurl.com/1gfug5xt (Access

## Asylum seekers in Belgium

Although Belgium has been a country of immigration for a long time, it has a relatively short history as a refugee receiving country. However, Filip Strubbe claims based on the archival research on central government archives between the years 1945-1957 that Belgium is the first European state which "recognizes refugees on its territory" by recruiting displaced persons from Germany in the late 1940s.[10]

Belgium ratified the Convention Relating to the Status of Refugees on 22 July 1953.[11] By the end of the 1970s, asylum applications in Belgium were extremely few (see table 1) compared to Germany, France, and Austria which were the most popular European states for asylum seekers. Belgium was one of the least attractive European states following Denmark, Portugal, and the UK. During the 1970s, in Belgium, most of the asylum seekers were Yugoslavs, Portuguese, Poles, Vietnamese, and Chileans. The asylum applications increased gradually after the 1980s. The applications generally came from Vietnam, Turkey, and Ghana in the first years of the 1980s. Similar to the previous period, in Europe Germany, France, and Austria were the main destinations of the asylum seekers.[12]

**Table 1.** The Number of First Asylum Applications in Belgium, 1970-1984[13]

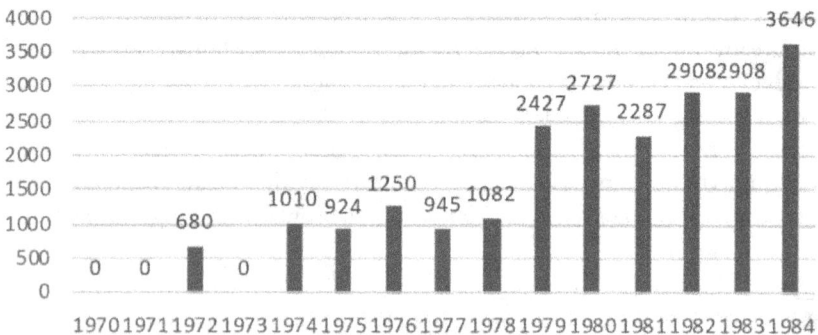

Note: Zero means that the data is not available.

Unlike the former worker migrants group between the 1940s and 1970s, a new category of migrants began to emerge in Belgium. This consisted of

17.11.2020)

[10] Filip Strubbe, "A Straightforward Journey? Discovering Belgium's Refugee Policy through Its Central Government Archives (1945-1957), **Historische Sozialforschung**, 2020, Vol. 45, No. 4, Special Issue: Violence Induced Mobility, p.69.

[11] **Convention relating to the Status of Refugees Geneva, 28 July 1951,**
https://tinyurl.com/3gnqvewo (Access 15.11.2020).

[12] UNHCR, "Asylum Applications in Industrialized Countries: 1980-1999", November 2001, https://www.unhcr.org/3c3eb40f4.pdf (Access: 15.11.2020).

[13] The graphic was created by the author with the data obtained from UNHCR Report. *See* Ibid.

asylum seekers coming from Eastern Europe, Africa, and Asia. Nationality within the Belgian population diversified and increased with this new group of migrants. Nevertheless, the increasing diversity of immigrant groups has unfortunately blurred the distinction between these groups in the public sphere. After that, in every crisis, immigrants started to be seen as scapegoats.[14]

With the number of asylum applications increasing since the late 1980s, Belgium changed its asylum system several times in order to simplify and quicken the process. However, the ultimate aim of the changes in the asylum policy was to reduce the number of asylum applications.

The 1980 Aliens Law establishing the rights of refugees was very generous, and the entry conditions of the asylum seekers were very liberal. According to the law, anyone who arrived at the Belgian border and stated that s/he wanted to enter the country as a refugee had the right to enter Belgium as one. In addition, anyone who came to Belgium legally, like for touristic purposes, s/he also had the right to seek recognition as a refugee during her/his stay. In the case of entering Belgium illegally people could request refugee status within 15 days of entering the country. People could stay in the country until their process of refugee claims ended. Institutionally, UNCHR had the ultimate power in Belgium to decide who was granted a refugee. However, the Belgian government gave their opinions on whether the file was acceptable or not after some examination of each.[15]

The period of liberalism in asylum policy began to change in 1987. The Belgian Parliament introduced a bill which mainly aimed to change the liberal entry requirements and the position of UNHCR in Belgium's asylum policy. With the 1987 revision, people who were seeking refugee status at the border could be turned away by the border police. The power to determine refugees was given to the newly established government Office for Refugees and Stateless Persons. Thus, 1987 was the year that ended Belgian liberal asylum policies.[16]

Since 1999, the Europeanization period has started in migration and asylum policies. The Amsterdam Treaty sought to create a common area of freedom, security, and justice that includes a common policy of asylum and

---

[14] Hassan Bousetta, Sonia Gsir and Dirk Jacobs, "Belgium", **European Immigration: A Sourcebook**, Anna Triandafyllidou and Ruby Gropas (Eds.), Ashgate, 2007, p. 34.

[15] Maryellen Fullerton, "Restricting the Flow of Asylum-Seekers in Belgium, Denmark, the Federal Republic of Germany, and the Netherlands: New Challenges to the Geneva Convention Relating to the Status of Refugees and the European Convention on Human Rights", **Virginia Journal of International Law**, Vol. 29, No. 33, 1988, pp. 39-41.

The examination process of the applications took long times during the 1980s-1990s. The decision was taken more than two years or even seven years, and most cases they were rejected. *See* Martiniello, op. cit, p. 228.

[16] Fullerton, op. cit, pp. 41-45.

immigration. This idea was further developed in the European Councils of Tampere and The Hague. Belgium was on the side of the EU by supporting these initiatives at the time, and the government then stated that they would implement an open economic migration policy. In 1999 the government announced a one-time plan which aimed to naturalize people illegally residing in the country. The nationality law was amended in 2000, and more than 50 thousand people were naturalized. Another significant change was in 2004. The right to vote for foreigners at local elections in Belgium was introduced.[17]

However, the Belgium government began to implement a restrictive asylum policy then. As can be seen below, the number of asylum applications decreased year by year. As a signatory to the Dublin Convention, Belgium has only examined case files handled in Belgium. In 2001, the asylum system underwent a major change. Asylum seekers did not have the right to any financial benefit during the first phase of the procedure. The government also decided to implement the Last In, First Out principle, which gives priority to the handling of new asylum applications and ensures the swift return of those who do not meet the criteria.[18]

**Table 2.** The Number of First Asylum Applications in Belgium, 1985-2010[19]

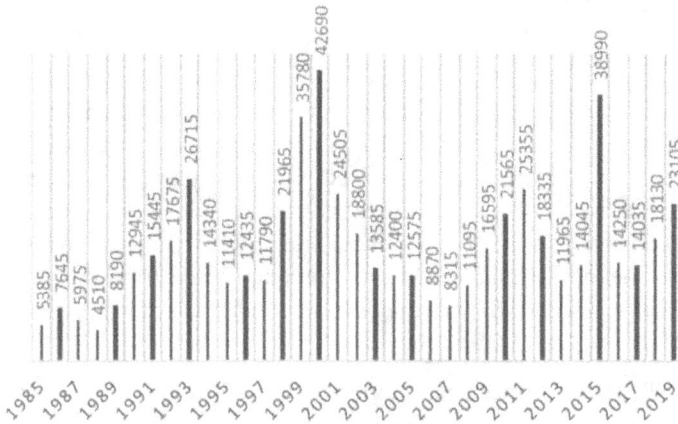

Source: Eurostat, 2020.

---

[17] **The Organisation of Asylum and Migration Policies in Belgium,** September 2012, p. 20, https://tinyurl.com/19sgppc1 (Access 10.11.2020).

[18] Ibid.

[19] The graphic was created by the author with the data obtained from Eurostat. The data between 1985-2007 is available on https://tinyurl.com/4f5g5e74 and the data between 2008-2019 is available on https://tinyurl.com/5fa5ke6c (Access 15.11.2020).

## Multi-level governance of migration and asylum in Belgium

Belgium declared its independence in 1830. Following several state reforms (1970, 1980, 1988-89) and with the revision of the Constitution on May 5, 1993, Belgium became a federal state. These reforms also continued in 2001, and 2012-14. Thus, currently, composed of communities and regions, Belgium is a federal state.[20]

In the federal state structure, responsibilities are divided between the federal and regional levels. Related to migration and asylum policies, the federal government is responsible for legislation, procedures, and reception. After refugee status is granted, the regional governments are responsible for integration issues like housing, education, and professional training. However, the integration initiatives can be taken by the regional governments while an asylum seeker is staying in reception centres.[21]

There are several institutions responsible for the issues in the migration and asylum policy field at the federal level. The Federal Secretary of State for Migration and Asylum Policies and the Director General of the Immigration Department are responsible for regulating the entry, settlement, and deportation of foreign nationals.[22] Asylum seekers are registered by the Immigration Office. The in-depth examinations of applications are done by the Office of the Commissioner General for Refugees and Stateless Persons (CGRS). The Council for Alien Law Litigation and the State Appeals Council are responsible for appeals. The last institution at the federal level is Federal Agency for the Reception of Asylum Seekers (Fedasil) which coordinates the reception centres and voluntary return of asylum seekers.[23] Municipalities and the local social welfare organizations such as Local Reception Initiatives take up important roles in the management of receptions and integration issues at the regional level. [24]

---

[20] **Belgium, a federal state**, https://tinyurl.com/ylcb7cjg (Access 13.11.2020).
[21] Elsa Mescoli et al., "Mobilizations and Opinions Regarding Asylum Seekers, Refugees and Undocumented Migrants in Belgium: Frames, Motivations and Actions", **The Refugee Reception Crisis in Europe: Polarized Opinions and Mobilizations**, Andrea Rea, Marco Martiniello, Alessandro Mazzola and Bart Meuleman (eds.), Brussels University Publishing, 2019, p. 179.
[22] At the level of the federal government, the Prime Minister systematizes the whole of Migration and Asylum Policies. The federal Secretary of State for Migration and Asylum Policies serves under the federal Minister of Employment and Equal Opportunities. *See* "Policy report regarding asylum and migration Belgium 2009", p. 7, https://tinyurl.com/yfv4tw7m (Access 13.11.2020).
[23] **Federal Agency for the Reception of Asylum Seekers**, https://www.fedasil.be/en (Access 13.11.2020).
[24] Policy report regarding asylum and migration Belgium 2009, op. cit.

## Asylum flows in times of crisis and policy responses

### The 2008 Global Financial Crisis

Like most of the EU Member states, Belgium was affected by the economic crisis in the late 2000s. In 2009, the economic growth rate fell to -3.0 %[25], and the debt ratio was recorded as 99.5 % of gross domestic products (GDP).[26] Belgium was exposed to economic downturn, resulting in risk of falling into an economic crisis with the other Member States such as Spain, Italy and Greece.[27] In the following years, Belgium gradually recovered, although its economic indicators remained unstable. The labour market was severely affected by the 2008 crisis. In the first two years, the net loss of jobs was 20.000.[28] The economic slowdown caused an increase in social security expenditures. In addition, austerity measures imposed by both the EU and Belgian federal government began to be implemented. To do this, public spending in some areas like education and health care were cut; taxes were increased and severe controls for beneficiaries of social assistance were introduced. Indeed, the restrictive measures targeted immigrant groups. Despite this relatively negative context, Belgium was not one of the Member States that suffered severely from the economic crisis[29] nor did it receive large numbers of asylum cases.[30] The number of asylum applications increased between 2008 and 2011[31], then decreased between 2012-2014[32] (see Table 2).

The government declared that to harmonize Belgium's asylum policy with the EU, legislative changes would be made in 2009.[33] The federal government approved a decree on 3 April 2009 which regulated access of asylum seekers

[25] OECD, "Restoring Public Finances",2011, p.80, https://tinyurl.com/2durtkno (Access 10.02.2021).
[26] **Belgian Debt Agency**, https://www.debtagency.be/en/datagovernmentdebtdebtratio (Access 10.02.2021).
[27] Jean-Michel Lafleur, Mikolaj Stanek, "Restrictions on Access to Social Protection by New Southern European Migrants in Belgium", **South-North Migration of EU Citizens in Times of Crisis,** Jean-Michel Lafleur, Mikolaj Stanek (eds.), IMISCOE Research Series, Springer Open, 2017, p. 101.
[28] Ibid.
[29] Ibid.
[30] However, the total number of migrants increased in Belgium during the economic crisis. Southern European States were the most severely affected by the economic crisis in the EU, and their citizens preferred to migrate to Northwestern European countries. Thus, the number of Southern European migrants increased in this period in Belgium. For more detailed information on Southern European migrants in Belgium and the effects of the economic crisis see Ibid, pp. 99-121.
[31] There is a positive correlation between unemployment and the number of asylum applications. However, the correlation between the unemployment and the recognition rate is negative. *See* **The impact of the global economic crisis on illegal migration to the EU,** https://tinyurl.com/bvfrewgi (Access 13.11.2020).
[32] The most significant development in this period was that for the first time in Belgian history Minister of Migration and Asylum Policy was appointed in the government when a new federal government came into office in March 2008. It was recognized that migration issues become an important area at federal level. *See* **Policy report regarding asylum and migration Belgium 2008**, https://tinyurl.com/7o0klexe, pp.4-7, (Access 15.11.2020).
[33] Ibid.
[33] Ibid.

to the Belgian labour market. This decision was based on the transposition of the European Reception Conditions Directive. If an asylum seeker applied for international protection before 31 May 2007 and did not receive a negative decision after 6 months of his/her application, he/she can apply for a work permit C. Work permit C, which is valid until the residence permit of this person is over, allows the people to apply any kind of job. However, with this decree, asylum seekers whose applications are being examined are not allowed to apply for a work permit C.[34]

Parallel with the increase in the number of asylum applications, the effects of the economic crisis began to be felt in 2010. There were two main reasons for the increase in the number of asylum applications. The first was the results of the federal government's regularization of its irregular migrants policy, ongoing since 2006-2007. In 2010, about 24.000 migrants were regularized. The introduction of visa-free travel in Schengen countries for citizens of Macedonia, Montenegro, and Serbia was recognised as the second reason for the increase in asylum applications. The number of applications from Macedonia and Serbia increased significantly in 2010. The increase caused debates among politicians regarding countermeasures. For example, Vice Prime Minister Guy Vanhengel stated that Belgium had reached capacity concerning asylum applications. State Secretary Melchior Wathelet declared in March 2010 that Belgium is the only Member States that accepts asylum applications from citizens of other EU states and must stop.[35]

The number of asylum applications began to increase in 2011. The Belgian government took several measures to limit the increase in asylum seekers. Firstly, the Belgian government adopted the bill of October 27, which stated that asylum seekers who were introducing another asylum claim in Belgium could not benefit from material assistance if their claim was not accepted by the Immigration Office. It aimed at the exclusion of some categories of asylum seekers, like those from other Member States or those applying the second time or third time for international protection, from the reception system. Another restrictive measure was taken on 24 November 2011. The parliament adopted a bill that introduced the concept of "safe countries of origin". The asylum application procedure was shortened for the safe countries and the decision had to be taken within 15 working days by the CGRS. The appeals were also limited to an annulment procedure. The Flemish political parties were also New Flemish Alliance (N-VA) and Open Flemish Liberals and Democrats (Open-VLD) highly supported forced removals during the year 2011.[36] The decrease in the number of asylum

---

[34] Ibid, p.19.
[35] **Policy report regarding asylum and migration Belgium 2010**, https://tinyurl.com/13uezzp0, pp.14-16 (Access 15.11.2020).
[36] **Policy report regarding asylum and migration Belgium 2011**, https://tinyurl.com/1lpmj58t

applications continued in 2012 and 2013 compared to 2011. Adoption of a list of safe countries of origin was accepted as a successful measure, and the same list was approved.[37] Another important development to support outflows was the transposition of the Return Directive into Belgian law. The Law of 19 January 2012 introduced the concept of a "return path" for rejected asylum seekers. When their file was under examination, asylum seekers were informed about voluntary returns. This information was given at the moment they requested asylum. If a negative decision was taken regarding their asylum request, they left the country in 5 days.[38] In 2014, attention was given to outflows based on the principle "*voluntarily if possible, forced if necessary*".[39] Although the priority was given to the return of irregular migrants, the Belgian government began to implement several measures to ensure the return of rejected asylum seekers. The target groups were mainly Afghan and Iraqi asylum seekers. As a result of the return path, voluntary return in Belgium in 2012 and 2013 increased compared to the following years.[40]

During the economic crisis, the increase of the unemployment rate was less than the increase in the number of asylum seekers. According to economists, immigration's effect on Belgian employment and salaries is negligible because asylum seekers' qualifications are different from locals in terms of education, specialization, etc. Thus, it is not possible to posit any kind of replacement. In addition, immigration contributes 0.3% fiscal gain of the GDP. Despite all the negative discourse regarding asylum seekers, they do not generate the economic costs on the Belgian economy if refugees are integrated economically and socially.[41] However, social policies became one of the most important instruments of controlling asylum in Belgium within the context of the economic crisis, and the federal government highly supported voluntary returns during the economic crisis.

### The 2015 Refugee Crisis

In 2015, the number of total asylum applications in Belgium was 44,760, and the number of asylum applications doubled compared to the previous year's total applications. The majority of the applicants were Syrians (10.415),

---

(Access 15.11.2020).

[37] **Policy report regarding asylum and migration Belgium 2012**, https://tinyurl.com/16hmg57t (Access 17.11.2020).

[38] Ibid, p.28.

[39] **Policy report regarding asylum and migration Belgium 2014**, p. 67, https://tinyurl.com/vevvh0lz (Access 17.11.2020).

[40] Voluntary return numbers are in 2011 (3870), 2012 (5650), 2013 (4707), 2014 (2936), 2015 (3395), 2016 (4667), 2017 (3827), 2018 (2994) and 2019 (2426). Data were obtained from the policy reports of the relevant year.

[41] **Refugee and immigration crises: at what cost to Belgium?**, https://tinyurl.com/d85p85my (Access 15.10.2020).

Iraqis (9.470), and Afghans (8.310).[42] Even though, as mentioned above, Belgium is a country that has accepted asylum seekers for many years, the sudden increase in the number of asylum applications in 2015 caused serious difficulties in Belgium's asylum and reception system.[43] Nevertheless, previous studies have indicated that the total number of asylum applications was not as many as recorded in 1993 Bosnia and the 2000 Kosovo crises.[44] Despite this, a so-called crisis environment occurred in Belgium, and like many other Members States, Belgium also began immediately making some amendments in the laws related to migration and asylum.

The first immediate response came from Immigration Office authorities. The Belgian Immigration Office imposed a quota of 250 registration per day at the end of summer 2015. The decision was rationalized by highlighting the crowd in waiting room of the office. Instead of being registered on the same day, people seeking international protection were informed on which day they must come back for registration. Coming back could take more than one or two weeks. It meant that as long as those people were not registered, they did not have the right to access reception facilities. This decision taken by Belgian authorities forced those people to stay at parks and streets until the Belgium government opened the pre-reception centres as a response in September.[45] However, in this situation, according to the EU Asylum Procedure Directive, after the application, registration must be done within three days. States can only extend the registration process to ten days in exceptional situations. Yet this directive was not transposed by the Belgium government.[46] The right to asylum is guaranteed in the 1951 Refugee Convention and also in Article 18 of the EU Charter of Fundamental Rights. Although Belgium is a part of these agreements, it has implemented practices that will put this right at risk in order to manage the so-called humanitarian crisis, and so the Belgian authorities introduced a pre-registration system.

Following an unexpected increase in asylum applications in 2015, the Belgian government began taking restrictive measures. For this purpose, first of all, a law proposal was prepared to limit the duration of residence permits of those with refugee status. Asylum-seekers used to have permanent residence permits after they gained refugee status. However, with this new law proposal, refugees will not be granted permanent residence permits and

---

[42] **Policy report regarding asylum and migration Belgium 2015**, https://tinyurl.com/qfs9hdg0 (Access 12.11.2020).
[43] Ibid.
[43] Koen Burggraeve and Céline Piton, "The economic consequences of the flow of refugees into Belgium", 2016, p. 43, https://tinyurl.com/4y6jr4ue (Access 13.11.2020).
[44] Ibid.
[45] **Europe's asylum policy in crisis: the case of Belgium**, https://tinyurl.com/oq8w2qy7 (Access 12.11.2020).
[46] Ibid.

temporary residence permits will be granted for only five years. At the end of five years, after their situation is re-evaluated, those refugees will be given a permanent residence permit if they are found suitable. [47] On 28 April 2016, the Belgian Parliament adopted this new law that shortens the duration of residence permits for refugees from permanent to a temporary 5 years. According to the Article 24 Qualification Directive of the EU, the minimum duration of the right to residence for recognized refugees must be at least three years.[48] While Czech Republic, Ireland, Lithuania, Latvia, Slovenia, and Slovakia have granted permanent residence for asylum seekers,[49] the Belgium government used both the EU's directive and crisis to change its existing permanent residence permit to limit asylum applications.

In January 2020, Belgian authorities issued some decisions to limit the right to reception of certain groups of asylum seekers. Asylum seekers who have already granted international protection in another EU Member State but made another application in Belgium, and have made an application based on the Dublin III Regulation were excluded from housing and food assistance, and they were only allowed to access medical support.[50]

### The 2020 Covid-19 Pandemic

The COVID-19 virus, which first appeared in China in November 2019, spread all over the world in the first months of 2020, and each country has started to take measures such as temporary restriction on non-essential travel and lockdowns to reduce the rate of contamination as much as possible. It is an undeniable fact that the pandemic has economic and psychological effects on the citizens of every state. However, these effects can be devastating for people seeking international protection, such as refugees and asylum seekers on the way to the EU. In order to restrict the spread of the virus in the EU, the Commission adopted a communication, "the Temporary Restriction on Non-Essential Travel on to the EU in view of COVID-19", on March 16. The Commission emphasized in the communication that people in need of international protection must be an exemption from these temporary restrictions.[51] On April 14 a communication from the Commission titled "COVID-19: Guidance on the implementation of relevant EU provisions in the area of asylum and return procedures and on resettlement" was released.

---

[47] Ibid.

[48] **Council Directive 2004/83/EC,** https://tinyurl.com/yjeuzorr (Access 21.11.2020).

[49] For further information on other EU Member States' duration of residence permits for beneficiaries of international protection *See* **Asylum on the Clock? Duration and review of international protection status in Europe,** https://tinyurl.com/hwbhe55m (Access 21.11.2020).

[50] **Country Report: Belgium, Asylum Information Database,** 2019, p.76, https://tinyurl.com/ry7kv4mb (Access: 21.11.2020).

[51] **COVID-19: Temporary Restriction on Non-Essential Travel to the EU,** https://tinyurl.com/qrms4bzk (Access 21.11.2020).

Basically, the Commission advises that while member states impose some measures and restrictions on asylum application processes in accordance with national law, they must be proportional, non-discriminatory and should not contradict the principle of non-refoulement in international law.[52]

The first death related to COVID-19 was recorded in Belgium on March 2[53] while it is stated that currently, this number picked up over 15 thousand.[54] As soon as the government realized that the cases were on the rise, it announced measures such as closing schools, restaurants, bars, day care, and sports facilities on March 17 to cut the spread of the virus. The government has also prohibited all non-essential travels.[55] With the number of cases that peaking in mid-April and decreasing at the beginning of May, it was announced that the measures to reopen the economy and stimulate social life will be implemented gradually from May 11.[56]

Regarding the people in need of international protection, the Belgian Immigration Office announced on March, 17 that it was shutting down the arrival and reception center (Petit-Château in Brussels) for newly arriving asylum seekers. The aim was to prevent gathering people outside the arrival centre or in the waiting rooms inside. Nevertheless, it means that asylum applications were temporarily suspended.[57] In the two following weeks, on April, 3 the Belgian Immigration Office declared that those who wish to apply for international protection must make an appointment at the Registration Centre by filling in an online form.[58] However, unfortunately, the civil society organizations helping applicants to arrange their appointments could not prevent an increase in problems related to language and internet access. Thus, civil society organizations conveyed their demands to the authorities that the standard application process should be pursued by taking necessary health measures at the Registration Centre. Regarding the examining process of applications, personal interviews were suspended. Decisions are also being made in ongoing cases, though.[59]

From June 8 onwards, interviews gradually started. To protect the health

---

[52] COVID-19: Guidance on the implementation of relevant EU provisions in the area of asylum and return procedures and on resettlement, https://tinyurl.com/ykt4ud6t (Access 21.11.2020).

[53] Toon Van Overbeke and Diederik Stadig, "High politics in the Low Countries: COVID-19 and the politics of strained multi-level policy cooperation in Belgium and the Netherlands", **European Policy Analysis**, 2020, p. 3.

[54] **Belgium COVID-19 Epidemiological Situation**, https://tinyurl.com/4ftphuco (Access 20.11.2020).

[55] Van Overbeke and Stadig, op. cit, p.3.

[56] Ibid.

[57] **The arrival center closes its doors**, https://tinyurl.com/wjn1ww14 (Access 20.11.2020).

[58] **Resumption of applications for international protection**, https://tinyurl.com/su28xyul (Access 20.11.2020).

[59] **COVID-19 Measures Related To Asylum And Migration Across Europe**, https://tinyurl.com/10f0rt64 (Access 20.11.2020).

of applicants and staff, some measures were taken. Each applicant must come at appointment time since the waiting room inside of the CGRS is closed. A face mask is mandatory while the applicant enters the CGRS; however, the applicant can choose whether or not to wear a face mask during the interview since protective screens are installed in the interview room.[60]

However, on April 11 the cabinet announced some additional socio-economic and health measures to mitigate the effects of the COVID-19. One of these measures was related to asylum seekers' access to the labour market. According to the decision, asylum seekers who submitted their applications are allowed to work for the examination duration.[61]

## Conclusion

In the first quarter of the 21st century, we have faced global crises that emerged one after another, and before the effects of one crisis disappeared, we started to feel the effects of another weigh heavily. In these periods of crisis, undoubtedly, immigrants felt the harsh conditions most of all. EU countries have been favorable countries for asylum seekers. Yet most of the EU Member States have been facing economic, political, and humanitarian crises, and these multiple crises have a combined effect on vulnerable policy realms like asylum and migration. Asylum applications are one of the means of legal migration about which all European states have settled on a compromise. However, almost all European states work for disincentive policies to make it more difficult. Thus, any kinds of postponement in application processes, long decision processes, limiting the residence permit, and so on might lead those who are seeking international protection to illegal means.

European governments are in a dilemma. On the one side, international treaties like the 1951 Refugee Convention and the European Convention on Human Rights push European states to open borders and welcome newcomers. On the other side, the newcomers weigh on welfare systems, and the possibility of possessing security threats push states to control and curb newcomers. Belgium is one of these EU Member States experiencing the dilemma. In this chapter, I have shown that asylum applications have increased since the 1980s gradually in Belgium. However, Belgian governments have perceived the growing number of refugees as a threat to social welfare; therefore, policies related to migration and asylum have been tightened to limit asylum seekers' access to housing, the labor market, and health services. From the 1980s to 2015, there were several peak periods of

---

[60] **European Migration Network, Belgium,** https://tinyurl.com/7dzwf5nj (Access: 21.11.2020).
[61] **Access to the labour market for asylum applicants in Belgium,** https://tinyurl.com/5bnmshyj (Access 23.11.2020).

asylum applications. Each of them caused major or minor changes in asylum policy in Belgium. With the non-explicit asylum policy of the 1980s, asylum seekers could settle in any municipality with their basic needs met by local social welfare services. However, this openness towards asylum seekers increased the tension and asylum seekers' registration began to be refused by the local government. In the end, in 1987 with the changes in the Immigration Act, asylum seekers' entry conditions became harder. Nevertheless, these changes did not prevent the increase in asylum applications at the beginning of the 1990s due to the unrest in the Balkans after the fall of the Berlin Wall. It was followed by the Kosovo War at the turn of the century.

Nevertheless, most of the changes in Belgium's asylum policy were the result of the EU framework. Belgium, in its history, followed the directions of its European partners. However, it is a fact that the Belgium government is even today making it harder to be legally admitted to Belgium, especially in times of crises. Changing the labor laws in addition to the application processes causes a difficult situation for asylum applicants. On the other hand, although Belgium does not stand against the directives of the EU in the field of common asylum and immigration policies, Belgium is transferring them to its domestic law by meeting the requirements of the EU's common asylum and migration policy at the minimum level. It should not be overlooked that although Europe has accepted large numbers of Syrian asylum seekers since the beginning of the conflict in Syria in 2011, only one in ten Syrians asylum seekers live in Europe. The greatest number of Syrians is still living as refugees in neighboring countries including Turkey and Lebanon.[62] Most of EU's measures show that responsibility is shifting to those countries shouldering a heavier load than the EU Member States. Belgium's long term intention of restriction of migration has not changed, however, Belgium's government have just diversified their political instruments to do that.

As I have shown in the chapter, a great number of asylum-seekers from the Middle East, Asia, and Africa have become a significant part of Belgium's immigration history, and they will continue to come to Belgium as long as there is unrest in their countries. Although the government has taken measures to limit their influx for years, and most of these refugees and their descendants occupy invisible positions in social life, they are great examples of what integration into society looks like when the proper rights and necessary conditions are given. Today, the most significant symbol of this is the Secretary of State for Asylum and Migration, Sammy Mahdi, who is the son of an Iraqi refugee who came to Belgium in 1970. What kind of policy

---

[62] **Number of Refugees to Europe Surges to Record 1.3 Million in 2015,** https://tinyurl.com/16jmfyw3 (Access 21.11.2020).

this Secretary of State for Asylum and Migration with an immigrant background has followed requires another study.

# CHAPTER 13

# HUNGARY'S ASYLUM POLICY BEFORE AND AFTER THE REFUGEE MOVEMENT IN 2015

N. Aslı Şirin[*]

## Introduction

**"The truth is that Europe is being threatened by massive immigration on an unprecedented scale.** (...) Today we are talking about hundreds of thousands, but next year we will be talking about millions, and that will never end. And **one morning we can wake up and realize that we are the minority on our own continent.** (...) **they can occupy Hungary** (...)"

"Now we are inundated with countless immigrants: there is an invasion, they break down fences, and it is clear to us all that they are not seeking refuge, and are not running for their lives. (...)"

"We are in a deep trouble. The migration crisis is able to destabilize governments, countries and the whole European continent (...). (...) what we have been facing is not a refugee crisis. This is a migratory movement composed of economic migrants, refugees and also foreign fighters. This is an uncontrolled and unregulated process..."

The words above belong to the Hungarian Prime Minister Viktor Orbán. He made these speeches in September and October 2015, a year quite challenging for the European Union (EU) as well as its members, particularly the ones acting as entry points and destination countries for migrants, most of whom were fleeing conflict-zones or internally destabilised countries. Europe has not experienced such a refugee movement since World War II. Asylum applications had already been increasing in the early 2000s but the movement in 2015 was even a bigger boom as there were over 1.2 million first time applications.[1] The asylum and immigration system both at the national and Union level were faced with its biggest challenge so far.

Having become an important transit country for nearly 800,000 migrants, most of whom were in need of international protection,[2] all eyes were on

---

[*] Asst. Prof. Dr., Marmara University, Institute of European Studies, Istanbul, Turkey.
[1] Eurostat "Record number of over 1.2 million first time asylum seekers registered in 2015", 44/2016 - 4 March 2016, https://ec.europa.eu/eurostat/documents/2995521/7203832/3-04032016-AP-EN.pdf/79 0eba01-381c-4163-bcd2-a54959b99ed6 Access 03.08.2020
[2] In legal terms, these people are not refugees as long as they are granted the refugee status in

Hungary during the influx that became a crisis for the EU in 2015. Starting in late 2014, Hungary was faced with an extraordinary situation regarding asylum. Many Kosovars were leaving their homes and crossing the border between Hungary and Serbia with the hope of reaching Western Europe, primarily Germany.[3] The main reason for Kosovar migration was poverty and unemployment. Since most of the applications were unfounded, it was not difficult for the Hungarian asylum system to cope with the situation and the Kosovar migration movement came to an end in a short time.[4] But the issue of migration and asylum turned out to be a hot topic for the Hungarian public as well as the government because there were new asylum claims and the number was increasing.

The scale of the refugee movement was enormous for a country like Hungary which had not experienced any significant migratory movement or asylum claims before.[5] In the decade after Hungary became an EU member, there was a slight increase in the number of asylum applications[6] but 2015 saw the highest number of asylum applications lodged in Hungary.[7] It was indeed a momentous shift for Hungary which has never been a country of destination for immigrants. But, at the same time, it was a reality that those asylum-seekers applied in Hungary out of formality and almost all of them moved on to the Western European countries, particularly Germany.[8] Nevertheless, being aware of anti-migration sentiment among the public, the government led by Orbán emphasised this major shift through media campaigns in 2015. From the very beginning, the refugee movement was framed as a migrant crisis by the government. In the eyes of the cabinet

---

accordance with the 1951 UN Convention Relating to the Status of Refugees but in sociological terms they are refugees because they are fleeing war.

[3] Reuters, "Dramatic surge in Kosovars crossing illegally into EU", 04.02.2015, https://www.reuters.com/ article/us-kosovo-eu-migrants-idUSKBN0L811120150204 Access 03.08.2020

[4] Gábor Vetö, "National interests in the European asylum policy - Hungary in the European migrant crisis: Persistent Objector or Agenda-setter?", UACES Conference, Brussels, 9-10 May 2016 (Access 04.08.2020)

[5] The flight of Hungarians following the uprising in 1956 is an exception in that regard.

[6] "According to the Eurostat, the Central Statistics Office and the Hungarian Immigration and Asylum Office, in 2005, a year after its accession to the EU, Hungary recorded 1610 asylum applications this increasing to 21157 in the year 2006 (Eurostat, Asylum applications in the European Union 2007), while in 2008 it recorded a smooth escalation to 3118, in 2009 reaching to 4672 applications, however in 2010 the number more than halved, decreasing to 2104. In 2011 it further decreased to 1693, in 2012 the number of claims increased to 2157 (Központi Statisztikai Hivatal, 2013), while in 2013 it raised to a record number of 18.900, and in 2014 to 42.777 (Hungarian Immigration and Asylum Office, Statistics 2014–2015)". See Edina Lilla Mészáros, "The Politicization, Mediatisation and the Visual Framing of the Refugee Crisis in Hungary", **Muslim Minorities and the Refugee Crisis in Europe** Katarzyna Górak-Sosnowska, Marta Pachocka, Jan Misiuna (Ed.), Warsaw, SGH Warsaw School of Economics Publishing House, 2019, p. 238

[7] The number of first time asylum applications Hungary received only in 2015 was 174.400 and it represented 14% of all asylum applications. See Eurostat, op cit.

[8] Attila Juhász, Bulcsú Hunyadi, Edit Zgut, "Focus on Hungary: Refugees, Asylum and Migration", Prague, Heinrich Böll Stiftung, 2015, p. 10.

members, most of the people coming to Europe through Hungary, who were posed as refugees, were actually economic migrants coming from different regions.[9] So there was no refugee crisis according to the Hungarian government because those people were not refugees at all.

Against this background, the present study examines the Hungarian asylum policy since the regime change in 1989 with a focus on the refugee movement in 2015 and the government's response. The purpose is to reveal how the Hungarian government has securitised migration and what kind of measures it has adopted accordingly. In order to understand the response of the Hungarian government to the refugee movement reaching high levels in the autumn of 2015, the first section briefly mentions Hungary's asylum policy from 1989 until the Arab uprisings. Then the growing scale of refugee movements as a result of the Arab uprisings in the recent decade is scrutinised. The last part focuses on the Hungarian government's draconian response to this movement generated by the Arab uprisings. The measures are extremely harsh and continue to be taken even though the number of asylum-seekers as well people transiting the country has declined significantly five years after the refugee movement in 2015.

## The asylum state of affairs and Hungary's asylum policy: 1989-2010

Hungary's asylum policy is based on the 1951 UN Convention Relating to the Status of Refugees to which it became a party in early 1989. Actually it was the first Eastern bloc country to sign the 1951 Convention and the 1967 New York Protocol. However, when ratifying Hungary made geographical reservation meaning that it would not give protection to non-European refugees. As Fullerton notes, this reservation allowed Hungary to limit its obligations under the Convention to a small population of refugees in the world, i.e. those who fear persecution only in Europe.[10] Nevertheless, signing the 1951 UN Convention and the 1967 Protocol was crucial in Hungary's transition process. Since European integration was the main aim of the country, the governments put their efforts to fulfil the basic requirements set out in the 1951 UN Convention which was supported by Hungary's membership of the European Court of Human Rights in 1993.[11]

When we look at Hungarian asylum policy in the late 1980s and 1990s, we see that it was not developed as there was a patchwork of legislation and government decrees in the field of migration and asylum.[12] The government tried to develop a modern asylum system in order to protect refugees with

---

[9] Meszaros, op. cit. p. 239.

[10] M. Fullerton, "Hungary, Refugees, and the Law of Return", **International Journal of Refugee Law,** Vol 8 No 4, 1996, pp. 499-531.

[11] Vetö, op.cit. p. 4

[12] Fullerton, op. cit.

Hungarian origins. The existing law and the administration of the refugee system was designed accordingly and the result was a de facto law of return for ethnic Hungarians.[13] The desire to protect refugees with Hungarian origins is understandable but the government was misusing the refugee system to achieve this objective and this is not acceptable. "Ethnic Hungarians who entered Hungary seeking refuge were not only channelled into the refugee system but were also eligible for Hungarian citizenship within one year, and all the rights that citizenship accords, while others who needed refuge were mainly provided temporary protection status. They received food, shelter, and other necessities, although in recent years these too are becoming scarce, but they lacked any substantial legal protection."[14]

In the meantime, war broke out in the former Yugoslavia and Hungary was faced with large groups of civilians who were fleeing the fighting between Croatia and Serbia, two of the constituent republics of the ex-Yugoslavia. Most of them were coming from an area close to Vukovar, a Croatian city that witnessed some of the bloodiest fighting between Serbs and Croats during the war. More than 400,000 people sought protection outside the former Yugoslav territories. Germany hosted 200,000 and provided temporary protection to them while Hungary admitted 60,000 refugees.[15] Towards the end of 1994, there were less than 8,000 refugees in Hungary. But new ethnic cleansing and renewed fighting in Bosnia-Hercegovina in the following year resulted in more displaced people, some of whom came to Hungary. A refugee camp which had been closed a long time ago had to be reopened.

The people displaced as a result of the war in the ex-Yugoslavia did not stay in Hungary permanently and the burden they caused in financial and social terms was minimal indeed. Nevertheless, as Vetö notes, it became a necessity for the government to create a functioning asylum system with its institutions, staff and the required legislation.[16] Since Hungary wished to become a member of the EU, this developing asylum system was to be in harmony with the *acquis* of the Union to which the Schengen *acquis*[17] was incorporated with the Treaty of Amsterdam.

After accession to the EU, the relevant EU asylum-related directives were

---

[13] E. M. Goździak, "Using Fear of the "Other," Orbán Reshapes Migration Policy in a Hungary Built on Cultural Diversity", Migration Policy Institute, 10.10.2019, https://www.migrationpolicy.org/article/orban-reshapes-migration-policy-hungary Access: 24.07.2020
[14] ibid. p.7
[15] ibid.
[16] Vetö, op. cit.
[17] The Schengen acquis was composed of the Schengen Agreement (1985), the Convention on Implementation of the Schengen Agreement (1990) and all of the accession protocols and agreements to the Schengen Agreement and the Convention, and the declarations and decisions adopted by the Executive Committee.

transposed into national legislation. The Law on Asylum was adopted for first time in 2007 and the Office of Immigration and Nationality would be responsible for determining the procedures of asylum and statelessness, providing reception services, and limited integration services to asylum seekers and refugees. In December 2010 came amendments to the legislation concerning asylum seekers and refugees. For example, we see the introduction of the maximum length of administrative detention from six to 12 months and the detention of up to 30 days of families with children.[18]

Being an EU member did not make Hungary a country of destination for the people displaced in conflict zones. The permanent refugee population was small as Hungary served as a transit country for the asylum-seekers. In that regard, the asylum burden of the country was rather moderate until the so-called refugee influx in 2015. However, migration had become politicised in the Hungarian public discourse in the early 21st century. At the beginning it was connected with the local interpretations of what were mainly foreign political developments and related media reports of the time.[19] Actually the developments in the early 1990s, i.e. the flight of refugees from the ex-Yugoslav territories, the resettlement efforts by ethnic Hungarians from the region and the first immigration from China,[20] were rather justifiable for the politicisation of migration in the country. But none of them moved to the centre of the political discourse; they received regular coverage in the Hungarian media at that time.[21] In the early 2000s, particularly after the 9/11 terrorist attacks in the USA, xenophobia towards Muslim refugees, who were the new Other, started rising in many countries and Hungary was no exception in that sense. As Gozdziak notes, although we see the implementation of minimum standards of refugee protection – at least on paper – xenophobia towards refugees was increasing and protection for asylum-seekers and refugees was virtually non-existent.[22] The uprisings in the Arab countries starting at the end of 2010 leading to mass refugee movements strengthened xenophobic sentiments even more. The Arab uprisings

---

[18] Gozdziak, op. cit. p.8.

[19] Juhász et al., op. cit. p. 23.

[20] In the post-1989 period, Russia and Hungary were the major reception area for Chinese immigration as well as trade to the rest of Eastern Europe. As Nyiri notes, two factors played a role in the surge of migration to the region. First, the private sector was anxious after the student democracy movement was harshly suppressed in Tiananmen Square in 1989. Entrepreneurs were searching for an escape path for their families as well as capital in case of a reversion of economic reforms by the government. Secondly, private entrepreneurs, workers and managers at state-owned companies were negatively affected by the recession of the economy in the 1989-91 period. In early 1990s, many Chinese moved on from Russia to Hungary in search of better economic opportunities. However, as a result of the anti-Chinese policy of the Hungarian authorities in 1992 and, subsequently, increasing competition, lower profits Chinese had to move to other Eastern European countries. See P. Nyiri, "Chinese Migration to Eastern Europe", **International Migration**, Vol. 41 No. 3 SI 1/2003, pp.239-265; P. Nyiri, "Chinese in Hungary", **Encyclopedia of Diasporas**, Melvin Ember, Carol R. Ember, Ian Skoggard, 2005, pp.664-672.

[21] Juhász et al., op. cit.

[22] Gozdziak, op. cit.

followed by those refugee movements and the response of the EU are examined in the following section.

## Refugee movements in the aftermath of the Arab Uprisings

The uprisings in the Middle East and North Africa (MENA) region first began in December 2010 in Tunisia as a street vendor set himself alight in public after he had been repressed by the police forces. With the help of social media, other groups came to know about this protest and uprisings spread to the whole country.[23] During the upheavals, the social mobilization was so vigorous and united in its aims that the President Zine El-Abidine Ben Ali was forced to resign after three weeks and he fled to Saudi Arabia.[24] Since the countries of region share similar culture, geography, life styles and mentality, developments in any one of them can affect all the others and it happened in that manner. Hence, as the mobilization was successful in Tunisia, the upheavals in the country created a domino effect for the whole region. In Egypt, for instance, the opponents of regime gathered in Tahrir Square and the uprisings resulted in resignation of Hosni Mubarak, who had been the president of Egypt since 1981.[25] Libya and Yemen were also influenced by the uprisings taking place in the other Arab countries. In Libya, the social unrest continued until the deposed leader Gaddafi was captured and killed in October 2011. In Yemen, after months of clashes between dissident groups and the security forces, President Saleh finally signed a deal that saw his deputy, Hadi, assume power.[26]

As briefly mentioned above, the uprisings and unrest in the MENA region resulted in coups or civil wars following political reconstruction in many of them. One of the most important results of those upheavals and regime changes was displacement and mass refugee movements. Thousands of people left their homes and sought refuge in the neighbouring countries as well as in Europe. Among the Arab countries experiencing unrest and upheavals, Syria is the one which has produced the highest number of refugees since the conflict was gradually transformed from a civil uprising to

---

[23] Katerina Dalacoura, "The 2011 Arab Risings in the Middle East: political change and geopolitical implications", **International Affairs**, Vol. 88 No.1, 2012 pp. 63-79, https://onlinelibrary.wiley.com/doi/ abs/10.1111/j.1468-2346.2012.01057.x Access 04.08.2020

[24] Gerardo Otero, Efe Can Gürcan, "The Arab Spring and the Syrian refugee crisis", **Monitor**, Vol.22, No. 5, February 2016, pp. 16-17, https://www.researchgate.net/publication/297289457_The_Arab_ Spring_and_the_Syrian_refugee_crisis Access 03.09.2020

[25] K. Nagarajan, "Egypt's political economy and the downfall of the Mubarak Regime", **International Journal of Humanities and Social Science**, Vol. 3 No.10, SI, 2013, pp. 22-39, https://www.ijhssnet. com/journals/Vol_3_No_10_Special_Issue_May_2013/3.pdf Access 03.09.2020

[26] **BBC News World**, "Arab uprising: Country by country – Yemen", 16.12.2013, https://www.bbc.com/ news/world-12482293 Access 14.09.2020

an armed rebellion, and later a full-scale civil war.

The wave of popular unrests that had swept through MENA region reached Syria relatively late, in March 2011. The first major protests took place in Dar'a, an impoverished drought-ridden rural province in the southern part of the country. After a group of children had been arrested and tortured by the security forces for writing anti-regime graffiti, enraged local people took to the streets to demonstrate for economic and political reforms. They demanded an end to the authoritarian practices of the Assad regime that had been continuing since 1971. The response of government was harsh as it used violence to oppress the demonstrators and made extensive use of security as well as paramilitary forces.[27] This violence used by the regime made the protesters' cause more visible and, gaining pace, the protests spread to other cities. Unfortunately, the regime responded even more harshly to the increasing protests. The cities or neighbourhoods which had become hubs of protest were encircled with tanks and artillery paving the way to some groups of protesters taking up arms against the regime.[28]

The civil uprising phase continued until July of the same year when the early insurgency phase began. In this phase, we see the beginning of armed rebellion against the Assad regime with the rise of armed oppositional militias and by September these militias were regularly combatting with government troops.[29] The fighting continued despite the efforts of international organizations to bring the conflict to an end[30] and in spring 2012 the conflict gradually escalated to a full-fledged civil war that still goes on, having left more than 500,000 people dead and thousands injured in the past nine years.[31]

Continuing with no end in sight, the war in Syria has caused the biggest refugee and displacement crisis since the World War II. Millions of Syrians fled their homes. Most of them sought refuge in the neighbouring countries while some made it to Europe, making up the biggest proportion of refugee population the European countries have encountered in the 2011-15 period. Over one million irregular migrants and refugees arrived in Europe only in 2015; most of them were from Syria, Africa and South Asia.[32] The

---

[27] Encyclopaedia Britannica, "Syrian Civil War", 2020, https://www.britannica.com/event/Syrian-Civil-War/Uprising-in-Syria-2011 (Access 04.09.2020)

[28] ibid.

[29] The Free Syrian Army claimed leadership over the armed opposition fighting in Syria, but its authority was largely unrecognized by the local militias. See ibid.

[30] The most significant efforts of the international community was the Kofi Annan Peace Plan launched in March 2012 by the Arab League and the UN. Al Jazeera, "Kofi Annan's six-point plan for Syria", 27.03.2012, https://www.aljazeera.com/news/2012/3/27/kofi-annans-six-point-plan-for-syria Access 04.09.2020

[31] The Syrian Observatory for Human Rights, "Syrian Revolution NINE years on: 586,100 persons killed and millions of Syrians displaced and injured", 14.03.2020, https://www.syriahr.com/en/157193/ Access 17.09.2020

[32] IOM, "Irregular Migrant, Refugee Arrivals in Europe Top One Million in 2015", 22.12.2015,

Mediterranean Sea routes were the most frequently used routes and since the main route went from the Aegean coast of Turkey to Greek islands, Greece was the major arrival country. The refugees were mostly from Syria. The Western Balkan route was preferred as well as the Mediterranean routes. The irregular migrants and refugees whose destination was Central Europe, particularly Germany and Austria, used this route. They passed through countries located en route like Slovenia, Hungary, Macedonia, and Serbia.[33]

The migration wave to Europe in 2015 brought with it the highest number of asylum applications. It was a record in the history of the Union. Over 1.2 million people applied as first-time asylum-seekers in the EU member countries.[34] Most of the applicants were the citizens of Syria, Afghanistan and Iraq. Among the EU member-countries, Germany received the highest number of asylum applications as well as in 2014. Germany was followed by Hungary, Sweden, Austria and Italy.

With deadly tragedies in the Mediterranean and Aegean Seas as well as arrivals in the European countries, the refugee movement was at the top of the agenda of the European Council throughout 2015.[35] The European Council bringing the heads of state and government of the member-states, decided to take many immediate actions with the aim of

> "saving lives at sea, targeting criminal smuggling networks, responding to high volumes of arrivals with the relocation of 160,000 refugees from Italy and Greece within the EU, granting protection to asylum seekers through an EU-wide resettlement scheme, and using EU tools such as the European Asylum Support Office (EASO), Frontex and Europol to help frontline Member States identify, register and fingerprint incoming migrants in dedicated 'hotspots'".[36]

---

https://www.iom.int/news/irregular-migrant-refugee-arrivals-europe-top-one-million-2015-iom Access 17.09.2020

[33] M. MacGregor, "Changing journeys: Migrant routes to Europe", 13.02.2019, https://www. infomigrants.net/ en/post/15005/changing-journeys-migrant-routes-to-europe Access 17.09.2020

[34] Eurostat, op.cit.

[35] Being the Union's High Representative and at the same time Vice-President of the European Commission responsible for the Commissioners' Group on External Action (CGEA), Mogherini has been engaged in intervention in the domain of 'migration'. "*On the occasion of the Foreign Affairs Council in March (the first in 10 years to discuss 'migration'), it was decided to organise an extraordinary meeting of Foreign Ministers and Interior Ministers on 20th April. This first-ever joint ministerial prepared the first 'special' European Council meeting on the refugee crisis on 23rd April, after the single-most deadly shipwreck on the Mediterranean claimed more than 800 lives. Mogherini has played an instrumental role in keeping the external dimension of the refugee crisis on the agenda since.*" S. Carrera et al., "The EU's Response to the Refugee Crisis Taking Stock and Setting Policy Priorities", Centre for European Policy Studies Essay, 2015, https://www.ceps.eu/wp-content/uploads/2015/12/EU%20Response%20to%20the%202015%20Refugee%20Crisis_0.pdf Access 18.09.2020

[36] F. Willermain, "The European Agenda on Migration, One Year on. The EU Response to the Crisis Has Produced Some Results, but Will Hardly Pass Another Solidarity Test", IEMed Mediterranean Yearbook 2016,

Not long after the shipwreck with the highest death toll in mid-April 2015, the European Agenda on Migration was proposed by the European Commission on May 13. The European Agenda on Migration was *"intended to address immediate challenges and equip the EU with the tools to better manage migration in the medium and long term in the areas of irregular migration, borders, asylum and legal migration"*.[37] Six "immediate (short-term) EU policy actions" were identified in the Agenda:

"1) A temporary and emergency-driven relocation mechanism for asylum-seekers within the EU for those member states confronting higher influx, based on a new redistribution key criteria for determining responsibility for assessing asylum applications; and the presentation of a legislative initiative for a permanent system before the end of 2015 2) A relocation mechanism for 20,000 refugees from outside the EU, and an extra €50 million budget 2015-16 to support this scheme 3) Tripling the capacities and budget of the EU External Border Agency (Frontex) joint border control and surveillance operations in the Mediterranean (called 'Triton' and 'Poseidon') 4) Increasing emergency funding to frontline EU member states by €60 million, and setting up a new 'hotspot approach in which EU home affairs agencies like Frontex, Europol and the European Asylum Support Office (EASO) would work on the ground to support 'frontline' member states in identifying, registering and fingerprinting migrants 5) Strengthening Europol's joint maritime information operation in the Mediterranean to deal with migrants' smuggling via CEPOL (European Policy College) 6) Establishing a Common Security and Defence Policy (CSDP) Operation in the Mediterranean to dismantle traffickers' networks and the 'business model' of smugglers, so as to identify, capture and destroy vessels used by smugglers".[38]

Additionally, 'medium-term levels of action' were identified in the Agenda. Those were the key 'pillars' necessary for a comprehensive EU migration policy: a) reducing the incentives for irregular migration; b) border management – saving lives and securing external borders; c) Europe's duty to protect – a strong common asylum policy; and d) a new policy on legal migration. Sets of specific policy actions were advanced in each 'pillar'.

In accordance with the 'immediate actions' outlined in the Agenda, the

https://www.egmontinstitute.be/content/uploads/2016/10/IEMed_MedYearBook2016 _Europe-Migration-Agenda_Fabian_Willermain.pdf Access 18.09.2020

[37] European Commission, "Communication From The Commission To The European Parliament, The European Council and The Council - Progress Report on the Implementation of the European Agenda on Migration", COM(2019) 481 final, 16.10. 2019, https://ec.europa.eu/home-affairs/sites/homeaffairs/files/what-we-do/policies/european-agenda-migration/20191016_com-2019-481-report_en.pdf Access 19.09.2020

[38] S. Carrera et al., op. cit. p.4

capacities and assets for the European Agency for the Management of Operational Cooperation at the External Borders of the Member States of the European Union's (Frontex) joint operations Triton in the Mediterranean Sea in 2015 and Poseidon in the Aegean Sea in 2016, were strengthened so that the level of intervention provided under the former Italian 'Mare Nostrum' search and rescue operation could be restored.[39] A number of "hotspots" were established in Italy and Greece where Frontex, Europol and EASO would work together for quickly identifying, registering and taking fingerprints of migrants who were arriving, expediting refugee screening and coordinating returns of the irregular migrants including the asylum-seekers whose applications have been rejected. A Regulation establishing a common list of safe third countries was adopted. In the Regulation, actual and potential EU candidates along the Western Balkan route, namely Serbia, Turkey, Montenegro, Bosnia-Herzegovina, Macedonia, and Kosovo were designated as safe third countries. An Action Plan against Migrants' Smuggling,[40] EU Action Plan on Return,[41] and a Recommendation on Common Return Handbook were adopted by the European Commission. The aim these measures was to return third country nationals who were irregularly entering and staying in Union territory and to cooperate with third countries on readmission of those irregular migrants. Moreover, it was decided by the EU Council of Ministers to relocate 160,000 asylum seekers in clear need of international protection from Italy and Greece to the territory of other Member States.[42] The member-states would also increase their operational support so that Italy and Greece could tackle the pressure on their asylum and migration systems due to the increasing number of migrant arrivals.[43]

The relocation from Italy and Greece was quite important in terms of solidarity and burden-sharing so the European Commission called on the member-states to commit to their duties and increase their efforts. However,

---

[39] F. Willermain, op. cit. p.2

[40] European Commission, "Communication From the Commission To The European Parliament, The Council, The European Economic and Social Committee and The Committee of The Regions EU Action Plan against migrant smuggling (2015-2020)",COM (2015) 285, 27.05.2015, https://ec.europa.eu/antitrafficking/sites/antitrafficking/files/eu_action_plan_against_migrant_smuggling_en.pdf Access 20.09.2020

[41] European Commission, "Communication from the Commission to the European Parliament and to the Council EU Action Plan on Return", COM(2015) 453 final, 09.09.2015, https://ec.europa.eu/home-affairs/sites/homeaffairs/files/what-we-do/policies/european-agenda-migration/proposal-implementation-package/docs/communication_from_the_ec_to_ep_and_council_-_eu_action_plan_on_return_en.pdf Access 20.09.2020

[42] The Council of Ministers Resolution on relocating from Greece and Italy 40,000 persons in clear need of international protection was adopted on 22 July 2015. The Resolution was complemented by an additional Council Decision on the temporary relocation of 120,000 asylum-seekers from Greece and Italy adopted on 22 September 2015 (Council Decision (EU) 2015/1601). The Council Decision in question is no longer in force; its validity came to an end in September 2017. Eur-Lex, https://eur-lex.europa.eu/legal-content/EN/TXT/?uri=celex%3A32015D1601 Access 19.09.2020

[43] F. Willermain, op.cit

there was disagreement among the member-states and they organised themselves into groups. On the one side, there was a coalition of the member states which were keen on relocation of the refugees from Greece and Italy to other EU countries. This group was composed of Austria, the Benelux countries, Finland, Germany. Together with Greece, they started meeting regularly. In addition, they were holding separate meetings with Turkey.[44] On the other side, the Czech Republic, Hungary, Poland and Slovakia made up the Visegrad Group. Emphasising that the EU member-states should solve the refugee problem themselves, these states were strictly opposed to the relocation of refugees. Through a focus on Hungary, their position is examined in detail in the following pages.

## Hungary's asylum policy following the Arab Uprisings

Except for the exodus of ethnic Hungarians following the uprisings in 1956 and the Chinese immigration in early 1990s, Hungary had not experienced any significant voluntary or forced migration on its territory. It has mostly been preferred as a country of transit so far. The asylum applications had increased after the accession to the EU but had never exceeded 5000.[45] Nevertheless, the legislation on asylum was tightened on par and it brought criticisms with it. In 2012, the UNHCR published a report which damned this tightening and the government halted detaining asylum-seekers in January 2013.[46] Yet, a couple of months later, there was a sharp increase in the number of people seeking refuge in Hungary. Accordingly, the legislation was redesigned with the new law on asylum going into force in July of that year, *"reintroduced the detention of asylum seekers, shortened appeal times in cases of negative decisions, and restructured the integration scheme for recognized refugees".*[47] Despite this tightened law, migrants continued crossing through Hungary. Many people sought protection in the country: the number of asylum-seekers was nearly 20,000 in 2013 while it exceeded 42,000 in 2014 and 177,000 in 2015.[48] As seen in the numbers, Hungary (particularly the border with Serbia) became an entry point to the EU territory.

When the countries of origin of asylum-seekers are examined, it is seen that most of the migrants were from Kosovo in late 2014 and early 2015, but the situation changed in the spring as there was a dramatic increase in the

---

[44] S. Lehne, "How the Refugee Crisis Will Reshape the EU", Carneige Europe, 04.02.2016, https://carne 238.gieeurope.eu/2016/02/04/how-refugee-crisis-will-reshape-eu-pub-62650 Access 18.09.2020

[45] Meszaros, op.cit p.238.

[46] A. Kallius et al., "Immobilizing mobility: Border ethnography, illiberal democracy, and the politics of the "refugee crisis" in Hungary", **American Ethnologist**, Vol. 43, No. 1, 2016, pp. 25–37

[47] ibid. p.35, footnote 2.

[48] Hungary National Directorate-General for Aliens Policing, "Statistics 2014–2015", http://bevandorlas.hu/index.php?option=com_k2&view=item&layout=item&id=492&Itemid=1259&lang=en Access 20.09.2020

number of migrants coming from zones of conflict such as Syria, Iraq and Afghanistan. The change is important due to the fact that, in the first half of 2015, the government officials claimed that most of the people coming to Hungary were actually 'economic migrants' instead of refugees. Actually, the anti-immigration rhetoric of the government and the governing party Fidesz had already started following the Charlie Hebdo attack in Paris in January of that year. Anti-immigration billboards reading 'We shall not allow economic migrants to jeopardise the jobs and livelihoods of Hungarians' and 'If you come to Hungary, respect our culture' were displayed all over the country.[49] As can be seen from the blue billboards with white letters written in Hungarian, the targeted group was Hungarians, not the economic migrants or refugees. Being shown as the main threat to the national economy and culture, migrants were the scapegoats. Thus, the populist anti-immigration discourse of the government was playing on welfare chauvinism[50] as well as fear.[51]

The anti-immigration discourse was showing itself in PM Orbán's speeches, as well. When he participated in the march to commemorate the victims killed in the attack, he stated to the Hungarian news Agency (MTI) that immigration was bad indeed because it was only bringing trouble and danger to the peoples of Europe. He said, *"We [Hungarians] do not want to see significantly-sized minorities with different cultural characteristics and backgrounds among us. We want to keep Hungary as Hungary"*.[52]

Furthermore, the Hungarian government launched wide-reaching campaigns throughout 2015. The first one was the "National Consultation on Immigration and Terrorism" launched in April 2015.[53] It was a survey accompanied by Orbán's letter which labelled asylum-seekers as "economic migrants" who were crossing the border illegally and showing themselves as refugees. Orbán thought that the increasing number of "economic migrants" posed a big threat to the Hungarian people and state so they had to be halted.

---

[49] C. Thorleifsson, "Disposable strangers: far-right securitisation of forced migration in Hungary", **Social Anthropology**, Vol. 25, No. 3, 2017, p. 321, https://onlinelibrary.wiley.com/doi/pdf/10.1111/14698676.12420 Access 30.08.2020

[50] As a concept, welfare chauvinism was first introduced in order to explain the success right-wing populist parties have achieved in elections held in European countries. According to Kitschelt and McGann, welfare chauvinism is the view that *"the welfare state [...] is a system of social protection for those who belong to the ethnically defined community and who have contributed to it"*. *People with this view believe that immigrants are not contributing sufficiently to the publicly funded club good but they are getting social benefits so they are "free-riders."* H. Kitschelt, A.J. McGann, **The Radical Right in Western Europe: A Comparative Analysis**, (USA, University of Michigan Press, 1995), *quoted in* B. Heizmann et al., "Welfare Chauvinism, Economic Insecurity and the Asylum Seeker 'Crisis'", **Societies**, Vol.8, Issue 3, 2018, p. 83, https://www.mdpi.com/2075-4698/8/3 Access 25.09.2020

[51] Thorleifsson, op. cit.

[52] Juhász et al., op. cit. p.24.

[53] The government spent 3.2 million Euros on this consultation. **Fenced Out: Hungary's Violations of The Rights of Refugees and Migrants**, Amnesty International, United Kingdom, 2015, p.5, www.amnestyinternational.org Access 11.08.2020

The survey was composed of 12 questions that reflected the anti-immigration rhetoric of the government. Some of the questions are as follows: *Question 3*: "There are some who think that mismanagement of the immigration question by Brussels may have something to do with increased terrorism. Do you agree with this view?", *Question 5*: "We hear different views on the issue of immigration. There are some who think that economic migrants jeopardise the jobs and livelihoods of Hungarians. Do you agree?", *Question 6*: "There are some who believe that Brussels' policy on immigration and terrorism has failed, and that we therefore need a new approach to these questions. Do you agree?", *Question 9*: "Do you agree with the view that migrants illegally crossing the Hungarian border should be returned to their own countries within the shortest possible time?", and *Question 12*: "Do you agree with the Hungarian government that support should be focused more on Hungarian families and the children they can have, rather than on immigration?" (The Hungarian Government, 2015).[54]

The second campaign was a billboard campaign on which the government spent 1.3 million Euros.[55] It was launched in June 2015. The posters that appeared across the whole country ran three types of messages: 1) "if you come to Hungary, you have to respect our culture." 2) "if you come to Hungary, you have to respect our laws." 3) "if you come to Hungary, you mustn't take work away from the Hungarians!".[56] The migrants were warned about coming to Hungary but all the posters were written in Hungarian. So the target was actually the domestic audience rather than the migrants or the human traffickers as the government officials claimed.

In summer came the Hungarian government's draconian response to the increasing number of irregular migrants, most of whom were refugees. First, fences were constructed along the borders with Serbia and Croatia. Secondly, there were amendments to the legislation concerning asylum. On August 1, an amendment to the Law on Asylum authorising the government to issue lists of safe countries of origin and safe third countries of transit came into effect. Accordingly, along with the EU countries including Greece, Serbia and Macedonia were declared as safe countries by the government authorities. This meant that *"asylum applications by people transiting through from these countries can be sent back to them following expedited proceedings"*.[57] As Serbia was declared a safe third country, people who have transited through that country on their way to Hungary, would not be able to apply for asylum

---

[54] National Consultation on Immigration and Terrorism, The Orange Files, 19.05.2015, https://theorangefiles.hu/?s=National+consultation+on+immigration+and+terrori Access 15.08.2020
[55] Amnesty International, op. cit p. 6.
[56] **The Budapest Beacon**, "Hungarian government launches xenophobic billboard campaign", 04.06.2015,https://budapestbeacon.com/hungarian-government-launches-xenophobic-billboard campaign/ Access 15.08.2020
[57] Amnesty International, op. cit p. 6.

because their applications would not be admitted and they would be deported.

While Hungary was taking strict measures against asylum-seekers, a proposal came from the European Commission about the relocation of 120,000 refugees from Greece and Italy in addition to 40,000 refugees which had been proposed on May 27.[58] Upon the European Commission's proposal, the heads of governments of Visegrad Group countries, namely Poland, Hungary, Czech Republic and Slovakia, held an extraordinary summit[59] in Prague on September 4. After the summit, the prime ministers released a joint statement in which they declared that the Visegrad Group would support the EU by making financial assistance to vulnerable people as a result of this mass refugee movement and third countries with high numbers of refugees generated by the unrest and uprisings in the MENA region and they made a remark that they would do whatever they could in terms of technical side of border protection and asylum procedures. However, the prime ministers were critical about the obligatory quotas for relocation from Italy and Greece and instead they recommended cooperation among member-states based on voluntariness. Despite the opposition of the Visegrad Group, the Council of the EU adopted the decision for the relocation of 120,000 refugees on September 22. Among the Visegrad Group states, Hungary as well as Slovakia and the Czech Republic voted against the decision.

In the meantime, another set of amendments to the Law on Asylum came into effect in Hungary. Being valid from September 15, a state of emergency was declared at the border, "allowing the deployment of troops in peace time and the right to search homes where migrants are thought to be sheltering".[60] People who entered Hungary "unauthorized" through the border fence, are

---

[58] On 27 May 2015, the European Commission came forward with a first package of implementing measures of the European Agenda on Migration, including an emergency relocation scheme to relocate 40,000 people from Italy and Greece, and a recommendation on a European Resettlement Scheme which was calling for Member States to resettle 20,000 people from outside the EU. European Commission, "Refugee Crisis – Q&A on Emergency Relocation", 22.09.2015, https://ec.europa.eu/commission/ presscorner/detail/en/MEMO_15_5698 Access 24.08.2020 Shortly after the adoption of this package, the heads of government of the Visegrad Group countries held a meeting in Bratislava in June 2015. Their Joint Statement is as follows: "*We recall to develop a more systemic and geographically comprehensive approach to migration. Therefore we regret that the Agenda fails to address and find adequate solutions to migration pressure from and via the Western Balkan route as well as the Eastern route. We also recall the voluntary options when emergency relocation and resettlement are concerned. We do not deny the spirit of solidarity but we firmly argue the contradictory effects and pull factors of a possible mandatory redistribution scheme for asylum seekers.*" Visegrad Group, "Joint Statement of the Heads of Government of the Visegrad Group Countries", 19.06.2015, http://www.visegradgroup.eu/calendar/2015/joint-statement-of-the Access 24.08.2020
[59] The Visegrad Group has been holding summit meetings at Presidential and Ministerial levels since the early 1990s when the Group was first established. For more about meetings and statements see the official website of the Visegrad Group http://www.visegradgroup.eu/
[60] A. Kallius et al., op.cit p. 33.

considered to be committing a criminal offence and they would be punished up to three years of prison and/or deportation. Giving damage to the border fence and giving aid to another person who is crossing the border in an illegal way are also criminalised. They are offences to be punished with between one to five years imprisonment.[61] Furthermore, with this asylum law the state was given the right to establish a transit zone at the border. Transit zone is "*an area where foreigners arriving in the event of a mass immigration crisis have the opportunity to initiate asylum procedures properly and to use the services provided in the transit zones until the asylum procedure is completed*".[62] As stated in a report of the Amnesty International, people in the "transit zones" may accede to Hungarian territory in case their application for asylum is deemed admissible.[63] There were two transit zones in Röszke/Horgoš crossing and Tompa,[64] and two in Beremend and Letenye along the Croatian border but the latter two did not become operational.[65]

On September 16, a day after a state of emergency was declared at the border meaning that Hungary closed its borders to migrants and refugees, "*hundreds of walkers, stranded at the Röszke/Horgoš crossing, …, attempted to break through the border fence that had been erected by the Hungarian authorities*".[66] The Hungarian police responded quite brutally to those people. They used tear gas and water cannons. This was not the first time the police acted like that and such actions were not limited with the police officials. As the UN Human Rights Commissioner had observed, the other Hungarian authorities were also violating international law as they were denying entry, arresting, summarily rejecting and returning refugees, and using disproportionate force on migrants and refugees.[67]

---

[61] Amnesty International, op. cit. p.20

[62] Hungary National Directorate-General for Aliens Policing, "Transit Zone", 2019, http://www.bmbah. hu/index.php?option=com_k2&view=item&id=1220:transit-zone&lang=en Access 25.08.2020

[63] Amnesty International, op. cit. p.17.

[64] Shortly after the opening of "transit zones" in mid-September, it was seen that they would not be able to process many asylum claims. As Amnesty International reported, very few people were let in to the "transit zone" in Röszke/Horgoš while thousands of others were waiting in Serbia without being informed about how they would apply for asylum. Moreover, even though the admissibility procedure in the "transit zones" at the border should take up to eight days according to the Law on Asylum, Amnesty International observed that the decisions were being made very quickly. The people entering the "transit zones" through Serbia, which was a safe third country, would quite possibly be rejected within the admissibility procedure. ibid. p.17.

[65] Asylum Information Database, "Country Report: Hungary", 31.12.2019, https://www.asylumineurope. org/reports/country/hungary Access 26.08.2020

[66] C. Cantat, "Governing Migrants and Refugees in Hungary: Politics of Spectacle, Negligence and Solidarity in a Securitising State", **Politics of (Dis)Integration**, S. Hinger, R. Schweitzer (Ed.), IMISCOE Research Series, 2020, https://doi.org/10.1007/978-3-030-25089-8_10, p. 186 Access 08.09.2020

[67] Furthermore, the UN Human Rights Commissioner found the amendments to the Law on Asylum and the Criminal Code incompatible with Hungary's human rights commitments. He said that neither seeking asylum nor entering a country in an irregular way could be considered a crime. Amnesty

Despite the UN Human Rights Commissioner's criticisms, another strict measure was taken. The Hungarian Parliament first passed legislation which made it possible for the military forces to act with the police in securing the Hungarian border and territory in cases of "crisis caused by mass immigration", and second a resolution calling for the use of "all available measures to defend Hungarian borders".[68] The humanitarian organisations including Amnesty International were rather worried because the Parliament's call to use "all available measures" could easily pave the way to excessive use of force which may cause serious injury and even death. However, the harsh anti-immigration rhetoric of the Government and Fidesz politicians as well strict measures taken by the state continued in the weeks following the Hungarian police's brutal response to the refugees attempting to break through the border fence in mid-September.

The terror attacks in Paris in mid-November brought more harshness to the government's anti-immigration rhetoric. Migrants, including refugees, were identified with terrorists. Orbán declared that Europe was under a grave threat because terrorism would spread in the continent as a result of the EU's obligatory refugee relocation quota system.[69] Accordingly, the government's third campaign was launched. In the national newspapers, there were

> "government-sponsored messages such as 'The quota increases the terror threat!' and 'An illegal immigrant arrives in Europe on average every 12 seconds.'", and other messages like "'We don't know who they are, or what their intentions are" and "We don't know how many hidden terrorists are among them.'"[70]

Fidesz began collecting signatures for a petition that was against the refugee redistribution quota system. As known, the Council of the EU adopted the decision for the relocation of a 160,000 refugees and Hungary was supposed to take in around 1,300 refugees.[71] Moreover, the Hungarian parliament passed a bill which accused the EU *"of ignoring the right of individual national governments to 'express their opinion' by trying to share 160,000 refugees across all 28 member countries based on population"*.[72] The legislation enabled the government to sue the European Union over its proposal to relocate refugees from Greece and Italy based on a quota system. Following its neighbour

---

International, op. cit p.7.

[68] ibid. p.22

[69] Juhász et al., op. cit. p.27.

[70] **Deutsche Welle**, "Hungary sues EU at European Court of Justice over migrant quotas", 03.12.2015, https://www.dw.com/en/hungary-sues-eu-at-european-court-of-justice-over-migrant-quotas/a-18892790 Access 29.09.2020

[71] **BBC News**, "Hungary PM claims EU migrant quota referendum victory", 03.10.2016, https://www.bbc.com/news/world-europe-37528325 Access 28.08.2020

[72] Deutsche Welle, "Hungary ready to sue EU over migrant plan", 17.11.2015, https://www.dw.com/en/hungary-ready-to-sue-eu-over-migrant-plan/a-18856469 Access 29.09.2020

Slovakia, Hungary filed a lawsuit at the European Court of Justice (ECJ) in early December. Orbán said that Hungary had protested enough and it was time to take action.[73] In the lawsuit, Hungary's argument was that the Council decision should be considered a legislative act rather than provisional measures, and that Art. 78(3) TFEU[74] does not provide an adequate legal basis for the Council to adopt it. The joined cases of Hungary and Slovakia against the provisional mechanism for the mandatory redistribution of refugees would be dismissed by the ECJ on September 6, 2017. With its judgment, the ECJ would confirm the Council's decision to relocate refugees from Italy and Greece.

The government continued to identify migrants/refugees with terrorists in 2016. In the eyes of the government officials, the migrants posed a serious threat to the Hungarian nation and the state. The anti-migrant understanding was reflected in government actions as well as legislation. First, in March, the national state of emergency that had been declared in September 2015 was extended for another six months because the Western Balkans migratory route had been closed and more than 14.000 migrants were stuck along the Greek-Macedonian border.[75] [76] Secondly, in June, a draconian counter-terrorism package including "a constitutional amendment and changes to the laws governing the police, national security services and defence forces" was passed and Hungary's new Counter Terrorism Intelligence and Criminal Analysis Centre (TIBEK) was established with this counter-terrorism package.[77] Hence, a series of oppressive and restrictive laws that would have an impact on all residents came into force in the name of protecting the Hungarian nation against the imagined threat posed by the migrants/refugees.

In early October of the same year, a referendum was held on the EU's mechanism of refugee redistribution. As known, the government was vehemently opposed to the mandatory migrant quota that was imposed by the EU, and the main aim of the referendum was to get public support and

---

[73] **Deutsche Welle**, "Hungary sues EU …"

[74] TFEU Art 78 (3): "In the event of one or more Member States being confronted by an emergency situation characterised by a sudden inflow of nationals of third countries, the Council, on a proposal from the Commission, may adopt provisional measures for the benefit of the Member State(s) concerned. It shall act after consulting the European Parliament."

[75] The extension of state of emergency was labelled by the government as "a safety and preventive measure to the unpredictable reactions that the 'tightened border restrictions in neighbouring nations' could generate among refugees and migrants" **NBCnews** "Europe's Refugee Crisis: Hungary Declares State of Emergency Over Migrants", 09.03.2016 https://www.nbcnews.com/storyline/europes-border-crisis/ europe-s-refugee-crisis-hungary-declares-state-emergency-over-migrants-n534746 Access 29.08.2020

[76] The Hungarian government continued extending the national state of emergency even though the number of arrivals and illegal crossings at the border had decreased significantly. It was extended in February and September 2018 as well as in 2017. Meszaros, op. cit. p. 248

[77] Cantat, op. cit. p.186.

thus to receive legitimacy for refusing the quota. The question asked in the referendum was a simple one: *"Do you want the European Union to prescribe the mandatory settlement of non-Hungarian citizens in Hungary without the consent of the National Assembly?"*.[78] The referendum results were presented as an overwhelming success because 98% of the voters said No to the EU's mechanism of refugee relocation. Yet, in reality, the referendum was not valid at all since the turnout was below the required percentage (it was only 40.4%).[79]

Even though the referendum was successful in the eyes of the government officials, they were still afraid of the possibility that the referendum would not be enough to deter potential asylum-seekers from coming to Hungary. Hence, in order not to experience the same situation as in 2015, shortly after the referendum the Orbán government started strengthening the borders even more than before and closing the refugee camps.[80] One of the camps shut down, which was in Bicske, had been serving refugees for more than two decades. With the opportunities provided to the asylum-seekers it was relatively easier to adjust to life in Hungary. When it was closed, there were only 75 asylum-seekers in the camp and they were relocated to a remote camp in Kiskunhalas in southern part of the country.[81] The Hungarian government shows that it does not want migrants/refugees. This can be observed in the treatment of refugees. Both asylum-seekers in reception centres and refugees who have received protection are not provided with many resources so the assistance that civil society organisations give is quite important for them.

In 2017, we come across two other consultations at the national level. One of them was on the EU policies and the other on the Soros Plan. The first one entitled "Let's Stop Brussels" was conducted in April and May. It contains six questions on a number of issues regarding Hungary's relations with the EU. The questions related to migration and asylum as well as the presence of international organisations in the country[82] are as follows:

---

[78] Gozdziak, op. cit. p. 10.
[79] **BBC News**, op cit.
[80] Gozdziak, op. cit. p.11.
[81] As of October 2016, only 529 asylum seekers were staying in the waiting centers: 318 at open reception centers such as Bicske and 211 in detention centers. ibid. p.12.
[82] "They refer to NGOs which receive funding from international sources, and against which the Fidesz government has begun drafting legislation: a bill leaked Sunday revealing government plans to require foreign-funded NGOs to register themselves with authorities". **The Budapest Beacon**, ""Let's Stop Brussels!": Here is the new National Consultation", 03.04.2017, https://budapestbeacon.com/lets-stop-brussels-new-national-consultation/ Access 29.08.2020
The Law on the Transparency of Organisations Receiving Foreign Funds, or the so-called NGO Law was adopted in mid-June 2017. According to the law, Hungarian Helsinki Committee, Hungarian Civil Liberties Union, and Transparency International which receive partial funding from George Soros' Open Society Foundation, have to register with government as "organisations receiving foreign funds", disclose their donors and show on all publications and web-sites that they receive foreign funding. **The**

*Question 2*: In recent times, terror attack after terror attack has taken place in Europe. Despite this fact, Brussels wants to force Hungary to allow illegal immigrants into the country. What do you think Hungary should do? (a) For the sake of the safety of Hungarians these people should be placed under supervision (felügyelet) while the authorities decide their fate. (b) Allow the illegal immigrants to move freely in Hungary. *Question 3*: By now it has become clear that, in addition to the smugglers, certain international organizations encourage the illegal immigrants to commit illegal acts. What do you think Hungary should do? (a) Activities assisting illegal immigration such as human trafficking and the popularization of illegal immigration must be punished. (b) Let us accept that there are international organizations which, without any consequences, urge the circumvention of Hungarian laws. *Question 4*: More and more foreign-supported organizations operate in Hungary with the aim of interfering in the internal affairs of our country in an opaque manner. These organizations could jeopardize our independence. What do you think Hungary should do? (a) Require them to register, revealing the objectives of their activities and the sources of their finances. (b) Allow them to continue their risky activities without any supervision.

The second consultation, which was on the so-called Soros Plan, was conducted in October-December 2017. Orbán claimed that, having the support of the EU, the Hungarian-American millionaire George Soros had a plan which would allow a foreign international organization on settling one million migrants in Europe thus Muslim refugees would flood the continent once Soros and his allies were successful in opening the borders.[83] Shown as 'the most successful national consultation ever', the National Consultation on the Soros Plan accused Soros of "*deliberately trying to destroy the national states and the national culture by planning to resettle at least 1 million immigrants in Europe one a yearly basis and to dismantle the borders fences together with Brussels in order to clear the way for the incoming immigrants*".[84] Hungarian citizens who receive the consultation via mail, are supposed to check one of two boxes on the questionnaire: one in favour of the "plan", and one against the "plan". The statements are as follows: 1. George Soros wants Brussels to resettle at least one million immigrants per year onto European Union territory, including in Hungary. 2. Together with officials in Brussels, George Soros is planning to dismantle border fences in EU Member States, including in Hungary, to open the borders for immigrants. 3. One part of the Soros Plan is to use Brussels to force the EU-wide distribution of immigrants that have accumulated in

---

**Budapest Beacon**, op cit.

[83] O. Vadhanavisala, "Radical Right-Wing Politics and Migrants and Refugees in Hungary", **European Journal of Social Sciences**, Vol. 2, Issue 3, 2019, http://journals.euser.org/files/articles/ejss_v2_i3_19/ Vadhanavisala.pdf Access 06.09.2020

[84] Meszaros, op. cit. pp.248-249.

Western Europe, with special focus on Eastern European countries. Hungary must also take part in this. 4. Based on the Soros Plan, Brussels should force all EU Member States, including Hungary, to pay immigrants HUF 9 million in welfare. 5. Another goal of George Soros is to make sure that migrants receive milder criminal sentences for the crimes they commit. 6. The goal of the Soros Plan is to push the languages and cultures of Europe into the background so that integration of illegal immigrants happens much more quickly. 7. It is also part of the Soros Plan to initiate political attacks against those countries which oppose immigration, and to severely punish them.[85] [86] The government spokesperson told at a press conference that the consultation on the so-called Soros Plan broke all previous records in terms of participation.[87] [88]

Shortly after the national elections in April 2018, which was easily won by Orbán,[89] the Hungarian parliament made use of the results of this consultation and approved the "Stop Soros" package of bills that "criminalise any individual or group that offers to help an illegal immigrant claim asylum".[90] With the law, the ability of NGOs to act in asylum cases is restricted. Moreover, the individuals or groups helping irregular migrants gain status to stay in Hungary will be imprisoned. Organisations such as the Council of Europe, Organisation for Security and Cooperation in Europe and the EU as well as human rights groups severely criticised the legislation but still the Hungarian parliament passed it in addition to a constitutional amendment "stating that an 'alien population' cannot be settled in Hungary".[91]

---

[85] **The Budapest Beacon,** "Here are the "Soros Plan" national consultation questions!", 28.09.2017, https://budapestbeacon.com/soros-plan-national-consultation-questions/ Access 06.10.2020
[86] The questionnaire had online as well as paper version. The online version, as HírTV showed, lacked basic security features. First, sending the answers required a valid email address but the site did not validate the entered email address. It means that, in theory, an infinite number of false responses may be submitted. Moreover, the online consultation form did not give any feedback once a response was published. **The Budapest Beacon,** ""Soros plan" national consultation open to abuse", 11.10.2017, https://budapestbeacon.com/soros-plan-national-consultation-open-to-abuse/ Access 06.10.2020
[87] About Hungary, "National consultation survey on the "Soros plan" attracted a record 2.3 million responses", News in Brief, 5.12.2017, http://abouthungary.hu/news-in-brief/national-consultation-survey-on-the-soros-plan-attracted-a-record-23-million-responses/ Access 06.10.2020
[88] In November 2017, the statements in the consultation were rebuted on George Soros' official website. "Rebuttal of the October 9 National Consultation in Hungary", 20.11.2017, www.georgesoros.com/ rebuttal/ Access 06.10.2020
[89] Orbán's party, the Alliance of Young Democrats-Civic Union (FIDESZ-MPP) made an electoral alliance with the People's Christian Democratic Party (KDNP). C. Deloy, "Viktor Orbán easily sweeps to victory for the third time running in the Hungarian elections", Fondation Robert Schuman, The European Elections Monitor, 10.04.2018, https://www.robert-schuman.eu/en/eem/1765-viktor-orban-easily-sweeps-to-victory-for-the-third-time-running-in-the-hungarian-elections, 08.10.2020
[90] **The Guardian,** "Hungary passes anti-immigrant 'Stop Soros' laws", 20.06.2018, https://www.theguardian.com/world/2018/jun/20/hungary-passes-anti-immigrant-stop-soros-laws Access 09.10.2020
[91] **The Guardian,** op. cit.

The year 2019 was marked by the continuation of "state of crisis due to mass migration".[92] [93] In other words, the state of emergency was still in force. In accordance with the special rules applied during the state of emergency, asylum could only be sought at the border, inside the transit zone, and asylum seekers were held in the transit zones for the entire asylum procedure. They were detained without any legal basis. Police were "*still authorised to pushback across the border fence irregularly staying migrants (including those who wish to seek asylum in Hungary) from any part of the country, without any legal procedure or opportunity to challenge this measure*" (Asylum Information Database, 2019).[94] [95] In July, the UN Special Rapporteur on the human rights of migrants paid a visit to Hungary and said that the state of emergency should be immediately ended as there was not a single migrant coming to the country from the Serbian side of the border, thus the extension was meaningless and not at all necessary.

Detention was still a frequent practice although it should be an exceptional measure. One may see many asylum-seekers arbitrarily detained in the transit zones of Röszke and Tompa. Unfortunately, those people inside the transit zones were staying in dire conditions and deprived of liberty. This was confirmed by various UN bodies such as the United Nations Working Group on Arbitrary Detention (UNWGAD) and the UN High Commissioner for Human Rights as well as the European Committee for the Prevention of Torture (CPT), the European Commission and the Council of Europe.[96]

Furthermore, the asylum claims were approved at quite a low rate (less than 9%) after very long procedures and the asylum-seekers had to stay in the transit zone during that time.[97] There were also institutional changes. As of July 1, the Asylum and Immigration Office was replaced by the National Directorate-General for Aliens Policing (NDGAP) which would be supervised by the Ministry of Interior and have its own budget but would operate under the Police Act. The NDGAP is in charge of the asylum procedure as well as operation of the transit zones, open reception centres

---

[92] Asylum Information Database, op. cit
[93] The state of emergency due to mass migration was in force in the two counties bordering Serbia and in the four counties bordering Croatia, Slovenia and Austria since September 2015. On 9 March 2016, the state of emergency was extended to the whole country. It has been extended ten times since that time and is in force until 7 March 2021. Asylum Information Database, op. cit; The Parliament Magazine, "EU warns Hungary not to discriminate against EU citizens during ongoing health crisis", 02.09.2020,https://www.theparliamentmagazine.eu/news/article/eu-warns-hungary-not-to-discriminate-against-eu-citizens-during-ongoing-health-crisis Access 10.10.2020
[94] Asylum Information Database, op. cit.
[95] In 2019, 11,101 people were pushed back from the territory of Hungary to the external side of the border fence and there were 961 people who were blocked entry at the border fence. ibid.
[96] ibid.
[97] ibid.

and closed asylum detention facilities for asylum seekers.[98]

The year 2020 was marked by the rulings of the European Court of Justice and another national consultation. The first of the ECJ rulings came in early April. The European Commission had initiated infringement proceedings against Hungary because of failing to fulfil its obligations concerning the Council Decision (EU) 2015/1601 on the relocation of refugees from Italy and Greece. Since it had found Hungary's response unsatisfactory, the Commission had moved on to the next step and, in late July 2017, sent Hungary a reasoned opinion. Yet Hungary's reply to the reasoned opinion of the European Commission was not satisfactory, too. Hence, in December 2017, the Commission decided to take Hungary to the ECJ for not fulfilling its relocation obligations.[99] Along with Hungary, Poland and the Czech Republic were taken to court by the European Commission for the same reason. On 2 April, the ECJ ruled that those three countries had violated their obligations by not acting in accordance with the Council Decision (EU) in September 2015. Actually the relocation programme has not been valid since 2017, thus it is not practically possible to make these three countries take in more asylum-seekers. In that case, as underlined in the ECJ statement, the European Commission will decide what to do as the next step. Hungary's Minister of Justice, J. Varga, expressed the discontent of the government with the following words: *"This is especially shocking in the light of the fact that almost none of the member states have fully implemented the 2015 'quota decisions'. ..."*.[100] Moreover, she declared on Twitter that the EU's compulsory relocation system of migrants was dead and the ECJ judgement would not change this fact.[101]

The second judgment of the ECJ was on the so-called NGO Law. According to the NGO Law adopted in mid-2017, NGOs which receive partial funding from Open Society Foundation, should register as "organisations receiving foreign funds". In December 2017, the European Commission had sued Hungary for *"failing to fulfil its obligations under the Treaty provisions on the free movement of capital, due to provisions in the NGO Law which indirectly discriminate and disproportionately restrict donations from abroad to civil society organisations"*.[102] It was the final step in the infringement proceedings. The

---

[98] ibid.

[99] InfoCuria Case-Law, "European Commission v Hungary (Case C-718/17)" 22.12.2017, http://curia.europa.eu/juris/document/document.jsf?text=&docid=200650&pageIndex=0&doclang=en&mode=lst&dir=&occ=first&part=1&cid=715470 Access 10.10.2020

[100] **The New York Times**, "E.U. Court Rules 3 Countries Violated Deal on Refugee Quotas", 02.02.2020, https://www.nytimes.com/2020/04/02/world/europe/european-court-refugees-hungary-poland-czech-republic.html Access 08.10.2020

[101] ibid.

[102] European Commission, "Infringements -European Commission refers Hungary to the Court of Justice for its NGO Law", Press Release, 07.12.2017, https://ec.europa.eu/commission/presscorner/detail/en/

ruling of the ECJ on 18 June was that the Hungarian legislation on the foreign funding of NGOs was in breach of the EU law: *"The restrictions imposed by Hungary on the financing of civil organisations by persons established outside that Member State do not comply with EU law"*.[103]

The last development of 2020 is the launch of a new national consultation in June. The focus is on the Covid-19 pandemic in the country and the best possible ways to overcome a new wave. There are thirteen questions in the consultation, *"asking people whether they agree with wearing masks, social distancing and maintaining a three-hour 'shopping slot' (between 9am and 12 noon) exclusively for the elderly in shops"*.[104] Other questions are about the control of nursing homes, the preference of Hungarian products over foreign goods and taxation of multinationals and banks to tackle the economic consequences of the Covid-19 pandemic. However, PM Orbán's two favourite enemies George Soros and migrants are also on target. For example, *Question 10* is about the former: "George Soros has come up with a new plan to handle the economic crisis that will follow the coronavirus epidemic. In it, he proposes that EU member states take up gigantic loans (perpetual bonds), on which we would have to pay interest for generations to come, perpetually. According to experts, this would force nations into bonded labour. Do you reject George Soros's plan, which would put our homeland in debt for an unforeseeably long period of time?" Questions 12 and 13 are about migration: *Question 12*: "According to a European Court of Justice ruling, it is illegal to have immigrants wait in the transit zone on the Hungarian border. The decision found that migrants should be allowed entry into our country during the epidemic. This ruling coincides with George Soros's old plan on migration, which proposed that one million immigrants must be allowed entry annually and at any cost. Do you agree that the government should continue to stand up against immigration and maintain strict protection of Hungary's borders?", *Question 13*: "Brussels is preparing an offensive against the immigration-related regulations of the Hungarian constitution. They want to force us to amend the Fundamental Law's articles that prevent migration. Do you agree that the Hungarian government must insist on its anti-immigration rules even at the price of an open conflict with Brussels?"[105] The consultation was supposed

---

IP_17_5003

[103] Court of Justice of the European Union, "The restrictions imposed by Hungary on the financing of civil organisations by persons established outside that Member State do not comply with EU law", Press Release

No 73/20, Judgment in Case C-78/18 Commission v Hungary, 18.06.2020, https://curia.europa.eu/jcms/upload/docs/application/pdf/2020-06/cp200073en.pdf Access 06.10.2020

[104] Reporting Democracy, "Orbán's 'National Consultation' Seeks to Set Hungary's Political Agenda", 09.06.2020, https://balkaninsight.com/2020/06/09/orbans-national-consultation-seeks-to-set-hungarys-political-agenda/ Access 08.10.2020

[105] About Hungary, "Here's the latest national consultation questionnaire in English", News in Brief, 09.06.2020, http://abouthungary.hu/news-in-brief/heres-the-latest-national-consultation-questionnaire-in-english/ Access 11.10.2020

to be completed by the mid-August.[106] Like the previous ones, this consultation will also serve hatemongering against migrants, the EU and Soros.

## Concluding remarks

As a country with no significant migratory movement or asylum claims before, Hungary was shocked by the relatively high number of asylum applications lodged in 2015. It was a momentous shift for the state as well as the public due to the fact that Hungary had not been a destination for migrants. The scale of forced migration movement was so enormous that Hungary could not accept it. Hence, although the majority of migrants used Hungary as a country of transit or nearly all of the asylum-seekers applying for protection out of formality moved to the Western Europe, the shift was used by the Orbán-led government to fuel the fear of public. The government considered and framed this forced migration movement as a migration crisis. Accordingly, its response was quite harsh. Wide-reaching campaigns were launched throughout the country. Fences were constructed along the borders with Serbia and Croatia. With an amendment to the Law on Asylum, safe third countries of transit and safe countries of origin were listed by the government. Among the safe third countries of transit Serbia comes to the fore. Since it was declared as a safe third country, people passing through that country on their way to Hungary would not be allowed to apply for asylum and would be deported. With another set of amendments coming into force in the mid-September 2015, a state of emergency due to mass migration was declared and the state was given the right to establish a transit zone at the border. Transit zones are places where people apply for asylum, and unless their applications are admitted they cannot enter the Hungarian territory. It was reported by the Amnesty International that very few people were let in to the transit zones and the duration of deciding on asylum applications was much shorter than it was supposed to be.

Moreover, the Hungarian authorities were violating international law because migrants were denied entry to Hungarian territory, arrested, deported without being given any chance to make an asylum claim, and disproportionate force was used on them. Particularly the police forces were

---

[106] The Orbán-led government has launched eight national consultations since 2010 and it is announced that each consultation is quite successful. However, there is a problem. The results of consultations cannot be really validated due to the fact that neither independent researchers or polling analysts have had access to them. There are eight million voters in the country but the highest number of questionnaires to be returned reached only 2.5 million. Moreover, they are criticised for being "hate campaigns" as well as being part of the governing party Fidesz's efforts to set the political agenda. Friedrich Naumann Foundation Europe, "'National Consultation' Campaigns in Hungary, 23.11.2017, https://fnf-europe.org/2017/11/23/national-consultation-campaigns-in-hungary/ Access 10.10.2020. Nevertheless, the results are presented as a big success by the Fidesz-led government.

acting quite brutally to prevent them from passing through the fence at the border.

Following the terror attacks in Paris in November 2015, the government's rhetoric and attitude towards migrants was even harsher. They were identified with terrorists thus seen as posing a big threat to the nation as well as the state. Actually this was quite paradoxical because most of them were using Hungary as a country of transit on their way to Western Europe. Yet, this framing was an important element of the securitisation of migration in Hungary. Migrants, especially refugees were being otherised in this way. Both the government action and legislation echoed the anti-immigrant rhetoric. The state of emergency due to mass migration declared in September 2015 started to be extended every six months and it was still in force at the time of writing. Oppressive and restrictive laws that would affect everybody in the country were put into force. Asylum-seekers were detained in the so-called transit zones with no legal basis at all. The police forces were authorised to push back the irregular migrants without any legal procedure. Instead of an exceptional measure, detention came out to be a frequent practice.

The border policies and criminalisation practices in Hungary are not compatible with EU law, particularly the Schengen rules because there are no walls that stop the asylum-seekers from applying for international protection. Hence, the EU is deeply concerned about the asylum applications being systemically dismissed, the asylum procedures lacking guarantees and remedies, the consideration of crossing the border as a crime, the closure of border crossing points and the excessive powers given to the military for managing the borders. Furthermore, Hungary has failed in fulfilling its obligations concerning the Council Decision on the relocation of refugees from Italy and Greece. Along with Poland and the Czech Republic, Hungary disregarded the EU's principle of solidarity. Thus, the European Commission took those member-states to the ECJ and the ECJ ruled that they had violated their obligations by not taking any refugees according to the Council Decision of September 2015.

As a last remark, it may be underlined that the asylum claims are approved at a very low rate because asylum-seekers continue to be considered as economic migrants. They are not seen as people in need of protection. This understanding affects the authorities' general attitude and treatment of asylum-seekers. The ones who have obtained refugee status or who are benefitting from subsidiary protection, on the other hand, are faced with dire circumstances. The camps they have been staying are being closed down and the integration services they have been receiving are cut off so they are left to destitution and homelessness. They can get integration assistance in the fields of housing, finding job, learning the Hungarian language and family reunification only from non-governmental organisations and church-based organisations. Hence, it may be said that the Hungarian asylum policy followed by the Orbán-led government is not at all refugee-friendly.

# CHAPTER 14

# ASYLUM POLICY OF REPUBLIC OF SERBIA: THE CASE OF THE HUMANITARIAN ROUTE

Ayşegül Bostan[*]

> "It's something that fades us one by one.
> They call it "war". Wars break and destroy.
> Not only our hearts ..."[1]

In a general sense the former Yugoslavia, including Serbia, Croatia, Bosnia-Herzegovina (BiH), Kosovo, Macedonia, Montenegro and Slovenia, has been regarded as a country of emigration in terms of internal and external migration. In the late 1970s, Slovenia was exposed to guest-workers coming from southern Yugoslavia. The reason of such internal migration was both the opportunity for ex-Yugoslavian people to find a job in industrial cities of Slovenia and the economy of Slovenia being better than other ex-Yugoslavian states.[2] When the civil war broke up in Yugoslavia in the 1990s, the world witnessed the forced displacements of Yugoslav citizens and the Western European countries were suddenly subjected to the wave of refugees. Therefore, it could be inferred that ethno-national conflict or deep economic crisis led to waves of migration and refugees.[3]

Recently internal conflict, one of the main drives of exodus, has also been a cause of mass refugee movement named as the Syrian migration crisis. The immigration wave started by people fleeing from Syria has caused the most serious migrant crisis that the world has witnessed after the 1994 refugee

---

[*]Research Assistant, Department of International Relations, Çankırı Karatekin University, Çankırı, Republic of Turkey. Email: aysegul_bostan@yahoo.com and abostan@karatekin.edu.tr. ORCID: 0000-0002-8731-2757.
[1] Merve Çirişoğlu Çotur, **Karton Kutu (The Box).** İstanbul: Uçan At Yayınları, 2018 , p. 13. The Box, the animated story of one of the millions of war children, got screened on over 240 film festivals in 52 different countries and won 44 awards worldwide. In order to watch the animation, please see the youtube address: https://www.youtube.com/watch?v=KwCtWfwYlkw&feature=youtu.be
[2] Chiara Milan, "Refugees at the Gates of the EU: Civic Initiatives nd Grassroots Responses to the Refugee Crisis along the Western Balkans Route", **Journal of Balkan and Near Eastern Studies**, Vol. 21, No. 1, 2019, pp. 44, 45; Şule Toktaş, Aspasia Papadopoulou, Mila Paspalanova and Natalija Vrecer, "Transit and Receiving Countries: Refugee Protection Policies in Belgium, Slovenia, Greece, and Turkey", **Alternatives: Turkish Journal of International Relations**, Vol: 5, No: 1, 2, 2006, pp. 28, 29. For further reading please, see the following article concerning the Serbian migrants in Slovenia. Mladena Prelić, "The Serbs in Slovenia: A New Minority", **Bulletin of the Institute of Ethnography SASA,**Vol. LVI, No. 2, 2009, pp. 53-68.
[3] Russel King and Nermin Oruc, "Editorial Introduction: Migration in the Western Balkans-Trends and Challenges", **Journal of Balkan and Near Eastern Studies**, Vol: 21, No: 1, 2018, p. 1.

crisis in Rwanda. The Syrian citizens abandoning their country in fear of death firstly took refuge in the neighbouring countries. In the succeeding period, their journey followed a dangerous path stretching to Europe. Arriving in Turkey and Greece with boats via sea, the refugees aimed to reach the countries like Germany, Sweden, and Austria by using the humanitarian corridor passing through the Balkan countries.[4]

In the beginning of the summer of 2015, the Western Balkan countries were exposed to massive flow of migrants and refugees fleeing from the African and Middle Eastern countries. Initially, it was perceived as a Syrian refugee crisis, but later the name was changed to a European migration crisis. The year 2015 was the peak of the migration crises on the Balkan Peninsula. Approximately 7.000.000 migrants and refugees travelled to the Western countries, and in the last month of 2015 the number of illegal arrivals increased to 760.000.[5] Due to the several reasons which will be mentioned later in the following pages, the European migration crisis was the most challenging problem for the Balkan countries as well as the European Union members.

This study concentrates on the asylum policy of the Republic of Serbia (RS) with a special focus on the Syrian refugee crisis. First, general information on Serbian asylum policies will be given. Then, a new asylum policy will discussed with Serbia's motivation to become an EU member. With the arrival of the Syrian asylum seekers on the Balkan peninsula, the asylum policy of the RS and policies of the Serbian government toward the asylum seekers will be analyzed in detail.

## Introduction to asylum policy of RS

Yugoslavia signed the Geneva Convention on the Protection of Refugees (1951) and New York Protocol (1967) which are key legal documents concerning refugees. The 1951 Convention defines the term 'refugee', refugee rights and the principle of 'non-refoulement'. With no discrimination based on race, religion, political ideologies, the tasks and responsibilities of the states are determined.[6] It is worth noting that the Yugoslav government transferred its responsibility related to asylum policy to the United Nations Refugee Agency (UNHCR). The Agency processed all asylum procedures and evaluated all claims and applications of asylum seekers in accordance with the gentlemen's agreement between Yugoslavia and UNHCR.[7] Due to the

---

[4] Suna Gülfer Ihlamur Öner, "Türkiye'nin Suriyeli Mültecilere Yönelik Politikası", **Ortadoğu Analiz,** Sayı 6, 2014, pp. 42-45.

[5] Milan, op. cit., p. 44.

[6] Convention and Protocol Relating to the Status of Refugees, The Official Website of the UN Refugee Agency, https://www.unhcr.org/3b66c2aa10.html (Access 01.11.2020).

[7] For the signed all agreement, protocol and convention by the Western Balkan states, see the document:

fact that asylum seekers were granted status by the UNHCR, not by the Serbian authorities, it was widely believed that Serbia did not have an independent asylum policy, except for opening an asylum centre located on the west border of Serbia, Banja Kovilijaca.[8]

However, there were two cases in which the Yugoslav government granted a status of asylum to people fleeing from Hungary after the Soviet intervention (1956) and Chile after the president's assassination (1973). According to the 1974 Constitution and the 1990 Constitution, asylum status would be granted to foreign citizens and stateless people supporting democratic ideologies, national liberality and individual freedom. The Serbian national law included a definition of asylum seekers, yet there was no information on what kind of asylum procedure would be followed. Therefore, the UNHRC was accepted as only responsible for all asylum procedures in Yugoslavia in accordance with the gentlemen's agreement.[9]

The 1974 Constitution declared that *"foreigners in Yugoslavia enjoy freedoms and human rights"* (Article 201) which is granted by the Constitution and international agreements. According to the Article 202 of this Constitution[10], *"the right to asylum is guaranteed to foreign citizens and stateless persons, who are persecuted for supporting of democratic ideas and movements, of social and national liberation, of human freedom and rights or of the freedom of scientific or artistic creation"*. The Article 202 of the 1974 Constitution was accepted as the Article 50 of the 1990 Constitution with no change.[11] The following article emphasized that these freedoms and rights could not be restricted or removed.[12]

Until the late 1980s, Serbia was generally considered as a transit country for asylum seekers because asylum seekers temporarily accommodated in asylum centers of the UNHCR were sent to a safe third country via the UNHCR. However, Serbia was subjected to inflows of internal displacements

---

Jelena Unijat (Ed.), "Common Western Balkan Migration Policy: Borders and Returns: Regional Policy Paper", Group 484 Sarajevo, Balkan Refugee and Migration Council, October 2019, http://azil.rs/en/wp-content/uploads/2019/11/FV-Borders_and_Returns_BRMC.pdf (Access 1.11.2020).

[8] There are two kinds of refugees for Serbians: (1) domestic refugee coming from ex-Yugoslavia and speaks Serbian language; (2) external refugee defined by the 1951 Geneva Convention. Marta Stojić Mitrović, "Presenting as a Problem, Acting as an Opportunity: Four Cases of Socio-Political Conflicts Taking the Presence of Migrants as a Focal Object in Serbia", **Glasnik Etnografskog Instituta SANU**, Vol. 62, No. 1, 2014, pp. 68-69.

[9] Marta Stojić Mitrović, "Serbian Migration Policy Concerning Irregular Migration and Asylum in the Context of the EU Integration Process", **Issues in Ethnology and Anthropology**, Vol. 9, No. 4, 2014, pp. 1107-1108.

[10] Note that the author made some reduction on translation of the Serbian law text. Ustav Socijalističke Federativne Republike Jugoslavije (1974), http://mojustav.rs/wp-content/uploads/2013/04/Ustav-SFRJ-iz-1974.pdf (Access 2.11.2020).

[11] Ustav Republike Srbije 1990. Godina, http://mojustav.rs/wp-content/uploads/2013/04/Ustav-iz-1990.pdf (Access 2.11.2020).

[12] Ustav Socijalističke Federativne Republike Jugoslavije (1974), http://mojustav.rs/wp-content/uploads/ 2013/04/Ustav-SFRJ-iz-1974.pdf (Access 2.11.2020).

of ethnic-Serbs fleeing from ex-Yugoslav republics during the civil war of the 1990s. Concerning this flow, the Serbian government adopted the Law on Refugees (1992) which is similar to the 1951 Convention. To admit the arrivals and provide them with health care, temporary accommodation, food, and other aids, the Commissariat for Refugees (KIRS- Komesarijata za Izbeglice Rebuplike Srbije)[13] was established under the Ministry of Interior.[14]

### The reformation of Serbian migration policy

The European Union (EU) has a significant role in the reform process of the Serbian asylum policy. At the beginning of the 2000s, the Serbian government and the EU improved and enhanced their mutual relations due to the fact that Serbian authorities regarded it as a high priority to join the EU. By normalizing the relations with the European Union in that period, the Serbian government signed Stabilization and Association Agreement on 29 April 2008.[15] According to the Article 82 of the Stabilization and Association Agreement[16], Serbia promises to cooperate with the EU on subjects of border control, visa, asylum, and migration policy. This cooperation is based on close coordination and mutual consultation. It also contains administrative and technical help such as the exchange of data and information, training of staff, monitoring of the EU and so on.[17] During the process of negotiations, Serbia made intensive efforts on asylum policy in order to harmonize with the European Union law. The Serbian government endeavored to construct a legal framework and regulations for asylum policies for the sake of visa liberalization process.[18]

Before the Stabilization and Association Agreement, the Serbian government agreed on the readmission procedures of persons residing without the Schengen authorization in the EU states and signed the Readmission Agreement with the EU in 2007. Serbia accepted to readmit the

---

[13] KIRS has several experiences in working for not only refugees and migrants but also natural disasters such as floods. KIRS functions the same as the Göç İdaresi (Directorate General of Migration Management) and AFAD (Disaster and Emergency Management Presidency) in the Republic of Turkey.
[14] Marta Stojić Mitrović, "The Reception of Migrants in Serbia: Policies, Practices and Concepts", **Journal of Human Rights and Social Work,** Vol. 4, 2019, pp. 18-19.
[15] The Ministry of Foreign Affairs of the Republic of Serbia, "Chronology of relations between the Republic of Serbia and the European Union", http://www.mfa.gov.rs/en/foreign-policy/eu/political-relations-between-the-republic-of-serbia-and-the-european-union/12452-chronology-of-relations-between-the-republic-of-serbia-and-the-european-union (Access 3.11.2020).
[16] Stabilization and Association Agreement, European Council, The Official Website of the European Union, https://ec.europa.eu/neighbourhood-enlargement/sites/near/files/pdf/serbia/key_document/saa_en.pdf (Access 2.11.2020).
[17] Komesarijat za izbeglice Republike Srbije, "Politika azila u Srbiji: usklađivanje sa EU i sprovođenje na teritoriji Republike Srbije", September 2012, p. 8. http://www.kirs.gov.rs/media/uploads/Migracije/Publikacije/Politika_azila_u_Srbiji_-_uskladjivanje_sa_EU_i_ sprovodjenje_na_teritoriji_Republike_Srbije.pdf (Access 2.11.2020).
[18] Mirjana Bobić and Marija Babović, "Međunarodne Migracije u Srbiji – Stanje i Politike", **Sociologija,** Vol. LV, No. 2, 2013, pp. 223-224.

illegal arrivals without demanding any formalities from the EU. Serbia, has contributed in order for the EU to combat illegal immigration more effectively.[19] In order to comply with the EU law, Law on Asylum (2007) and the Alien Law (2008)[20] were adopted and implemented by the Serbian government. This shows that the Serbian authorities could grant refugee status and have an independent asylum policy. While the legal procedure remains similar to asylum procedure of UNHCR, the Serbian government opened new asylum centers[21] (under the responsibility of the Commissariat for Refugees and Migration), an asylum office and a Commission.[22]

Due to the reforms of the Serbian asylum policy, KIRS became the most prominent institution in terms of implementation of the Serbian asylum policy while the UNHCR has solely an advisory role on the asylum procedure. In accordance with the 2001 Law on Asylum, KIRS became the only institution responsible for admitting illegal arrivals to the asylum centers and readmission of Serbian citizens from the Schengen Area. Also KIRS can cooperate with NGOs[23] (national and international) and international organizations to deal with the issues of refugees and migration. Until the emergence of the Syrian refugee crisis, the asylum issue was not considered as a significant topic for Serbian citizens. This reformation remained the only condition for visa liberalization.[24]

In December 2009, Serbia achieved visa-free travel towards the EU so that Serbian citizens could travel with no Schengen visa for 3 months.[25] After

---

[19] Note that the readmission obligation does not contain some certain cases. For further information, visit the website. See 2007/819/EC: Council Decision of 8 November 2007 for the conclusion of the Agreement between the European Community and the Republic of Serbia on the readmission of persons residing without authorisation, The Official Journal of the European Union, Document 32007D0819 dated on 19.12.2007, https://eur-lex.europa.eu/legal-content/EN/TXT/?uri=CELEX%3A32007 D0819 (Access 2.11.2020).

[20] The Aliens Act describes conditions for the legal entry. Without legal entry, arrivals are regarded as illegal because they cannot fulfil and provide these conditions even any document. For the consequences of the illegalised migrants or migrant illegality, please see the article: Marta Stojić Mitrović and Ela Meh, "The Reproduction of Borders and the Contagiousness of Illegalisation: A Case of a Belgrade Youth Hostel", **Glasnik Etnografskog Instituta SANU**, Vol.63, No. 3, 2015, pp. 625-635.

[21] The asylum entres (AC) and reception centers (RC) in Serbia are AC Banja Koviljaca, AC Bogovadja, AC Sjenica, AC Tutin, AC Krnjaca, RC Presevo, PC Obrenovac, RC Adasevci, RC Principovac, RC Sid-Stanica, RC Pirot, RC Bujanovac, RC Vranje, RC Divljana, RC Dimitrovgrad, RC Bosilegrad, RC Subotica, RC Sombor, RC Kikinda. The Commissariat for Refugees and Migration, Republic of Serbia, "Asylum and Reception Centres". http://www.kirs.gov.rs/eng/asylum/asylum-and-reception-centers (Access 4.11.2020).

[22] Mitrović, "Presenting as a Problem, Acting as an Opportunity: Four Cases of Socio-Political Conflicts Taking the Presence of Migrants as a Focal Object in Serbia", op. cit., pp. 69-70.

[23] For instance, Group 484, the Regional Center for Minorities, Belgrade Center for Human Rights, Asylum Protection Center, No Borders Group, Adventist Development and Relief Agency (ADRA), Miksalište Centre-Refugee Aid Miksalište, Info Park Initiative, Refugee Aid Serbia.

[24] Zakon O Upravljanju Migracijama – Law on Migration Management, http://www.parlament.gov.rs/upload/archive/files/lat/pdf/predlozi_zakona/3118-12Lat.pdf (Access 4.11.2020) and Mitrović, "The Reception of Migrants in Serbia: Policies, Practices and Concepts", op. cit., pp. 18-19.

[25] The European Union Commission, "Brussels, 30 November 2009 Visa Liberalisation for Western

the liberalization process of visa regime, Serbia applied for membership of the European Union[26]; was granted a candidate status of the EU on 1 March 2012; and accession negotiation of the EU started on 28 June 2013.[27] With the encouragement of the EU and Serbia's newly acquired candidate status, the Law on Migration Management was adopted in 2012. The 2012 Law is mainly about migration management and exchange of updated data concerning refugees and migrant flows with the European authorities. For the effective accomplishment of responsibilities, it was important for Serbia to adopt a clear definition of migration (mainly economic migrants) and refugee (forced displacements) in order to distinguish both concepts. So, the aforementioned arrangements provided a clear definition of economic migrant and refugee.[28]

### The Emergence of the Syrian Refugee Crisis

Millions of Syrian citizens crossed the borders during the Syrian war because of fear of death. By these crossings caused the biggest refugee crisis in the world because this resulted in the arrival and accumulation of a great number of asylum seekers to the Europe and caused them to accumulate along the EU borders. In recent years the EU therefore has become one of the major refugee-hosting continents.[29]

The illegal entries to the EU are mainly from Italy, Greece, and Turkey. After passing the border of Greece and Turkey, the illegal arrivals followed migration routes over the Balkan Peninsula. Travelling by illegal routes on the path of the Western Balkans, the Syrian asylum seekers could reach the Schengen area. In fact, the Balkan region was a basin for refugees to take them to Western Europe, yet the Syrian refugee crisis has turned the peninsula into the largest transit route of illegal migrants and refugees. There are mainly two itineraries of illegal arrivals in the Balkan region. The first itinerary is the route of Turkey – Bulgaria – Serbia – Hungary. The second itinerary is the route of Turkey - Greece - Macedonia - Serbia - Hungary /

Balkan Countries", The Official Website of the European Union, 30 November 2009, https://ec.europa.eu/commission/presscorner/detail/en/PRES_09_349 (Access 5.11.2020).

[26] The European Council, "Serbia is Granted EU Candidate Status", EUCO 35/12, PRESSE 84, Brussels, 1 March 2012, https://www.consilium.europa.eu/uedocs/cms_data/docs/pressdata/en/ec/128445.pdf (Access 5.11.2020).

[27] The Ministry of Foreign Affairs of the Republic of Serbia, "Chronology of relations between the Republic of Serbia and the European Union", http://www.mfa.gov.rs/en/foreign-policy/eu/political-relations-between-the-republic-of-serbia-and-the-european-union/12452-chronology-of-relations-between-the-republic-of-serbia-and-the-european-union (Access 5.11.2020).

[28] Mitrović, "Serbian Migration Policy Concerning Irregular Migration and Asylum in the Context of the EU Integration Process", op. cit., pp. 1110-1111.

[29] Nazan Öztürk and Serkan Ayvaz, "Sentiment Analysis on Twitter: A Text Mining Approach to the Syrian Refugee Crisis", **Telematics and Informatics**, Vol. 35, 2018, p. 138.

Croatia.[30]

When Bulgarian government built a fence along the Turkish border in order to prevent illegal migrants, the migration flow of the first itinerary deescalated dramatically. While Bulgaria has lost its importance for illegal migrants and refugees, the second itinerary (Macedonia-Serbia-Hungary/Croatia) has become attractive to refugees.[31]

The second itinerary shows that Serbia is the final departure point of the migration route for the illegal migrants and asylum seekers whose destination is the Schengen area. In this sense, while Serbia was a sending country of economic migrants and refugees to the Western Europe in the past, now it is transit country for the refugees.[32]

Regarding the number of the illegal arrivals to Serbia as a transit country, the 2019 data of the UNHCR shows that the number of asylum seekers and migrants in Serbia was 5.833.[33] Yet this number reached 7.950 people in October 2020.[34] It is necessary to note that these figures can show differences monthly or annually.

### Construction of Humanitarian Route and White Cards

Due to the density of illegal arrivals along the Macedonian-Greek border, a local *imam* took an initiative in constructing a humanitarian corridor from Preševo (close to the Greek-Macedonian border) to Subotica (close to the Serbian-Hungarian border). The aim of the Macedonian imam was to facilitate the journeys of the asylum seekers on foot and help them safely reach the Schengen area. The starting point of this humanitarian corridor was the town of Preševo. The imam persuaded the owners of crop fields so that the asylum seekers could walk on the fields first through Miratovac (the Serbian village) and then use transportation through Preševo (a Serbian town). This route was a starting point of the journey from Macedonia to Serbia, and then Hungary. The humanitarian corridor was mainly financed by the Doctors Without Borders. In addition, the Macedonian government amended its asylum law in order to enable them to travel with no requirements. Thanks to these amendments of the Macedonian asylum law,

---

[30] Ferruccio Pastore, "From Source to Corridor: Changing Geopolitical Narratives about Migration and EU-Western Balkans Relations", **Journal of Balkan and Eastern Studies,** Vol. 21, No. 1, 2019, pp. 18-19.

[31] Rick Lyman, "Bulgaria Puts Up a New Wall, but This One Keeps People Out", **The New York Times,** 5 April 2015, https://www.nytimes.com/2015/04/06/world/europe/bulgaria-puts-up-a-new-wall-but-this-one-keeps-people-out.html (Access 6.11.2020).

[32] Milan, op. cit., p. 44.

[33] The website of the UNHCR, "Serbia Update", December 2019, https://data2.unhcr.org/en/documents /details/73432 (Access 6.11.2020).

[34] The Website of the UNHCR, "Serbia: October 2020", https://data2.unhcr.org/en/documents/details /83083 (Access 6.11.2020).

the asylum seekers gained the 72-hour permission to travel freely throughout the country. Therefore, they could benefit from public transportation (such as bus, train) freely and leave the country in three days and enter into the Serbian border.[35]

To be frank, the humanitarian corridor was reconstructed as a *de facto* route by the suspension of the EU law and national law because the legal right of entry is not granted to illegal arrivals without a valid visa and an official travel document in accordance with the Article 5(1) of the Schengen Border Code.[36] In terms of daily practices, the corridor, however, provided a right of entry into the EU for the asylum seekers.[37]

Whenever the asylum seekers came to Serbia, the Serbian authorities implemented a 72-hour permission policy (White Cards) to the asylum seekers. The White Cards granted the asylum seekers a *"semi-regular legal status"*. The final aim of the White Cards was to expel the SAI[38] asylum seekers from the Schengen countries and to prevent them from settling there. Accordingly, the SAI asylum seekers could cross the Hungarian-Serbian border semi-legally. Hungary was an entry-point to the Schengen and European Union countries in the path of Balkan route. Therefore, Hungary was appealing for the asylum seekers who want to reach the European Union region. In this sense, Subotica became the final destination for the asylum seekers to reach Hungary, and then Austria. The service of free-of-charge transportation was financed by international NGOs.[39] Also, in accordance with the official procedure in Serbia, when the illegal person with the 72h permission was admitted to one of the asylum centers, the asylum procedure was initialized for her/him. The asylum seeker could still enjoy some rights such as the provision of clothes, health care, food, accommodation, accession to free legal assistance.[40]

The highest number of illegal arrivals in the summer of 2015 in the region

---

[35] Mitrović, "The Reception of Migrants in Serbia: Policies, Practices and Concepts", op. cit., p. 19.

[36] Neža Kogovšek Šalamon and Kaja Šeruga, "Refugees and the "Disorganised State of Exception: EU and States' Responses to Mass Arrivals Through the Western Balkans Migration Route", **The Disaster of European Refugee Policy: Perspectives from the Balkan Route,** Igor Ž. Žagar, Neža Kogovšek Šalamon and Marina Lukšič Hacin (Ed.), Cambridge: Cambridge Scholars Publishing, p. 39.

[37] Except for the SAI countries, all asylum seekers are considered as the economic migrants and pushed back to Greece and Macedonia. Mirjana Bobić and Danica Šantić, "Forced Migrations and Externalization of European Union Border Control: Serbia on the Balkan Migration Route", **International Migration**, Vol. 58, Vol. 3, 2020, p. 7.

[38] SAI: Syria, Afghanistan and Iraq.

[39] For briefly migration policy of Hungarian, please see: Szilveszter Póczik and Eszter Sárik, "Law and (B)order: Will Border Fence and Transit Zones Stop the Asylum Seekers' Wave on the Balkan Route?", **Refugees and Migrants in Law and Policy: Challenges and Opportunities for Global Civic Education,** Helmut Kury and Sławomir Redo (Ed.), Cham: Springer, 2018, pp 75-107; Milan, op. cit., pp. 45-52.

[40] Mitrović, "Presenting as a Problem, Acting as an Opportunity: Four Cases of Socio-Political Conflicts Taking the Presence of Migrants as a Focal Object in Serbia", op. cit., p. 71.

urged the Balkan countries unanimously to construct an organized corridor, yet this state-organized corridor was an opportunity for the illegal arrivals.[41] In fact, the humanitarian corridor was considered as a path for the desired asylum seekers to cross the borders in accordance with the agreed number by the European states.[42] In addition, the desired asylum seekers were people coming from Syria, Iraq, and Afghanistan.[43] The opening of the EU's border via the humanitarian corridor triggered the influx of SAI asylum refugees. Thus, illegal arrivals increased dramatically in the Balkan region. The rapid growth in the number of illegal arrivals led the Hungarian government to close the borders to the illegal arrivals. As a result, the asylum seekers headed towards the Croatian border. The Croatian authorities accepted the SAI asylum seekers illegally crossing the Croatian border for a short time. However, the Croatian government also closed her border to the illegal arrivals as well as the Hungarian government.[44]

The Syrian refugee crisis was a problem of the EU and *"separate incidents"* for the Serbian citizens until 2015. With the activation of the humanitarian corridor, Serbia functioned as solely a transit state for the asylum seekers for a short time. The Serbian authorities, however, faced the reality that Serbia was considered as a buffer zone and dumping ground of the EU with the closure of the Hungarian and Croatian borders and and the continuously increased numbers of asylum seekers in Serbia.[45]

### The Legalization of Humanitarian Corridor

The European Union law does not include the right to enter the Schengen countries on a daily basis. According to provisions of the Article 5.1 of the Schengen Borders Code, the entry of non-Schengen country nationals to the Schengen area is not allowed. During the Syrian refugee crisis, thousands of migrants might have entered the European Union area without fulfilling the requirements for the Schengen visa. This entry of the asylum seekers was

---

[41] Milan and Pirro, "Interwoven Destines in the 'Long Migration Summer': Solidarity Movements Along the Western Balkan Route", **Solidarity Mobilizations in the 'Refugee Crisis': Contentious Moves**, Donatella Della Porta (Ed.), Basingstoke : Palgrave Macmillan, 2018, p. 125.

[42] Damir Josipovič, "Contemporary Geography of Migration Refugees, Middle East, Syria, Europe", **The Disaster of European Refugee Policy: Perspectives from the Balkan Route**, Igor Ž. Žagar, Neža Kogovšek Šalamon and Marina Lukšič Hacin (Ed.), Cambridge: Cambridge Scholars Publishing, 2018, p. 88.

[43] Milan and Pirro, op. cit., p. 125.

[44] Marta Stojić Mitrović, "The Reception of Migrants in Serbia: Policies, Practices and Concepts", op. cit., p. 20.

[45] Milan and Pirro, op. cit., p. 136; Marta Stojić Mitrović, Nidžara Ahmetašević, Barbara Beznec and Andrej Kurnik, **The Dark Sides of Europeanization: Serbia, Bosnia and Herzegovina and the European Border Regime**, Belgrade: Research Paper Series of Rosa Luxemburg Stiftung Southeast Europe, 2020, p. 20; Claudio Minca, Danica Šantić and Dragan Umek, "Managing the "Refugee Crisis Along the Balka Route: Field Notes from Serbia", **The Oxford Handbook of Migration Crises**, Cecilia Menjivar, Marie Ruiz and Immanuel Ness (Ed.), Oxford: OUP, 2019,p. 454 and Marta Stojić Mitrović, "The Reception of Migrants in Serbia: Policies, Practices and Concepts", ibid., p. 20.

considered as a transit entry by the Balkan states. According to the EU law, transit right is defined as right of entry to the Schengen area with aviation, not on foot. In other words, airports are regarded as transit zones for the passengers who want to transit to another European country. Consequently, passengers are not allowed to cross the border of another European country on foot in accordance with Article 2.1.3 of the Schengen Borders Code. Unfortunately, both the European Union and national law do not meet the needs of mass migration movements. With the beginning of the accumulation of a huge number of people on the Western European borders, the right of transit entry was granted to the SAI refugees for a short time. The reason for granting them illegal permission for crossing to the Schengen area was to prevent the accumulation of high numbers of people in one country (such as Greece and Macedonia) and to protect them from inhumane conditions. To provide basic human rights and prevent human abuse, this permission was vehemently called *"emerging entry rights"* and *"emerging right of transit"* for mass arrivals.[46]

The aforementioned reasons (such as the inability to provide basic human needs, activities of human smugglers and lack of a proper law for mass migration) facilitated the construction of a de facto humanitarian corridor on the territory of the Western Balkan countries that are the border neighbors of the European Union. It could be said that there were some advantages of the humanitarian corridor as well. One of them was to help the refugees travel safely to their preferred destination with no travel document and Schengen visa. The route of this humanitarian corridor also shortened the duration of the journey. They could reach the countries they preferred much faster and in a safer way. In addition, the humanitarian corridor provided a much

---

[46] Neža Kogovšek Šalamon, "Legal Implications of the Humanitarian Corridor", **Razor-Wired: Reflections on Migration Movements through Slovenia in 2015**, Ljubljana: Peace Institute, 2016, pp. 40, 41, 48. https://www.mirovni-institut.si/wp-content/uploads/2016/03/Razor_wired_publikacija_web.pdf, (Access 11.11.2020). For further information, see these articles: Julija Sardelić, **From Temporary Protection to Transit Migration: Responses to Refugee Crises Along the Western Balkan Route**, EUI Working Papers, RSCAS 2017/35, Fiesole: 2017, https://cadmus.eui.eu/handle/1814/47168 (Access 11.11.2020); Drago Župarić-Iljić and Marko Valenta. "Opportunistic Humanitarianism and Securitization Discomfort Along the Balkan Corridor: The Croatian Experience", Refugee Protection and Civil Society in Europe, Margit Feischmidt, Ludger Pries, Celine Cantat (eds). Cham: Palgrave Macmillan, 2019, pp. 129-160; Barbara Beznec and Andrej Kurnik, "Old Routes, New Perspectives: A Postcolonial Reading of the Balkan Route", The Frontier Within: The European Border Regime in the Balkans, Barbara Beznec, Marijana Hameršak, Sabine Hess, Andrej Kurnik, Marc Speer, Marta Stojić Mitrović (Ed.), Journal for Critical Migration and Border Regime Studies, Vol. 5, No. 1, 2020, pp. 33-54 and Duška Petrović, "Humanitarian Exceptionalism: Normalization of Suspension of Law in Camp and Corridor", Formation and Disintegration of the Balkan Refugee Corridor: Camps, Routes and Borders in the Crotian Context, Emina Bužinkić and Marijana Hameršak (Ed.), Institute of Ethnology and Folklore Research Centre for Peace Studies Faculty of Political Science University of Zagreb – Centre for Ethnicity, Citizenship and Migration, bordermonitoring.eu e.V. (Munich), Zagreb-Munich, 2018, pp. 43-62 https://bordermonitoring.eu/wp-content/uploads/2018/09/Formation_and_Disintegration_of_the_Balkan_Refugee_Corridor-2018.pdf (Access 11.11.2020).

cheaper journey for the refugees because there was no need to pay human smugglers any money for illegal transportation to the Schengen area where entry was allowed via the humanitarian corridor. The ultimate advantage of the Balkan corridor was that the refugees would not have to accumulate in only one country. Therefore, the refugees and migrants could pass the borders via the humanitarian corridor from Greece to Macedonia, from Macedonia to Serbia, from Serbia to Croatia or Hungary and so on. If the border crossings had been not constructed by the Balkan states, a huge number of arrivals would have accumulated at the border sites. As a result, even the basic humanitarian care such as food, shelter, health, clothes, sanitary systems could have not been provided to the refugees and migrants by the Western European states because of lack of financial support and small budgets of the Western Balkan states. This situation could have led to difficult humanitarian problems, such as famine, hygiene problems, security problems, physical injury (with the police or among themselves), and even loss of human life because the Hungarian borders were secured by a razor-wired fence and barrier.[47] Therefore, the construction of the Balkan humanitarian corridor has seemed a satisfactory solution for mass migration movements.

### The Close-up of the Humanitarian Corridor

Illegal border crossing became one of the national security problems in Hungary, and some Hungarian elites and the media started to use securitization discourse towards the refugees and migrants.[48] Due to the density of illegal arrival on the Hungarian-Serbian borders, an increase in incidents between asylum seekers and police forces was reported, particularly in the summer of 2015. According to the discourse of the Hungarian government, the Hungarian president was ready to deploy the army to the Serbian border if necessary. In this regard, the Hungarian government decided to build a fence along the Serbian border to prevent illegal crossings and protect the integrity of the national border. In addition to this policy, the government introduced strict penalties for illegal asylum seekers. The construction of the new border fence was completed in September 2015. The border is 4 m in height and 175 km in length. It is secured by razor wire outside and a sturdy barrier inside. This razor-wired fence shows that the Hungarian authorities perceived the illegal arrivals coming from the Serbian border as a serious threat for the Hungary.[49]

---

[47] Neža Kogovšek Šalamon, "Mass Migration, Crimmigration and Defiance: The Case of the Humanitarian Corridor, **Southeastern Europe Journal**, Vol. 41, No. 3, 2017, pp. 270-271.
[48] İrem Karamik, "Securitised Migration of the Other in Hungary: A Fantasy Created by the Politics of Fear", **Political Reflection Magazine**, Vol. VI, No: IV, Issue: 25, 2020, p. 37.
[49] Senada Šelo Šabić and Sonja Borić, "At the Gate of Europe: A Report on Refugees on the Western Balkan Route", Friedrich Ebert Stiftung, Zagreb, http://library.fes.de/pdf-files/bueros/kroatien/13059.

With the closure of the Hungarian border in the middle of October 2015, illegal crossing border was not allowed by the Hungarian government. The asylum seekers crossing the border illegally were arrested and put under custody. In 2015 the number of detentions was 2.393 persons. The number of affected persons affected by the strict policy of Hungary increased to 2.621 persons in a few months. The illegal arrivals were immediately sent back to Serbia, but the Serbian authorities refused to take them back.[50] On top of that, there was a tendency for the denial of asylum applications by the Hungarian authorities because Serbia was considered as safe third country as claimed by the Hungarian government. Therefore, the Hungarian authorities implemented the policy of the denial of the asylum seekers and deported them to Serbia.[51]

Following Hungary's policy of closing its borders, some Balkan countries such as Macedonia and Croatia officially declared the closure of the humanitarian corridor. Consequently, no one could pass the borders of Western countries illegally. The authorities implemented a new strict border policy and abolished the Balkan route. However, it should be noted that the policy was for only illegal crossings. Undoubtedly, the SAI refugees could legally cross the border even if the Balkan states closed the borders. Nevertheless, this permit was strictly limited to approximately ten asylum seekers as passengers per week. The Hungarian authorities determined these numbers in accordance with their asylum policy. There was a list of the asylum seekers who applied for asylum protection to the Hungarian asylum centers and the authorities chose the passengers from this list. There was no explanation regarding to selection criteria of this list.[52] It could be said that this caused an exclusionary situation among asylum seekers.

Hungary's asylum policy led the Balkan states to have a harsh policy towards the Syrian asylum seekers. While the Macedonian authorities pushed the asylum seekers back to the Greek border by using tear gas and police force, the Slovenian and Croatian governments deployed police forces and armed forces to secure the national borders. In addition, the Croatian and Slovenian armed forces were appointed new tasks for border security.

---

pdf. pp. 9, 19 (Access 12.11.2020).

[50] The European Parliament of the European Union, "Integration of Regugees in Greece, Hungary and Italy Comparative Analysis, Directorate-General for Internal Policies, Policy Department: Economic and Scientific Policy A, p. 20 https://www.europarl.europa.eu/RegData/etudes/STUD/2017/ 614194/ IPOL_STU(2017)614194 _EN.pdf (Access 12.11.2020).

[51] Aleksandra Ilić, "Media Reporting on Refugees and Related Public Opinion in Serbia", **Refugees and Migrants in Law and Policy: Challenges and Oppurtinities for Global Civic Education,** Helmut Kury, Sławomir Redo (Ed.), Cham: Springer, p. 140.

[52] Robert Rydzewski, "Hope, Waiting and Mobility: Migrant Movement in Serbia After the EU-Turkey Deal", **Journal for Critical Migration and Border Regime Studies,** Vol. 5, No. 1, 2020, p. 77 and Claudio Minca, Danica Šantić and Dragan Umek, Managing the "Refugee Crisis Along the Balkan Route: Field Notes from Serbia", **The Oxford Handbook of Migration Crises,** Cecilla Menjivar, Marie Ruiz and Immanuel Ness (Ed.), Oxford: OUP, 2019, pp. 451-453.

Because of the closure of the border and the abolishment of the humanitarian route, the asylum seekers were obliged to stay in Serbia for a while. During the second period of 2015, the reception centers became full and some asylum seekers had difficulty in finding accommodation. On one hand, Slovenian, Serbian, and Croatian authorities built new transit reception centers.[53] On the other hand, the asylum seekers tried to find a place at the parks in Belgrade. Day by day, the number of asylum seekers who lived in the parks increased. They became more visible in public areas, particularly the parks near the bus stations and the train station in Belgrade. Serbian citizens witnessed the density of people speaking non-Serbian in the parks and their tents pitched in these parks.[54]

### Securitization of the Syrian refugee crisis

In a general sense, the Serbian government has made inclusive statements for the refugees. This inclusive discourse has been built mostly on human solidarity, common experience (in the Yugoslavian war in the 1990s), empathy with the asylum seekers, and responsibility for humanity.[55] The Serbian President Aleksandar Vučić stated that "*if no common European solution is found, we will behave humanely and respect the principles of solidarity*".[56]Serbia openly tries to take care of the refugees and shows her solidarity with the refugees.[57] The Serbian public discourse has been designed in such a way that Serbia tried to provide as much food, health service, and accommodation to the asylum seekers as possible.[58]

Behind the refugee-friendly behavior towards the illegal arrivals, there were three reasons. The first reason was the empathy of the Serbian citizens with the Syrian asylum seekers because "*Serbs were refugees themselves, and therefore, as a nation, should help*".[59] The second reason is the fact that the asylum seekers would not stay in Serbia longer and their desirable destination was the European Union countries. In this regard, Serbia was just a transit country for them. Having the 72-hour permission, the asylum seekers who pitched their tents in the parks in Belgrade could leave Serbian territories as soon as possible. The last reason is the desire of the Serbian government for Serbia

---

[53] Drago Župarić-Iljić and Marko Valenta, "Refugee Crisis in the Southeastern European Countries: The Rise and Fall of the Balkan Corridor", **The Oxford Handbook of Migration Crises**, Cecilla Menjivar, Marie Ruiz and Immanuel Ness (Ed.), Oxford: OUP, 2019, pp. 373-377.

[54] Milan and Pirro, op. cit., p. 137.

[55] Šabić and Borić, op. cit., p. 10.

[56] "Vucic on migrant crisis: Egoism reigns among EU countries", The Official Website of the B92 New media, 30 March 2016, https://www.b92.net/eng/news/politics.php?yyyy=2016&mm=03&dd=30&nav_id=97526 (Access 13.11.2020).

[57] Michael Wetzel, "Serbian PM Vucic: 'EU Still the Best Place to Belong to'", Deutsche Welle (DW), 19 January 2017, "https://www.dw.com/en/serbian-pm-vucic-eu-still-the-best-place-to-belong-to/a-37188933 (Access 13.11.2020).

[58] Milan and Pirro, op. cit., p. 138.

[59] Aleksandra Ilić, op. cit., p. 158.

to prove to be a trustworthy partner and earn the membership status of the EU.[60]

Despite the inclusive discourse, some harassment and human abuse against the asylum seekers were reported. According to the reports of Human Rights Watch[61], the police forces victimized the asylum seekers rather than protecting them, particularly in Subotica town and Belgrade. The Serbian asylum authorities felt alone on the issue of solving the Syrian refugee crisis as well. Therefore, the Serbian government insistently emphasized that Serbia could not carry this burden alone and assume the responsibility of the refugee crisis alone.[62]

This situation led the way to securitization discourse against the asylum seekers in Serbia. The Syrian refugees are seen as one of the most serious problems today.[63] Some Serbian politicians believed that Serbia has nearly been "*the biggest migrant centre*" in Europe.[64] The President Aleksandar Vučić declared that "*(n)o one will unnecessarily enter Serbia. But we will make our own judgments. We will certainly not be a parking lot for migrants.*".[65] The asylum seekers pitched their tents at the central parks located close to railway stations and bus stations in Belgrade. However, they struggled for life outside due to the full capacity of the asylum centers. On top of the closing up of the humanitarian route, the number of people living outside dramatically raised in the country. More asylum seekers started to live in public areas that are close to public transportations. Because of this situation, the presence of asylum seekers in public areas caused the Serbian citizens to feel disturbed. This discomfort transformed the positive perception toward the SAI asylum seekers into the exclusive discourse.

In the context of the securitization of Syrian refugees, another argument is the possibility of the infiltration of some terrorist groups into the group of refugees on the Western Balkan route. There is a controversial argument suggesting that the humanitarian corridor presented some advantages for terrorist groups to reach the Western European countries and the Balkans.[66]

---

[60] Milan and Pirro, op. cit., pp. 138-139.
[61] Human Rights Watch, "Serbia: Police Abusing Migrants, Asylum Seekers", 15 April 2015, https://www.hrw.org/news/2015/04/15/serbia-police-abusing-migrants-asylum-seekers (Access 13.11.2020).
[62] Šabić and Borić, op. cit., p. 10.
[63] "Serbian PM 'shocked' at Hungary's Plan for Migrant Fence", The Official Website of BBC, 18.06.2015, https://www.bbc.com/news/world-europe-33168125 (Access 13.11.2020).
[64] Milica Stojanovic, "Right-wing Serbian Party Launches Anti-Immigration Campaign", The Official Website of the Balkan Sight, 28.02.2020, https://balkaninsight.com/2020/02/18/right-wing-serbian-party-launches-anti-immigration-campaign/ (Access 13.11.2020).
[65] Talha Öztürk, "Serbia not a 'Parking Lot' for Migrants, Says President", The Offical Website of the Anadolu Agency, 04.03.2020, https://www.aa.com.tr/en/europe/serbia-not-a-parking-lot-for-migrants-says-president/1754836 (Access 13.11.2020).
[66] Milan and Pirro, op. cit., 126.

Serbian people believed the government should close the borders and refuse the entry of new asylum seekers into the country. They also believed that the European institutions should finance the current arrivals.[67] To prevent new entries and defend the borders, the Serbian government considers sending the security forces to the borders as an alternative solution like Austria and Croatia.[68]

## Conclusion

Both the Syrian refugee crisis and the Europeanization process contributed to reshaping the asylum policy of Serbia. In the process of the membership negotiation, the Serbian government implemented new regulations on migration and asylum law. Until 2000, refugee concept was perceived as a displaced person who is an ethnic Serb or speaks the Serbian language. Therefore, the Serbian citizens consider the arrival of the displaced etnic Serbs as a kind of return to the motherland. In the 2000s, the Serbian authorities implemented a series of legal amendments due to the conditionality of the harmonization with the EU law. One of the advantages of these amendments was a clear definition of asylum seekers and migrant concepts. Another advantage was that the role of KIRS became powerful for the management of migration and refugee and assumed new responsibilities for handling migration and refugee issues in Serbia. The Serbian government had the opportunity to test the asylum policy in the case of the Syrian refugee crisis. Accordingly, Serbia has been transformed into a buffer zone rather than a sending country or transit country, although Serbia played a proactive role in handling the refugee crisis with the construction of the humanitarian corridor and the application of 72-hour permission.

---

[67] Ilić, op. cit., p. 158.
[68] Talha Öztürk, "Serbia not a 'Parking Lot' for Migrants, Says President", The Offical Website of the Anadolu Agency, 04.03.2020, https://www.aa.com.tr/en/europe/serbia-not-a-parking-lot-for-migrants-says-president/1754836 (Access 13.11.2020).